# Vegetarian Planet

# Vegetarian Planet

## 350 Big-Flavor Recipes for Out-of-This-World Food Every Day

### DIDI EMMONS

Illustrations by Melissa Sweet

### THE HARVARD COMMON PRESS
Boston, Massachusetts

To my Mom, Roz Emmons,
who always gave me creative license,

and to Ann O'Brien,
who gave me unbridled support

**THE HARVARD COMMON PRESS**
535 Albany Street
Boston, Massachusetts 02118

Printed in the United States of America
Printed on acid-free paper

Library of Congress Cataloging-in-Publication Data

Emmons, Didi.
Vegetarian planet : 350 big-flavor recipes for out-of-this-world food every day / Didi Emmons.
    p.   cm.
Includes index.
ISBN 1-55832-114-4 (hardcover  :  alk. paper). — ISBN 1-55832-115-2
(pbk.  :  alk. paper)
1. Vegetarian cookery.  2. Cookery, International.   I. Title.
TX837.E49  1997
641.5'636—dc21                                                          97-3654

Special bulk-order discounts are available on this and other Harvard Common Press books.
Companies and organizations may purchase books for premiums or resale, or
may arrange a custom edition, by contacting the Marketing Director at the address above.

*Cover and book illustrations by Melissa Sweet*
*Cover and book design by Kathleen Herlihy-Paoli, Inkstone Design*

10 9 8 7 6 5 4

# Contents

# Acknowledgments

### MANY THANKS TO:

Steven Raichlen, who encouraged me, humored me, and inspired me.

Kevin Sheehan at the Delux Cafe, whose trust and generosity have been invaluable to this book as well as to my work as a chef.

Bruce Shaw at the Harvard Common Press, who was willing to let me do what I wanted to do.

Dan Rosenberg and Laura Christman at the Harvard Common Press, two uncommonly good people who are totally committed to their work.

Linda Ziedrich, whose editing is razor sharp at all hours of the day.

Melissa Sweet, the splendid illustrator whose work graces my pages and cover.

Kathleen Herlihy-Paoli for her wonderful design, and Joyce C. Weston for helping to bring the pages to life.

David Strymish, who helped me cross the treacherous bridge from cook to cookbook writer.

Doe Coover, my agent, who is as fantastic as everyone says she is.

Jon Strymish, who gives me tons of support, tests my recipes, and eats everything I make.

My big-boned cat, Henry, who slept diligently next to my keyboard while I wrote, and who also eats everything I make.

Walter Clay, for his amazing wine prowess.

Rob and Amy, my upstairs neighbors and friends, who frequently doubled as a 24-hour convenience store.

Scott, my roommate, who responded to my mood swings with grace and good humor.

Joan Maxfield, who helped me with my research and gave me unswerving support.

My sister Polly, for being an awesome sounding board.

My sister Lisa, for her optimism, savvy, and artful eye.

Germana Fabbri Day, for her enthusiasm, warmth, and lifelong friendship.

Tim Towner, for his intelligence and patience.

Pat Kopperl, for her careful reading of the manuscript.

Ihsan, Matt, and the rest of the staff at Formaggio's Kitchen, for cheese info.

Lane Gifford, who has bestowed upon me her support and wisdom.

Judith Barrett, for her testing techniques and risotto insight.

Gregg Zoske, for her unmatched and thoughtful support.

Liz First, for her many efforts to help me in any way possible.

My California Cooking Contingent and late-night-support phone line, Deirdre Davis and Laurel Koledin.

The students at the Cambridge School of Culinary Arts who cheerfully helped me test recipes: Bonnie Churbuck, Liz Quinn, Bettina Messana, Walter Moore, and Elinor Boutin.

All my trusty testers who double-tested my recipes over the last 18 months: My mom, Roz Emmons, and Lynn Burlham, Marina Kvitnitsky and Dan Cohen, Maria Hecht, Greg Foley, Marie Noelle Ducett, Gary Stout, Greg Rahal and Melodie Wertelet, Lynn Roulo and Eric Enders, Barbara Magill, Melissa Manolis, Ann Gallager, Julia Shanks, Maria Copses, Hilary Farber, Risa Evans, Deborah Mutchler, Chris Gant, Alison Gant and Kim MacKenzie, Anne Cortissoz, Colleen Tucker and Bill Weinscheuk, Paul Lewis, Brenda Conoway, Ginny Pasternak, Teresa Chick, Clare and Dave Perry, Sarah Winkley, Joan Cohen, Shirley Hirshorn, Leigh Houser, Susan Schon, Michelle Itzkowitz, Andy and Marilyn Lehren, Kate Boyd, Cathy Macchiarola, and Kathleen Iacabocci.

Four truly inspiring people who have helped me along the way: Robin Hall, Claude Vauget, Chris Schlesinger, and Michael Ehlendfelt.

# Introduction

Cooking without meat is as natural to me as breathing. I've always been more interested in ways to dress greens than ways to roast chickens. Creating soups from roasted garlic and butternut squash, or from white beans and Swiss chard, gets me charged like no broiled tenderloin can. And it is because of my interest in cooking with vegetables, spices, grains, and the like that I am now nearly a full-time vegetarian. Although I've never thought much about reducing the amount of meat in my diet, I eat meat just once or twice a month now.

Part of the reason it's easy to eat vegetarian these days is that the variety of foods available is bigger now than ever before. Products that only fifteen years ago were nearly impossible to find in the United States are now in our supermarkets. Goat cheese, dried cranberries, coconut milk, fresh oregano, shiitake mushrooms, elephant garlic, hazelnuts, and a large selection of olive oils all sit unassumingly in my local grocery store. What's more, many of the ingredients we now buy are from countries where people eat relatively small amounts of meat. Vietnam, China, India, and the Middle East are just a few of the places where vegetables, grains, and spices play larger culinary roles than meats do. Foods like jasmine and basmati rice, lemongrass, bulgur, pomegranates, rice noodles, nappa cabbage, and sesame oil are widely available in our country now because they are important in the diets of recent immigrants. New immigrants are even growing and producing some of their native foods here; tortillas, mangoes, fresh Chinese noodles, chiles, flat breads, bok choy, fresh mozzarella cheese, ginger, and cilantro are but a few examples. Also on the increase is the variety of spices and herbs available; fresh rosemary and mint, for example, have become standard items in supermarkets. The explosive increase in new foods has allowed me to explore the meatless culinary traditions of many, many countries, and to enjoy as many flavor combinations as until a few decades ago only a wealthy traveler could do.

My interest in food and cooking started around the age of twelve, when my good friend Gigi told me that she was going

to spend her allowance—one dollar—on Brie cheese. I'd never tasted Brie, and I thought it odd that she would spend her precious dollar on anything but candy. Besides, cheese was something our mothers regularly bought, anyhow.

But we went downtown and stopped into the cheese shop before heading to the candy store. In a businesslike manner, Gigi asked for exactly one dollar's worth of Brie cheese. The counterperson took a disc of cheese and cut a sliver from it. Secretly hoping the white coating on the cheese was powdered sugar, I tried a piece. It didn't taste sweet, nor did it taste like the cheddar my mom bought. It was definitely better.

I was so turned on to Brie cheese that I decided to spend my own dollar allowance on it the following week. A few weeks later, I started tasting other cheeses. Eventually I decided to split the dollar. First I got 50 cents' worth of Brie and 50 cents' worth of Italian fontina. Then I dropped the Brie and tried Danish havarti; I dropped the fontina for Swiss Gruyère; and then French Comté came onto the scene. Before long, I was one of the cheese shop's most frequent customers. The staff always gave me much more than 50 cents' worth of cheese, and they never spoke down to me. Completely in love with cheese and the shop workers, I asked them if I could have a job when I was old enough.

The staff had turned over by the time I turned sixteen. But I told the new people my story, and for some reason they hired me. The new staff was just as good as the old one. I began a three-year, fun-filled education about cheese, spices, and herbs (the shop sold over two hundred spices and herbs by the pound), coffees, teas, fresh breads, and imported foods.

I went through a vegan phase when I was seventeen, sidestepping sugar as well as all dairy products and meat. Unfortunately, I made Christmas cookies that year for all of my friends. These cookies were devoid of any sugar or dairy products but instead had rice syrup, sunflower seeds, and carob powder. According to my friends, they tasted worse than dog biscuits. A few months later, I quit the vegan diet, mainly because I couldn't resist all of the cheeses I was selling.

It was about this time that I developed the habit of perusing cookbooks and magazines. When I went to college, and my roommate would be out dancing late at night, I would be sit-

> **"** *A nickel will get you on the subway, but garlic will get you a seat.* **"**
> —OLD NEW YORK YIDDISH SAYING

ting on my bed flipping through *Gourmet* magazines. When *Cook's* magazine came out in the early eighties, I became even more mesmerized. *Cook's* introduced me to cuisines more exotic than those of Benihana and the Chinese take-out restaurants I grew up with in Connecticut. I was thrilled to discover how a Spanish stew is enriched with grated bittersweet chocolate, or how a baklava can be sweetened with squash and raisins. I wanted to be a part of the world that created these foods.

Still in college, I bought and read books from used bookstores about cuisines in various countries. I volunteered myself as an assistant at two of New York City's cooking schools. I bought roller skates and skated all over New York, scouring the Polish, Italian, Indian, Chinese, and Central American neighborhoods looking for food shops. As I traveled around the globe within the confines of New York, I found that in many countries people don't eat much meat. Moreover, I saw that most cuisines do not revolve around meat, but are instead shaped by the ways that particular vegetables, grains, and spices are cooked and combined. From Provençal sandwiches, chickpea fritters, and tamales to kimchi, gazpachos, and quesadillas, the myriad of exciting meatless dishes from around the planet stunned me.

After college, cooking turned into my vocation. As a result, my world of food has grown even larger. For the next twelve years I worked in restaurants, in cooking schools, and with food writers. I saw how temperamental gnocchi dough can be, and I learned why a Korean pancake is more tender than a Chinese scallion pancake. I came to understand why Salvadorans squeeze lime juice on their yuca and why the French fuss over the preparation of an omelet. And I witnessed time and time again that cuisines all over this planet can be at their best when meat isn't around. The flavors of herbs and spices come through clearer in meatless dishes, and the personalities of vegetables and grains are more vivid. With a choice of tantalizing food combinations and spice mixtures from all corners of the world, meatless eating can be satisfying beyond words. Today, vegetarians who like to cook enjoy endless creative possibilities.

These are the ideas that spurred me to write this book. In *Vegetarian Planet*, I have explored ways to cook some of my favorite foods. My style is not fusion cooking—I don't try to mix various cuisines. But I do invent twists on traditional concepts and dishes. In *Planet*, I've tried to offer a repertoire of full-flavored dishes that will entice you to try them and leave you satisfied at the end of the meal. I hope that you will enjoy these dishes, and, when you have finished one, that you will not think about the fact that it was meatless. I hope you will enjoy, as I do, the great variety of foods our planet has to offer.

# CHAPTER 1

# Splendid Breads

# Dried Cranberry–Pecan Coffeecake

I love the tart flavor of the dried cranberries in this sweet, moist coffeecake. Toasted pecans are combined with brown sugar, fresh gingerroot, flour, and butter to create a delicious crumble that sits atop the cake. Although this recipe has more steps than others, it is not difficult, and it's certainly worth trying if you're a fan of coffeecakes.

**CRUMBLE:**
3 tablespoons minced fresh ginger
3/4 cup brown sugar, lightly packed
1/4 cup unbleached white flour
1/4 cup unsalted butter, melted
1 1/2 cups chopped pecans, lightly toasted

**CAKE:**
1/2 cup orange juice
1 1/2 cups dried cranberries
2 3/4 cups unbleached white flour
1 1/2 teaspoons baking soda
1 1/2 teaspoons baking powder
1 teaspoon salt
1 1/2 cups sugar
10 tablespoons (1 1/4 sticks) unsalted butter,
    softened
3 eggs
1 teaspoon vanilla extract
1 teaspoon grated lemon rind
2 teaspoons ground ginger
1 cup buttermilk or plain yogurt
1 cup whole, low-fat or nonfat sour cream

**1.** In a bowl, combine the ingredients for the crumble. Set the bowl aside.

**2.** Preheat the oven to 375°. Butter and flour a 9-by-13-inch pan.

**3.** In a small saucepan, bring the orange juice to a simmer. Stir in the cranberries, and cover the pan. Let the cranberries simmer for about 3 minutes, then remove the pan from the heat, and let the mixture cool.

**4.** In a small bowl, stir together the flour, baking soda, baking powder, and salt for the cake.

In a large bowl or in an electric mixer, blend the sugar with the butter until the mixture is light and fluffy. Beat in the eggs, one by one, and the vanilla, lemon rind, and ginger. Blend in the buttermilk or yogurt, then fold in half the flour mixture. Stir in the sour cream. Strain the cranberries, and add them to the batter. Then fold in the remaining flour mixture, being careful not to overmix.

**5.** Spoon the batter into the casserole pan. Sprinkle the crumble evenly over the batter. Bake the cake for 60 to 70 minutes, or until a knife inserted into the center comes out clean.

**6.** Let the cake cool for 10 minutes before cutting it. This coffeecake keeps well, wrapped and refrigerated, for up to 4 days. Well wrapped, it freezes well, too.

**Variation:** Use 2 cups fresh cranberries instead of the dried cranberries, and omit the orange juice and step 3.

Makes 12 servings

# Fruited Sherry Bread

This recipe combines two ideas. First, I wanted to make a quick bread that didn't have a lot of fat, and second, I wanted to make a bread that showcased dried fruits. After I made a few versions, I realized that this would be a lovely hol-

On airplane eating:

"I dislike eating at a restaurant that's 30,000 feet in the air. You can't walk out."
—ALAN KING, COMEDIAN

iday bread, which made me feel I was helping society at large. Unlike the completely inedible fruitcake of legend, which travels from house to house, year after year, this fruited bread gets eaten. It is better on the second day, and, when well wrapped and refrigerated, it lasts for at least two weeks.

2½ cups mixed dried fruits, such as figs, pitted
    prunes or dates, raisins, dried apricots,
    currants, dried cranberries, or dried cherries
3 tablespoons chopped crystallized ginger
    (optional)
²/₃ cup sherry
1 teaspoon grated orange rind
2 tablespoons unsalted butter, softened
3/4 cup sugar
1 egg, beaten
1 cup milk
2¼ cups unbleached white flour
1½ teaspoons baking powder
½ teaspoon ground allspice
1 teaspoon salt
1 cup walnuts, lightly toasted

**1.** Cut the figs and the prunes in half. Place them in a small saucepan with the other dried fruits, the crystallized ginger, the sherry, and the orange rind. Bring the mixture to a boil, remove the pan from the heat, cover it, and let it rest for 30 minutes.

**2.** Butter and flour a 9-by-5-by-3-inch loaf pan. Preheat the oven to 350°. In a mixing bowl, cream the butter and sugar. Beat in the egg, then the milk.

**3.** In a large bowl, combine the flour, baking powder, allspice, and salt. Make a well in the center and pour the egg mixture into it. With a wooden spoon, slowly incorporate the liquid, but do not overmix. Stir in the walnuts, the macerated fruit, and the accompanying liquid. Transfer the batter to the loaf pan.

**4.** Bake the bread for 1 hour to 1 hour and 10 minutes, checking it after 1 hour by inserting a knife into the loaf (if it comes out clean, the bread is ready). Let the loaf cool in the pan 15 minutes before removing it. When the bread has cooled completely, wrap it in plastic. It tastes better if left to sit for a day, and it's especially good with butter or cream cheese.

Makes 1 loaf

# Carrot Coffeecake
# with
# Poppy-Seed Streusel

Nothing can beat a Sunday morning with coffeecake, a good cup of coffee, and the newspaper. This carrot coffeecake is one of my all-time favorites. The carrots are ground in the food processor, not grated, and I think this allows the carrot flavor to come through better. The poppy seeds and walnuts in the streusel give the cake an enjoyable crunch and nutty flavor.

3 large carrots (about 3/4 pounds), peeled and
    chopped
2 cups plus 3 tablespoons unbleached white flour
1½ teaspoons ground cinnamon
½ teaspoon ground nutmeg
½ teaspoon ground cardamom (optional)
2 teaspoons baking powder
1 teaspoon baking soda
1 teaspoon salt
4 eggs
3/4 cup sugar

$^2/_3$ cup canola or corn oil
2 tablespoons poppy seeds
$^1/_4$ cup sour cream

**STREUSEL:**
$^1/_2$ cup poppy seeds
2 tablespoons butter, softened, plus a bit for
    greasing the pan
$1^1/_3$ cups walnuts
$^1/_2$ cup brown sugar, lightly packed
3 tablespoons unbleached white flour

**1.** Preheat the oven to 350°. Grease a tube or Bundt pan.

**2.** In a food processor, grind the carrots for 1 to 2 minutes, almost to a purée. Transfer them to a small bowl, and set it aside.

**3.** Grind the streusel ingredients in the food processor for 1 minute.

**4.** In a large bowl, combine the flour, cinnamon, nutmeg, cardamom (if you like), baking powder and soda, and salt. In a smaller bowl, whisk together the eggs, sugar, oil, ground carrots, poppy seeds, and sour cream. Add the liquid mixture to the dry, stirring with a wooden spoon. Transfer half the batter to the cake pan. Sprinkle half of the streusel onto the batter, then pour the remaining half of the batter over the streusel. Top with the remaining streusel.

**5.** Bake the cake for 1 hour or until a knife inserted into the center comes out clean. Let the cake cool in its pan for 30 minutes before inverting it onto a serving dish. Serve the coffeecake at room temperature.

Makes 1 Bundt or tube cake,
about 12 to 16 slices

# Cardamom Banana Bread

This tastes better than the banana bread I had as a kid, and it doesn't contain that typical cup of vegetable oil. If you have no cardamom on hand, substitute ground nutmeg, which also makes for a delicious bread.

2/3 cup raisins or currants
1/3 cup dark rum or apple cider
1 cup unbleached white flour
3/4 cup whole-wheat flour (or more white flour)
2 teaspoons baking powder
1 teaspoon baking soda
1 teaspoon salt
1 teaspoon ground cardamom
3 ripe bananas
1/3 cup canola or corn oil
3/4 cup light brown sugar, firmly packed
2 eggs
1/2 cup chopped walnuts, lightly toasted

**1.** Preheat the oven to 350°. Grease a 9- or 10-inch loaf pan.

**2.** In a small saucepan, combine the raisins or currants with the rum or cider, and bring the mixture to a simmer. Turn off the heat, and let the pan sit for 10 minutes.

**3.** While the raisins or currants are soaking, combine in a large bowl the flours, baking powder, baking soda, salt, and cardamom. Mix well. In a smaller bowl (or the bowl of an electric mixer), mash the bananas with a fork. Add the oil and brown sugar, and beat for 1 minute. Add the eggs, and beat 1 minute more. With a spoon, stir this mixture into the flour mixture until the ingredients are well combined. Stir in the walnuts, the soaked raisins or currants, and their liquid. Pour the mixture into the greased loaf pan.

**4.** Bake the bread 50 to 60 minutes, until a knife inserted in the middle comes out clean. Remove the pan from the oven, place

## Cardamom

There is no other spice that I enjoy smelling as much as cardamom. A member of the ginger family, cardamom has an aroma that is intensely assertive, sweet, flowery, and peppery all at once. The spice is best known for its use in Scandinavian pastries and breads, and Indian savory and sweet dishes. I like cardamom in carrot cakes and quick breads.

Cardamom seeds are available ground, whole, and in their intact pods. I prefer to crack the pods and grind the seeds myself, or use the pods whole in rice and grain dishes and sweet custards. Try floating a pod or two in your coffee, as the Turkish do. Cardamom can be found in many supermarkets as well as Indian and Middle Eastern markets.

it on a rack, and let the bread cool for 10 minutes before you remove it from the pan. Wrapped well, this bread keeps at room temperature for 5 days, and longer if refrigerated.

Makes 1 loaf

# Granny's Oatmeal Bread

My upstairs neighbor, Rob, occasionally cooks up a storm to relieve the pressure of finishing his grad school dissertation. This recipe, one of his favorites, came from his grandmother, Dorothy Wilson McElroy. Even when it's a week old, her oatmeal bread makes excellent toast.

Rob prefers Br'er Rabbit or Plantation molasses. He also likes blackstrap molasses, but says it is probably too strong for most people's tastes.

2 cups rolled oats
2 cups boiling water
1 cup scalded whole milk
1 tablespoon canola or corn oil
2/3 cup molasses
1/3 cup sugar
1 tablespoon dry yeast
6 cups unbleached white flour
1 tablespoon salt

**1.** Put the oats into a very large bowl, or into a mixer with a dough hook. Pour the boiling water over them. Then add the scalded milk, and stir. Pour in the oil and molasses, and stir.

**2.** In another bowl, mix the sugar with the yeast and 1 cup of the flour. When the oatmeal mixture has cooled to lukewarm, add the yeast-flour mixture. Stir, and add the salt. Stir in the remaining 5 cups of flour.

**3.** If you are using a mixer, knead on the lowest setting for 5 minutes. Otherwise, beat the dough with a sturdy spoon (preferably a metal one) for 8 minutes, holding the bowl tight with one arm. If you use a spoon, make sure you work all the dough. This is hard on the wrists; if 8 minutes is longer than you can manage, just beat as long as you can.

Cover the bowl with a damp towel, and place the bowl in a warm spot until the dough has doubled in bulk, about 1½ hours.

**4.** Punch the dough down. Knead briefly with a spoon, then divide it in half, and place it in two greased 9-by-5-by-3-inch loaf pans. Cover the pans with a damp towel, and let the dough rise in a warm spot until it has almost doubled in bulk.

**5.** While the dough rises, preheat the oven to 350°.

**6.** Bake the loaves for about 1 hour. To make sure they're done, turn them out of the pans and tap them on the bottom; they should sound hollow. Let the loaves cool on a rack. When the loaves have cooled thoroughly, wrap them well, and store them in a cool spot.

**Variations:** Use 2 cups whole-wheat flour and 4 cups unbleached white flour instead of the 6 cups white flour. Or substitute 1 cup cornmeal for 1 cup of the flour.

Makes 2 loaves

# Irish Soda Bread

After many soda bread failures, I called upon Boston's soda bread expert, Eileen Hanlon, to help me out. She has been baking soda bread since her youth in Galway. Now a grandmother in Belmont, Massachusetts, she still bakes soda bread every Saturday morning.

Speckled with raisins and caraway seeds, this soda bread is delicious fresh from the oven with a bit of butter, or toasted and buttered a few days later.

1 3/4 cups raisins

4 cups unbleached white flour

1/2 teaspoon salt

1 tablespoon caraway seeds

1/4 teaspoon baking soda

2 1/2 teaspoons baking powder

2 eggs

1/3 cup sugar

1 tablespoon whole, low-fat, or nonfat sour
   cream, or yogurt

1/2 cup whole or low-fat milk

3/4 cup buttermilk

**1.** In a small bowl, cover the raisins with warm water, and let them sit for 15 minutes. Preheat the oven to 335°.

**2.** In a large bowl, stir together the flour, salt, caraway seeds, baking soda, and baking powder.

In a smaller bowl, whisk together the eggs, sugar, and sour cream or yogurt. Beat in the milk and the buttermilk.

**3.** Drain the raisins. Spread them on a towel, and pat them dry with another towel. Stir them into the egg mixture.

Make a well in the flour mixture, and pour in the egg mixture. Stir with a strong wooden spoon until the dough comes together. Then transfer the dough to a clean work surface, and knead the dough lightly with your palms (not forcefully with the heal of your hand, as for yeast dough) for about a minute. Work in a bit of flour if the dough is too sticky to handle. When the dough is smooth, form it into a round about 7 inches in diameter. Sprinkle flour onto the round of dough, then gently flatten it with your hands to 9 inches in diameter. Turn the round over, and pat its sides to form an 8-inch round of dough.

**4.** Heat a heavy 8-inch cast-iron skillet until it is warm. Remove the pan from the heat, and coat it with a thin film of butter, using a paper towel to distribute the butter. Dust the skillet with flour, and shake out the excess. Swiftly place the round of dough top side up in the pan. With a sharp knife, cut 1/2 inch deep through the center of the round from one side to the other, then make another cut like the first but perpendicular to it.

**5.** Bake the loaf for about 1 hour and 10 minutes, until it is lightly browned on top. Serve the bread warm or cold, with butter.

Makes 1 large round loaf

# Brown Soda Bread

Hearty and wholesome, brown soda bread is everyday fare for the Irish. I wish it were for Americans, too. Toasted and topped with butter, it is a terrific breakfast bread. This recipe is based on one from Boston's master soda bread baker, Eileen Hanlon.

In Ireland, cooks use a coarse stone-ground whole-wheat flour for their brown soda bread. Unfortunately, such flour is hard to find in the United States, so to approximate the texture and flavor of Irish brown soda bread I've added toasted wheat bran and wheat germ to finer stone-ground whole-wheat flour.

2 cups stone-ground whole-wheat flour (I use
    Arrowhead Mills)
1/3 cup wheat bran
1/4 cup toasted wheat germ
2 cups unbleached white flour
1/2 teaspoon salt
1 tablespoon baking powder
1/4 teaspoon baking soda
1/3 cup sugar
1 tablespoon sour cream
1 large egg
1 1/2 cups buttermilk
1 cup milk

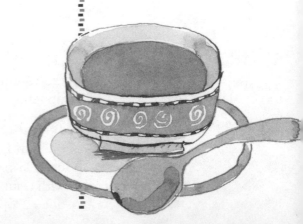

**1.** Preheat the oven to 350°. Butter two 9-by-5-by-3-inch loaf pans or one large Dutch oven. (Eileen likes to heat her pans slightly in the oven before buttering them, so the butter forms a thinner, more uniform film; the bread sticks less this way.)

**2.** In a large bowl, stir together the whole-wheat flour, bran, wheat germ, white flour, salt, baking powder, and baking soda. In another bowl, combine the sugar, sour cream, and eggs, and whisk well. Add the buttermilk and milk, and whisk again.

**3.** Make a well in the flour mixture, and pour the egg mixture into it. Stir well with a wooden spoon until the ingredients are incorporated. Spoon the batter into the prepared pan or pans. Bake regular loaves for 40 to 45 minutes, or a large loaf for about 1 hour and 10 minutes. The bread is done when a knife inserted in the middle comes out clean.

**4.** Turn the bread out of the pan. Let the bread cool for 15 minutes, then serve it with butter, or let it cool completely and serve it toasted. The bread will keep for 4 to 5 days if it is wrapped well and refrigerated.

*Makes 2 medium loaves,
or 1 large loaf*

# Three-Seed Anadama Bread

This is a traditional New England bread made from cornmeal and wheat flour. The story behind the bread's name comes in many versions; the most common concerns a hungry fisherman in Gloucester, Massachusetts, who was fed up when his wife, Anna, didn't have any bread in the house. He begrudgingly made his own bread, adding some cornmeal and molasses on a whim, and when he sat down to eat it he cursed, "Anna, damn her!"

This bread is just as good without seeds, but it is more healthful with them. It is especially good toasted.

1¼ cups cornmeal

2 cups water

2 tablespoons unsalted butter

¼ cup molasses, preferably blackstrap

1 tablespoon dry yeast

½ cup warm water

3¼ cups unbleached white flour

1 cup whole-wheat flour

1½ teaspoons salt

¼ cup sunflower seeds

3 tablespoons poppy seeds

3 tablespoons sesame seeds

1 tablespoon flax seeds (optional)

**1.** Mix ¾ cup cornmeal with the 2 cups water in a heavy saucepan over medium heat. Stir the mixture with a whisk until it bubbles. Add the butter, the molasses, and the remaining ½ cup cornmeal. Cook for another 2 minutes while stirring. Transfer the mixture to a plate, and let it cool for 15 minutes.

**2.** Meanwhile, dissolve the yeast in ½ cup lukewarm water. In a large bowl, combine 2¾ cups of the white flour, the whole-wheat flour, the salt, and all the seeds.

**3.** Add the cornmeal mixture and the yeast mixture to the large bowl. Stir well with a sturdy spoon until the dough forms a solid mass. Transfer the dough to a floured work surface, and knead it for 7 minutes, adding some or all of the remaining ½ cup flour, if necessary.

**4.** Place the dough in a large, lightly oiled bowl, cover the bowl with a damp towel, and let the dough rise in a warm spot until it has doubled in bulk, about 1 hour.

**5.** Punch the dough down, and knead it in the bowl for 1 minute or so. Grease two 9-by-5-by-3-inch loaf pans. Cut the dough in half with a sharp knife, and shape the halves into two

## Spices Separated at Birth

*S*tar anise, anise, and fennel. One would think they all come from the same family, because they all have a distinct licorice flavor. Fennel and anise, like cumin, caraway, dill, parsley, and carrot, belong to the family Umbelliferae. Star anise, however, is unrelated. The dried, star-shaped brown fruit of an evergreen tree, it has the strongest flavor of the three, almost like bitter caramel. Anise seed is less intense in flavor than star anise, but somewhat sweeter and stronger than fennel. Both fennel and anise contain the oil anethole, which accounts for their similar flavors. All three spices, when ground, can substitute for any of the others if you use a careful hand.*

loaves. Place them in the pans, cover with the damp towel, and let the loaves rise until they have almost doubled in bulk, about 45 minutes. While the dough is rising a second time, preheat the oven to 375°.

**6.** Bake the bread for 45 to 55 minutes, until the loaf sounds hollow when tapped on the bottom.

**7.** Remove the bread from the oven, and let it cool on a rack. This bread freezes well. It also keeps well at room temperature, wrapped, for 3 days.

Makes 2 loaves

# Paximade

*T*his Greek bread, perfumed with anise, tastes almost like a cake, although the sugar content is much lower. Melissa Manolis, who introduced me to this bread, keeps it for days, toasting it for breakfast morning after morning.

2½ cups unbleached white flour
2 teaspoons baking powder
½ teaspoon salt
1 teaspoon anise seed; or 2 star anise, ground in a spice mill
½ cup unsalted butter, softened
½ cup sugar
2 eggs
½ cup whole or low-fat milk

**1.** Preheat the oven to 350°. Butter a 9-by-5-by-3-inch loaf pan. Sift the flour with the baking powder and salt. Add the anise to the flour mixture.

**2.** In a large bowl, beat the butter and the sugar until the mixture is light and fluffy. Add an egg, beat well, then add the other egg. Beat until the mixture lightens in color, about 1 minute. Add the milk and the sifted flour mixture alternately, the flour in three parts and the milk in two. Fold with a rubber spatula until they are incorporated. Spoon the batter into the loaf pan.

**3.** Bake the bread for 50 minutes or until a knife inserted in the middle comes out clean. Let the bread cool in the pan 10 minutes before inverting the loaf onto a rack. When the bread has cooled completely, wrap it well in plastic. Store it in the refrigerator for up to 10 days. (After the second day, toast the bread to revive it.)

Makes 1 loaf

# Naan

Naan is a flatbread that is eaten in India, western China, Iran, Afghanistan, and Pakistan. The bread is traditionally cooked in a tandoor oven, which often exceeds 700° Fahrenheit. Pieces of dough are slapped onto the burning hot sides of the clay oven and are left to bake for 7 to 8 minutes. Lacking a tandoor oven, you can bake naan on a baking stone, on unglazed quarry tiles, or even on a metal baking sheet. Incorporating the scallions into the dough is not traditional, but I prefer them this way rather than tossed on top, where they tend to burn.

1 teaspoon dry yeast

1¼ cups warm water

3 cups unbleached white flour, plus a bit more for kneading

1½ teaspoons salt

1 tablespoon olive oil

1¼ cups minced scallions

1 egg beaten with 2 tablespoons water

1 teaspoon cumin seeds

**1.** Dissolve the yeast in the warm water, and let the mixture sit for 10 minutes. In a large bowl, combine 3 cups flour and the salt.

**2.** Add the olive oil to the yeast water. Pour the yeast water over the flour, and stir well with a sturdy spoon. Once the dough comes together, spoon it out onto a floured surface.

**3.** Knead the dough for 5 to 8 minutes, adding flour as needed to keep the dough from sticking. But be careful not to add too much flour; the dough should remain quite soft and slightly tacky. Once the dough is smooth and supple, place it in a greased bowl and cover it with a damp towel. Let the dough rise in a warm place until it is doubled in bulk, which usually takes a little over an hour.

**4.** Punch the dough down, and turn it out onto a lightly floured surface. Put the scallions on top, and knead the dough to incorporate them well. Cut the dough into three equal pieces. Form each piece into a ball, and let the balls of dough rest for 20 minutes.

**5.** Place a baking stone, quarry tiles, or two baking sheets in the oven. Preheat the oven to 500°. Sprinkle the cumin seeds onto your work surface, and roll each ball of dough into the seeds so that they are transferred to the dough. With a rolling pin, flatten the balls into 9-inch rounds with the seeds all on one side. Place the rounds on well-floured baking sheets, seed side up. Let them rest for 10 minutes.

**6.** Slide the dough onto the baking stone, quarry tiles, or heated baking sheets. Bake the rounds in the oven for 8 to 10 minutes, rotating them in the oven, if necessary, for even cooking. Eat the bread warm with olive oil, if you like.

Variation: For extra texture, color, and flavor, try sprinkling 1 tablespoon nigella seeds (found in Indian markets) into the flour and salt in step 1.

Makes 3 9-inch
flatbread rounds

# Ten-Minute Cornbread

Buttermilk is the magician at work here; I'm continually impressed at its ability to lighten and moisten baked goods. This one-bowl batter can be combined and placed in the oven in about 10 minutes. The bread is best served hot from the oven, or at least served the same day it is baked (it goes stale quickly and does not freeze well). If there is still some left on the second day, I recommend toasting it.

2 cups cornmeal, preferably labeled organic or
   stone-ground
1 cup whole-wheat flour or unbleached white
   flour
1/2 teaspoon salt
2 teaspoons baking powder
1 teaspoon baking soda
3 cups buttermilk
2 tablespoons honey
4 eggs
6 tablespoons canola oil, corn oil, or melted
   butter
1 bunch scallions, both white and green parts,
   minced (about 1 1/2 cups)

**1.** Grease a 9-by-5-by-3-inch or a 13-by-9-inch pan. Preheat the oven to 400°. In a large bowl, combine the cornmeal, flour, salt, baking powder, and baking soda. In another bowl, whisk together the buttermilk, honey, eggs, and oil or butter. Make a well in the cornmeal mixture, and pour the liquid mixture into it. With a whisk, stir the liquid mixture slowly, gradually incorporating the cornmeal mixture. Once it is totally incorporated, stir in the scallions.

**2.** Pour the batter into the prepared pan. Bake the bread 45 minutes if you are using a loaf pan, 35 minutes if you are using

## Mahleb

*T*raditionally used in Turkish and Syrian cooking, mahleb *(or* mahlab*) is the core of the sour cherry pit. Once ground in a spice mill, it adds a sour, nutty flavor to grain salads, rice dishes, and even cookies and pound cake. Paula Wolfert, in her book* The Cooking of the Eastern Mediterranean, *recommends adding* mahleb *to breads to impart a terrific aroma.*

*This spice is not easy to find. One reliable source is the mail-order spice company, Penzeys, in Waukesha, Wisconsin. The phone number is 414-574-0277.*

the larger pan. The bread is ready when a knife inserted into the center comes out clean. Serve and eat the bread as soon as possible.

*Makes 1 loaf*

# Spelt Walnut Bread

*T*his recipe combines rye, white, and spelt flours. An ancient type of wheat, spelt is used in many Italian breads, especially in Tuscany. Spelt flour produces a delicate, moist loaf. It can be found at many whole-foods stores.

▪▪▪▪▪▪▪▪▪

1 3/4 cups warm water
1 teaspoon sugar
2 teaspoons (1 package) dry yeast
1 egg
2 cups unbleached white flour
2 cups spelt flour
1 cup rye flour
1 1/2 teaspoons salt
1 1/2 cups walnut pieces

▪▪▪▪▪▪▪▪▪

**1.** Place the water and sugar in a small bowl. Sprinkle the yeast over the water, and let the yeast proof for about 5 minutes. Add the eggs, and whisk the mixture well. Set it aside.

**2.** In a large bowl, combine the white flour, spelt flour, rye flour, and salt. Make a well in the center, and pour in the liquid mixture. Stir well with a large wooden spoon until the dough begins to come together. Turn the dough out onto a lightly floured surface, and knead lightly for about 5 minutes, adding more flour if the dough becomes sticky (the gluten in spelt is fragile, and can be broken down by rough or long kneading).

**3.** Place the dough in a lightly oiled bowl, and cover with plastic wrap or a damp cloth. Place the bowl in a warm spot, and let it rise until it is doubled in bulk, about 1 hour.

**4.** Punch the dough down, and put the walnuts on top. Knead the dough for 3 to 4 minutes, incorporating the walnuts throughout the bread. If you want to make two loaves, cut the dough in two, shape the two halves, and then place them in two lightly oiled 9-by-5-by-3-inch loaf pans. If you want to make one large round loaf, sprinkle a baking sheet with flour, and form the dough into a large ball. Place it on the baking sheet.

Cover the dough with a damp cloth, and let the dough rise until it is almost doubled in bulk, about 45 minutes. Sprinkle the dough with a bit of flour.

While the dough rises, preheat the oven to 350°.

**5.** Bake the bread for 1 hour if you are making two small loaves, or for 1 hour and 20 minutes if you are making one large loaf.

Variation: About 80 percent of those who are allergic to regular wheat flour can tolerate spelt flour without any problems. If this is true for you, you can substitute spelt flour for the unbleached white flour, using a total of 4 cups spelt. The bread will be denser, but will taste quite good.

Makes 2 loaves or
1 large round loaf

# Dark Boston
# Brown Bread

After making many successful loaves of traditional Boston brown bread, I one day doubled the original recipe but forgot to double the amount of rye flour. The bread came out much moister, albeit a little gummy. I was intrigued, so I made

# Raisins to the Rescue

*Rich in iron, potassium, and fiber, raisins are a versatile food. Use them in chutneys, in stuffings for vegetables, and in grain salads as well as cookies, scones, muffins, and breads. Several kinds of raisins are common. The pale yellow raisins often called sultanas are dried from the same grape (Thompson) as the conventional raisin, but are treated with sulphur dioxide to prevent darkening. Black Monukka raisins are larger than Thompsons and slightly crunchy. California Red Flame raisins are twice the size of Thompson raisins, and can add elegance to many a dish. The little raisins called currants are dried Zante grapes, not fresh currants that have been dried.*

the bread again with a smaller quantity of rye flour than the original recipe called for. This time it was perfect—moist but not gummy. Boston brown bread is perfect alongside any of the chilis and stews in chapter 17.

1 cup rye flour
1½ cups cornmeal, preferably labeled organic or
    stone-ground
1 teaspoon baking soda
½ teaspoon salt
½ cup dark molasses, warmed
2 cups whole or low-fat milk
1 egg, beaten
1 cup raisins
2 empty 1-pound coffee cans

**1.** Combine the rye flour, cornmeal, baking soda, and salt in a bowl. In another bowl, combine the warmed molasses, milk, and egg, and stir well. Combine all of the ingredients, and mix them well. Stir in the raisins.

**2.** Butter two 1-pound coffee cans. Pour the batter evenly into the two cans. Seal the cans tightly with foil. Pour 2 inches of water into a stockpot wide enough to fit the two cans. Place the cans in the stockpot, then cover the stockpot with a lid or with foil.

**3.** Turn the heat to high. As soon as the water begins to boil, turn the heat to low. Steam the bread for 2 hours, checking occasionally to make sure at least 1 inch of water remains in the pot.

**4.** Remove the cans from the stockpot. Remove the foil lids, and let the bread cool for 15 to 20 minutes. With a butter knife, loosen the bread around the sides. Then, holding the can upside down, shake the bread out. Slice the bread, and serve it with butter.

Makes 2 6-inch
cylindrical loaves

# Chutneys, Ketchups, Salsas, & More

# Roasted Corn and Garlic Salsa

You might think that a recipe using such ordinary ingredients as corn, garlic, and tomatoes would taste ordinary, but the quick roasting of the sliced garlic and corn makes for a sophisticated salsa. Serve it with chips and sour cream, or with quesadillas or burritos.

The easiest way to cut corn without sending the kernels in all directions is to lay the ear flat on a cutting board and make lengthwise cuts with a large chef's knife.

Kernels from 3 ears corn (about 2 cups)
15 large garlic cloves, peeled and sliced thin
2 tablespoons olive oil
2 tablespoons water
1/2 teaspoon salt
Fresh-ground black pepper to taste
3 ripe round tomatoes or 6 small plum tomatoes,
    cored and chopped fine
1/4 cup lime juice (from about 2 limes)
1 to 2 jalapeños, minced, with seeds included if
    you like a lot of heat
1/4 cup chopped cilantro

**1.** Preheat the oven to 375°. Put the corn kernels in a roasting pan with the garlic, and mix well. Drizzle the olive oil over the corn, and add the water, salt, and pepper. Mix well. Roast the corn and garlic, uncovered, for 20 minutes.

**2.** In a bowl, combine the tomatoes, the corn and garlic mixture, the lime juice, the jalapeño, and the cilantro. Stir well, and let the salsa stand for 1 hour at room temperature so the flavors can develop.

Serve the salsa immediately, or store it in a sealed container in the refrigerator for up to 4 days. It is best the day it is made.

Makes 3 cups salsa

# Soused
# Salsa

Here salsa gets to drink tequila and have a good time. I call for plum tomatoes because even the imported ones available in winter are tolerably flavorful, but by all means use local tomatoes of any kind when you can get them. I particularly enjoy this salsa with Homemade Tortilla Chips (page 411) and, of course, a margarita.

8 plum tomatoes, chopped fine
4 scallions, both green and white parts, chopped fine
1 green bell pepper or poblano pepper, seeded and chopped fine
1/4 cup chopped cilantro (stems can be included)
1 large garlic clove, minced
1 jalapeño pepper, minced, with seeds included if you like a lot of heat (optional)
1/4 cup lime juice (from about 2 limes)
2 tablespoons tequila
1 tablespoon olive oil
1/2 teaspoon salt
Fresh-ground black pepper to taste

**1.** In a small bowl, combine the tomatoes, scallions, pepper, cilantro, and garlic. If you're using bell pepper or want extra heat, add the jalapeño, with or without seeds. Mix well.

**2.** Add the lime juice, tequila, and olive oil. Stir well, and add the salt and pepper. Serve the salsa immediately, or store it in a sealed container in the refrigerator for no more than 24 hours.

Makes 3 cups salsa

# Apple-Chipotle Salsa

For a quesadilla topping or burrito accompaniment, I believe one can do no better than a bit of apple-chipotle salsa. Use a sweet apple that will retain its crunchiness and flavor. I prefer Fuji or Golden Delicious.

> 3 sweet apples (such as Fuji, Golden Delicious, Cortland, or Northern Spy), cored and chopped
> 1 cup minced red onion
> 2 green bell peppers, seeded and cut into 1/2-inch squares
> 2 chipotle peppers (dried and soaked in hot water 30 minutes, or canned in adobo sauce), chopped fine
> 1/2 small garlic clove, minced
> 1/4 cup lime juice (from about 2 limes)
> 1 tablespoon apple cider vinegar
> 1 tablespoon olive oil
> 2 tablespoons chopped cilantro
> 1/2 teaspoon salt
> Fresh-ground black pepper to taste

**1.** Combine the apples with the onion and bell peppers in a large bowl.

**2.** In a smaller bowl, combine the chipotles with the garlic, lime juice, cider vinegar, olive oil, and cilantro, and stir. Add this mixture to the fruit mixture. Stir well, and add the salt and pepper. It's best to serve this salsa on the day it is made, but you can store it in a covered container in the refrigerator for up to 3 days.

**Variation:** Substitute poblano, serrano, Anaheim, or any other chile pepper for the bell pepper. Be careful how many chiles you use, because the salsa can quickly become too hot.

*Makes 4 cups salsa*

# Rasta Salsa

The bright colors you see on Rastafarian hats, scarves, ankle bracelets, and rugs are displayed just as beautifully in this fruity salsa.

4 ripe nectarines or peaches, cut into $1/2$-inch cubes

$1/2$ pound green seedless grapes, stemmed and coarsely chopped

$1/2$ cup minced red onion

1 green bell or poblano pepper, seeded and cut into $1/2$-inch squares

1 red bell pepper, seeded, and cut into $1/2$-inch squares

1 to 3 jalapeños, or 1 to 3 canned chipotle peppers in adobo sauce

$1/4$ cup chopped cilantro

$1/3$ cup lime juice (from about 3 limes)

1 tablespoon olive oil

$1/2$ teaspoon salt

Fresh-ground black pepper to taste

**1.** In a large bowl, combine the nectarines or peaches, grapes, onion, and bell or poblano peppers.

**2.** If you're using jalapeños, char them directly on a hot electric burner or, using a fork, over a gas flame. Either way, let the pepper partly blacken, then rotate it so it becomes a bit charred all over. Mince the charred pepper or the chipotles, and add them to the salsa.

**3.** Stir in the cilantro, lime juice, and olive oil. Add the salt and pepper. It's best to serve the salsa on the day it is made, but you can store it in a covered container in the refrigerator for up to 3 days.

Makes 5 cups salsa

# Salsa Verde

This classic salsa is still one of the best. You can grind the ingredients in a food processor or blender, but let the machine run for only a few seconds, so the salsa does not become a purée. If the consistency is too thin, the salsa won't hold onto chips or any other food well. This salsa is good with Homemade Tortilla Chips (page 411) or quesadillas.

2 quarts water
1 pound tomatillos, husked
3 large garlic cloves
½ cup chopped onion
1 tablespoon olive oil
¼ cup lime juice (from about 2 limes)
1½ teaspoons sugar
½ cup chopped cilantro
½ to 1 jalapeño pepper, minced
½ teaspoon salt
Fresh-ground black pepper to taste

**1.** Bring the water to a boil in a saucepan. Add the tomatillos, and boil them for 3 minutes. Drain the tomatillos, and put them into a blender or food processor.

**2.** Add the remaining ingredients to the tomatillos. Blend for only a few seconds, leaving the salsa a bit chunky (small pieces of onion and tomatillo should be evident). Store the salsa in a sealed container in the refrigerator until you are ready to serve it. It will keep for 4 days.

Makes 3 cups salsa

# Salsa City

### ✺✺✺

The salsa craze has hit every town in the union. No longer exclusively Mexican, salsa is also part of the American way of life. At the restaurant, I spend a portion of every day making gallons of salsa. It's a wonderful outlet for my creative side.

The first and most important step is choosing a combination of fruits and vegetables. I am fortunate in that I go to the market for produce, so I have more control than chefs who order produce by phone. Also, at the market I can spot overripe fruit and buy it at a discount. Or, I'll get inspired by what I see—fat nectarines, ruby-red grapes, crunchy jícama, sweet basil.

Once the produce is home, you can slice the vegetables and fruits, chop them coarsely, grind them, or vary the treatment depending on the ingredient.

The basic ingredients common to most salsas are lime juice, some kind of chile pepper, salt, and a fresh herb, usually cilantro. I like to add a splash of extra-virgin olive oil and often some minced garlic.

The balance of ingredients is important. The amount of lime juice will vary according to the acidity of the produce, but usually one to two limes are used for every two cups of salsa. The heat depends on your tastes and how the salsa will be eaten. If you're serving it in a big burrito, the salsa can be on the hot side—the other foods in the burrito will quell the fire. If the salsa will accompany chips, though, try to keep the heat down.

What do you do with salsa after you have made it? Try the Homemade Tortilla Chips, page 411, or serve your salsa with quesadillas (pages 412 to 416) or enchiladas (pages 399 to 407). Sometimes I put a big scoop of salsa on shredded romaine lettuce, with a bit of olive oil over all. A grilled portobello mushroom topped with salsa is wonderful. Or grill zucchini and eggplant, place them on a bed of rice, and top with some salsa.

## HERE ARE SOME OF MY FAVORITE SALSA COMBOS:

◆ *Poblano chile, apple, red onion, chipotle peppers, cilantro, lime juice, and a touch of apple cider vinegar*

◆ *Grated carrot, red bell pepper, grilled red onions, habanero peppers, and lime juice*

◆ *Cut corn, puréed blanched tomatillos, scallion, chipotle peppers, green bell pepper, cilantro, and lime juice*

◆ *Plum, red onion, red pepper, basil, jalapeño, lime juice, and extra-virgin olive oil*

◆ *Honeydew melon, mango, grilled serrano pepper, shallot, mint, and lime juice*

◆ *Peach, red onion, ancho peppers (soaked and chopped), cilantro, and lime and lemon juice*

◆ *Chopped red grapes, apple, scallion, poblano pepper, cilantro, and lime juice*

◆ *Chopped green grapes, cucumber, jalapeño, fresh oregano, and lime juice*

◆ *Tangerine, avocado, poblano pepper, red onion, cilantro, tangerine juice, and lime juice*

# Harissa

This is my version of a fiery hot sauce found in Tunisia, Morocco, and Algeria. It is traditionally used as a condiment for the many stews of this region. I like it with the Tagine of Eggplant and Olives (page 476) and the African Potato Stew (page 478). But its uses go beyond this; I like it with veggie burgers, alongside curries, with fried plantains, and in barbecue sauces.

5 tablespoons chile flakes, chiltepín peppers, or
    other dried red hot peppers
1 tablespoon coriander seeds
1 tablespoon caraway seeds
1 teaspoon cumin seeds
1 cup chopped fresh jalapeño or other chile
    peppers
15 whole garlic cloves
2 tablespoons apple cider vinegar
2 tablespoons water
1/4 cup canola oil
1 teaspoon salt

**1.** Soak the dried chiles or chile flakes in hot water for 25 minutes.

**2.** Lightly toast the coriander, caraway, and cumin seeds in a skillet over low heat, shaking the pan frequently. When they become slightly fragrant, grind them in a spice grinder or mortar.

**3.** In a food processor or blender, purée the fresh hot peppers with the garlic, adding the vinegar while the machine is running. Drain the soaking chiles, and add them to the machine with the ground spices. While the machine is running, slowly pour in the water and then the oil in a thin stream. Mix in the salt. Store the sauce in a tightly sealed jar in the refrigerator for up to 6 weeks.

Makes 1 cup sauce

# Roasted Garlic

Peeling a cup full of garlic cloves will seem well worth the effort once you have this roasted garlic at your disposal. For starters, try whole roasted cloves on pizzas, in pasta dishes, or in grain dishes. Or try it blended in risotto cakes, mashed potatoes (page 191), or puréed vegetables. It's also delicious as a sandwich spread. Roasted garlic will keep in the refrigerator for at least two weeks.

1 cup garlic cloves, unpeeled
¼ cup olive oil or other vegetable oil
¼ cup water

**1.** Preheat the oven to 350°. Loosen the skins on the cloves by placing the flat side of a chef's knife or cleaver over them and pressing with the heel of your hand.

**2.** In a small, heavy casserole, combine the garlic, oil, and water. Toss well with a spoon to coat the garlic cloves with oil. Then cover the pan with foil, and place it in the oven.

**3.** After 25 minutes or so, take the pan out of the oven, and stir the garlic so it will cook evenly. Return the garlic to the oven, and bake it for another 25 minutes, or until the cloves are soft when squeezed and just beginning to brown in spots. Remove the casserole from the oven, and let the garlic cool.

**4.** Leave the cloves whole in the oil mixture, or peel the garlic and purée it with the oil. Either way, store the garlic in a tightly sealed container in the refrigerator.

Makes about
1 cup roasted garlic

# Chinese Preserved Garlic

Letting garlic sit for three weeks in a sweet and salty marinade can do wonders for your cooking. Pickled garlic is used much as fresh garlic is. I like to mince it and add it to rice and grain dishes and slaws. Although this is a Chinese recipe, the garlic works well in many curries and Japanese dishes. And you can use the pickling liquid to marinate other foods, such as tofu before pan-frying or vegetables before grilling.

¹/₄ cup soy sauce

¹/₄ cup sherry or Chinese rice wine

¹/₄ cup cider vinegar

¹/₄ cup sugar

¹/₄ teaspoon chile flakes

1 cup peeled garlic cloves (from about 2 large heads of garlic)

**1.** In a small saucepan, heat the soy sauce, sherry or rice wine, cider vinegar, sugar, and chile flakes over medium heat. Remove the pan from the heat as soon as the sugar dissolves.

**2.** Put the garlic cloves into a container with a tight-fitting lid and pour the liquid over. Let the mixture cool at room temperature, then seal the container. Refrigerate the garlic for at least 3 weeks. It will keep well for at least 1 month beyond the 3-week marinating period.

Makes 1¹/₂ cups preserved garlic

# Pickled Cucumbers and Daikon

In this recipe, garlic, cloves, cinnamon, and coriander seeds come together to create a powerful pickle. It can be eaten five hours after you make it, and it will keep three weeks in the refrigerator (I don't bother canning it). I usually make this pickle to serve alongside sandwiches or even pilafs, but it would be a perfect addition for a picnic or a buffet table.

1 cup water
3 cups red wine vinegar
3/4 cup sugar
1/2 teaspoon whole cloves
2 cinnamon sticks
1 teaspoon Sichuan peppercorns or black peppercorns
1 tablespoon whole or ground coriander seeds
2 salad cucumbers or 3 small pickling cucumbers
3 garlic cloves, peeled
1 quart daikon radish in 1/8-inch rounds (about 1 radish)
3 tablespoons salt

**1.** In a saucepan, combine the water, vinegar, sugar, cloves, cinnamon sticks, peppercorns, and coriander seeds. Let the mixture come to a boil. Turn the heat down, and simmer the mixture for 15 minutes, uncovered.

**2.** Meanwhile, peel the cucumber if the skin is waxed (pickling cucumbers are rarely waxed, so they need only to be washed). Slice the cucumbers thin.

**3.** After the spiced vinegar has simmered for 15 minutes, add the daikon radish, cucumbers, and salt. Transfer the mixture to a container with an air-tight lid. Let the pickle cool, then seal the container and refrigerate it for at least 5 hours. The pickle is best after 24 hours.

Makes 4 cups relish

## Stu's Very Special Spice Paste

❀

**M**y brother-in-law, Stuart Tilghman, is just as intrigued by spices and condiments as I am. When he can find it, he buys fresh galangal at Asian markets. Stu has come up with a simple paste that is delightful when added to rice, Asian soups, and tofu stir fries (in all cases, add it at the end of the cooking). In a mortar or food processor, combine 1 tablespoon minced peeled galangal with 1 tablespoon minced garlic. Add 1 tablespoon fresh-ground black pepper and 1 tablespoon minced cilantro root and stems. Add 2 tablespoons fish sauce or 1 teaspoon salt, and blend well.

# Pickled Carrots with Ginger

**A**fter I pickled some ginger for sushi one day, the leftover sweet and sour cooking syrup seemed too good to throw out, so I peeled some carrots and simmered them whole in the liquid. Once these carrots were chilled, they were delicious, especially alongside spicy Asian dishes. Other vegetables—green beans, radishes, cucumbers, zucchini—can be pickled in the same way. Try experimenting with your favorite vegetables. And once the vegetables are eaten, don't throw out the sweet, gingery pickling liquid. Strain it, chill it, and use it as a vibrant no-fat dressing for a slaw made from grated carrot, scallion, thinly sliced cabbage, peanuts, and mung bean sprouts.

1 cup sugar
1 cup rice vinegar
1 cup water
1 teaspoon salt
1 3-inch piece fresh ginger, sliced 1/4 inch thick
1 pound carrots, preferably small, peeled

**1.** In a large saucepan, combine the sugar, vinegar, water, salt, and ginger. Bring the mixture to a simmer, and add the carrots. Make sure the carrots are completely immersed, then cover the pan. Simmer the carrots for 15 to 20 minutes, or until they can be easily cut with a fork. Transfer the carrots and their liquid to a container with a lid, and let them cool.

**2.** Cover the container, and refrigerate the carrots in their liquid until you are ready to use them. They will keep well for over a week.

Makes 8 to 9 small
pickled carrots

# Kitchen Cupboard Curry

You may have heard that the curry powders sold in super-markets are a far cry from those made in Indian kitchens. Once you try making your own curry powder, you'll see that this is true. Supermarket brands often use too much turmeric, which doesn't have a lot of flavor or aroma. Also, curry bought in a store could be months old. If you put your homemade curry powder beside the commercial product and took in a large whiff, you wouldn't think they were the same thing. So if you enjoy curry dishes, it's definitely worth blending your own spice mix.

1 tablespoon black or brown mustard seeds

2 tablespoons cumin seeds

4 tablespoons coriander seeds

1 tablespoon fenugreek seeds (optional)

1 teaspoon cardamom seeds, or 2 teaspoons ground cardamom

1 tablespoon ground turmeric

1 teaspoon fresh-ground black pepper

**1.** In a dry skillet over medium heat, toast the mustard seeds, cumin seeds, and coriander seeds. Shake the skillet over the heat continuously so that the seeds cook evenly. When the mustard seeds turn gray and all the seeds are fragrant, remove the pan from the heat.

**2.** Grind the toasted seeds in a spice grinder or mortar along with the fenugreek and cardamom. Transfer the mixture to a container with a tight-fitting lid, and stir in the turmeric and black pepper. In a sealed container, curry powder will keep for at least 2 months.

Makes about ¹/₂ cup
curry powder

## Crazy for Curry

*There are hundreds of ways to use curry powder. Here are just a few ideas:*

◆ *Whisk curry powder into olive oil, and toss vegetables in the mixture before roasting or grilling them.*

◆ *Add a pinch or two of curry powder to pasta dishes. (I like to combine curry, olive oil, garlic, a squeeze of lemon, and broccoli with hot pasta.)*

◆ *Add curry powder to chutneys and ketchups as they cook.*

◆ *Sprinkle a little curry powder into vinaigrettes and other dressings.*

◆ *Add curry powder to hummus.*

# Garam Masala

Garam masala is a fragrant, woodsy spice mixture from India. Usually containing cinnamon, cardamom, and cloves, it may include as many as seven additional spices. It is often mixed into a dish at the last minute to boost flavor. I like to add it to sautéed vegetables and mashed sweet potatoes. It is also nice in pilafs and similar grain dishes. Here are some other ideas:

- Add 1 teaspoon garam masala along with the other spices to Tomato-Raisin Chutney (page 45).
- Add 1 teaspoon garam masala to Curried Cauliflower Bisque (page 110). Omit the fenugreek, and use only 1½ teaspoons curry powder.
- Add 1 teaspoon garam masala to the onions before sautéing them for Felicia's Kasha Burgers (page 375).
- Add 1 teaspoon garam masala to Baba Ghanoush (page 54), mixing it in step 2 with the tahini, garlic, and other ingredients.

1 tablespoon white peppercorns
1 teaspoon whole or ground cloves
1 teaspoon cardamom seeds, or 2 teaspoons ground cardamom
2 teaspoons cumin seeds
1 tablespoon coriander seeds
1 tablespoon ground cinnamon
1 teaspoon freshly grated nutmeg

**1.** Grind the peppercorns, cloves, cardamom seeds, cumin seeds, and coriander seeds in a spice grinder. Cloves are very hard, so this may take a minute or two.

**2.** Transfer the mixture to a container with a tight-fitting lid, add the cinnamon and nutmeg, and cover the container. Store it in a cool, dark place. The mixture will keep for at least 2 months.

Makes about ¼ cup

# Five-Spice-Plus-One Powder

I sneak one more spice—coriander—into Chinese five-spice powder. But the five spices aren't carved in stone anyhow; they often vary both in cookbooks and in commercial packages. I use five-spice powder in both savory dishes, such as marinades and dipping sauces, and sweet dishes, like coffeecakes, muffins, and cookies. Sometimes I like to just open the jar, smell the intoxicating aroma, then put the jar back on the shelf.

You can use five-spice powder for different twists on recipes in this book:

- Add 1 teaspoon five-spice powder to Cardamom Banana Bread (page 8). Omit the cardamom.
- Add 1 teaspoon five-spice powder along with the other spices to Sweet-Potato Muffins (page 537).
- Add 1 teaspoon five-spice powder along with the other spices to Carrot Coffeecake (page 6).
- Add 1 teaspoon five-spice powder along with the other spices to Dark Boston Brown Bread (page 20).
- Add 2 teaspoons five-spice powder to Yellow Split-Pea Burgers (page 370). Omit the 1½ teaspoons cumin.

Sichuan peppercorns and star anise are available in Asian markets.

¼ cup Sichuan peppercorns
12 whole star anise or ¼ cup fennel seeds
1 tablespoon coriander seeds
2 teaspoons whole or ground cloves
2 teaspoons ground ginger
1 tablespoon ground cinnamon

**1.** Put the peppercorns, the star anise or fennel, the coriander, and the cloves into a small skillet, and place the skillet over low

## How to Use Sichuan Pepper

*If you are like me, you'll be looking for more ways to use Sichuan peppercorns once you taste them. Woodsy and perfume-like, Sichuan peppers are berries from a prickly ash tree that grows in China. For the best flavor, toast the peppercorns in a dry skillet until they darken before you grind them. Once ground, they are delicious in many dishes, such as Chinese stir-fry dishes, winter-squash soup, and veggie burgers. For a good all-purpose seasoning, combine 1 tablespoon ground Sichuan pepper, 1 tablespoon ground black pepper, 3 tablespoons coarse salt, and 1 teaspoon cayenne pepper.*

heat. Toast the spices, stirring, for 3 minutes or until they brown slightly and become fragrant. Transfer these spices to a spice grinder. Grind the mixture fine.

**2.** Transfer these spices to a container with a tight-fitting lid, and stir in the ginger and cinnamon. Cover the container. The spices will stay fresh at room temperature for at least 2 months.

*Makes about ¹/₂ cup spice powder*

# Winter Cranberry Ketchup

I once included a cranberry-plum ketchup on a fall menu only to realize, once the menus were printed, that it was too late in the season to get plums. I resorted to using prunes, hoping that the plum flavor would come through. Fortunately, this was one of those mistakes that led to a new and better recipe. I serve this ketchup with the Portobello Burgers (page 367), but it would be nice with any of the burgers.

2 teaspoons canola oil
1 tablespoon minced fresh ginger
2 cups chopped onions
1 12-ounce bag cranberries
³/₄ cup sugar
¹/₂ teaspoon ground allspice
1 teaspoon ground coriander seeds
1 cup pitted prunes, coarsely chopped
¹/₃ cup red wine vinegar
Salt and fresh-ground black pepper to taste

**1.** In a heavy saucepan, heat the oil with the ginger and the onions over low heat for 10 minutes. Add the cranberries, sugar, allspice, coriander, prunes, and vinegar. Let the sauce simmer gently for 25 minutes, stirring two or three times. Stir in the salt and pepper to taste.

**2.** In a blender or food processor, purée the cooked mixture.

Transfer it to a container with a tight-fitting lid, and let the ketchup cool. Keep it in the refrigerator, covered, for up to 1 month.

Makes about 3½ cups ketchup

# Mango Ketchup

Mangoes are now grown in California as well as Florida, and they are also imported year-round into the United States. But the supplies increase and the prices fall during the summer, so this is when I cook with mangoes.

Mangoes come in dozens of varieties, but two kinds— Haitian and red—are especially popular in the Northeast. Haitian mangoes are flattish and oval and quite sweet. They are great for desserts or eating out of hand. But for cooking I prefer the larger, rounder red mangoes, which are imported from Mexico or Brazil. Their tart flavor complements savory foods, and their size and shape yield more pulp per pound.

1 tablespoon canola or corn oil
2 cups chopped onions
1 teaspoon Kitchen Cupboard Curry (page 36)
    or commercial curry powder
1 teaspoon ground cumin seeds
1 teaspoon ground coriander seeds
6 plum tomatoes, coarsely chopped
3 ripe mangoes, peeled and coarsely chopped
⅔ cup apple cider vinegar
1⅓ cups sugar
Salt and fresh-ground black pepper to taste

**1.** Heat the oil in a large saucepan over medium heat. Add the onions, and sauté them 5 minutes, stirring occasionally. Stir in the spices, and sauté another 2 minutes.

**2.** Add the tomatoes and mangoes to the onions. Add the vinegar, sugar, and salt and pepper. Stir the mixture, and let it simmer for 1 hour over low heat, stirring every 20 minutes or so to make sure the bottom is not scorching. Remove the pan from the heat, and let the mixture cool.

**3.** With a food processor or immersion blender, purée the mixture. Transfer the ketchup to a container with a tight-fitting lid. Store the ketchup in the refrigerator, covered, for up to 1 month.

*Makes 2 cups ketchup*

# Strawberry Guava Jam

The first time I made this jam I was surprised at how delicious it was. Guava paste has always been too sweet for me, but when mixed with fresh strawberries it loses its intensity. It also adds a new and welcome note to an otherwise conventional jam. Tightly sealed in the refrigerator, this jam keeps for at least 1 month.

Guava paste is sold in short, round tins in Latin American markets.

5 tablespoons guava paste
1 pint strawberries, stemmed and halved
3/4 cup water
1 cup plus 2 tablespoons sugar
2 tablespoons granulated pectin
1 heaping teaspoon grated lime rind

**1.** In a heavy saucepan, combine the guava paste, the strawberries, the water, and 1 cup of the sugar. Bring the mixture to a boil, and let it simmer for 10 minutes.

**2.** In a cup, combine the 2 tablespoons sugar and pectin. Stir well. Add this mixture to the boiling guava-strawberry liquid.

## Cool Guava

Guava fruit is very popular in India and South America. In India, people sell guava on the street, hours after it is picked, cut into pieces and sprinkled with lime juice.

In the United States, guavas are grown in California, Florida, and Hawaii. Although sometimes available elsewhere, they do not travel well. A guava more than a day or two old will have lost much of its flavor.

Guavas are also available canned whole, in jams and jellies, and in guava paste, sold in wheels in many supermarkets and Latin American markets. To provide a fruity zing in chutney, add a tablespoon or two of guava paste during the cooking, and reduce the amount of sugar proportionately.

Stir well, and let the mixture boil for at least 2 minutes to activate the pectin.

**3.** Remove the pan from the heat, and add the lime rind. With a potato masher or immersion blender, mash the jam well. Pour it into a sturdy plastic container with a tight-fitting lid. Let the jam cool, then cover it. Chill it for at least 2 hours before serving. The jam will keep in the refrigerator for at least 1 month.

*Makes 2½ cups jam*

# Green Tomato Chutney

When frost threatens, do you find that you have hundreds of green tomatoes sitting in your garden, all refusing to ripen? Make a chutney! The tartness and texture of green tomatoes make for a delectable chutney, one you'll want to use in sandwiches, on top of veggie burgers, and alongside grain dishes such as Fragrant Millet Pilaf (page 269). This chutney will keep in the refrigerator, tightly sealed, for about 1 month.

2 cups minced onions
1 tablespoon canola or corn oil
2 tablespoons minced fresh ginger
1 tablespoon ground coriander seeds
½ teaspoon ground allspice
1¾ pounds (about 5 to 6) green tomatoes, cored and chopped
1 cup sugar
¼ cup apple cider vinegar
½ cup water
1 cup raisins

## When to Eat Chutney

There are many ways to enjoy chutney besides as an accompaniment for curry. Here are some ideas: Try chutney in sandwiches, such as grilled white cheddar and pear or smoked mozzarella with sliced and seared portobello mushroom. Serve chutney instead of ketchup with veggie burgers. Try Spinach Patties (page 347) with a homemade chutney instead of raita. Or set a bowl of chutney next to grilled vegetables, such as red onion, zucchini, and eggplant, along with some basmati rice. Two books that offer terrific chutney recipes are The Art of Indian Vegetarian Cooking, by Yamuna Devi, and Salsas, Sambals, Chutneys, and Chowchows, by Chris Schlesinger and John Willoughby.

**1.** In a large saucepan, combine the onions and the oil over medium heat. Add the ginger, coriander, and allspice. Cook the onions with the spices for 5 minutes, stirring often.

**2.** Add the green tomatoes, sugar, and vinegar. Add the water, and let the chutney simmer for 1 hour, stirring once or twice.

**3.** Remove the pan from the heat, and add the raisins. Let the chutney cool, then transfer it to a container with a tight-fitting lid. Store the chutney, covered, in the refrigerator.

**Variation:** Add 2 chopped pears or apples along with the tomatoes, and increase the amount of vinegar to ½ cup.

*Makes 2 cups chutney*

# Peach and Five-Spice Chutney

Five-spice powder seems to have been invented for this chutney. You can buy the five-spice powder at well-stocked supermarkets or Asian markets, or, better yet, make your own. If you have the spices on hand, the recipe (page 38) takes only a few minutes. The small, pungent, mildly hot Sichuan peppercorns are also available at Asian markets.

2½ pounds (about 8) ripe peaches
1 tablespoon canola or corn oil
2 cups chopped onions
1 tablespoon minced fresh ginger
1 teaspoon five-spice powder
1 teaspoon ground allspice
1 teaspoon ground Sichuan peppercorns
    (optional)
⅔ cup apple cider vinegar
1 cup sugar
Lemon juice to taste

**1.** If the peaches are ripe but hard enough to peel with a vegetable peeler, then peel them in this way. If they are softer, bring 3 quarts water to a boil, and, with a knife, cut a cross on the bottom of each peach. Immerse the peaches in the boiling water for about 30 seconds, then remove them. Slip the skins off the peaches. Cut the peach flesh off of the pits.

**2.** In a large pot, heat the oil over medium-high heat. Add the onions, and sauté them until they have softened, about 5 minutes, stirring occasionally. Add the ginger and the ground spices. Sauté another minute or two, then add the peaches, vinegar, and sugar. Stir. Turn the heat to low, and let the chutney cook for 45 minutes, stirring every now and then.

**3.** Mash the chutney with a potato masher, or use an immersion blender, but leave the chutney somewhat lumpy. Add the lemon juice. Transfer the chutney to a container with a tight-fitting lid. Let the chutney cool, then cover it. It will keep, refrigerated, for 3 weeks.

Makes 2½ cups chutney

# Banana-Ginger Chutney

This is a no-fuss chutney; there's no sautéing or puréeing. Try this simple but delicious relish with curry dishes, with rice pilafs, in sandwiches, or with veggie burgers. I particularly like it with Jamaican Rice Mix-Up (page 208).

½ cup lime juice (from about 4 limes)
1 cup minced onion
2 tablespoons minced fresh ginger
1 Granny Smith or other tart apple, chopped
   into ½-inch pieces
8 ripe bananas, cut into 1-inch chunks

²/₃ cup sugar
¹/₃ cup chopped walnuts, lightly toasted
2 tablespoons chopped mint (optional)

**1.** In a large, heavy-bottomed saucepan over medium heat, combine all of the ingredients except the walnuts and mint. Let the chutney simmer for 30 minutes, stirring occasionally.

**2.** Remove the pan from the heat, and stir in the walnuts and mint. Transfer the chutney to a container with a tight-fitting lid, and let the chutney cool uncovered. When it is cool, cover and refrigerate it. It will keep well in the refrigerator for 2 weeks.

Makes 4¹/₂ cups chutney

# Tomato-Raisin Chutney

I particularly like this mild chutney with Curried Poached Eggs (page 526) for brunch. Make the chutney in late summer, when gardens and markets are full of flavorful vine-ripened tomatoes. Feel free to halve the recipe, if you like, since it makes a large batch. The chutney will keep in the refrigerator for up to 3 weeks.

1 tablespoon canola or other vegetable oil
3 cups chopped onions
1 teaspoon fennel seeds
1 teaspoon ground coriander seeds
3 pounds tomatoes (about 15 plum tomatoes or
    8 medium round tomatoes)
1 cup apple cider vinegar
1 cup sugar
¹/₂ teaspoon salt
2¹/₄ cups raisins
1 cup chopped walnuts, lightly toasted (optional)

**1.** In a large saucepan, heat the oil over medium heat. Add the onions, and sauté them, stirring occasionally, for 15 minutes or until they begin to brown. Add the fennel seeds and coriander, and cook for another 2 minutes.

**2.** Add the tomatoes, vinegar, and sugar. Simmer for 1 hour.

**3.** In a blender or food processor, or with an immersion blender, blend the chutney, leaving it a bit chunky if you prefer it that way (as I do). Stir in the salt, the raisins, and, if you like, the walnuts. Let the chutney cool, then seal it in a tightly-lidded container and refrigerate it. The chutney will keep for 3 weeks.

Makes 6 cups chutney

# CHAPTER 3

# Small Bites

# Spinach Dip

Even though I've lived in cities for the past ten years, I've encountered this dip only at homes in the suburbs. Why is this, I wonder? Because I'm a cook and not an anthropologist, I'll just say that this dip makes for good eating in any part of the world.

My mother uses a package of Knorr vegetable soup mix instead of the cut vegetables. If you want to try her version, leave out the ½ teaspoon salt.

I suggest serving the dip with carrot sticks or bland crackers, such as Wheat Thins.

1 10-ounce package frozen chopped spinach, thawed
1 cup minced onion
2 garlic cloves, minced
1 cup minced vegetables, such as carrot, red pepper, or cucumber
¹/₂ cup whole, low-fat, or nonfat sour cream
¹/₂ cup mayonnaise
1 teaspoon ground cumin seeds
¹/₂ teaspoon salt
Fresh-ground pepper to taste

1. Squeeze the water out of the spinach, and put the spinach into a bowl.

2. Add the onion, garlic, vegetables, sour cream, mayonnaise, and cumin. Season with salt and pepper. Let the dip stand at room temperature for ½ hour for the flavors to mix, and stir again before serving. This dip keeps well in the refrigerator, covered, for up to 1 week.

Makes 3¹/₂ cups dip

# Hot Artichoke and Goat Cheese Dip

This is the delicious artichoke and mayo dip one often spots at cocktail parties, but with goat cheese in lieu of the sour cream. This dip is surprisingly good when made with low-fat or nonfat cream cheese and mayonnaise. The recipe will serve 12 partygoers.

1 14-ounce can water-packed artichoke hearts, drained, or 10 ounces frozen artichoke hearts
1½ cups chopped onions
1 large garlic clove, minced
½ cup mayonnaise
8 ounces cream cheese, softened
⅔ cup grated Parmesan cheese
6 ounces soft goat cheese
Crackers, bruschetta, or Homemade Tortilla Chips (page 411)

**1.** In a food processor, combine the artichoke hearts, onions, garlic, mayonnaise, cream cheese, Parmesan cheese, and goat cheese. Blend the ingredients, leaving some texture in the dip. Spoon the dip into a 7- or 8-inch casserole dish. (At this point you can refrigerate the dip, covered, for up to 2 days if you like.)

**2.** Preheat the oven to 350°.

**3.** Bake the dip, uncovered, for 30 minutes or until it is browned on top. Serve it hot with crackers, bruschetta, or chips.

**Variation:** Try using this dip as a tart filling. Spread the uncooked mixture about ¾ inch thick on a prebaked pie shell, then top with chopped olives and parsley. Bake the tart for 10 minutes at 350°, and serve it hot.

Makes 3½ cups dip

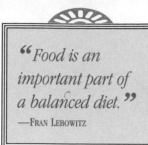
# Smoky Black-Bean Dip

The complex flavors of this dip will have your guests believing that you labored over it. But with a food processor, you can make it fast in only 5 to 10 minutes. So open that bag of chips, and get ready to dip. (If you have a few more minutes, try the Homemade Tortilla Chips, page 411, or Sweet Fried Plantains, page 57.)

1 15-ounce can black beans
3 tablespoons chopped fresh cilantro
½ cup chopped onion
2 large garlic cloves
1 tablespoon chopped chipotles in adobo sauce, 1
    dried chipotle pepper soaked in hot water 30
    minutes and chopped, or ½ teaspoon liquid
    smoke (I like Gerwer Tex-Mex Mesquite
    Liquid Smoke)
1 pinch cayenne
2 tablespoons lime juice (from about 1 lime)
Salt and pepper to taste
¼ cup unsalted hulled pumpkin seeds, toasted
    (available in Mexican markets; optional)

**1.** Pour the black beans into a large strainer, and run cool water over them for a few seconds.

**2.** In a food processor, combine the cilantro with the onion, garlic, and chipotles, and run the machine in short spurts to mince the vegetables. Add the black beans, cayenne, lime juice, and salt and pepper, and run the machine for 5 seconds or so, until most of the beans are puréed.

**3.** Transfer the mixture to an attractive dipping bowl, sprinkle with the toasted pumpkin seeds, if you like, and serve.

Makes about 2 cups dip

# Avocado-Lime Dip

Avocado, the Jekyll and Hyde of fruits. So beautiful and green when first cut, then ugly and brown just a few hours later. This happens even when avocados are made into guacamole. But this creamy avocado dip will not turn on you, even after four days. Try it with tortilla chips or fresh vegetables, or spooned on tacos.

1 Haas avocado (the dark, bumpy kind), peeled and pitted
3 tablespoons lime juice (from about 1½ limes)
3 tablespoons whole, low-fat, or nonfat sour cream
3 tablespoons chopped cilantro
1 teaspoon ground coriander seeds
1 garlic clove
⅓ cup canola or corn oil
¼ teaspoon salt
Fresh-ground black pepper to taste

**1.** In a blender or food processor, combine the avocado, lime juice, sour cream, cilantro, ground coriander, and garlic. Blend well.

**2.** With the machine running, slowly pour in the canola oil. Add the salt and pepper. Serve the dip immediately, or store it, refrigerated, in a container with a tight-fitting lid. It will keep for 5 days.

Variation: For a less fatty dip, substitute silken tofu or plain yogurt for the sour cream.

Makes 1½ cups dip

## The Avocado

*B*esides its subtle, sweet flavor and unctuous texture, one virtue of the avocado is that only one-sixth of its fat is saturated, a much smaller proportion than in meats, butter, cheese, or sour cream. If I have a ripe avocado hanging around, I use it instead of butter on my morning toast or bagel (with a slice of tomato), and I'll use avocado instead of cheese with my tomato and watercress sandwich at lunch. I also love avocado sliced in salads (especially with Belgian endive) and in burritos, with black beans and grilled or pan-fried vegetables.

# Rockin' Guacamole

This is a chunky, low-fat guacamole that I invented when I had to bring an hors d'oeuvre to a party, but had only a small amount of edible food in my refrigerator. (This is, I think, how many recipes are born.) On this particular day I had a ripe avocado, an eggplant, a red and a green pepper, some cilantro, and not much else. After roasting the eggplant, I mashed its flesh with the avocado, chopped peppers, chopped cilantro, lime juice, garlic, and red onion. One of my friends said that it tasted better than traditional guacamole, but I'll just say it's really good.

1 1-pound eggplant
1 ripe Haas avocado (the dark, bumpy kind), peeled and pitted
1 red bell pepper, minced
2 mildly hot peppers (such as Italian or Anaheim), minced, or 1 green bell pepper, chopped, and a pinch of cayenne
1 garlic clove, minced
1/2 cup minced red onion
1/4 cup minced cilantro
1 tablespoon extra-virgin olive oil
1/4 cup lime juice (from about 2 limes)
1/2 teaspoon salt, or more, to taste
Fresh-ground black pepper to taste

**1.** Preheat the oven to 425°. Cut the eggplant in half and lay the two halves on a baking sheet, cut side up. Bake the eggplant for 30 minutes. Remove it from the oven, and let it cool.

**2.** In a bowl, combine the avocado, red bell pepper, hot peppers, garlic, red onion, cilantro, olive oil, and lime juice. Spoon the eggplant from its skin, and add it to the bowl. With a potato masher or a fork, mash the mixture coarsely. Add the salt and pepper. Chill the dip for at least 30 minutes, then serve it with tortilla or pita chips.

Makes 4 cups dip

# Baba Ghanoush

This is a classic Middle Eastern "puréed salad," made from eggplant and sesame paste. Baba Ghanoush is wonderful spread on lavash (a very flat bread) and wrapped along with foods such as tomatoes, cucumbers, watercress, and feta cheese. Or use the mixture as a dip for triangles of pita bread. The smoky flavor produced by grilling the eggplant adds character to Baba Ghanoush, but you can also roast the eggplant in the oven.

⬛▪⬛▪⬛▪⬛▪⬛

1 large firm eggplant (about $1\frac{1}{3}$ pounds)
$1\frac{1}{2}$ tablespoons tahini (sesame paste)
1 large garlic clove, minced
$\frac{1}{3}$ cup minced shallots or onion
$\frac{1}{4}$ cup fresh lemon juice
2 tablespoons extra-virgin olive oil
$\frac{1}{2}$ teaspoon salt, or more, to taste
About $\frac{1}{4}$ teaspoon fresh-ground black pepper, to taste
3 tablespoons chopped cilantro

⬛▪⬛▪⬛▪⬛▪⬛

**1.** Grill or roast the eggplant. To grill it, bring a gas grill to medium heat, or prepare a medium hot charcoal fire. Prick the eggplant all over with a fork, then cut it in half lengthwise. Lay the eggplant halves on the grill cut side down, and let them cook for 20 minutes. Then turn the eggplant halves over, and grill them an additional 5 minutes. The eggplant should be soft and sagging a bit.

To roast the eggplant: Preheat the oven to 375°. Cut the eggplant in half lengthwise and place the halves in a roasting pan cut side down. Bake them 30 minutes or until they are soft.

Transfer the eggplant to a plate, and let it cool.

**2.** In a large bowl, mix the tahini, garlic, shallots or onion, lemon juice, olive oil, salt, pepper, and cilantro. Spoon the eggplant flesh onto a cutting surface, and mince the eggplant. Add

## In Praise of Chickpeas

❁

$S$ome people say chickpeas are so named because each bean resembles the head of a baby chick, with the pointed part resembling the chick's beak. Also called garbanzos, these legumes are a good source of protein and calcium, and they are particularly high in iron. Although they take over two hours to cook, a less ambitious person can use them canned, as I usually do. Combine chickpeas with brown rice or other grains in pilafs. Or coarsely chop chickpeas, pan-fry them with some olive oil and garlic, and toss them with hot pasta and grated Parmesan cheese.

it to the bowl, stir, and correct the seasoning, adding a bit more lemon juice, salt, or pepper, as needed.

**3.** You can use Baba Ghanoush immediately, but I like to chill it for an hour or two first. It will keep in the refrigerator, covered, for up to 4 days.

Makes 2 1/2 cups

# Toasty Hummus

$F$reshness can make a big difference. In this recipe, you toast and grind sesame seeds yourself rather than use a canned sesame paste. Pita bread, bagel chips, and raw vegetables are all great for dipping in this hummus.

▪▪▪▪▪▪▪▪▪▪▪

1 cup hulled white sesame seeds
2 teaspoons minced garlic
1/2 teaspoon salt
1 teaspoon sumac powder (available in Middle
    Eastern markets; optional)
1/4 cup olive oil
2 cups cooked chickpeas (garbanzo beans)
2/3 cup lemon juice (from about 3 lemons)
3 tablespoons minced shallots
About 1/3 cup water

▪▪▪▪▪▪▪▪▪▪▪

**1.** Preheat the oven to 350°. Spread the sesame seeds on a baking sheet, and toast them for 10 to 15 minutes, until most of the seeds have turned a rich brown (but do not let them burn). In a spice mill or blender, grind the sesame seeds to a paste. You will have to do this in two batches if you use a spice mill, and you may need to add a bit of the olive oil if you use a blender. If you're using a blender, leave the sesame paste in the blender jar as you proceed with the directions.

**2.** In a blender or food processor, combine the sesame seed paste, garlic, salt, and, if you're using it, sumac. Slowly add the olive oil while the machine is running. Then add the chickpeas in two batches, puréeing well after each addition. With the machine still running, add the lemon juice and shallots. Add enough water to thin the hummus to the desired consistency.

**3.** Store the hummus in a container with a tight-fitting lid. It will keep in the refrigerator for at least 1 week.

## Variations:

◆ Use toasted cashews (1¼ cups) instead of sesame seeds (grind them in a blender, not a spice mill).

◆ Make curried hummus: Add 1 tablespoon curry powder along with the lemon juice.

◆ Add ⅓ cup chopped cilantro along with the lemon juice.

*Makes 3 cups hummus*

# No-Fry Spicy Potato Skins

Many of us adore fried potato skins, but are reluctant to indulge too often. When I tested a less rich version of the fat-laden classic, I was pleasantly surprised. The flavor is excellent, and little, if any, of the crispiness is lost. I suggest serving these skins with sour cream mixed with chopped scallions, a good ketchup, or both. Save the insides of the potatoes for mashing or for Harry's Famous Home Fries (page 540).

4 large russet potatoes
¼ cup olive oil
1 teaspoon salt
½ teaspoon black pepper
1½ teaspoons chili powder
1½ teaspoons curry powder
1½ teaspoons ground coriander seeds

## Life as a Plantain

*Plantains can be eaten at any stage from quite green to very ripe. Green plantains are often peeled with a knife, cut into rounds, then deep-fried. They are also added to stews and soups like potatoes, since before the plantains' starch has converted to sugar they are similarly bland. Yellow, medium-ripe plantains keep their shape when cooked and have a slightly sweet taste. They are served fried or in dishes like mofongos (a Puerto Rican dish of fried plantains mashed with fried pork rinds). Black-skinned plantains, which have converted all their starch to sugar, are sweet like ripe bananas and good in puddings and cakes.*

**1.** Preheat the oven to 400°. Bake the potatoes for 1 hour.

**2.** Remove the potatoes from the oven, but keep the oven on. Slice the potatoes in half lengthwise, and let them cool for 10 minutes.

**3.** Scoop out most of the potato flesh, leaving about ¼ inch of flesh against the potato skin (save the potato flesh for another use). Cut each potato half crosswise into 3 pieces. Place the olive oil in a small cup. Dip each potato piece into the olive oil, and place it on a baking sheet. Repeat this with the remaining potato pieces. Combine the salt and the spices, and sprinkle the mixture over the potatoes.

**4.** Bake the potato skins for 15 minutes or until they are crispy and brown. Serve them immediately, with small bowls of ketchup or sour cream.

Makes 24 hors d'oeuvres

# Sweet Fried Plantains

Plantains are often fried when they are green and underripe. In Puerto Rico these are called *tostones,* in Mexico *plátanos fritos.* They are first fried in slices, then flattened with a pan or mallet and fried again. Another popular Puerto Rican plantain dish is *maduros* or *amarillos,* sliced ripe plantains fried in oil. This recipe also uses ripe plantains but they are rolled in fresh bread crumbs to create a crispy exterior. Although quite a bit of oil is called for in this recipe, the plantains absorb only a small portion of it. They are good served with a dipping bowl of hot sauce.

2 yellow or black medium-ripe plantains
6 slices white or whole-wheat sandwich bread
½ teaspoon fresh-ground black pepper
½ cup canola or corn oil
Salt to taste

**1.** Cut 3 slits down the length of each plantain skin, without cutting into the flesh. Cut the ends off the plantain, then peel away the skin in 3 long strips. Cut each plantain diagonally into 8 pieces.

**2.** Cut the crusts off the bread slices. Lightly toast the bread, then either chop it fine or whirl it in a food processor to make bread crumbs. Put the bread crumbs onto a large plate, and stir in the pepper.

**3.** In a large skillet, heat the oil over medium-high heat. Dredge the plantains in the bread crumbs, pressing the plantains into the crumbs so they stick. When the oil is hot, add one plantain slice. If it burns on the bottom after 10 seconds or so, then the oil is too hot; adjust the heat as necessary. Add as many plantain slices as will fit in the pan without crowding. When the slices are golden brown on the bottom, turn them over. Cook them until they are golden on the other side. With a slotted spoon, transfer the fried plantains to paper towels. Continue cooking until all of the slices are fried, keeping the cooked slices in a warm oven for up to 20 minutes, if necessary.

**4.** Salt the fried plantains, and serve them immediately with a small bowl of your favorite hot sauce.

Makes 16 fried slices

# High-Tea Cucumber Sandwiches

Cucumber sandwiches are no longer on the party circuit. Perhaps they are considered old-fashioned, but I don't see how anything that tastes so good can go out of style. In this version of the classic, the cucumber slices are briefly soaked in a dill marinade to boost the flavor. Try these sandwiches for hors d'oeuvres, a tea party, or a summer lunch or picnic.

3 cucumbers, peeled and sliced as thin as possible
⅓ cup red wine vinegar
1 bunch dill, chopped (about 1½ cups)
½ teaspoon salt
Fresh-ground black pepper to taste
1½ cups mayonnaise
30 thin slices good white bread

**1.** In a shallow bowl or casserole dish, combine the cucumbers, the red wine vinegar, ¾ cup of the dill, and the salt and pepper. Toss the cucumbers well, and let them sit for 5 minutes.

**2.** Meanwhile, in a small bowl, combine the remaining ¾ cup dill with the mayonnaise. Cut the crusts off the bread.

**3.** Drain the cucumbers. Spread the mayonnaise generously on one piece of the bread. Lay 4 to 6 slices of cucumber (depending upon the size of the slices) on top. The cucumber slices may overlap slightly. Spread another slice of bread with the mayonnaise, and place it mayonnaise-side down on top of the cucumbers. Press down lightly. Cut the sandwich into 4 squares or triangles. Continue making sandwiches until all the bread and cucumbers are used.

Makes 60 mini-sandwiches

# Technicolor Tapenade on Toast

I've been playing around with tapenade, a popular Provençal paste made from olives, anchovies, and capers, among other things. I've added finely chopped yellow and red pepper, minced basil, and scallions (and I've omitted the anchovies). Traditional tapenade is a classic, a dish that can't be improved upon, but this version is pretty to look at and tastes great.

20 large Kalamata olives, pitted
3 tablespoons extra-virgin olive oil
2 teaspoons lemon juice
3 garlic cloves, minced
¼ cup minced basil
¼ cup minced scallions (use mostly the green part)
1 heaping tablespoon capers
½ small red bell pepper, seeded and minced
½ small yellow bell pepper, seeded and minced
Salt and fresh-ground black pepper to taste
⅓ loaf French bread

**1.** In a food processor or by hand, chop fine (do not purée) all of the ingredients except the salt, pepper, and bread. Season with salt and pepper, and add a little more lemon juice, if you like. Store the tapenade in the refrigerator, covered, for up to 2 days, but bring it to room temperature before serving it.

**2.** Preheat the oven to 350°. Slice the bread diagonally ½ inch thick. Lay the slices on a baking sheet, and toast them in the oven for about 5 minutes. Remove the pan from the oven, and let the slices cool. (You can make the toasts up to 4 hours ahead.)

**3.** Spoon the tapenade onto the toasts. Place them on a plate, and serve them with napkins.

Makes about 10 tapenade-topped toasts

# Charred-Tomato Salsa with Grilled Bread

This summer salsa is quick to make, especially if you have the grill revved. The recipe calls for grilling fresh pita bread, but feel free to use other kinds of bread. Sliced baguette, boule, and focaccia would all work quite well.

## Keeping Fresh Herbs Fresh

*The life of fresh herbs can be extended quite a bit with proper care. Parsley, basil, cilantro, dill, sage, tarragon, rosemary, and thyme are best stored unwashed, with their stems left on. Place them in a plastic bag with a damp, folded paper towel, and refrigerate them with the bag open until you are ready to use them. If the herbs have been washed, store them in an open plastic bag with a dry paper towel; they should stay fresh for a few days.*

**SALSA:**

1 jalapeño pepper

5 medium round tomatoes, or 10 plum tomatoes

2 large garlic cloves, minced

2 tablespoons extra-virgin olive oil

2 tablespoons chopped basil

1/4 cup lime juice (from about 2 limes)

1/2 teaspoon salt

Fresh-ground black pepper to taste

4 8-inch rounds of pita bread

**1.** Make the salsa: Over a low gas flame or directly on a hot grill, char the jalapeño until it has darkened evenly. Then, using tongs, grill the tomatoes whole until the skins develop large black spots. Cut the tomatoes (including the skin) into 1/2-inch chunks, and put them into a bowl. Mince the jalapeño, seeding it first if you prefer less heat, and add it to the bowl. Add the garlic, olive oil, basil, lime juice, salt, and pepper. Chill the mixture in the refrigerator for at least 15 minutes.

**2.** Meanwhile, split the pita bread, and lay the halves on a hot grill. Turn the bread over once the bottom side has been marked by the grill. Take the bread off the grill once both sides have been marked. Cut the bread into small triangles. Serve them, preferably warm, with the salsa. (You can hold the bread, covered with a kitchen towel, at room temperature for 2 to 3 hours, if necessary. Rewarm the bread before serving.)

Makes 3 cups salsa

# Pepper-Masa Cheesesticks

Cheesesticks that taste of more than just cheese, these delicate hors d'oeuvres are made with masa harina—ground parched corn treated with lime—as well as wheat flour. Masa harina contributes an earthy flavor as well as a tender, slightly crumbly texture.

1½ cups unbleached white flour
1 cup masa harina (available at Latin American
    markets and many supermarkets)
1 teaspoon salt
1 teaspoon baking soda
1 teaspoon fresh-ground black pepper
⅔ cup grated Parmesan cheese
½ pound (2 sticks) cold unsalted butter
1 egg, beaten

**1.** Preheat the oven to 400°. Combine the flour, masa harina, salt, baking soda, pepper, and Parmesan cheese either in a bowl for hand mixing, or in a food processor.

**2.** If you're mixing by hand, stir until the ingredients are well mixed. Chop the butter into tiny pieces, and, with a pastry blender or two forks, work the butter into the flour mixture. Add ½ cup very cold water, and stir until a mass forms, adding more water if necessary.

    If you're using a food processor, turn the machine briefly on and then off until the ingredients are thoroughly mixed. Chop the butter into 15 to 20 pieces, and add them. Turn the machine on and off until the mixture has a sand-like consistency. Add ½ cup very cold water to the mixture. Turn the machine on and off again until the dough begins to come together.

**3.** Transfer the dough to a clean, floured surface. Form the dough into a ball. With a rolling pin, roll it into a large rectangle, about 10 by 24 inches. Brush the entire surface with the egg (you won't need all the egg). Cut the dough into strips ¾ inch wide and 10 inches long. Cut the strips in half crosswise. Carefully lift them one by one, and place them on an ungreased baking sheet.

**4.** Bake the sticks for 10 minutes, or until they are golden but not brown. They are best served while they are still warm, but they will keep for at least a week in a sealed container, to be reheated or eaten at room temperature.

Makes about 50 5-inch cheesesticks

# Cheddar-Pecan Balls

This is my own version, but variations on this recipe have been in Junior League cookbooks since the Middle Ages. My version is easy, especially if you have a child or two around. Kids love to get their hands into the sticky mixture to form the balls, which is the part we adults could do without.

It's important to use an aged sharp cheddar for this recipe.

1²/₃ cups grated aged sharp white or yellow
    cheddar cheese
8 ounces cream cheese, softened
2 tablespoons minced parsley
1 heaping tablespoon prepared horseradish,
    or 2 teaspoons grated fresh horseradish
2 tablespoons minced shallots or onion
2 tablespoons grated Parmesan cheese
1¹/₄ cups finely chopped toasted pecans

**1.** In a large bowl, combine everything except the pecans. Stir with a large wooden spoon until the ingredients are well combined.

**2.** Put the chopped pecans onto a large plate. Form the cheese mixture into small balls, using about 2 teaspoons for each ball (rubbing some oil on your hands can make the job less messy). Roll the balls into the pecans, and then place the balls on a baking sheet. Continue until you have used all of the cheese mixture.

**3.** Chill the cheddar balls for at least 1 hour. They will keep, covered and refrigerated, for up to 4 days. They do not freeze well.

Makes 40 bite-size
cheddar balls

# Mexican Slowboats
# (Deviled Eggs)

This is my tribute to deviled eggs, because I enjoyed them so much as a kid. I loved them especially at cocktail parties, where I could down three or four of them in just one conversation. Sadly, they aren't very popular anymore. Here is a south-of-the-border version, using sour cream, cumin, lime juice, and other Mexican flavors.

6 large eggs
1/2 jalapeño pepper, minced with or without seeds
3 tablespoons mayonnaise
2 tablespoons whole, low-fat, or nonfat sour
    cream (or more mayonnaise)
2 tablespoons finely chopped chives or scallion
1/2 teaspoon ground cumin seeds
Grated rind of 1/2 lime
1/2 teaspoon salt
Fresh-ground black pepper to taste
3 tablespoons chopped cilantro or parsley

**1.** In a saucepan, bring about 2 quarts water to a simmer. Gently lower the eggs into the simmering water with a large spoon. Simmer the eggs for 12 minutes. Then place the eggs in a large bowl of ice water for 5 minutes.

**2.** In a medium bowl, combine the jalapeño, mayonnaise, sour cream, chives or scallion, cumin, lime rind, salt, pepper, and 2 tablespoons of the cilantro or parsley.

**3.** Peel the eggs, then carefully cut them in half lengthwise. Add the yolk halves to the sour cream mixture. With a fork, mash the yolks, distributing them throughout the sour cream. Spoon the mixture into the cavities in the whites. Place the eggs on a platter, and sprinkle them with the remaining cilantro or parsley.

## Food Flicks

❀

Here is a list of good movies in which food plays a major role. Some are decidedly un-vegetarian, but I think all are worth seeing.

Babette's Feast
Tampopo
Delicatessen
Chunking Express
Duck Soup
Diner
Big Night
Like Water for
    Chocolate
Eat Drink Man Woman
Willy Wonka and the
    Chocolate Factory
Satyricon
Baghdad Cafe
Tom Jones

**4.** You can make these up to 1 day ahead. Store them, covered, in the refrigerator.

*Makes 12 deviled egg halves*

# Tiny Curried Empanadas

Fun-filled food is here. These Mexican short pastries filled with potatoes, butternut squash, pine nuts, currants, and onions always make good party food. Like any pastries made in single-serving pieces, they take some time to prepare, but they always leave the hors d'oeuvre tray like hot cakes—well, more like hot empanadas.

▪▪▪▪▪▪▪▪▪

1 large potato (about ²/₃ pound)
1 small butternut squash (about 1¹/₂ pounds)

DOUGH:
1¹/₂ sticks cold unsalted butter
2¹/₄ cups unbleached white flour
1 teaspoon salt
1 egg
5 tablespoons cold water
1 egg yolk mixed with 1 tablespoon water

2 teaspoons olive oil
1 cup chopped onion
1¹/₂ teaspoons minced fresh ginger
2 teaspoons curry powder
1 teaspoon ground coriander seeds
¹/₄ cup currants
2 tablespoons pine nuts
1 teaspoon salt
Fresh-ground black pepper to taste

**SPICY SOUR CREAM:**
1 cup sour cream
1/2 teaspoon cayenne
1 teaspoon chili powder
Salt and fresh-ground black pepper to taste

**1.** Preheat the oven to 375°. Peel the potato, then cut it in half. Cut the butternut squash in half lengthwise. To do this, cut ½ inch off the base of the squash, stand it upright (the base cut should make it stable), then carefully, with a strong chef's knife, cut from the top down. Bake the squash and the split potato for 45 minutes or until both are tender.

**2.** Make the dough while the vegetables are baking: In a large bowl combine the butter, flour, and salt. With a pastry cutter, cut the butter into fine bits, smaller than peas. Beat the egg with the water, and add this mixture to the butter and flour mixture. Stir with a wooden spoon until the dough comes together, adding a bit more water if the dough looks too dry. Transfer the dough to a floured work surface. Knead the dough for a minute to smooth it. Let the dough sit at room temperature for 15 minutes (unless your kitchen is over 70 degrees, in which case you should refrigerate the dough).

**3.** In a skillet, heat the olive oil over medium heat. Add the onions, and cook them for 5 minutes, stirring occasionally. Add the ginger, curry powder, and coriander, and cook, stirring often, for another 3 minutes. Take the skillet off the heat.

Spoon out the seeds of the butternut squash, and discard them. Then scoop out the flesh. Add half the flesh to the skillet, and save the other half for another use (see the note following this recipe).

Cut the baked potato into ¼-inch cubes, and add them to the skillet as well. Stir well with a wooden spoon, mashing the squash so it is fully integrated in the filling. Add the currants, pine nuts, salt, and pepper.

**4.** Roll the dough quite thin on the floured surface. With a large glass or a biscuit cutter (3 to 3½ inches in diameter), cut as many rounds as possible. Spoon about 1 teaspoon filling onto the middle of each round. Fold the rounds in half, and

press the semicircle closed. Form a loose ball from the scraps of dough, then roll this out thin. Continue making empanadas until all the dough is used.

Place the empanadas on a baking sheet, and brush them with the egg yolk–water mixture (don't let too much of this drip onto the baking sheet, because it will burn). Press with a fork along the sealed edge, making a ridged design and further sealing the empanadas. Bake the empanadas at 375° for 20 to 25 minutes, until they are golden brown at the edges.

**5.** To make the Spicy Sour Cream, put the sour cream into a bowl, and mix in the cayenne and chili powder. Add salt and pepper to taste. Serve this dip with the hot empanadas.

*Makes 40 2½-inch long empanadas*

# Sushi Party Balls

Rolled in sesame seeds and served with a perky wasabi-ginger dipping sauce, these ping-pong–size balls are perfect to pass around at a cocktail party. You can count on each guest eating two, so this recipe is perfect for a party of eight. You can make the balls up to 2 days before serving them.

Hijiki seaweed and dried, powdered wasabi (Japanese horseradish) are available in Japanese markets and whole-foods stores. Cook the hijiki according to the package directions.

**SUSHI BALLS:**
2 cups uncooked sushi-style white rice (I like to use Kokuho, a short-grain rice grown in California and available in Asian markets)
2 cups water
⅓ cup rice vinegar
2 tablespoons sugar
1½ teaspoons salt
¼ cup chopped cooked hijiki sea vegetable (optional)

2 carrots, minced
5 scallions, green part only, chopped fine
1/4 cup hulled black or white sesame seeds

**WASABI-GINGER SAUCE:**
1 tablespoon wasabi powder
1/4 cup water
1 garlic clove
1 inch fresh ginger, peeled and sliced
2 tablespoons canola or corn oil
1 teaspoon sugar
3 tablespoons rice vinegar
3 tablespoons soy sauce

**1.** Make the sushi balls: Thoroughly rinse the rice in a sieve until the water runs clear, about 5 minutes. Let the rice drain for a minute or two.

In a saucepan with a tight-fitting lid, combine the rice and water. Bring the rice to a boil, then reduce the heat to medium, and cook for 5 minutes. Reduce the heat again to low, and cook for 15 minutes more. Don't open the lid at any point during the cooking. Take the pot off the heat, and let the rice stand, covered, for 10 minutes.

**2.** While the rice is cooking, combine the rice vinegar, sugar, salt, sea vegetable (if you're using it), carrots, and scallions in a large nonreactive bowl.

**3.** Toast the sesame seeds to bring out their flavor: Place a heavy skillet over medium heat. Add the seeds, let them sit for 30 seconds, then begin to shake the pan periodically. If you are using white seeds, toast them until they are uniformly browned; if you have black seeds, toast them until they taste nutty and toasted. Transfer the seeds to a small plate, and let them cool.

**4.** Turn the rice out into the bowl that contains the vinegar-scallion mixture. Stir with a wooden spoon for 3 minutes to cool the rice. (At this point you can leave the rice to sit for 1 to 2 hours.) When the rice has cooled, form a ball from a large

## Wasabi Fever

Wasabi is every-where. First it was just in sushi, but then American chefs started coming up with dishes like seared tuna with arugula and wasabi, chilled melon soup with wasabi, and lobster with wasabi oil. As trendy as it may be, I love wasabi. It has a clean heat that vanish-es in seconds. I particu-larly enjoy wasabi in sandwiches. I like to make a paste of wasabi powder and water, and spread it on one side of a pita pocket or on a slice of toast. Then I'll spread mayo on the other side of the pita, or on a sec-ond slice of toast. I'll fill the sandwich with watercress, tomatoes, roasted eggplant, cu-cumbers, or whatever else appeals to me. Then I am satisfied, until I am struck again with wasabi fever.

spoonful, then roll the ball in the sesame seeds to lightly coat it. Place the sushi ball on an oiled baking sheet. Continue in this fashion until the rice mixture is all used. Refrigerate the balls, well wrapped, for up to 2 days, but let them sit at room temperature for 10 minutes or so before serving.

**5.** Make the sauce: In a food processor or blender, combine all of the sauce ingredients. Blend until the garlic and ginger are chopped fine. Serve the sauce with the sushi balls.

*Makes about 16 large rice balls*

# Asparagus Wasabi Tempura

I held a party for my kitchen-savvy friends who helped me test recipes for this book. (I believe they conspired to starve themselves for a day before the party so they could wipe out all my food, in compensation for their recipe testing.) This hors d'oeuvre was the big hit of the party. The tempura needs no dipping sauce, because the wasabi in the batter provides plenty of flavor. Dried, powdered wasabi, or Japanese horse-radish, is available in Japanese markets and whole-foods stores.

16 asparagus spears
3/4 cup unbleached white flour
2 tablespoons cornstarch
1 teaspoon salt
1 teaspoon sugar
1 teaspoon baking powder
1 teaspoon ground ginger
1 to 2 teaspoons wasabi powder, to taste
1/4 cup water
1/2 cup beer (any kind will do)
About 2 cups canola or corn oil

**1.** Break off the tough ends off the asparagus, and discard the end pieces.

**2.** In a bowl, mix together the flour, cornstarch, salt, sugar, baking powder, ginger, and wasabi.

**3.** Add the water and beer to the flour mixture, and whisk slowly until the batter is smooth. Transfer the batter into a pan at least 8 inches wide.

**4.** In a saucepan or skillet at least 8 inches in diameter, heat the oil over medium-high heat. Test the oil by dropping in ½ teaspoon of the batter. If it immediately bubbles and fizzes, the oil is ready. Dip one asparagus spear into the batter, then drop it into the oil, being careful not to splash the oil too much. Add 7 more batter-dipped asparagus spears, and let them fry for 2 to 3 minutes. Remove them to paper towels with a large slotted spoon. Dip and fry the remaining asparagus spears, and blot them on the paper towels. Serve the tempura immediately.

Makes 16 tempura pieces

# Korean Vegetable Pancakes

These exotic pancakes are a festive way to start a dinner party. Every guest gets his or her own vegetable pancake and a dish of sesame-soy dipping sauce. Follow this course, perhaps, with an Asian noodle dish.

Glutinous rice flour is found in Chinese, Korean, and Vietnamese markets. It is usually sold in 10-ounce bags.

1¹/₃ cups unbleached white flour
1¹/₂ cups glutinous rice flour (or more white flour)
1 teaspoon salt
3 eggs
1 3/4 cups water

**VEGETABLES:**

1 bunch scallions (about 6), halved lengthwise,
   then cut into 3-inch lengths
4 medium carrots, cut into thin 3-inch sticks
1 red bell pepper, seeded and cut into thin
   julienne strips

**DIPPING SAUCE:**

1 tablespoon hulled white sesame seeds
2 teaspoons dark sesame oil
6 tablespoons soy sauce
2 tablespoons water
3 tablespoons rice vinegar
1 teaspoon sugar
1 teaspoon minced fresh ginger
1 garlic clove, minced

4 to 6 tablespoons canola or corn oil

**1.** In a large bowl, mix the white flour, rice flour, and salt together. In a smaller bowl, whisk together the eggs and the water. Make a well in the flour mixture, and, slowly, stirring with a whisk, add the liquids to the flour. Continue to whisk until the mixture is smooth. The consistency should be thinner than regular pancake batter but thicker than heavy cream.

**2.** Combine the cut scallions, carrots, and peppers in a bowl. Set the bowl aside.

**3.** Place a heavy skillet over medium heat. Add the sesame seeds. Let them sit until they just start to brown, then begin shaking the pan now and then until they are uniformly toasted.

**4.** Combine all of the dipping sauce ingredients in a bowl, and stir. Set the bowl aside.

**5.** Over medium heat, heat a griddle or a heavy skillet at least 12 inches in diameter. Pour on 1 tablespoon of the oil, then scatter a handful of the vegetables into the oil, over a roughly 8-inch circular area. Immediately ladle about ⅔ cup of the batter over the vegetables, to form a large pancake. Let the pancake cook for 3 to 4 minutes, until it is browned on the bottom side, then flip the pancake (I use two spatulas for this), and cook it for 2 minutes on the other side.

**6.** Transfer the pancake to a plate. Continue to make the 5 remaining pancakes as in step 5, using about 1 tablespoon oil for each pancake. If you'd like, hold the cooked pancakes in a warm oven until all are made. Serve each pancake with a small bowl of the dipping sauce.

Makes 6 pancakes

# Shiitake Spring Rolls with Peanut Dipping Sauce

To have such a lovely morsel to offer your friends is worth the amount of time this recipe requires (about 1 to 1½ hours). Besides, the spring rolls can be prepared ahead; all you need to do at the last minute is pan-fry them. Dried mushrooms and spring roll skins can be found in Asian markets. Spring roll skins are also called egg roll skins and lumpia wrappers. My favorite brand is Shanghai Egg Roll, from New York.

25 dried shiitake mushrooms
4 tablespoons canola or corn oil
6 cups finely chopped green cabbage
5 carrots, coarsely grated
8 scallions, minced
2 tablespoons minced fresh ginger
Salt and pepper to taste
40 7- to 8-inch spring-roll skins
2 batches Peanut Sauce (page 336), at room
    temperature

## Dried Shiitakes

*A*lmost all the dried mushrooms one sees in plastic packages in Asian stores are shiitake mushrooms, also called black mushrooms. These mushrooms range in grades and sizes. The more expensive grades do have a superior flavor, although the less expensive ones are certainly good as well. Dried mushrooms need to be reconstituted. I usually pour boiling water over them and let them sit for 20 to 30 minutes. The tough stems need to be cut off and discarded once the mushroom is reconstituted. It is becoming more frequent to find the dried shiitake mushrooms in supermarkets. The price will be higher but worth it if you don't live near an Asian market.

**1.** Bring 1 quart water to a boil. Put the mushrooms in a bowl, and pour the water over them. Soak the mushrooms for 20 minutes.

**2.** Drain the mushrooms, saving ½ cup of the soaking liquid. Cut off and discard the mushroom stems, and slice the caps thin.

**3.** In a large pot, heat 2 tablespoons of the oil over medium-low heat. Add the cabbage, and cook it for 5 minutes, stirring occasionally. Add the reserved soaking liquid, and cook for about 20 minutes more, stirring occasionally. When the cabbage is tender, add the carrots, scallions, and ginger. Cook for another 5 minutes, and add salt and pepper to taste. Stir in the sliced shiitakes, and let the mixture cool.

**4.** Place a spring roll skin on a work surface, with one of the corners pointed toward you. Place 2 tablespoons of the filling 2 inches from the corner closest to you. Roll the skin fairly tightly from this corner, folding in the two side corners as you roll. Make the rest of the rolls in the same fashion.

**5.** In a large skillet or on a griddle, heat the remaining 2 tablespoons oil over medium heat. Add the spring rolls, and cook and turn them until the rolls are golden. Serve them with the Peanut Sauce.

Makes 40 thin spring rolls
(serves 20 as an appetizer)

# Vietnamese Rice-Paper Rolls

*C*old rice-paper spring rolls are one of the most refreshing foods I know. Coupled with zesty Cilantro-Chile Dipping Sauce (page 75), they can be habit forming.

Most Vietnamese cookbooks tell the reader to soak the rice paper in cold water. This method softens the rice paper but makes it slippery, so that it's hard to form a tight and secure roll. A Vietnamese chef showed me a different method: He dipped the rice paper in boiling water before rolling it. The hot water made the rice paper tacky, so it sealed tightly. But it weakened the rice paper and created tears, forcing me to throw out every other piece. Then a friend who had worked with some Chinese cooks showed me that doubling the rice paper after it's dipped in water creates a stronger, sturdier roll. Finally, Vietnamese rolls that don't fall apart!

The rice paper and rice vermicelli can be found at Southeast Asian and most Chinese markets.

4 ounces dried rice vermicelli
3 large carrots
1 small jícama (about 12 ounces)
20 basil leaves
1½ cups mint leaves, minced
½ cup ground dry-roasted, unsalted peanuts
½ package (10) 14-inch round rice papers
½ package (10) 8-inch round rice papers

**1.** Bring a large stockpot of water to a boil. Boil the rice vermicelli for 1 minute. Drain the noodles in a fine-mesh colander or sieve, and rinse them well with cold water. Then heat another large pot of water, to use for dipping the rice paper.

**2.** Meanwhile, peel the carrots and jícama. Coarsely grate them, or slice them into very thin julienne strips with a mandoline or by hand. Assemble the vegetables, herbs, vermicelli, and peanuts around your work area.

**3.** Pour the boiling water into a large bowl, and place the bowl close at hand. Take one large rice paper, and quickly dip it into the hot water. Lay it on your work surface. Dip the small rice paper in the water, and place it in the center of the large paper. Let the papers sit for a minute to become tacky. (I lay out papers for three rolls at a time and let them rest together. You can do as many at once as you have space for.)

**4.** Sprinkle a teaspoon or two of peanuts across the middle of the papers, leaving 2 inches clear on either end. Spread a large handful of noodles over the peanuts. Spread a small handful each of carrots, jícama, and mint on top of the noodles. Finally, place two basil leaves at one end of the mound, 1 inch below the outer edge of the rice paper. Starting from the other end, roll the paper tightly around the stuffing. Halfway up, fold the sides of the paper towards the center, and continue rolling to the end of the paper. The basil leaf should be visible at the top of the roll. Transfer the roll to a plate. Make the remaining rolls the same way. (You can refrigerate the rolls for up to 5 hours before serving. Wrap them tightly with plastic, or seal them in a plastic container.)

Serve the rolls with Cilantro-Chile Dipping Sauce (recipe follows).

**Variation:** Pan-fry the rolls in a bit of oil, and serve them hot with the sauce.

Makes 10 large rolls

# Cilantro-Chile Dipping Sauce

**a** fantabulous sauce. Besides being a perfect foil for the Vietnamese Rice-Paper Rolls (page 73), it's great as a dipping sauce for crudités, fried tofu, and various sorts of Asian deep-fried or pan-fried rolls. Strict vegetarians can substitute salt for the fish sauce, which is available at Asian markets.

1 tablespoon minced garlic
2 cups minced cilantro (about 1 bunch)
⅓ cup lime juice (from about 3 limes)
½ cup sugar
¼ cup Thai or Vietnamese fish sauce, or
    ¾ teaspoon salt
¼ cup water
1 tablespoon hot chile sauce (such as a Vietnamese tuong or Indonesian sambal sauce)

**1.** In a large bowl, combine all of the ingredients. Add a bit more chile sauce if you like.

**2.** Store the sauce in a sealed container in the refrigerator. Because of the fresh cilantro, this sauce keeps only 3 to 4 days.

Makes 1½ cups sauce

# CHAPTER 4

# Soups–
## Some Cold,
## Some Hot

# Soup Stocks

## Basic Vegetable Stock

This stock is different from most vegetable stocks in that the vegetables are sautéed over high heat before they are simmered in water. This caramelizes the vegetables, bringing out their natural sugars. I recommend making the full batch of stock and freezing it in small quantities, such as 2 or 4 cups. This way you'll have some on hand when you need it at the spur of the moment.

Feel free to make substitutions and to experiment with this recipe. If you have any herbs in the house, use them (I love plenty of cilantro in stocks, but be sparing with the stronger herbs, such as rosemary, marjoram, or tarragon). If your vegetable bin has three bunches of scallions that you don't need, then add them. Many other vegetables can be added in lieu of or in addition to the basic vegetables in the recipe. Appropriate vegetables include parsnips (my favorite), leeks, zucchini, watercress, lettuce (but not endive or radicchio), red and yellow peppers, carrots, turnips, mushrooms, shallots, kale, Swiss chard, bok choy, corn on the cob (or just the stripped cobs), eggplant, cucumbers, celeriac, green beans, and fennel. (It's important to take the skins off eggplant and any vegetables that may be waxed, like cucumbers and turnips.) Also winter squash—butternut, acorn, or delicata—contribute great flavor, but they cloud the stock, so if your stock will be turned into a minestrone or consommé you may want to avoid these. In Indian cuisine, legumes are often added to stocks. Try adding ½ cup of soaked navy, broad, or black beans. Also, try an Asian twist by adding any of the following ingredients: chopped lemongrass, chopped fresh ginger, Thai basil, chiles, cilantro, kaffir lime leaves, bean sprouts, and dried orange peel. In other words: Experiment!

2 tablespoons canola, corn, or olive oil
6 carrots, chopped
4 medium onions, peeled and chopped
8 celery stalks, chopped
4 tomatoes, quartered
2 potatoes, chopped
Any other vegetables you have on hand, except
    green peppers, cauliflower, artichokes,
    brussels sprouts, broccoli, beets, or spinach
1 garlic head, peeled of outer skins and cut in
    half horizontally
1 bunch parsley
1 teaspoon peppercorns
3 bay leaves
4½ quarts of water
1 cup white wine

**1.** Heat the oil in a stockpot over high heat. Add all the vegetables except the garlic and parsley, and sauté them for 15 minutes, stirring frequently. Add the garlic, parsley, peppercorns, bay leaves, and water. Bring the mixture to a boil, and turn down the heat. Simmer for 35 minutes.

**2.** Add the wine, and simmer for another 10 minutes.

**3.** Strain out the vegetables, and let the broth cool. It will keep in the refrigerator, tightly covered, for 1 week. The stock also freezes well; just be sure to leave room in the container for expansion.

Makes 4 quarts stock

# Roasted Vegetable Stock

In this recipe, the vegetables are all roasted together in a hot oven, then simmered in water for an hour. The resulting stock is better than the sum of its parts; I use it instead of Basic

Vegetable Stock whenever I want a big, rich flavor and don't need perfect clarity. This stock tastes as rich as the chicken or veal stock that I depended on years ago.

5 carrots, cut into 1-inch lengths
3 medium onions, quartered
10 garlic cloves, peeled
1/2 butternut squash, peeled and cut into
    chunks
1 turnip or 1/2 rutabaga, peeled and cut into
    chunks (optional)
2 red bell peppers, seeded and quartered
3 tomatoes, quartered
2 tablespoons olive oil
1 tablespoon fresh thyme or 1 teaspoon dried
    thyme, or 1 teaspoon fennel seeds or any
    favorite herb
4 1/2 quarts water
1 cup sundried or other dried tomatoes

**1.** Preheat the oven to 400°. Put all of the fresh vegetables (including the garlic) into a large roasting pan or two smaller roasting pans, and toss them with the olive oil and thyme or other herb. Roast the vegetables for 1 hour.

**2.** Transfer the hot vegetables to a large stockpot, and add the water and the dried tomatoes. Simmer gently for 1 hour.

**3.** Strain the stock. When it has cooled, cover it, and refrigerate it for up to 1 week. The stock freezes well, but be sure to allow room in the container for expansion.

Note: For a quick but tasty soup, purée the strained vegetables in a food processor, and sieve them. Then add 4 to 5 cups of the stock, some light cream, and salt and pepper to taste. Serve it up.

Makes approximately
4 quarts stock

*"Auntie was fond of food and when she was offered only a vegetarian diet she was indignant, she said she could not eat any old filth and demanded that they give her meat and chicken. The next time she came to dinner she was astonished to find a live chicken tied to her chair and a large knife on her plate.... 'You wanted chicken,' Tolstoy replied, scarcely restraining his laughter. 'Not one of us is willing to kill it. Therefore we prepared everything so that you could do it yourself.'"*

—ALEXANDRA TOLSTOY,
    TOLSTOY, A LIFE OF MY
    FATHER

# Mushroom Stock

I like this Asian-inspired stock plain, or with a bit of miso stirred in, when I'm feeling under the weather. Try cooking rice in this broth instead of in water; black sweet rice (available in Chinese markets) is especially good this way.

1 1-inch piece fresh ginger
1 garlic head, cut in half horizontally
2 cups chopped onions
2 cups dried shiitake mushrooms
½ cup Chinese rice wine, sherry, or sake
2 tablespoons soy sauce
3 quarts water

**1.** Slice the ginger into 5 or 6 pieces. In a 3-quart saucepan, combine all of the ingredients. Bring the mixture to a boil, and let it simmer, covered, for 1½ hours.

**2.** Strain the stock (reserve the mushrooms for another use, such as Shiitake Spring Rolls, page 72). Let the liquid cool, then cover and refrigerate it. It will keep well for 1 week. This stock also freezes well, but be sure to allow room in the container for expansion.

Makes 2½ quarts stock

# Carrot-Fennel Broth

This simple broth, when used in soups and rice dishes, renders delicious flavor. I use Carrot-Fennel Broth in Carrot-Fennel Soup (page 116). I also sometimes substitute this broth for Basic Vegetable Stock in Saffron Risotto with Mushrooms (page 220) and Fennel Risotto (page 215).

1 tablespoon olive oil
2 small fennel bulbs, including stalks and leaves, cut into 1-inch pieces
6 medium carrots, cut into 1-inch pieces
2 medium onions, coarsely chopped
1 garlic head, skins left on and cut in half horizontally
2 teaspoons fennel seeds
4 quarts water
1 cup white wine

**1.** Heat the olive oil in a stockpot over low heat, and add the fennel bulb, carrots, onions, garlic, and fennel seeds. Cook for 10 minutes, stirring occasionally.

**2.** Add the water, bring the mixture to a boil, and cover the pot. Let the mixture simmer for 30 minutes. Add the wine, and simmer another 10 minutes. Strain the stock, let it cool, then cover it. Refrigerate it for up to 1 week. This stock freezes well, but be sure to leave room in the container for expansion.

Makes 3½ quarts stock

# Cold Soups

## Tomato, Corn, and Black-Bean Gazpacho

This chunky and refreshing gazpacho is best made in summer. There is no substitute for the flavor of fresh, locally grown corn and tomatoes.

3 ears corn, shucked

½ cup coarsely chopped onion

7 medium round tomatoes or 14 plum tomatoes, cut into chunks

2 slices bread, toasted or left out to dry for a day, then cut into ½-inch squares

1½ cups cooked black beans, or 1 15-ounce can black beans

3 tablespoons minced onion

3 tablespoons lime juice (from about 1½ limes)

1 tablespoon olive oil

3 scallions, green part only, minced

1 teaspoon salt

½ teaspoon fresh-ground black pepper

¼ cup chopped cilantro

1½ cups water

1 jalapeño pepper, minced, seeds included (optional)

**1.** Bring 3 quarts salted water to a boil in a stockpot. Drop in the corn. Boil the corn for 2 minutes, then drain it, and rinse it with cold water. Cut the kernels off of the cob.

**2.** In a food processor, combine the ½ cup chopped onion, tomatoes, and bread. Run the machine in short spurts until the ingredients are puréed. Transfer the purée to a large bowl.

**3.** Put the beans into a strainer, and rinse them well with cold water.

**4.** Add to the puréed ingredients the rinsed beans, minced onion, lime juice, olive oil, scallions, salt, pepper, and 3 table-spoons of the cilantro. Add the corn kernels and the water. Stir well, and taste for seasoning. Add the jalapeño if you like a little heat.

**5.** Serve the soup well chilled, garnished with the remaining cilantro. It will keep for up to 4 days, covered, in the refrigerator.

Serves 6

# Green Grape and Tomatillo Gazpacho

In this recipe, I have taken a twist on *ajo blanco,* a cold Spanish soup I learned about from Steven Raichlen, a friend and cookbook author. Combining grapes, garlic, bread crumbs, olive oil, and almonds, the soup lingers in my mind as a truly divine gastronomic creation. This Mexican-inspired version combines tomatillos, pumpkin seeds, and grapes.

4 slices sandwich bread, chopped well

2 large garlic cloves, peeled

1/4 cup toasted pumpkin seeds (or almonds)

1/2 cup loosely packed cilantro

1 tablespoon extra-virgin olive oil

1 tablespoon red wine vinegar

5 small tomatillos (about 1/2 pound), chopped

3 cups water

1 pound seedless green grapes

Salt and fresh-ground black pepper to taste

4 teaspoons whole, low-fat, or nonfat sour cream
    (optional)

**1.** Put the bread pieces into a food processor or blender. Whirl until crumbs are formed. Transfer the crumbs to a bowl, and set the bowl aside.

**2.** In the empty food processor or blender, combine the garlic, pumpkin seeds or almonds, cilantro, olive oil, and vinegar. Blend the ingredients almost to a purée. Add the tomatillos and 1½ cups of the water. Blend until the tomatillos are coarsely chopped. Pour out most of the soup into a large bowl, then add to the processor or blender the grapes, the bread crumbs, and the remaining 1½ cups water. Blend until the grapes are chopped but not puréed. Pour this into the bowl containing the rest of the soup.

**3.** Add salt and pepper to taste. Chill the soup. Garnish with sour cream, if you like, and serve.

Serves 4

# Watermelon Gazpacho

Watermelon is by no means a traditional gazpacho ingredient, but it can make this chilled soup even more refreshing on a sultry day.

## Squirrel Away Your Bread

*D*on't pitch leftover or stale bread! Start a stash of frozen bread for bread crumbs. In a plastic bag in your freezer, save end slices from sandwich loaves, stale bagels or pita pockets, leftover dinner rolls, or even focaccia crusts. When you need crumbs, take out a few pieces of bread, let them thaw, and cut them into smaller pieces. Then grind the bread to crumbs in the food processor.

*Bread crumbs can be used in dozens of ways. Crumbs pan-fried with olive oil and garlic are delicious in salads, soups, and pasta dishes. Use your crumbs in veggie burgers, Crumbed Zucchini (page 187), or Sweet Fried Plantains (page 57).*

7½ pounds watermelon, preferably seedless
2 slices white bread, toasted or left out to dry for a day
1 green bell pepper, seeded and minced
1 red bell pepper, seeded and minced
1 jalapeño pepper, seeded and minced (optional)
1 medium onion, minced
2 garlic cloves, minced
1 cucumber, peeled, seeded, and minced
½ cup chopped parsley
¼ cup red wine vinegar
2 tablespoons olive oil
About 1 teaspoon salt, or to taste
Fresh-ground black pepper to taste
1 or 2 pinches cayenne

**1.** Cut the hard green skin and white underflesh off the watermelon. (I do this as I would peel an orange: I lay a watermelon half on its cut side, cut a bit off the top, then, with a large knife, cut down the top and sides while rotating the melon, until only the red flesh is left.) Cut the melon into 1-inch cubes, removing any seeds; you should have about 9 cups. Then, in a food processor or blender, purée the melon. Transfer the purée to a large bowl.

**2.** Put the bread into the processor or blender, and blend until crumbs form.

**3.** Stir into the watermelon purée the bread crumbs, the green and red pepper, the jalapeño (if you're using it), the onion, the garlic, the cucumber, the parsley, the vinegar, and the olive oil. Add salt, pepper, and cayenne. Chill the soup before serving. It will keep for 2 days in the refrigerator, but it is best the day it is made.

*Serves 6*

# Beet and Cucumber Gazpacho

My upstairs neighbor grows beets in his community garden plot. Although he loves beets, his recipe ideas run dry long before his supply of beets runs out. I developed this soup to help. It's a refreshing gazpacho that features beets but retains traditional Spanish ingredients such as bell peppers, tomatoes, and olive oil.

2 large or 4 small fresh beets, trimmed
1 teaspoon ground coriander seeds
1 teaspoon cumin seeds
2 red bell peppers, seeded and cut into chunks
2 cups cold water
1 cucumber, peeled and chopped
1 cup chopped onion
5 plum tomatoes, chopped
3 tablespoons lime juice (from about 1½ limes)
2 tablespoons olive oil
3 tablespoons chopped cilantro or basil
1 teaspoon salt
Fresh-ground black pepper to taste
6 tablespoons yogurt or whole, low-fat, or nonfat
　　sour cream

**1.** If the beets are large, cut them in half. Put the beets into a large stockpot and cover them with water. Bring the water to a boil, and simmer until the beets can be pierced with a butter knife (depending on the size of the beets, this can take anywhere between 25 and 45 minutes). Drain the beets, and, under cold running water, squeeze off the skins and cut the beets into quarters.

**2.** Place the beets in a food processor or blender. Toast the coriander and cumin in a small dry skillet, shaking it often until they release their fragrance. Add the spices and peppers to the beets. Add ½ cup of the water, and blend the mixture until the large chunks are gone, but not to a smooth purée (you want some texture to this soup). Transfer the beet mixture to a large bowl.

**3.** In the processor or blender, combine the cucumber, onion, and tomatoes. Add ½ cup of the water. Process until the mixture is only slightly chunky. Add this mixture to the beet mixture. Add the remaining 1 cup water, the lime juice, the olive oil, the cilantro or basil, and the salt and pepper. Chill the soup for at least 1 hour. Then ladle it into bowls, garnish each bowl with a tablespoon of yogurt or sour cream, and serve.

Variation: Instead of the red bell peppers, try poblano peppers. But don't purée the poblanos; instead, chop them fine. They will add a nice contrast in color to the red of the beets, and a little heat besides.

Serves 6

# Spiced Tomato Soup

This soup is a cool treat during hot summer weather. I like the way the sweetness of the tomatoes checks the acidity of the yogurt. The chipotles provide zip, and the cumin and cinnamon subtle earthy notes. This recipe comes from my former sous-chef at the Delux, Matthew Campbell.

2 garlic cloves

½ to 1 chipotle pepper (dried and soaked in hot
    water 30 minutes, or canned in adobo sauce)

20 plum tomatoes, coarsely chopped

1¼ cups plain yogurt

¼ teaspoon ground cinnamon

½ teaspoon ground cumin seeds

1 teaspoon ground coriander seeds

1 teaspoon sugar

1 cup water

1 teaspoon salt

Ground white pepper to taste

2 tablespoons lime juice (from about 1 lime)

2 tablespoons chopped cilantro (optional)

**1.** Purée the garlic, chipotle, and half of the tomatoes in a food processor or a blender. Force the mixture through a sieve into a large bowl, pressing with a rubber spatula or spoon, to remove the skin and seeds. Purée the rest of the tomatoes, and force them through the sieve into the bowl, too.

**2.** Whisk in the yogurt, spices, and sugar. Stir in the water, salt, white pepper, and lime juice. Chill the soup for at least 1½ hours. Serve it garnished with the cilantro, if you like.

Serves 6

# Chilled Mango Soup

Most fruit soups I try I'd rather have for dessert than for a first or main course. This soup is different; it has a slight sweetness, but most of the presiding flavors, including onion, curry, and cilantro, are savory. Because the "cream" in this soup is really yogurt, this dish is deceptively low in fat and calories.

## Pepper: White, Black, and Green

Pepper is nearly the perfect spice; it improves almost every dish. Sometimes I get excited about black pepper and give it a little more importance, as in Kasha Burgers (page 375) or the dumplings in Wild Mushroom Stew (page 319). White and black peppercorns start as the same berry, but white peppercorns are skinned and sun-dried. Their flavor is slightly different, with a touch of pine. I buy them in Asian markets, where they are less expensive. Green peppercorns are picked young and pickled in brine to stay soft. Delectable but expensive, they can be used whole in pasta sauces or sauces for risotto cakes.

Tuong chile sauce is available in Southeast Asian and Chinese markets, and in some supermarkets as well.

∎∎∎∎∎∎∎∎

1 tablespoon olive oil
1 large sweet onion, chopped
1 teaspoon curry powder, store-bought or
    homemade (page 36)
2 teaspoons minced fresh ginger
2 large or 3 small ripe mangoes, peeled and
    pitted
2½ cups water
⅔ cup orange juice
2 cups yogurt
1 teaspoon salt
1 pinch fresh-ground black pepper
1 tablespoon chopped cilantro
2 teaspoons tuong chile sauce or other red chile
    sauce
4 lime wedges

∎∎∎∎∎∎∎∎

**1.** In a large saucepan, heat the olive oil over medium heat. Add the onions. Cook them, stirring frequently, for 5 minutes or until they soften. Add the curry and the ginger, and cook another 5 minutes, letting the onions brown along the edges.

**2.** Add the mango flesh to the cooked onions. Add the water and orange juice, and let the mixture simmer for 15 minutes.

**3.** Purée the mixture in a food processor or blender, in batches if necessary. Then pass the purée through a sieve into a bowl, pressing with a rubber spatula or spoon to extract all the liquid.

**4.** Stir in the yogurt, salt, pepper, and cilantro. Chill the soup for at least 1 hour, preferably 2.

**5.** To serve, fancifully squirt or lightly spoon hot sauce on top of each bowl of soup. Accompany each serving with a wedge of lime, and urge your friends to squeeze the lime into the soup.

Serves 4

# Spinach Vichyssoise

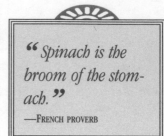
For those of us who love spinach, it can make its way into most any recipe. This vichyssoise is simple and—except for the spinach—traditional. It makes a nice start to a summer meal.

1½ tablespoons butter
2½ cups chopped onions or leeks
3 medium russet potatoes, peeled and chopped to make 3 cups
6 cups whole or low-fat milk
4 cups washed and stemmed spinach, firmly packed
1 large pinch fresh nutmeg
About 1 teaspoon salt, to taste
½ teaspoon fresh-ground black pepper
4 teaspoons sour cream
Chopped chives

**1.** Heat the butter in a stockpot over medium heat. Add the onions, and cook them, stirring frequently, for 5 minutes or until they have softened. Add the potatoes and milk, and bring the mixture to a simmer over high heat. Cover the soup, and turn the heat to low. Simmer for 30 minutes or until the potatoes are tender. Stir in the spinach, and simmer the soup 5 minutes more.

**2.** Purée the soup in batches in a food processor or blender. Season the soup with the nutmeg, salt, and pepper. Serve it either hot or cold (chilled for at least 1½ hours), with a dollop of sour cream and a sprinkling of chives.

Variation: For a more imaginative, if somewhat offbeat, vichyssoise, add 2 teaspoons curry powder to the onions or leeks after they have cooked for 5 minutes.

Serves 6

# Sweet-Potato Vichyssoise

Very similar in taste to traditional white-potato vichyssoise, this lovely soup has a bright orange color and a mellow sweetness. I call for shallots instead of leeks, since the green of the leeks would gray the orange color. I also add celery, garlic, and white wine to create a built-in stock. Unlike many cold soups, this one is equally good served hot.

2 tablespoons olive oil
4 shallots, chopped
2 inner celery stalks, chopped
2 garlic cloves, minced
1 large sweet potato (3/4 pound), peeled and
    chopped into 1-inch chunks
2 small potatoes (3/4 pound total), peeled and
    chopped into 1-inch chunks
1 quart water
1/2 cup white wine
5 tablespoons whole, low-fat, or nonfat sour
    cream
1/2 teaspoon salt, or more, to taste
Fresh-ground black pepper to taste
Chopped chives

**1.** In a heavy pot, heat the olive oil over medium heat. Add the shallots and celery, and sauté them, stirring often, for about 5 minutes or until the shallots soften. Add the garlic, sweet potato, and white potatoes, and stir. Add the water and wine, and simmer the soup until the potatoes are tender, about 15 to 20 minutes.

**2.** With a blender or food processor, blend the soup (in two batches, if necessary) until it is almost but not quite smooth. Transfer the soup to a container with a tight-fitting lid. Whisk in the sour cream, salt, and pepper (overseason the soup a bit, because the flavors will dull when the soup is chilled).

**3.** Chill the soup for at least 2 hours. Before serving it, check the seasonings, and add more salt and pepper, if you like. Serve the soup chilled, sprinkled with the chopped chives.

*Serves 4*

# Cream of Cucumber Soup

This soup can be made with any type of cucumbers available. You don't need to seed pickling or English (greenhouse) cucumbers since their seeds are relatively small and few. I use shallots instead of onions in this mellow soup because shallots are less harsh in flavor when raw.

2¹/₂ pounds cucumbers (about 4, if they're salad size), peeled, seeded if necessary, and chopped
2 tablespoons chopped shallots
1 tablespoon lime juice (from about ¹/₂ lime)
1 tablespoon extra-virgin olive oil
3 tablespoons chopped dill
2 cups plain whole, low-fat, or nonfat yogurt
¹/₂ teaspoon salt
1 pinch ground juniper berry (optional)
Fresh-ground black pepper to taste
4 small dill sprigs

**1.** In a blender or food processor, combine all of the ingredients except the 4 dill sprigs. Blend for at least 2 minutes, or until the soup is well puréed.

**2.** Transfer the soup to a bowl, and chill the soup for 30 minutes. Serve it with a dill sprig floating on the top of each bowl.

## Getting to Know Juniper Berries

*I used to think that juniper berries were only good for making gin and marinating venison and lamb. But when I smelled the berries, I thought of more possibilities. Juniper berries have a refreshing, intriguing piney scent with a hint of cloves. I now enjoy adding a pinch of ground juniper to squash soups and to balsamic vinaigrette for green salads. Ground juniper also works well with nutmeg to spice pumpkin pies.*

*If you can't find juniper berries at whole-foods or specialty food stores, you might order them from Penzeys spice company (414-574-0277).*

**Variation:** Try this soup with other vegetables—watercress or arugula (use 3 cups leaves), or even tomatoes (use 4 ripe ones)—instead of the cucumbers.

Serves 4

# Minty Melon Soup

Melon soup has long been popular. In this version, ground cumin and mint flavor the melon purée, and yogurt acts as the base. Make this soup from melons that are fully ripe— soft to the touch and fragrant when held close to the nose.

Flesh of 1 large cantaloupe or 1 small honeydew
    or Crenshaw melon
1/2 cup white wine
1 teaspoon ground cumin seeds
4 cups plain low-fat yogurt
1/2 cup minced onion
3 tablespoons chopped mint
Salt and fresh-ground black pepper to taste
6 tiny mint sprigs

**1.** In a blender or food processor, purée the melon flesh with the wine (you may need to do this in two batches).

**2.** In a small, dry skillet, heat the cumin over low heat, shaking the pan frequently until the cumin becomes fragrant. Transfer the soup to a large bowl, and whisk in the yogurt, onion, cumin, and mint. Add salt and pepper and some water, if needed, to thin the soup.

**3.** Chill the soup until it is very cold. Serve it in bowls garnished with tiny mint sprigs.

Serves 6

# Hot Soups

## African Tomato and Peanut Soup

A favorite of my friends, this soup is inspired by the many vegetable and meat stews of West Africa. These stews are traditionally served over rice or millet, but one can more fully enjoy the texture of the ground peanuts and the intriguing interplay of spices in a soup like this.

1 tablespoon canola or corn oil

1 large onion, chopped

2 garlic cloves, minced

2 teaspoons minced fresh ginger

1½ teaspoons ground cumin seeds

1½ teaspoons ground coriander seeds

½ teaspoon ground cinnamon

1 pinch ground cloves

3 ripe medium tomatoes, chopped

2 large (about 1½ pounds) sweet potatoes, peeled and coarsely chopped

1 carrot, coarsely chopped

4½ cups water

1 teaspoon salt

1 pinch cayenne (optional)

¼ cup chopped dry-roasted, unsalted peanuts

2 tablespoons peanut butter

1 tablespoon chopped cilantro

**1.** In a large saucepan or small stockpot, heat the oil over medium-high heat. Add the onion, and cook, stirring occasionally, for 10 minutes or until the onion browns around the edges. Add the garlic, ginger, and spices, and cook for 3 more minutes, stirring often.

**2.** Add the tomatoes, sweet potatoes, and carrot, and cook for 5 minutes.

**3.** Add the water and salt. Bring the mixture to a boil. Reduce the heat, cover the pot, and simmer the soup for 30 minutes.

**4.** With a food processor or blender, blend the soup (in batches, if necessary) almost to a purée. Taste, and add the cayenne, if you like. Add the peanuts and the peanut butter, and whisk until the peanut butter is fully incorporated.

**5.** To serve, reheat the soup, and ladle it into bowls. Top with the chopped cilantro.

Serves 6

## Blender Safety

*When puréeing hot soup in a blender, fill the blender only halfway, take the middle piece out of the lid so the soup can breathe, and run the machine in short spurts. Otherwise the soup may explode out of the blender and scald you.*

# Garlic Soup with Bread

This soup is especially welcome in the wintertime when the produce aisle is uninspiring. In fact, I seldom have to do any shopping for this soup, because all of the ingredients are usually in my pantry.

2 tablespoons olive oil
2 cups thinly sliced onions
16 large garlic cloves, minced
2 quarts water
1/2 teaspoon dried rosemary
1 teaspoon dried thyme
1 teaspoon fennel seeds, ground

2 medium russet potatoes, peeled and sliced thin
    crosswise, then cut in half lengthwise
2 large carrots, peeled and sliced into
    thin rounds
½ cup sherry
1 teaspoon salt
Fresh-ground black pepper to taste
4 thick slices of bread (mild sourdough or
    French bread is especially good)
¼ cup grated Parmesan cheese (optional)

**1.** In a stockpot, heat the olive oil over medium heat. Sauté the onions for 10 minutes, stirring frequently. Add the garlic, and sauté for another 5 minutes.

**2.** Add the water and the dried herbs, and let the soup simmer for 15 minutes. Then add the potatoes and carrots, and simmer until the potatoes are tender, about 15 minutes. Add the sherry, and simmer for another 5 minutes.

**3.** Season the soup well with salt and pepper. Place a slice of bread on the bottom of each soup bowl. Ladle the soup over the bread. Garnish with Parmesan cheese, if you like.

Serves 4

# Carrot, Ginger, and Beet Soup

This soup is great hot or cold. Subtle flavorings tend to be overpowered by beets, but the strength of ginger works well with them. Orange rind adds another interesting dimension to this soup.

## How to Beat the Mess of Beets

*The lovely, sweet flavor of beets works well in many dishes, including salads, soups, and risotto. But some cooks avoid beets because of the mess they leave behind. Here are a couple of ways to prepare beets without a lot of mess: Do not peel the beets, but scrub them with a brush under running water. Cut them into quarters, toss them with some salt, pepper, and olive oil, and roast them in a 400° oven until they are tender. Or boil the beets whole until they are tender (about 30 to 40 minutes), then rinse them under cold running water while you press the skins off with your hands.*

3 medium beets (about 1 pound)
1 tablespoon canola or corn oil
1 cup chopped onion
1 pound carrots, coarsely chopped
1 tablespoon minced fresh ginger
1 large garlic clove, minced
6 cups water or Basic Vegetable Stock (page 79)
1 teaspoon grated orange rind
3/4 teaspoon salt
Fresh-ground black pepper to taste
4 teaspoons sour cream (optional)

**1.** Under running water (this is very messy otherwise), peel the beets with a vegetable peeler. With a chef's knife, cut the beets in half, then lay them flat side down and cut them into large chunks.

**2.** In a stockpot over medium heat, heat the oil. Sauté the onion until it is translucent. Add the carrots, ginger, and garlic. Cook for 5 minutes, stirring frequently. Add the beets and the water or stock. Simmer the soup, covered, for 50 minutes. Add the orange rind, and stir well.

**3.** In a food processor or blender, purée the soup in batches. Transfer the puréed soup to a large container, and stir in the salt and pepper. Taste the soup, and adjust the seasonings, if you like. Serve the soup hot or chilled, garnished with dollops of sour cream.

Serves 4

# Gumbo Soup

Traditionally gumbo is a stew containing poultry, sausage, seafood, or a combination of these. A vegetarian version, being considerably lighter, works best as a soup. This gumbo does include a dark roux—that is, flour and fat are cooked to a deep tan. Watch carefully, because a roux can quickly cross the line between brown and burnt.

1 tablespoon butter
1 tablespoon unbleached white flour
3 garlic cloves, minced
2 cups chopped onions
1 teaspoon dried thyme
3 bay leaves
5 cups water or Basic Vegetable Stock (page 79)
3 1/2 cups (1 28-ounce can) chopped plum tomatoes
2 green bell peppers, seeded and finely chopped
3/4 cup uncooked long-grain white rice, rinsed well
1 1/2 cups sliced okra, cut crosswise into 1/2-inch-thick rounds
1 teaspoon salt, or more, to taste
Fresh-ground black pepper to taste
4 cups coarsely chopped mustard greens or kale
Hot chile sauce, to taste

**1.** In a large, heavy-bottomed saucepan, heat the butter over medium heat. Add the flour, and stir with a wooden spoon until the roux turns light brown (it will brown further over the next few minutes). Add the garlic, onions, spices, and thyme. Stirring constantly with a spoon, cook the mixture for another 2 to 3 minutes, being careful not to burn it.

**2.** Add the water or stock a cup at a time, stirring with a whisk to prevent any lumps from forming. Then add the tomatoes, peppers, rice, okra, and salt and pepper. Bring the soup to a boil, then turn the heat to low, cover the soup, and simmer it for 30 minutes. Add the mustard greens or kale, and simmer for another 10 minutes. Taste, add the hot sauce, and adjust the seasonings if you like. Serve the soup hot.

Variation: Add the kernels from two ears of corn 5 minutes before the soup is done.

Serves 6

## Leftover Herbs

*Often recipes call for only a table-spoon of this or that herb. And most herbs wither quickly, so there's not much time to make use of them if you've bought or picked a whole bunch. Here are a couple of options:*

*◆ Mince one or more herbs, and mix them with half their volume of olive oil. Keep the mixture refrigerated in an airtight container. Add balsamic vinegar to the mixture to use it as a vinaigrette.*

*◆ Mince one or more herbs, and mash them into some unsalted butter. Use the herb butter with roasted or steamed vegetables, soups, rice, or bread.*

# Potage Bonne Femme

A large crouton with melted Gruyère on top floats on this hearty, ever-popular potato soup. The beer in the soup provides good flavor, although it's hard to detect that the beer is there at all. This is a fitting soup for a cold night.

2 tablespoons olive oil
3 cups chopped onions
6 garlic cloves, minced
3 pounds russet potatoes, peeled and cut into
    ¼-inch cubes
1 cup light-colored beer (I use Rolling Rock;
    a dark beer would make the soup bitter)
7 cups water
2 teaspoons minced fresh rosemary, or
    1 teaspoon dried rosemary
2 teaspoons minced fresh tarragon, or 1 teaspoon
    dried tarragon
2 teaspoons minced fresh thyme, or 1 teaspoon
    dried thyme
1 teaspoon salt
Fresh-ground black pepper to taste
6 slices good white or whole-wheat sandwich
    bread
4 ounces imported Gruyère cheese, sliced thin
    into 6 slices

**1.** In a large pot over medium heat, heat the olive oil and the onions. Cook the onions for 10 to 15 minutes, or until the onions begin to caramelize. Add the garlic, and cook another 2 minutes. Add the potatoes, beer, water, rosemary, tarragon, thyme, salt, and pepper. Bring the soup to a boil, then turn the heat to low, and cover the pot. Let the soup simmer for 40 minutes.

**2.** While the soup is simmering, make the croutons: Preheat the oven to 400°. Cut the crusts off the bread slices. Toast the bread in the oven until it is golden. Remove the toast, but keep the oven on if you're going to serve the soup as soon as it is finished.

**3.** Just before serving the soup, lay the cheese slices on the croutons. Place the croutons on a baking sheet, and bake them at 400° just until the cheese has melted. Ladle the soup into bowls, lay one crouton atop each bowl, and serve.

**Variation:** For a richer soup, add ⅓ cup heavy cream at the end of step 1.

Serves 6

# Cream of Tomato Soup

I was a major tomato soup fan as a kid. The problem is, I'm an adult now and I don't like the canned tomato soup I once loved (sadly, this is also true with instant chocolate milk). Here I've created a cream of tomato soup that is more in tune with adult palates, but still definitely comforting.

3 tablespoons butter
2 cups chopped onions
3 garlic cloves, minced
3 tablespoons unbleached white flour
¼ cup Madeira or Marsala
7 cups (2 28-ounce cans) peeled plum tomatoes; drain and reserve their juice
1 pinch cayenne
Salt and fresh-ground pepper to taste
¼ to ½ cup light cream

**1.** In a heavy pot, melt the butter over medium heat. Add the onions, and cook for 5 minutes, stirring frequently, until they have softened. Add the garlic, and cook another minute or two. Add the flour, and cook, stirring constantly, for 1 minute. Stirring with a whisk, add the Madeira or Marsala. Then slowly add the juice from the plum tomatoes, whisking all the while so that lumps won't form. Add the tomatoes, and stir well.

**2.** Bring the soup to a boil, and let it simmer for 20 minutes, stirring occasionally. Purée the soup with a blender or food processor, in batches if necessary. Add the cayenne, salt, and pepper. Blend in as much cream as you like, and serve the soup hot.

Serves 6

# Corn and Sweet-Potato Chowder

This chowder tastes rich and creamy, partly because corn tortillas are included. They break down and thicken the soup, and they also boost the corn flavor.

2 tablespoons butter
1 tablespoon olive oil
2 cups chopped onions
3 garlic cloves, minced
1/2 teaspoon ground cumin seeds
1 teaspoon paprika
2 1/2 tablespoons unbleached white flour
6 cups whole or low-fat milk
3 corn tortillas, cut into small pieces
Kernels from 3 ears corn (about 2 cups) and the shaved cobs
1 large or 2 small sweet potatoes (about 1 pound), peeled and cut into 1/2-inch cubes
1 teaspoon salt

Fresh-ground black pepper to taste
Squeeze of lime
2 tablespoons chopped cilantro (optional)

**1.** In a stockpot or large saucepan, melt the butter with the olive oil over medium heat. Add the onions, garlic, cumin, and paprika. Cook for 5 minutes, stirring frequently.

**2.** Add the flour, and, stirring constantly with a whisk, cook for 30 seconds. Slowly add the milk, ½ cup at a time, while continuing to stir with a whisk so the flour doesn't lump. Add the tortillas, the shaved cobs, and the sweet potatoes, and simmer the mixture over low heat, stirring occasionally, for 20 minutes or until the sweet potatoes are tender.

**3.** Add the corn kernels, and let the soup simmer 2 minutes more. Add the salt, pepper, and lime. Remove the shaved cobs, then ladle the soup into bowls, and sprinkle it with cilantro, if you like.

Serves 4

# Corn and Tomato Chowder

Although this is a chowder, it is very light and refreshing, since it contains milk but no cream or flour. The soup is also quick to make—the only difficulty may be finding fresh corn on the cob. You can substitute frozen corn but the crunchy and sweet taste of fresh corn really makes a difference in this soup.

2 tablespoons olive oil
2 cups chopped onions
2 teaspoons finely minced garlic
4 ears corn

3½ cups whole milk
2 tablespoons tequila
3 tablespoons chopped cilantro
½ jalapeño pepper or 1 or 2 Thai chile peppers,
    minced
2 ripe tomatoes, cut into ½-inch pieces
½ teaspoon salt, or more, to taste
Fresh-ground black pepper to taste

**1.** In a large saucepan, heat the olive oil over medium heat. Add the onions and the garlic, and cook them, stirring frequently, for 5 minutes or until the onions have softened.

**2.** While the onions and garlic are cooking, shuck the corn, and cut the kernels off the cob. Then hold the cobs vertically, one by one, and scrape down the sides, collecting the milky solids that are still on the cob. Add these and the kernels to the saucepan with the onions and garlic.

**3.** Add the milk, bring the mixture to a simmer, and let it simmer lightly (do not boil) for 10 minutes. Add the tequila, cilantro, and chile peppers, and continue to simmer for 5 minutes more. Take the soup off the heat. Add the tomatoes, salt, and pepper. Ladle the soup hot into bowls. If you want to reheat it, do so gently, or it may break down and separate.

Serves 4

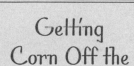

## Getting Corn Off the Cob

*An easy way to cut corn kernels from a cob is to lay the cob flat, and slice horizontally across the top. Then rotate the corn a quarter turn, and cut across the top again. Continue in this manner twice more, until all the kernels have been removed.*

# Tomato-Lentil Soup

This simple, healthful soup may be a possibility even if your refrigerator is nearly empty, since it requires little in the way of fresh produce.

2 tablespoons olive oil
1 cup chopped onion
2 garlic cloves, minced
2 teaspoons ground coriander seeds
1 teaspoon ground cumin seeds
1 green or red bell pepper, seeded and minced
2 cups dried brown lentils
1 jalapeño pepper, minced (optional)
6 cups water or Basic Vegetable Stock
    (page 79)
1 3/4 cups (1 14-ounce can) peeled plum tomatoes
1/4 cup lemon juice (from about 1 lemon)
1/2 teaspoon salt
Fresh-ground black pepper to taste

**1.** Heat the oil in a large saucepan over medium heat. Add the onion, garlic, coriander, cumin, and bell pepper, and sauté for 10 minutes, stirring frequently. Add the lentils, the jalapeño if you like, and the water or stock.

**2.** Pour the tomatoes into a small bowl, and squeeze them with your hands so they break into small pieces. Add the tomatoes to the soup. Let the soup simmer over low heat for 45 minutes.

**3.** Take the soup off the heat, and add the lemon juice and salt and pepper. Ladle the soup into bowls and serve.

Serves 4

# Yellow Split-Pea Soup

In my youth, I was never able to eat split peas. Always appearing in the form of split-pea soup with ham, they made ham taste worse than it already was. But with age, fortunately, comes maturity—and an appreciation of yellow split peas! They have a less intense flavor than green split peas, and they are great in soups. This soup combines them with carrot, onions, tarragon, thyme, and garlic, all simmered together and then puréed into a split-pea soup that I can not only eat, but enjoy.

2 tablespoons butter
1½ cups chopped onions
1 cup minced carrot
3 garlic cloves, minced
1 pound dried yellow split peas
6½ cups water
2 teaspoons fresh tarragon, or 1 teaspoon dried
    tarragon
1 teaspoon fresh thyme leaves, or ½ teaspoon
    dried thyme
½ cup white wine
1 teaspoon salt
Fresh-ground black pepper to taste

**1.** In a large saucepan, melt the butter over medium heat. Add the onions and carrot, and cook, stirring occasionally, for 10 minutes or until the onions soften and brown a bit on the edges. Add the garlic, and cook another 2 minutes.

**2.** Add the split peas, water, tarragon, and thyme. Let the soup simmer over low heat, covered, for 50 minutes, stirring 3 or 4 times to prevent any burning on the bottom of the pot.

**3.** Add the wine, and continue to cook the soup, uncovered, for 10 more minutes. Add the salt and pepper. Ladle the soup into bowls, and serve.

Serves 4

# Tuscan White-Bean Soup

This Italian soup traditionally combines a ham bone, white beans, vegetables, rosemary, and a lot of olive oil. After hours of stewing, the soup is partly puréed to give it a delicious creaminess. To gather the flavor traditionally provided by the ham bone, my vegetarian version slow-cooks fennel, leeks, celery, and carrots. I also add fennel seed and lemon to give the soup more depth. As in the original, Parmesan cheese and olive oil are stirred in at the end, creating a soup that is creamy and rich.

1 pound white navy beans
4 tablespoons olive oil
3 leeks (about 1 pound), both green and white
    parts, chopped fine; or 3 cups chopped onions
5 celery stalks, chopped
3 garlic cloves, minced
1½ cups minced carrots (about 3 carrots)
1 small fennel bulb, cored, trimmed, and minced
5 cups water, Roasted Vegetable Stock (page
    80), or Carrot-Fennel Broth (page 83)
1½ teaspoons chopped fresh rosemary, or
    1 teaspoon dried rosemary
½ to 1 teaspoon ground fennel seed (optional)
1 teaspoon salt, or more, to taste
Fresh-ground black pepper to taste
2 tablespoons lemon juice (from about ½ lemon)
⅓ cup grated Parmesan or Asiago cheese

**1.** Soak the beans overnight in at least 3 quarts of water, or use the quick-soak method: Bring a large pot of water to a boil, and add the beans. Boil them for 5 minutes, then let them soak in the water for 1 hour. After soaking the beans according to either method, drain them and rinse them well.

## How to Wash Leeks

To clean leeks, pull off the tired-looking outer leaves, and trim off the roots and about 1 inch of the green tops. Then make a slit at about the middle, where the leaves turn green, and cut through all the way to the top. Roll the leek a quarter turn, and again cut from the middle to the top of the leek, forming a kind of brush. Fill a large bowl with water, plunge the leeks in, and shake them to loosen any dirt.

**2.** In a heavy stockpot, heat 2 tablespoons of the olive oil over medium heat. Add the leeks or onions, and cook for 5 minutes, stirring frequently. Add the celery, garlic, carrots, and fennel. Cook for 10 minutes, stirring frequently. Add the water or stock, the rinsed navy beans, the herbs, and the salt and pepper. Bring the soup to a boil, then reduce the heat and let the soup simmer over low heat, covered, for 1 hour.

**3.** Ladle 3 cups of the soup into a blender or food processor. Purée this portion, then pour it back into the pot of soup. Correct the seasonings, adding the lemon juice and perhaps more salt or pepper. Ladle the soup into bowls, spoon the remaining olive oil over, and sprinkle on the cheese. Serve at once.

**Variation:** Instead of spooning 2 tablespoons olive oil over the soup, pan-fry six small pieces of bread in the oil, then float a slice on top of each bowl of soup. Sprinkle the Parmesan over.

Serves 6

# Lima Minestrone

Move over French onion, and watch out oxtail—this minestrone can contend with the richest meat-based soups around. It is chock-full of three vegetables—corn, red bell pepper, and lima beans. You need to make a simple vegetable stock beforehand, but once you've made the stock, you're only 20 minutes away from serving the soup.

2 tablespoons extra-virgin olive oil
1 cup chopped onion
3 garlic cloves, minced
1/2 cup white wine
6 cups Roasted Vegetable Stock (page 80)

2 cups water
2 teaspoons chopped fresh rosemary or
   1 teaspoon dried rosemary
1½ cups fresh or frozen lima beans
1 red bell pepper, seeded and cut into 1-inch
   julienne strips
2 cups corn kernels
1 teaspoon salt
1 squeeze lemon juice
1 or 2 dashes balsamic vinegar
Fresh-ground black pepper, and more salt, to
   taste
½ cup grated Parmesan cheese, for garnish

**1.** In a stockpot or large saucepan, heat the olive oil over medium-high heat. Add the onions, and let them cook for 10 minutes, stirring occasionally, or until they begin to brown at the edges. Add the garlic, and cook 1 minute more. Stir in the wine, stock, water, and rosemary. Bring the mixture to a simmer, and cook, covered, for 10 minutes.

**2.** Add the lima beans, red pepper, corn, and salt. Let the soup simmer another 5 minutes. Then squeeze a bit of lemon into the soup, add a dash or two of balsamic vinegar, and stir in the salt and pepper to taste. Serve the soup topped with Parmesan cheese.

Serves 6

# Curried
# Cauliflower
# Bisque

Despite the bouquet of ginger, curry, and onion in this bisque, the flavor of the cauliflower doesn't get lost. The roux (flour cooked in butter) thickens the soup a little and gives it a silky smooth consistency.

2 tablespoons butter
1 teaspoon ground fenugreek (optional)
1 tablespoon curry powder, store-bought or
　　homemade (page 36)
1 teaspoon ground coriander seeds
2 cups chopped onions
2 garlic cloves, minced
1 tablespoon minced fresh ginger
2 tablespoons unbleached white flour
7 cups whole or low-fat milk
1 head cauliflower, cut into small pieces
1 teaspoon salt, or more, to taste
Fresh-ground pepper to taste

**1.** In a stockpot, melt the butter over medium heat. Add the fenugreek, if you're using it, and the curry powder and coriander. Cook, stirring, for 1 minute. Add the onions, garlic, and ginger. Cook, stirring frequently, for 10 minutes.

**2.** Add the flour, and cook 3 minutes more, stirring continuously. Slowly add the milk, continuing to stir so that lumps don't develop. Then add the cauliflower. Bring the soup to a boil, then turn the heat to low, and simmer the soup for 40 minutes. Add the salt and pepper.

**3.** In a food processor or blender, blend the soup in batches, but not to a purée; leave it a little chunky. Taste the soup, and add salt or pepper if needed. Serve the soup hot.

Variation: For a lovely sweetness, add 2 peeled and chopped parsnips along with the cauliflower in step 2.

Serves 6

## A Handsome Seed: Fenugreek

Mustard brown and box-shaped, these attractive seeds come from small leguminous plants native to Asia and southern Europe. Fenugreek seeds need to be ground before they are used (in a spice mill, for about a minute), and I like to toast them lightly first. Slightly bitter and slightly sweet, they add a rich, deep flavor to curry powders. Besides being used throughout India, especially in the south, these seeds are used in Georgian and South African cuisines. Look for them in Indian groceries, whole-foods stores, and supermarkets.

# Shiitake Consommé with Transparent Noodles

The flavor of a consommé usually depends almost entirely upon meat, be it beef or poultry. But the essence of dried shiitake mushrooms can create a strong, heady stock. This is a perfect soup to serve at the beginning or end of a rich meal.

Dried shiitake mushrooms and bean-thread noodles (sometimes called "clear" or "cellophane" noodles) are available at Asian markets and some supermarkets.

4 carrots

11 cups water

1 cup Chinese rice wine, sherry, or sake

2 cups dried shiitake mushrooms

1 large onion, chopped

2 celery stalks, chopped

2 inches fresh ginger, sliced thin

6 garlic cloves, cut in half

3 1.5- to 1.8-ounce packages bean-thread noodles

3 tablespoons soy sauce

1 tablespoon rice vinegar

2 teaspoons dark sesame oil

4 scallions, cut into 2-inch lengths, then into julienne strips

1 red bell pepper, cut into 2-inch julienne strips

1 jalapeño pepper, seeded and cut into thin rounds (optional)

**1.** Peel two of the carrots. Cut them into 2-inch lengths, then into very thin julienne strips. Set them aside. Cut the remaining carrots into large pieces. Put these pieces into a stockpot with the water, wine, dried mushrooms, onion, celery, ginger, and garlic, and set the heat on high. Bring the mixture to a boil, reduce the heat, and let the consommé simmer gently for 1 hour.

**2.** While the consommé simmers, soak the noodles in warm water for 30 minutes.

**3.** Strain the consommé into a clean stockpot. (You can save the mushrooms in the sieve for another use, such as Shiitake Spring Rolls, page 72.) Heat the consommé to a simmer. Strain the cellophane noodles, and add the noodles and the julienned carrots to the soup. Let the soup simmer for 2 to 3 minutes or until the noodles are tender. Add the soy sauce, rice vinegar, and sesame oil. (At this point the soup can stand for up to 30 minutes, although the noodles will overcook some.)

**4.** Just before serving, add the julienned scallions and red pepper, and, if you like, the jalapeño.

**Variation:** For a more substantial soup, add 8 ounces of firm tofu, cubed, along with the noodles in step 3.

*Serves 6*

# Miso Soup

Miso, the flavorful fermented soybean paste, has become the chicken bouillon cube for many vegetarians. It is purported to aid digestion, and it needs only to be diluted with water to make a tasty soup. This version is a bit more complex, but still takes only about 15 minutes to prepare.

3 garlic cloves, peeled
2 quarts water
1¹/₂ inches fresh ginger, sliced thin
²/₃ cup red, brown-rice, or barley miso
8 ounces silken tofu, cut into ¹/₂-inch cubes
4 scallions, chopped fine
2 carrots, grated or minced

**1.** Slightly crush the garlic cloves with a whack of a cleaver or chef's knife. Heat the water with the crushed garlic and the sliced ginger. Bring the water to a boil, turn down the heat, and simmer for 10 minutes. Remove the ginger and garlic from the water.

**2.** Add the miso, and stir until it breaks down. Add the tofu cubes, scallions, and carrots, and simmer for another 2 minutes. To serve, ladle the soup into bowls.

*Serves 4*

# Parsnip Soup with Garam Masala

I love parsnips so much that I eat them raw, like carrots. Their lovely sweet flavor develops after the first frost of winter, when the parsnip's starch converts to sugar. This soup requires no vegetable stock, because the parsnip, the spices, and the wine provide plenty of flavor.

2 tablespoons butter
2 cups chopped onions
3 garlic cloves, minced
1½ teaspoons garam masala, store-bought or
    homemade (page 37)
1 teaspoon fennel seeds, ground (optional)
2 pounds parsnips, peeled and chopped into
    ½-inch pieces
6 cups water
3/4 cup white wine
½ teaspoon salt
Fresh-ground black pepper to taste
1 tablespoon chopped parsley

**1.** In a large pot, melt the butter over medium heat, and add the onions. Cook them for 10 minutes or until they brown a bit, stirring occasionally. Add the garlic and the spices, and cook, stirring, for 2 minutes more.

**2.** Add the parsnips and the water, cover the pot, and simmer for 30 minutes. Add the wine, and simmer, uncovered, for 10 minutes more.

**3.** Purée the soup in batches in a food processor or blender. Season with the salt and pepper. Serve the soup sprinkled with chopped fresh parsley.

*Serves 5*

# Root Soup with Three Herbs

Rutabaga looks like a giant turnip with a yellowish exterior often streaked with purple. Sharing the genus *Brassica* with cabbage and turnip, rutabaga has a flavor reminiscent of both. In this soup, parsnips add a certain sweetness that the rutabaga lacks. Parsley, rosemary, and thyme (sorry, no sage) add to the soup's character and aroma.

1 medium rutabaga (about 3 pounds)
1 pound parsnips
1½ tablespoons olive oil
3 cups chopped onions
3 large garlic cloves, minced
2 quarts water or Basic Vegetable Stock
    (page 79)
1 tablespoon chopped fresh thyme, or
    1½ teaspoons dried thyme
1 teaspoon chopped fresh rosemary, or
    ½ teaspoon dried rosemary
½ cup half-and-half
2 tablespoons chopped parsley
1 teaspoon salt
Fresh-ground black pepper to taste

## Rutabaga-ville

Rutabagas are the wrecking balls of root veggies. Looking like jumbo turnips and weighing up to 4 pounds, rutabagas belong to the cabbage family (just take a whiff once you peel one). Often labeled as turnips in supermarkets, rutabagas have pale yellow and purple skin and are usually waxed to extend their shelf life. They have a beguiling sweet flavor.

To prepare a rutabaga, peel it with a knife, then cut it into cubes or thin slices. I like to mix rutabaga cubes with a spoonful of olive oil, two or three cloves of sliced garlic, and ½ cup salted water in a skillet, then simmer the rutabaga until it is tender. I adore this dish with kasha on the side.

**1.** With a large chef's knife, cutting away from yourself, peel the hard skin from the rutabaga. Peel the parsnips with a vegetable peeler. Chop both of the vegetables into 1-inch pieces.

**2.** Heat the olive oil in a stockpot over medium heat. Add the onions, and cook them, stirring frequently, until they have softened, about 5 minutes. Add the garlic, the rutabaga, and the parsnips. Cook for another 2 minutes. Add the water or stock and the thyme and rosemary. Bring the mixture to a boil, then turn down the heat and simmer the soup, partially covered, for 45 minutes, or until the vegetables are soft.

**3.** Purée the soup in batches in a blender or food processor. Stir in the half-and-half, 1 tablespoon of the parsley, and the salt and pepper. Before serving, reheat the soup, and garnish it with the remaining parsley. The soup will keep well, refrigerated, for up to 5 days.

Serves 6 to 8

# Carrot-Fennel Soup

Vegetable purées add great body, flavor, and nutritional power to a soup. Here fennel and carrot are braised with wine, garlic, and onions to make a soup that needs no accompaniment other than a slice of hearty bread.

1 tablespoon olive oil
2 cups chopped onions
4 garlic cloves, minced
6 large carrots, chopped
2 fennel bulbs, cored and chopped
1¹/₂ teaspoons fennel seeds
1 cup white wine
1 teaspoon salt
6 cups water or Carrot-Fennel Broth (page 83)
1 teaspoon balsamic vinegar
Fresh-ground black pepper to taste

## Saffron

To vegetarian dishes, saffron can impart that rich, warm, pungent flavor and aroma that one often associates with meat dishes.

Traditionally used in rich Indian curries and Mediterranean stews and soups, saffron makes any food tempting. To make the most of saffron's flavor and color, soak or simmer the threads in water for 10 minutes before adding them to a dish. Try saffron in cornbread (soak the threads in 1 tablespoon water, and reduce the liquid in the recipe by 1 tablespoon), in squash soups, and even in desserts such as cakes and flans.

**1.** In a large saucepan, heat the olive oil over medium heat. Add the onions and garlic. Cook, stirring frequently, for 5 minutes or until the onions soften. Add the carrots and the fennel, and cook for 2 more minutes.

**2.** Add 1 teaspoon of the fennel seeds and the wine, salt, and water or broth. Simmer over medium heat for 50 minutes or until the vegetables are very tender. Add the balsamic vinegar.

**3.** Purée the soup in batches in a food processor or a blender. Stir in plenty of pepper.

**4.** Toast the remaining fennel seeds in a small dry skillet until they brown slightly. Serve the soup with the toasted fennel seeds floating on top.

Serves 6 to 8

# Saffron-Scented Plantain Soup

No, this does not taste like banana soup. The plantains are used green here, so their flavor is more potato-like than banana-like. This soup is best, I think, when the plantains are just beginning to yellow.

2 mostly green plantains
1 tablespoon olive oil
1 medium onion, chopped
1 tablespoon chopped fresh ginger
1 garlic clove, minced
1 teaspoon fresh-ground coriander seeds
2 russet potatoes, peeled and chopped into
   ½-inch cubes
5 cups water or Basic Vegetable Stock (page 79)
1 cup coconut milk
1 pinch saffron threads (about ⅛ teaspoon)

About 1 teaspoon salt, to taste
Fresh-ground black pepper to taste
6 teaspoons sour cream
Toasted and chopped cashews

**1.** Cut four slits in the skin of the plantain, from end to end. Cut the ends off the plantain, then, with a paring knife, peel the skin away in four strips. Cut the plantains into 1-inch chunks.

**2.** In a heavy saucepan, heat the olive oil over medium heat. Cook the onion, stirring occasionally, until it is slightly browned, about 10 minutes. Add the ginger, garlic, and coriander. Cook another 2 minutes, stirring often. Add the potatoes, plantains, water or stock, coconut milk, and saffron. Season the soup with salt and pepper. Bring the soup to a boil, and then turn down the heat, and cover the soup. Simmer it for 25 minutes.

**3.** Purée the soup in batches in a food processor or blender, adding a bit of water if the soup is too thick. Reheat the soup before serving it. Garnish each bowl with sour cream and chopped cashews.

Serves 6

# Roasted Squash Soup

I love to use winter squashes in the colder months. This smooth and creamy soup combines three of my favorites— acorn, butternut, and spaghetti squashes—with some green apple. The soup is simple to make, since the squash roasts in the oven while you cook only the onions, spices, and apples on the stovetop. The flavors of sherry, curry, and fresh ginger enhance the soup.

1 small butternut squash (about 1¹/₂ pounds), cut
    in half
1 acorn squash, cut in half
¹/₂ spaghetti squash (about 1¹/₂ pounds)
3 tablespoons butter or olive oil
1 large onion, chopped
3 garlic cloves, minced
1 tablespoon minced fresh ginger
1 teaspoon curry powder, store-bought or
    homemade (page 36)
2 Granny Smith or other tart apples, peeled and
    cut into ¹/₂-inch chunks
²/₃ cup sherry
5 cups water or Basic Vegetable Stock (page 79)
1 teaspoon salt
Fresh-ground black pepper to taste
1 pinch cayenne (optional)

**1.** Preheat the oven to 400°. Lay the squash halves cut side down on baking sheets, and roast them for 45 minutes or until the flesh is soft (the spaghetti squash may take a bit longer). When the squash has cooled a little, scoop out the seeds and discard them. Then, with a large spoon, scoop out the flesh of the squash into a bowl.

**2.** Heat the butter and oil in a medium saucepan over medium heat. Add the onion. Cook for 5 minutes, stirring frequently, until the onion softens. Add the garlic, ginger, and curry powder, and cook, stirring, for 1 minute. Add the apples and the sherry, and simmer for 10 minutes, or until the apples soften.

**3.** Purée the squash flesh with the water or stock in batches in a blender or food processor. Transfer the squash purée to a large saucepan, then purée the apple-sherry mixture, and add this to the puréed squash.

**4.** Heat the soup, and season it with the salt, pepper, and, if you like, cayenne. Ladle the hot soup into bowls, and serve.

*Serves 6*

# Thai Coconut Soup

*T*ome kha gai is a favorite of many people who enjoy Thai food. This soup can be either very rich and sweet, using both coconut milk and coconut cream, or more broth-like, with less coconut milk and no coconut cream, as in this version. The traditional soup includes chicken, but here I use tofu, water chestnuts, and red bell pepper to accompany the flavorful broth.

Kaffir lime leaves add a unique citrusy flavor and aroma to this soup. They come dried in small, clear packages in well-stocked Asian markets, and they keep well for a year if wrapped and stored in a cool, dark place. If you search them out, you can use them in two other recipes in this book, Malay Rice Salad (page 234) and Thai Tofu with Red Curry Sauce over Coconut-Scallion Rice (page 213).

Lemongrass, added for its delicate lemony perfume and flavor, is also available in many Asian markets.

Galangal, a member of the ginger family with a strong citrusy flavor and scent, may be harder to find, but it's worth seeking out, also in Asian markets.

---

1 14-ounce can coconut milk

5 quarter-size slices fresh ginger or galangal

4 dried kaffir lime leaves, or 2 2-inch-long strips lime rind

2 lemongrass stalks, stripped of tough outer leaves and cut into thirds (optional)

2 garlic cloves, minced

6 cups water

1 red bell pepper, seeded and chopped

8 ounces firm tofu, cut into ½-inch cubes

1 8-ounce can water chestnuts, drained and cut in half

2 to 4 Thai peppers, sliced thin, or 1 jalapeño

## Galangal

*A*lthough galangal, or galanga, is related to ginger and looks a bit like it, its flavor and fragrance are reminiscent of lemon and black pepper as well as ginger. Galangal holds an important place in Thai cooking, much more so than ginger. Although fresh galangal is preferable to dried galangal in Thai cooking, I have come to love dried and ground galangal in various foods. I like to add ground galangal to carrot cake, banana bread, and chutneys, and ground galangal can substitute for ground ginger in just about any recipe, with great results. Both fresh and dried galangal are available in Southeast Asian and some Chinese markets.

pepper, seeded, if you like, then sliced thin

1½ cups chopped scallions, both green and white parts

2 tablespoons Thai or Vietnamese fish sauce, or 1 teaspoon salt

1 tablespoon lime juice (from about ½ lime)

3 tablespoons chopped cilantro

**1.** Combine the coconut milk, ginger or galangal, lime leaves or rind, lemongrass (if you're using it), garlic, and water in a large saucepan. Place the pan over high heat. When the soup comes to a boil, turn the heat down. Simmer the soup, covered, for 20 minutes.

**2.** Add the red pepper, tofu, water chestnuts, chile peppers, and scallions. Simmer the soup for 3 to 4 minutes more. Take the pan off the heat, and add the fish sauce or salt, lime juice, and cilantro. Serve the soup immediately.

Serves 6

# CHAPTER 5

# Artful Salads & Slaws

## Kimchi

*I first tasted kimchi when I had a college roommate whose parents were from Korea. On top of her dresser she kept four one-gallon jars of kimchi. She was following a two-thousand-year-old tradition. Korean pickled cabbage is traditionally stored in large ceramic pots, kept on the rooftop during the warm season, and buried in the garden during the winter months. Not only salt helps preserve the kimchi; hot chiles, fresh ginger, and garlic act as natural preservatives as well. Other vegetables besides cabbage—such as eggplant, cucumbers, and radishes—work well in kimchi, too. What is important in any kimchi is the mix of these properties: spiciness, saltiness, sweetness, sourness, bitterness, and astringency.*

# Tame Kimchi

I've always wanted to eat kimchi as a salad. But it's a pungent, super-spicy condiment, not a salad, and after three mouthfuls I am defeated. So I have departed from the classic recipe a bit to create a mellow, more friendly kimchi. I now have no problem consuming copious amounts.

꒰꒱꒰꒱꒰꒱꒰꒱

½ medium red onion, sliced thin

2 small carrots, julienned, grated, or sliced fine

1¼ to 1½ pounds nappa cabbage (half a medium head), cored and sliced into 1-inch strips

¼ cup kosher or sea salt

5 to 6 garlic cloves, minced

1 tablespoon minced fresh ginger

1 to 3 teaspoons hot chile sauce, or 1 teaspoon chile flakes

2 teaspoons sugar

3 tablespoons rice vinegar

2 tablespoons canola or corn oil

꒰꒱꒰꒱꒰꒱꒰꒱

**1.** In a large bowl, combine the red onion, carrots, cabbage, and salt. Add just enough water to cover the vegetables. Let them sit at room temperature overnight.

**2.** The next day, drain the vegetables. Add the remaining ingredients, and toss well. Chill the salad for at least 1 hour before serving. It will keep in a sealed container in the refrigerator for up to 7 days.

**Variation:** This kimchi doesn't undergo a fermenting process, as real kimchi does. If you'd like to ferment this kimchi, omit the oil, and put the mixture into a large sterilized jar. Let the kimchi stand at room temperature for 2 to 4 days, opening the jar once a day to let out the gases that build up. Store the kimchi in the refrigerator after this period. It will keep for several weeks.

*Serves 6*

# Syrian Bread Salad

A versatile pita-bread salad from the Middle East, *fattoush* seems well suited for the creative cook. Traditionally the salad includes many different vegetables, such as cucumbers, tomatoes, scallions, arugula, and green or red peppers. Various fresh herbs such as parsley, mint, and oregano are also commonly used in *fattoush*. Be whimsical; use this recipe as a loose guide, substituting or adding the vegetables and herbs that you like.

1 large garlic clove, minced
1½ teaspoons sumac powder (available in
  Middle Eastern markets), or 1 tablespoon
  lime juice
3 tablespoons red wine vinegar
2 tablespoons olive oil
½ red onion, sliced thin
1 cucumber, peeled and chopped
2 large or 3 medium very ripe tomatoes,
  chopped, or 2 cups halved cherry tomatoes
2 Belgian endive heads, the leaves cut into thin
  julienne strips
½ cup chopped parsley
2 large pita bread rounds, split and cut into
  1-inch squares, to make 5 cups
½ teaspoon salt, or more, to taste
Fresh-ground black pepper to taste

**1.** In a large bowl, whisk together the garlic, sumac or lime, red wine vinegar, and olive oil. Add the vegetables, parsley, and bread. Toss well, and season with salt and pepper.

**2.** Before serving, let the salad sit for at least 20 minutes so the bread can soften.

Serves 6

# Italian Bread-and-Tomato Salad

With Americans' growing passion for high-quality bread, good bakeries seem to be popping up all over; even many supermarket chains now sell firm, crusty loaves. Yet these artisanal products lack the keeping quality of the preservative-packed, plastic-wrapped ones. Still, you needn't throw great bread away once it's gone stale—you can recycle it into bread salad.

2 tablespoons red wine vinegar
3 tablespoons extra-virgin olive oil
2 tablespoons water
2 garlic cloves, minced
6 cups cubed stale or lightly toasted bread (almost any type will do)
2 large round tomatoes, or 6 plum tomatoes, cut into wedges
1 small red onion, sliced as fine as possible
1 cup (combined) chopped basil, dill, and cilantro
1/2 teaspoon salt
Fresh-ground black pepper to taste

**1.** In a large bowl, mix the vinegar, olive oil, water, and garlic. Add the bread, and let it soak for 5 to 10 minutes.

**2.** Add the rest of the ingredients, taste, and add more salt and pepper if you like. Serve the salad immediately (after about 15 minutes it will become too soggy).

**Variations:** Try mint or chervil in place of basil, dill, and cilantro. Or try thyme, oregano, rosemary, or sage, but use just a little of these much stronger herbs.

Serves 4

# Fruit and Nut Tabouli

Like many things, tabouli is much better when made at home than when store-bought. This is because store-bought tabouli often skimps on the expensive stuff, like parsley, mint, and olive oil. Here tabouli takes a bit of a turn, with oranges, walnuts, and currants embellishing the traditional recipe.

1 cup fine bulgur
2¼ cups boiling water
2 seedless oranges
¼ cup lemon juice (from about 1 lemon)
¼ cup olive oil
1 garlic clove, minced
½ cup minced onion
½ cucumber, peeled, seeded, and chopped
1½ cups chopped parsley
½ cup chopped mint
¼ cup chopped walnuts, toasted
¼ cup currants
½ teaspoon salt, or more, to taste
Fresh-ground black pepper to taste

**1.** Put the bulgur into a medium bowl. Pour the boiling water over. Cover the bowl with a plate, and let the bulgur sit for 20 minutes. Then drain it with a fine mesh strainer.

**2.** Meanwhile, section the oranges with a paring knife: First cut away the peel and pith, then cut out the flesh by sections, leaving the membranes. Cut the sections in half, and add them to the bulgur. Then add the lemon juice, olive oil, garlic, onion, cucumber, parsley, mint, walnuts, and currants, and mix well. Season with salt and pepper. Serve the tabouli at room temperature (or even while the bulgur is still warm from its cooking, the way I like it).

**Variation:** Add ½ cup crumbled feta cheese.

Serves 6

---

## Tabouli Possibilities

Traditional tabouli is, no doubt, delicious stuff. But if you make tabouli fairly often, why not have a little fun? Here are some ingredients that I often use along with or instead of the traditional parsley, mint, bulgur, tomatoes, onion, cucumber, lemon juice, and olive oil:

- Wheat berries, millet, or quinoa (instead of bulgur)
- Dill, basil, or chopped fennel tops (instead of parsley or mint)
- Cooked french lentils (lentilles du Puy)
- Cilantro (instead of parsley)
- Lime juice (instead of lemon juice)
- Chopped hot peppers
- Ground Sichuan pepper

## Wheat Berries

*Because they are unprocessed, wheat berries are very good for you. They are rich in protein, vitamin E, riboflavin, thiamin, iron, and phosphorus. But part of the cost for all these nutrients is time. Wheat berries need two hours of simmering before they are soft enough to eat. (Soaking them overnight reduces the cooking time by an hour.) If you make a large batch, you can use them in numerous ways; their nutty flavor and chewy texture make them a good addition to soups, pilafs, salads, breads, even your morning cereal. Wheat berries are available in whole-foods stores and some supermarkets.*

# Wheat Berry Salad

High in nutrients, wheat berries are also quite chewy, even after an afternoon of cooking. The best way to enjoy them—and they *can* be enjoyable—is to mix them with softer foods. In this salad they are combined with tomatoes, fresh corn, capers, feta, and basil. Serve the salad alongside a sandwich or on its own, as a light lunch or dinner on top of some dressed mesclun or bibb lettuce. Wheat berries can be found at health-food stores. I prefer soft wheat berries, but hard wheat berries are fine, too.

1 quart water
1¹/₃ cups wheat berries
Kernels from 2 ears corn
3 tablespoons olive oil
1¹/₂ tablespoons balsamic vinegar
2 tablespoons drained capers
3 plum tomatoes, chopped
¹/₄ cup crumbled feta cheese
3 tablespoons minced basil
¹/₂ teaspoon salt, or more, to taste
Fresh-ground black pepper to taste

**1.** In a saucepan, combine the water and the wheat berries. Cover with a tight-fitting lid, and set the pan over medium-high heat. When the water comes to a boil, turn the heat to low. Simmer the wheat for 2 hours, checking from time to time to make sure that some water remains, and adding a bit if necessary. When the berries are tender but still chewy, add the corn kernels, and simmer for 1 minute more. Pour the berries and the corn into a colander, and run cold water over them to stop the cooking.

**2.** In a large bowl, combine the olive oil, balsamic vinegar, capers, tomatoes, feta, and basil. Add the wheat berries, corn, salt, and pepper. Chill the salad for at least 1 hour before serving. Well covered in the refrigerator, the salad will keep for 3 to 4 days.

Serves 6

# Roasted Beets with Oranges and Basil Vinaigrette

I think beets taste best when they're roasted. Roasting them is easy, too—there's no messy peeling or stained hands. In this salad the beets and the oranges look like glistening jewels. Serve the salad at room temperature as a first course, or as an intermezzo between the main dish and dessert.

3 medium or 2 large beets, cut into eighths
3 tablespoons olive oil
Salt and fresh-ground black pepper to taste
1 seedless orange
2 tablespoons balsamic vinegar
3 tablespoons chopped basil, and some whole
    leaves for garnish

**1.** Preheat the oven to 400°. Place the beets on a roasting pan, and dribble 1 tablespoon of the olive oil over them. Season the beets with salt and pepper. Bake them for 35 to 40 minutes, or until they are tender when pierced with a sharp knife. Remove them from the oven, and let them cool for 10 minutes.

**2.** While the beets cool, grate the rind from the orange, and, with a paring knife, section the orange: First cut away the peel and pith, then cut out the flesh by sections, leaving the membranes. In a bowl, combine the grated orange rind, the balsamic vinegar, and the basil. Whisking constantly, drizzle in the remaining 2 tablespoons olive oil. Add salt and pepper. Place the beet and orange pieces on a large plate, and spoon the vinaigrette over. Serve the salad when the beets have cooled completely.

**Variation:** Try substituting 2 tablespoons truffle oil for the 2 tablespoons olive oil in the vinaigrette. (Truffle oil, available at specialty food stores, is made from black or white truffles steeped in olive oil. Truffle oil has a rich, fruity flavor. I prefer white-truffle oil, which is less intense than the black-truffle variety.)

*Serves 4*

# Caribbean Sweet-Potato Salad

Sweet potatoes can do wonders for a potato salad. Here sweet and russet potatoes are combined with chopped peanuts, corn, and red onion, and dressed with a perky cilantro-lime vinaigrette. This is a perfect side dish to any of the veggie burgers in chapter 13.

1 large russet potato, peeled and quartered
1 large sweet potato, peeled and quartered
1 cup corn kernels (from about 1½ ears)
1 teaspoon Dijon mustard
2 tablespoons lime juice
3 tablespoons chopped cilantro
1 garlic clove, minced
3 tablespoons canola or corn oil
½ teaspoon salt, or more, to taste
¼ teaspoon fresh-ground black pepper
1 cucumber, peeled, halved lengthwise, and sliced into thin half-rounds
½ red onion, sliced thin
¼ cup finely chopped dry-roasted, unsalted peanuts

**1.** Put the russet potato pieces into a large saucepan, and cover them with salted water. Bring the potatoes to a boil. Turn the heat down to medium, and simmer the potatoes for 10 minutes. Add the sweet potato pieces, and cook about 15 minutes more. Remove a piece of each potato, and cut it in half to see if it has cooked enough. You should feel a bit of resistance with both potatoes; don't let them cook until they are breaking apart. Once the potatoes are tender, promptly add the corn kernels, and cook another 30 seconds. Quickly drain the vegetables in a colander, and fill the saucepan with cold water. Drop the potatoes and corn into the cold water, and leave them for 5 minutes to stop the cooking.

**2.** In a large bowl, combine the mustard, lime juice, cilantro, and garlic. Stir with a whisk. Slowly add the oil while whisking. Add the salt and pepper.

**3.** Drain the cooled sweet and white potatoes, and cut them into 1-inch cubes. Add the potatoes, the cucumber, and the red onion to the vinaigrette. Toss well.

Serve the salad at room temperature or chilled. Toss the peanuts in just before serving. Well covered in the refrigerator, this salad keeps for 3 days.

*Serves 5*

# Yuca "Potato" Salad

"This is the best potato salad I've had," my friend Jon said on taking a bite of this salad. But it was a yuca salad, not a potato salad. Yuca, also called cassava and manioc, is a large brown tubular root that is becoming more available in the United States every day. With a mild flavor and an appealing and slightly sticky texture, yuca is a staple for most of the people of South America. It can be found in many supermarkets and in Latin American markets.

■·■·■·■·■·■·■

1 medium yuca (about 1¹⁄₂ pounds, or about
    9 inches long)
2 large garlic cloves, minced
2 teaspoons sugar
1 teaspoon salt
¹⁄₄ teaspoon fresh-ground black pepper
¹⁄₃ cup lime juice (from about 3 limes)
¹⁄₄ cup olive oil
¹⁄₂ cup cilantro leaves
4 scallions, chopped fine
2 carrots, peeled and coarsely grated

■·■·■·■·■·■

**1.** Bring a large pot of salted water to a boil. While the water heats, cut the ends off the yuca with a large chef's knife (I use the "ax" method, lifting the knife into the air and making one strong hack). Then cut the yuca crosswise into 4 or 5 pieces, again with a strong hack of the knife. Stand each piece on end, and cut away the skin. While still holding the piece of yuca vertically, cut away pieces from about ½ inch away from the tough, stringy core. Discard the core. Cook the yuca pieces in boiling water for about 45 to 55 minutes, or until the flesh is soft but not falling apart. Drain the yuca, but do not rinse it. Let it cool for at least 10 minutes.

**2.** While the yuca cools, make the dressing: In a large bowl, whisk together the garlic, sugar, salt, pepper, and lime juice. Slowly add the olive oil, whisking constantly (to keep the dressing emulsified. (If you prefer, you can instead mix the dressing in a blender or food processor.)

**3.** Cut the yuca into smaller pieces if it has not already broken apart. Add the yuca, cilantro leaves, scallions, and carrots to the dressing. Toss well, and chill the salad for at least 1 hour before serving.

Serves 4

# Roasted New Potato Salad

As a kid, I loved roasted new potatoes with leg of lamb. In this dish the potatoes can stand on their own, without meat. They are roasted with a bit of olive oil, then tossed with a sherry vinaigrette, tomatoes, and cut green beans.

1½ pounds new potatoes (about 9 to 10), cut in half
5 tablespoons extra-virgin olive oil
1 teaspoon salt
Fresh-ground black pepper to taste
1½ cups green beans, trimmed and cut in half
    lengthwise
1 garlic clove, minced
1 tablespoon sherry vinegar or red wine vinegar
1 small red onion, sliced thin
1 cup chopped parsley
2 plum tomatoes

**1.** Preheat the oven to 425°. Put the potatoes into a roasting pan. Drizzle them with 2 tablespoons of the olive oil, and sprinkle them with ½ teaspoon of the salt and the pepper. Roast the potatoes for 40 to 50 minutes, or until they are tender. Let them cool for 10 to 15 minutes.

**2.** While the potatoes roast, bring 1 quart salted water to a boil in a small saucepan. Add the green beans, and boil them for 1 to 2 minutes, no longer. Drain them, and rinse them with cold water.

**3.** In a large bowl, combine the garlic, the vinegar, and the remaining 3 tablespoons olive oil. Add the onion, parsley, tomatoes, and green beans to the vinaigrette.

**4.** Add the potatoes to the bowl, and then add the remaining ½ teaspoon of salt and pepper to taste. Toss well. Serve the potato salad warm, or let it cool, cover it with plastic wrap, and chill it to serve cold later.

*Serves 6*

# White Bean and Fresh Mozzarella Salad

*T*his simple salad is simply as good as the ingredients that go into it. Fresh-cooked white beans, light and fruity olive oil, tomatoes bought vine-ripened, and mozzarella bought fresh in its liquid—these are the things that will make this a wonderful salad. When I can afford to, I buy organic ingredients, because I think they taste better.

1½ cups dried navy or Great Northern beans
1 tablespoon chopped oregano leaves
4 ounces fresh mozzarella, cut into ½-inch cubes
1 ripe tomato, chopped
¼ cup chopped red onion
1 tablespoon balsamic vinegar
2 tablespoons extra-virgin olive oil
½ teaspoon salt, or more, to taste
Fresh-ground black pepper to taste
2 tablespoons chopped basil (optional)

**1.** Soak the beans overnight in cold water, or use the quick-soak method: Bring the beans to a boil in a large saucepan, and cook them for 5 minutes. Remove the pan from the heat, and let the beans soak for 1 hour.

**2.** Drain the beans, and rinse them well. Put them into a saucepan, and cover them with water. Bring them to a simmer, and cook them, replenishing the water as needed, for at least 1 hour, until they are just tender (they should have a very slight bite in the middle). Drain the beans, and rinse them well.

**3.** In a large bowl, combine the cooked beans, chopped oregano, mozzarella, tomato, and red onion. In a smaller bowl, combine the balsamic vinegar and the olive oil. Pour this dressing over the salad, and stir gently but well. Add the salt and pepper.

**4.** Chill the salad, and toss it before serving. If you like, add chopped fresh basil just before serving.

*Serves 4*

# Bibb Salad with Anise Croutons

When I'm eating out and I'm given fresh-made croutons, I always sit up and take notice. So I did at a sweet inn and restaurant called L'Iris Bleu, in Bolton Centre, Quebec. The croutons were not only homemade; they were speckled with anise seeds. They were a welcome change from the standard garlic crouton, and a nice match for the soft goat cheese in the salad.

5 tablespoons extra-virgin olive oil
1 teaspoon anise or fennel seeds
1 small garlic clove, peeled and crushed with a
    chef's knife
8 baguette slices, cut on the diagonal, about 1
    inch thick and 4 inches long
4 teaspoons balsamic vinegar
Salt and pepper to taste
1 head bibb or Boston lettuce, broken apart
¼ cup crumbled soft goat cheese

**1.** Preheat the oven to 375°. In a small bowl, combine 3 tablespoons of the olive oil, the anise or fennel, and the garlic. Stir well, and let the mixture sit for 10 minutes so the garlic can flavor the oil.

**2.** Place the bread on a baking sheet. With either a spoon or a brush, coat the top side of the bread pieces with the seeds and the flavored oil. Reserve the bowl, even if only the garlic is left in it. Bake the croutons for 8 to 10 minutes, or until they are golden. Let them cool.

## Composing a Green Salad

*For a perfect tossed salad, choose the freshest greens you can find. Mixed greens are particularly nice. Some of my favorite combinations are watercress with red-leaf lettuce, arugula with Boston lettuce, and young mixed greens (mesclun) with endive. Store the greens in the refrigerator in a rigid airtight container or in plastic bags (line the container with paper towels if the greens are damp). When you're ready to use them, rinse the greens in a large bowl of cold water, then dry them in small batches in a salad spinner. Before serving, lightly coat the greens with extra-virgin olive oil, a splash of your favorite vinegar, and fresh-ground black pepper.*

**3.** Into the bowl in which you mixed the oil, anise or fennel, and garlic, put the remaining 2 tablespoons of olive oil and the balsamic vinegar. Stir well, and add salt and pepper.

**4.** Assemble the salad: Divide the lettuce among four plates. Lay the croutons on the lettuce, then drizzle the dressing (holding back the garlic clove) over the lettuce and croutons. Sprinkle with the goat cheese, and serve.

*Serves 4*

# French Lentil Salad with Caramelized Balsamic Vinaigrette

I'd be hard pressed to come up with a salad more sophisticated than this one. It's perfect for a special picnic, perhaps with Pan Bagna sandwiches (page 395), or alone as a light lunch spooned onto delicate greens and served with some good sourdough bread.

French lentils, or *lentilles du Puy,* can be found at specialty food stores, some supermarkets, and some whole-foods stores.

2 cups French lentils (or brown lentils)
5 cups water
¼ cup currants
5 tablespoons Caramelized Balsamic Vinaigrette
   (page 158)
1 large ripe round tomato or 3 plum tomatoes,
   cut into ½-inch cubes
2 tablespoons minced shallots
¼ cup chopped walnuts, lightly toasted
½ teaspoon salt
Fresh-ground black pepper to taste
¼ cup basil leaves, sliced thin (optional)

**1.** Put the lentils into a saucepan, and cover them with the water. Bring the water to a boil, and turn down the heat. Simmer the lentils for 20 minutes, uncovered, adding more water if necessary to prevent scorching. When the lentils are tender but slightly chewy, add the currants, and simmer 2 minutes more.

**2.** Drain the lentil-currant mixture well, and transfer it to a bowl. While the mixture is still hot, add the Caramelized Balsamic Vinaigrette. Stir well with a spoon.

**3.** Add the tomato pieces, shallots, walnuts, salt, and pepper to the lentil mixture. Stir well. Serve the salad warm, or chill it. Sprinkle on the basil leaves just before serving. This salad will keep for 2 days, covered, in the refrigerator.

Serves 4 to 6

# Bistro Avocado Salad

Here cubed avocado is bathed in a lime-and-olive-oil dressing that's spiked with mustard seeds and ground coriander. Cubes of red pepper and tomato brighten the salad and provide a pleasing medley of textures and flavors.

1 ripe Haas avocado (the dark, bumpy kind), cut into 1/4-inch cubes

2 tablespoons lime juice (from about 1 lime)

1 yellow or red medium tomato, cut into 1/4-inch cubes

1/2 cup minced red onion

1 red bell pepper, seeded and cut into 1/4-inch squares

1 teaspoon brown mustard seeds

1/2 teaspoon ground coriander seeds

2 tablespoons extra-virgin olive oil

1/2 teaspoon salt

Fresh-ground black pepper to taste

1 small bibb or Boston lettuce head, broken apart

**1.** Put the avocado into a medium bowl and stir in the lime juice. Add the tomato, red onion, red pepper, mustard seeds, coriander, and olive oil. Add the salt and pepper, and toss well. If you like, you can refrigerate the mixture for a few hours.

**2.** Create a bed of lettuce leaves on each of four small plates. Spoon the salad onto the beds of lettuce, and serve.

Serves 4

# Long and Winding Bean Slaw

Long beans are just that—over a foot long. They are also less sweet than our conventional string beans, and their texture after cooking is softer. Because they are pliable, long beans can be formed into various shapes. In this dish, the long beans are formed into a donut shape on each plate, and the slaw is mounded in the center. The salad makes a nice first course before an Asian-inspired main dish. Long beans can be found at Chinese and Southeast Asian markets.

1 pound long beans (about 20), trimmed

⅓ cup rice vinegar

1 tablespoon sugar

1 teaspoon hot chile sauce

2 teaspoons minced fresh ginger

1 bunch scallions (about 6), cut in half
    lengthwise, then cut into 2-inch lengths

2 cups very thinly sliced green cabbage

2 carrots, peeled and cut into julienne strips

1 red bell pepper, seeded and cut into thin
    julienne strips

1 tablespoon toasted sesame seeds (optional)

## Becoming a Slaw Chef

*Slaw has evolved far beyond cabbage with a heavy, mayonnaise-based dressing. A slaw is an opportunity for creative culinary expression. Pick your vegetable combo— perhaps carrot and cabbage, or endive and red onion, or scallions, bok choy, and red pepper. Slice the chosen vegetables thin. Make a dressing from lemon juice, lime juice, or any vinegar, a few spoonfuls of sugar, and perhaps a splash of oil or some yogurt, mayonnaise, or sour cream. Season with spices, minced garlic, chopped ginger, or fresh herbs, as well as salt and fresh-ground pepper. When you find you have created a sublime slaw, go ahead and declare yourself a slaw chef.*

**1.** Bring a large pot of salted water to a boil. Add the long beans, and boil them for 5 minutes. Drain them, and rinse them well with cold running water.

**2.** Make the dressing: In a large bowl, combine the rice vinegar, sugar, hot chile sauce, and ginger. Stir well. Add the vegetables (except the long beans) to the dressing, and toss well.

**3.** On each small salad plate, form about 3 long beans into a circle 4 inches wide. Mound the salad inside the bean circle. Sprinkle the salad with toasted sesame seeds, if you like, and serve.

Serves 6

# Snappy Snap-Pea Salad

Lime juice mixed with a good olive oil can make anything taste good. Here they combine forces with snap peas, red onion, and nappa cabbage. Sumac powder, made from dried sumac berries, can be found in Middle Eastern markets (and no, it will not give you a skin rash as a poison sumac plant will). Sumac powder sports a bright magenta color and has a terrific, tart flavor, for which lime juice can easily substitute.

2 cups snap peas
1/2 cup thinly sliced red onion
2 cups thinly sliced nappa cabbage or bok choy
1 1/2 teaspoons sumac powder, or 1 tablespoon
    more lime juice
3 tablespoons extra-virgin olive oil
3 tablespoons lime juice (from about 1 1/2 limes)
1 teaspoon sugar, or more, to taste
1 small garlic clove, minced
1/2 teaspoon salt
Fresh-ground black pepper to taste

**1.** In a large bowl, combine the snap peas, red onion, and nappa cabbage or bok choy. In a smaller bowl, whisk together the sumac, olive oil, lime juice, sugar, and garlic.

**2.** Pour the lime dressing over the vegetables, season with salt and pepper, and toss well. Let the flavors marry for 30 minutes, and serve. This salad keeps for up to 3 days, covered, in the refrigerator.

Serves 4

# Pear Salad with Stilton Dressing

Smooth, creamy Stilton dressing imparts the wonderful Stilton flavor into this salad. An English blue cheese, Stilton contains the same mold, *Penicillium roqueforti,* as Roquefort cheese. The flavors of the two cheeses are similar, but Stilton, aged longer and made from whole cow's milk rather than sheep's milk, is slightly less salty and usually creamier. If you can't find Stilton, however, Roquefort or Gorgonzola cheese can make a delicious substitute in this recipe.

**DRESSING:**

3 ounces Stilton cheese
1 teaspoon honey
1 garlic clove
3 tablespoons whole, low-fat, or nonfat sour cream
2 tablespoons sherry vinegar, white wine vinegar, or champagne vinegar
1/4 cup half-and-half
Salt and fresh-ground black pepper to taste

**SALAD:**

2 Belgian endive heads, halved lengthwise, cut
   into 1-inch crosswise slices
1 bunch watercress, stems trimmed
1 large ripe pear, sliced thin
3 tablespoons chopped walnuts or pecans, lightly
   toasted
Thin slices of red onion (optional)

**1.** In a blender or food processor, combine two-thirds of the Stilton, and all of the honey, the garlic, the sour cream, and the vinegar. Blend until the mixture is smooth. With the machine running, slowly add the half and half. Transfer the dressing to a bowl, and add salt and pepper. Cover and refrigerate the dressing until you are ready to use it.

**2.** When you are ready to serve the salad, put the half rings of endive into a bowl, add the watercress, and toss. Place a large handful of the greens onto each of four large salad plates.

Lay the pear slices over the salad, and drizzle about 3 tablespoons dressing over each plate. Crumble the remaining Stilton, and garnish the salad with the cheese, the walnuts or pecans, and, if you like, the red onion. Serve immediately.

Serves 4 (you'll have
leftover dressing)

# Hot-and-Sour
# Slaw

Hot-and sour soup isn't nearly as much fun as hot-and-sour slaw. There's a lot of wonderful crunchiness here, thanks to the bok choy and red peppers. And the dressing contains all the hot-and-sour elements—vinegar, chiles, and sugar.

1 bunch bok choy (about 2 pounds), both stems
    and leaves, sliced thin
1 large red bell pepper, seeded and sliced
    very thin
4 scallions, both green and white parts, chopped
    fine
2 teaspoons chile paste, or 1 tablespoon hot chile
    sauce, or 1/2 teaspoon chile flakes
1 teaspoon Dijon mustard
3/4 cup apple cider vinegar
2 garlic cloves, minced
1 tablespoon minced fresh ginger
1 tablespoon sugar
1 teaspoon salt
1 tablespoon canola or corn oil

**1.** Combine the bok choy, red pepper, and scallions in a large bowl.

**2.** In a smaller bowl, whisk together the remaining ingredients. Pour this dressing over the chopped vegetables, and toss well. Let the slaw sit in the refrigerator for 1 hour, then toss it again. Taste the chilled salad, and add more chile or salt or sugar to your liking before serving. This slaw will taste good for at least 3 days if kept tightly sealed in the refrigerator.

**Variation:** Chopped cilantro is a nice addition. You can also try other sliced vegetables instead of the bok choy—thin-sliced fennel bulb, carrots, snow peas, red onion, or nappa cabbage. (The flavor of green or red head cabbage, however, is too intense; it would compete with the hot-and-sour dressing.)

Serves 6

# Green Slaw

This happy-go-lucky slaw goes well with almost any sandwich, burger, or entrée. Chopped herbs and spinach make the slaw very green, but also more perishable, so eat it up within a day or two of making it.

½ small green cabbage head, cored and sliced as thin as possible
2 cups thinly sliced onions
3 cups fresh spinach leaves, cut into julienne strips
1 cup basil leaves, chopped fine
1½ cups parsley leaves, chopped fine
1 tablespoon Dijon mustard
⅓ cup lime juice (from about 3 limes)
3 tablespoons olive oil
2 teaspoons sugar
1 teaspoon salt
Fresh-ground black pepper to taste

**1.** Put the sliced cabbage and onions into a large bowl. Add the spinach.

**2.** Put the chopped herbs into another bowl, and add the mustard and lime juice. Stir with a whisk. While whisking, slowly add the olive oil. Whisk in the sugar, salt, and pepper.

**3.** Add the dressing to the cabbage mixture, and toss well (I use my hands). Refrigerate the slaw for at least 1 hour so the flavors can marry, then serve.

*Serves 6*

## Seeds in Slaws

*Slaw always benefits from some seeds. Whether you choose sesame, poppy, caraway, celery, sunflower, mustard, or even flax, seeds add texture and visual appeal. One of my favorite slaw additions is black sesame seeds, found at Asian markets; they jazz up any slaw, whether the other flavors are Asian or not.*

*Whatever seeds you choose, it's best to toast them in a dry skillet over medium heat for a couple of minutes to bring out their flavor before adding them to the slaw.*

# Jícama Slaw

a crunchy, slightly sweet root vegetable with a texture and flavor reminiscent of both apple and turnip, jícama, grown in Mexico, is generally available during the winter months. Try this jícama slaw on a snowy day for a quick burst of summer sun.

■ ■ ■ ■ ■ ■ ■ ■ ■

1 medium jícama, peeled (with a sharp paring knife) and cut into 1/4-inch cubes
1 large carrot, peeled and cut into 1/4-inch cubes
1 cup seedless grapes, chopped
1 cup arugula leaves, chopped fine
1 cup minced red onion
1 teaspoon Dijon mustard
1 garlic clove, minced
3 tablespoons lime juice (from about 1 1/2 limes)
1 tablespoon apple cider vinegar
1 to 2 tablespoons olive oil
1 teaspoon salt
Fresh-ground black pepper to taste
1/4 cup chopped dry-roasted, unsalted peanuts
2 tablespoons chopped cilantro (optional)

■ ■ ■ ■ ■ ■ ■ ■ ■

**1.** In a large bowl, combine the jícama, carrot, grapes, arugula, and red onion.

**2.** In a small bowl, whisk together the mustard, garlic, lime juice, vinegar, and olive oil.

**3.** Pour the dressing over the slaw, and toss well. Mix in the salt, pepper, and peanuts. Chill the salad for at least 1 hour. Just before serving, toss the salad again.

*Serves 6*

# Toasted Sesame Slaw

The strong flavors of sesame oil and green cabbage harmonize well in this salad. The sesame seeds reinforce the sesame flavor and, along with the peanuts, provide good texture. If possible, use black sesame seeds; available in Asian markets, they are delicious when toasted.

You can make this slaw in less than 15 minutes. Don't rush, though—you want to slice the cabbage really thin. Use a sharp chef's knife. And be sure to toss in the sesame seeds and peanuts just before serving, because they lose their all-important crunch if added too early.

½ small green cabbage head, cored and sliced as
    thin as possible
½ medium red onion, sliced thin
1 large carrot, grated or cut into thin julienne
    strips
1½ tablespoons dark sesame oil
⅓ cup rice vinegar
1 tablespoon sugar
2 teaspoons Dijon mustard
1 teaspoon salt
3 tablespoons sesame seeds
3 tablespoons dry-roasted, unsalted peanuts

**1.** Put the cabbage into a bowl with the red onion, and fluff the cabbage and onion with your hands to separate the pieces. Add the carrot, and mix well.

**2.** In a small bowl, combine the sesame oil, vinegar, sugar, mustard, and salt. Add the dressing to the cabbage and onion, and mix well. Refrigerate the slaw for at least 1 hour so the cabbage can soften.

## The Knobby Roots

Celery root, also called celeriac and celery knob, comes from a variety of celery cultivated for its large, bulbous root rather than its stalks. Celery root usually appears in the market without its stalks, looking like a softball. Its brownish-white exterior has crevices and rootlets, making it difficult to clean. Choose small, firm roots with no soft spots, and peel them with a knife.

The flavor is reminiscent of celery stalks and parsley. It is good raw as well as cooked. Try roasting it: Cut it into 1-inch cubes; toss the cubes with olive oil, minced garlic, salt, and pepper; and bake them at 400° for 40 minutes or until they are tender.

**3.** Toast the sesame seeds to bring out their flavor: Place a heavy skillet over medium heat. Add the seeds, let them sit for 30 seconds, then begin to shake the pan periodically. If you are using white seeds, toast them until they are uniformly browned; if you have black seeds, toast them until they taste nutty and toasted. Transfer the seeds to a small plate, and let them cool.

**4.** Just before serving, add the sesame seeds and peanuts to the slaw, and toss well.

**Variation:** Spice up this slaw with hot chile sesame oil, available in many supermarkets and in Asian markets.

Serves 6

# Celery Root and Apple Slaw

It's difficult for me to cut into a celery root, or celeriac, because I hate to destroy its fascinating mass of rootlets and knobs. Each celery root, like a snowflake, is so different from the rest. A few months ago I bought a really large and beautiful celery root with dozens of squiggly rootlets. So I cut them off in one large piece, and nailed it to the kitchen wall to admire. Unfortunately, my roommate threw it away after a couple of days.

This slaw is at its prettiest when the celery root and apples are cut with a mandoline or processor that has a julienne attachment, so the vegetables are in thin strips rather than grated.

1 celery root (celeriac) (about 1½ pounds)
1 small red onion, sliced thin
1½ tablespoons smooth Dijon mustard
1 teaspoon mustard seeds
¼ cup lemon juice (from about 1 lemon)
1 garlic clove, minced
1 tablespoon sugar
1 teaspoon salt
Fresh-ground black pepper to taste
4 tablespoons extra-virgin olive oil
1 large red apple, skin left on, cut into ¼-inch
cubes just before serving

**1.** With a chef's knife, cut the skin and knobby roots off the celery root. Cut the root in half, then cut each piece in half again. Grate the pieces by hand, or julienne them with the julienne blade of a food processor or a mandoline. Combine the celery root in a big bowl with the sliced onion.

**2.** Make the vinaigrette: In a small bowl, combine the mustard, mustard seeds, lemon juice, garlic, sugar, salt, and pepper. Slowly add the olive oil, whisking constantly.

**3.** Mix the vinaigrette into the slaw. Chill the slaw if you won't be serving it right away.

**4.** Just before serving, add the apple. (This must be done at the last minute because apples brown very quickly.) Toss the slaw, and serve it.

Serves 8

# Gunsmoke Slaw

This is dynamite stuff! The smoky chipotles, the cider vinegar, and the tangy mustard really get these vegetables jumping. But you can control the smoke and heat by starting with a small amount of chipotles and adding more as you see fit.

2 tablespoons smooth Dijon mustard
2 garlic cloves
3 tablespoons sugar
1 teaspoon salt
1 to 2 tablespoons chopped chipotle peppers
    (dried and soaked in hot water for 30
    minutes, or canned in adobo sauce)
1/2 cup apple cider vinegar
1/4 cup canola or corn oil
2 seedless oranges
1/2 green cabbage head, cored and sliced as thin
    as possible
2 carrots, grated
5 scallions, both green and white parts, minced

**1.** Make the vinaigrette: Mix the mustard, garlic, sugar, and salt in a food processor, then blend in the chipotles and cider vinegar. Or mince the garlic and chipotles, and whisk them together in a bowl with the mustard, garlic, sugar, salt, and vinegar. While running the processor or whisking, add the oil in a slow, steady stream.

**2.** Section the oranges with a paring knife: First cut away the peel and pith, then cut out the flesh by sections, leaving the membranes. Put the cabbage into a large bowl, and add the grated carrots, oranges, and scallions.

**3.** Pour the vinaigrette over the vegetables, and toss well. Taste, and add more adobo sauce or salt, if you like. Let the slaw sit for at least 2 hours in the refrigerator before serving. The slaw will keep 4 to 5 days, covered, in the refrigerator.

Serves 6 to 8

# Radicchio Slaw

Radicchio and cauliflower seem like a very unlikely pair, I know. But with the help of crumbled feta, sliced red onion, Dijon mustard, and red wine vinegar, these vegetables are transformed into a winning slaw.

1 radicchio head, quartered lengthwise, then
    sliced crosswise into thin strips
1 small cauliflower head, cut into small florets
1 red onion, sliced thin
4 ounces feta cheese
1 garlic clove, minced
¼ cup red wine vinegar
1 tablespoon Dijon mustard
2 tablespoons olive oil
½ teaspoon salt, or more, to taste
Fresh-ground black pepper to taste

**1.** In a large bowl, mix the radicchio, cauliflower, and red onion. Crumble the feta over the salad.

**2.** In a small bowl, whisk together the garlic, vinegar, and mustard. Slowly whisk in the olive oil. Season with the salt and pepper, and mix the dressing into the salad. Let the salad sit for at least 1 hour in the refrigerator before serving.

Serves 4 to 6

# Double Radish Delight

In this elegant slaw, all the vegetables are cut into thin matchstick pieces and then tossed with a horseradish-spiked creamy dressing.

A daikon radish looks like an overweight white carrot. Its flavor is similar to that of a round red radish, but it's milder, juicier, and a bit sweeter. Daikon radishes are available in many supermarkets as well as Asian markets.

6 scallions, cut lengthwise into quarters, then crosswise into 2-inch strips
1 large daikon radish (about 1½ pounds), peeled
2 medium carrots, peeled and cut into thin julienne strips
6 teaspoons prepared horseradish, or 3 tablespoons grated fresh horseradish
2 tablespoons sugar
½ cup whole, low-fat, or nonfat sour cream
3 tablespoons red wine vinegar
3 tablespoons olive oil
1 teaspoon salt
½ teaspoon fresh-ground black pepper
1 teaspoon celery seeds, or ½ teaspoon caraway seeds (optional)

**1.** Put the scallions into a very large bowl. Cut the daikon with a mandoline or a food processor with a julienne blade, or by hand into ⅛-inch rounds, then cut 8 to 10 rounds at a time into matchstick pieces. Put the daikon into the bowl with the scallions, and add the julienned carrots.

**2.** Make the dressing: Combine the horseradish, sugar, sour cream, and vinegar in a small bowl. Stir with a whisk until the mixture is smooth. Continuing to whisk, drizzle in the olive oil, then add the salt, pepper, and, if you like, the celery seeds or caraway seeds.

**3.** Add the dressing to the vegetables, and toss well. Serve the salad right away, or chill it in the refrigerator. This slaw stays fresh for 2 to 3 days if kept covered in the refrigerator.

Serves 6 to 8

## Roasting Pumpkin Seeds

*B*oth carving and sugar (pie) pumpkins have seeds that are delicious when roasted. Although these seeds are not a substitute for the hulled, green pumpkin seeds used in Mexican cooking, they are a tasty garnish for all kinds of dishes.

To prepare the seeds, put them with the attached strings into a colander, and separate the strings from the seeds under cold running water. Spread the seeds on a baking sheet, and bake them at 325° for 20 minutes. Stir in 1 tablespoon olive oil, some ground black pepper, and salt. Bake the seeds 40 minutes more, stirring from time to time.

# CHAPTER 6

# Dressed to Thrill

# Three-Citrus Vinaigrette

Lime, lemon, and orange all do their part to create this vibrant and creamy dressing. It is lovely tossed with delicate greens such as bibb or Boston lettuce. Or try it in a slaw made from thinly sliced endive, jícama, and red onion, with a touch of mint or basil.

Grated rind of 1 lemon
Grated rind of 1 orange (optional)
1 tablespoon lime juice (from about ½ lime)
3 tablespoons lemon juice (from about 1 lemon)
2 tablespoons red wine vinegar
1½ teaspoons Dijon mustard
1 tablespoon sugar
1 cup olive oil
½ cup whole, low-fat, or nonfat sour cream
Salt and fresh-ground black pepper to taste

**1.** Place a mixing bowl on a damp, folded towel to secure the bowl to your work surface. In the bowl, combine the first seven ingredients with a whisk. While whisking, slowly pour the oil in a stream the width of a pencil. Whisk in the sour cream, and add salt and pepper.

**2.** Store the dressing in a covered container in the refrigerator. It will keep for 1 week.

Variation: For even more citrus flavor, add ½ teaspoon each of grated tangerine and grapefruit rind to the dressing.

Makes about
1 ¾ cups dressing

# Lemongrass-Peanut Vinaigrette

I like this slightly sweet, zippy dressing tossed with romaine lettuce, tomatoes, and cucumbers, or mixed with cold Chinese wheat noodles and raw vegetables (such as chopped scallions, mung or soybean sprouts, and shredded carrot).

1 lemongrass stalk, white part only, stripped of
   dry leaves and sliced very thin (save the
   green part to flavor a soup or stock)
1 large garlic clove
1/2 teaspoon tamarind concentrate (optional)
1 tablespoon Thai or Vietnamese fish sauce, or
   1/2 teaspoon salt
1 tablespoon Dijon mustard
2 tablespoons creamy peanut butter
4 teaspoons sugar
1/3 cup rice vinegar
1/4 cup dry-roasted, unsalted peanuts
1/3 cup canola or corn oil

**1.** In a blender or food processor, combine the sliced lemongrass with the garlic, tamarind, fish sauce or salt, mustard, peanut butter, sugar, vinegar, and peanuts. Purée the mixture.

**2.** With the machine running, slowly add the oil, in a stream the width of a pencil. Store the dressing in a covered container in the refrigerator. It will keep for 2 weeks.

Variation: For a hot version, add 1 teaspoon hot chile paste in step 1.

Makes about 1 cup
dressing

## Tamarind

With its slightly sweet and very tart flavor, tamarind is a welcome flavoring in dozens of dishes. I like to add tamarind to chutneys and Thai and Indian curries. I also use tamarind instead of vinegar in salad dressings, or add it to soups such as Tomato-Lentil (page 105). The pulp from tamarind pods is sold in two forms, pressed into blocks (with the seeds still intact) in East Asian markets, and in a convenient jelly-like concentrate in Indian markets. Soak the blocks in boiling water (2 cups water to each 8-ounce block) for 30 minutes, then strain out the seeds. Approximately 2 tablespoons of the soaked block equals 1 teaspoon of the concentrate.

# Lime-Cilantro Dressing

A very tasty dressing, perfect for a simple romaine salad or a fancy salad of avocado, red onion, and curly endive (or frisée). You can use low-fat or nonfat sour cream in this recipe at no expense to the character of the dressing.

2 garlic cloves, minced
2 teaspoons sugar
1 cup coarsely chopped cilantro
1/2 cup lime juice (from about 4 limes)
1 cup canola or corn oil
1 cup whole, low-fat, or nonfat sour cream
1/2 teaspoon salt, or more, to taste
Fresh-ground black pepper to taste

**1.** In a blender or food processor, purée the garlic, sugar, cilantro, and lime juice. With the machine running, add the oil in a thin stream. Then add the sour cream, ½ cup at a time, blending the dressing between additions.

**2.** Season the dressing with salt and pepper. It will keep, covered, for up to 1 week in the refrigerator.

*Makes about 2 cups dressing*

# Chile-Cumin Dressing

This simple but sublime vinaigrette ranks near the top of my list of salad dressings. Delicious tossed with romaine lettuce or watercress, drizzled over steamed asparagus, as a dip for artichokes, or perhaps mixed in a salad of corn, scallion, and black beans, this dressing is endlessly versatile.

1½ teaspoons cumin seeds
1 garlic clove, cut in half
1 teaspoon Dijon mustard
1 teaspoon mild red chili powder
2 teaspoons honey
⅓ cup apple cider vinegar
⅔ cup canola or corn oil
Salt and fresh-ground black pepper to taste

**1.** Toast the cumin seeds in a small, dry skillet, shaking the pan often, until they release their aroma. Grind the seeds in a spice mill. In a blender or food processor, blend the garlic, mustard, cumin, chili powder, and honey to a paste.

**2.** Pour the vinegar and oil into a bowl. With the blender or processor running, slowly pour the vinegar-oil mixture into the paste. When all of the vinegar-oil mixture has been incorporated, add salt and pepper. Store the dressing in a covered container in the refrigerator. It will keep for up to 3 weeks.

Makes about 1 cup
dressing

# Caramelized Balsamic Vinaigrette

The day my peppy sous-chef Matthew Campbell told me he'd invented a caramelized balsamic vinaigrette, I asked him to make it for me. When he did, the flavor threw me straight into food heaven. This dressing is wonderful drizzled over greens, tomatoes, roasted or grilled vegetables, or probably anything that's edible—or even eaten with a spoon. Caramelized Balsamic Vinaigrette is also used in French Lentil Salad (page 137). Thanks, Matthew!

> **"** *Remember, you're all alone in the kitchen and no one can see you.* **"**
> —JULIA CHILD

1 cup sugar
6 tablespoons water
5 tablespoons balsamic vinegar
1 cup olive oil
3 garlic cloves, minced
1 teaspoon salt
Fresh-ground black pepper to taste

**1.** Combine the sugar and 4 tablespoons of the water in a heavy saucepan that can hold at least 2 quarts liquid. Bring the mixture to a boil, and continue to boil it until it turns a light golden color. Once it turns this color, immediately take the pan off the heat. While beating with a whisk, slowly pour in the balsamic vinegar, keeping your body and face as far away from the pot as possible in case the caramel should sputter. If you see little sugar balls in the syrup, some of the sugar has crystallized; if this happens, put the pan back on the heat, and stir until the sugar balls dissolve (and remove any that don't dissolve).

**2.** Off the heat, whisking constantly, slowly add the olive oil, in a stream the width of a pencil. Then whisk in the remaining 2 tablespoons water. (The dressing may appear incompletely emulsified through most of this process, but by the time you've finished adding the water the dressing should be fully emulsified.) Add the garlic, salt, and pepper.

**3.** The vinaigrette is now ready to use. If you need to store it, chill it in a covered container until you need it, then heat it slowly in a pan over low heat until it thins. It will keep in the refrigerator for at least 2 weeks.

**Variation:** Try the chilled, thick vinaigrette over brie or soft goat cheese, on crackers or on apple or pear slices. (You may need to heat the dressing slightly if it is too solid to drizzle.)

Makes 1 3/4 cups
dressing

# Vinegar: The Sour Truth

A splash of vinegar in a soup, stew, pasta sauce, or stir-fry dish can sometimes make the difference between a bland and an exciting meal. Vinegar is essential for balancing the sweetness in chutneys and for offsetting the intense flavor of cabbage in slaws. I often use vinegar to perk up a sauce or soup. But I add vinegar slowly, by the half-teaspoon or teaspoon, because, as with salt, you can always add more but you can't take any back. Too much vinegar can overwhelm more subtle flavors. Used sparingly, however, vinegar can enhance a dish and also reduce the amount of salt needed. Even if a sauce is already acidic—tomato sauce, for example—vinegar can bring out the sweetness as well as the tartness.

Vinegar is made from fermented liquids, such as cider, beer, or wine. Although commercial vinegars generally fall within the range of 4 to 6 percent acidity, the different kinds really do taste different. Getting acquainted with various vinegars can truly refine your cooking.

## HERE ARE SOME OF THE MOST COMMON VINEGARS:

**RED WINE VINEGAR**—This slightly sweet yet mellow vinegar is great for dressing greens, and it's good in slaws, vegetable salads, and chutneys. Adding a dash of red wine vinegar to chili and stew can help bring the flavors to life. I also use red wine vinegar as a basic component of many of my gazpachos.

**CIDER VINEGAR, OR APPLE CIDER VINEGAR**—Made from apple juice, this sweet-tasting vinegar has more punch than red wine vinegar, but it is less harsh than distilled white vinegar. Cider vinegar is a natural in chutneys and fruit salsas. It's also good in slaws, curries, moles and other Mexican sauces, chutneys, and, of course, pickles and relishes.

**SHERRY VINEGAR**—Usually aged in wooden casks, this vinegar made from fermented sherry has a smooth, full flavor. I like to add a dash of sherry vinegar to stews, soups, and sauces (from tomato to cream). I also like to combine sherry vinegar with Dijon mustard and extra-virgin olive oil to drizzle over bibb lettuce and arugula.

**BALSAMIC VINEGAR**—This very dense, sweet, dark-colored vinegar is made from Trebbiano, an Italian white grape. The vinegar is aged in wooden barrels for as long as 25 years. Most balsamic vinegars available in supermarkets, although they are aged for a much shorter time, are quite good and fairly inexpensive. Combined with extra-virgin olive oil, balsamic vinegar is terrific in salads, especially with the more assertive greens. Try balsamic vinegar and olive oil over grilled or roasted veggies. This vinegar also enhances many tomato-based sauces, stews, and soups, such as vegetarian chili.

RICE VINEGAR—Made from fermented rice, rice vinegar has a light, clean flavor and is indispensable in many of the Chinese-, Japanese-, and even American-inspired dishes I make. Rice vinegar seems to have a natural affinity with fresh ginger; the two are delicious together in slaws and in salad dressings. This vinegar can also be used in dipping sauces, stir-fry dishes, Chinese and Japanese soups, and fruit chutneys. Brown rice vinegar, sold in whole-foods stores, is interchangeable with conventional rice vinegar.

RASPBERRY VINEGAR—This very light and fruity vinegar is best mixed with light olive oil to make a dressing for mild-flavored greens such as Boston lettuce or mesclun.

BLACK VINEGAR—Made from glutinous rice and malt, black vinegar comes from Zhejiang, in western China. I've found that the Chinkiang brand, sold in Chinese markets, is much better than the others available. It is smooth-tasting, less acidic than cider vinegar, sweet, and a bit smoky in flavor. It's particularly good mixed with soy sauce and a touch of sesame oil in a dipping sauce, for wontons, dumplings, egg rolls, Peking ravioli, or even sliced daikon radish. Add black vinegar also to wok-seared vegetables (such as bok choy, green beans, and eggplant) with a teaspoon or two of sugar. Many people recommend using black vinegar instead of balsamic vinegar in vinaigrette. Like balsamic vinegar, some of the best black vinegars are aged for years.

MALT VINEGAR—This fermented liquid extract of sprouted barley has a distinctive, somewhat nutty flavor, and is best known as a condiment for fish and chips. Malt vinegar is also good added to braised cabbage. And try a dash on pan-fried potatoes. Malt vinegar is available in whole-foods stores and some supermarkets.

DISTILLED WHITE VINEGAR—Made from grain alcohol, this vinegar has a very harsh flavor. I almost never use distilled vinegar in cooking, but it is the norm in pickles and barbecue sauces. I think this vinegar is best for dyeing Easter eggs and, diluted, for cleaning coffee machines.

# Pomegranate-Poppy Vinaigrette

Pomegranate molasses contributes both a sweet and sour note to this vinaigrette, which is especially good on peppery greens such as arugula or watercress. Pomegranate molasses can be found at Middle Eastern and some Indian grocery stores. I always buy the Lebanese brand, Cortas.

1 tablespoon Dijon mustard
1 garlic clove, cut in half
2 tablespoons pomegranate molasses
2 tablespoons lime juice
1 tablespoon sugar
¼ cup apple cider vinegar
1¼ cups canola or corn oil
2 tablespoons poppy seeds
Salt and fresh-ground black pepper to taste

**1.** In a blender or food processor, blend the mustard, garlic, pomegranate molasses, lime juice, and sugar. Add the cider vinegar, and blend well.

**2.** With the machine running, slowly pour in the oil, in a stream the width of a pencil. Once the oil is fully incorporated, add the poppy seeds, salt, and pepper. Store the dressing in a covered container in the refrigerator. It will keep for 1 week.

Makes 1¾ cups dressing

# Caesar Revamped

Because tofu rather than egg yolk is the binding agent in this Caesar dressing, it has two advantages over the traditional version. First, the amount of saturated fat is much lower,

## Coriander Seed

*his is a good friend to many other spices and foods, because coriander seed never overwhelms or masks other ingredients in a dish. The dried fruit of cilantro, coriander seed has an entirely different personality from the leaves and stems of the plant. The aroma of the seed is lemony and floral. Coriander is used whole in pickling, and in India it is an essential spice in curries and many other dishes. Around the Mediterranean, ground coriander enhances stews, often accompanying chickpeas, tomatoes, onions, and eggplant.*

*Buy whole rather than ground coriander seed to ensure the best flavor. Lightly toast the seeds in a dry skillet, then grind them in a spice mill.*

and, second, there is no worry of salmonella. The tofu, having so little taste, barely affects the dressing's flavor. Although the recipe isn't an authentic Caesar, it's more healthful and just as delicious.

4 large garlic cloves, cut in half
1 tablespoon smooth Dijon mustard
6 ounces silken tofu
1/4 cup lemon juice (from about 1 lemon)
1/2 teaspoon salt
1 pinch fresh-ground black pepper
1 cup olive oil
1/2 cup grated Parmesan cheese

**1.** In a food processor or blender, purée the garlic, mustard, silken tofu, and lemon juice. Add the salt and pepper.

**2.** With the machine running, slowly add the olive oil, in a stream the width of a pencil. When the dressing is fully emulsified, stir in the Parmesan cheese. The dressing will keep in the refrigerator, covered, for up to 1 week.

Variation: Here is a vegan option. Pour boiling water over a 5-inch piece of wakame seaweed (available in whole-foods stores and Japanese markets), and let it soak for 5 minutes. Drain the wakame, then chop it and add it to the food processor before you add the oil. Omit the Parmesan cheese, and increase the salt to taste.

Makes 2 cups dressing

# Coriander-Honey Dressing

oriander and honey harmonize in this sweet and aromatic dressing. It goes well with both simple greens and grain salads. Hot or cold steamed quinoa or bulgur tastes wonderful when mixed with fresh tomatoes and dressed with this vinaigrette.

1½ teaspoons coriander seeds
1½ teaspoons Dijon mustard
1 tablespoon honey
1 small garlic clove, minced
3 tablespoons lemon juice (from about 1 small
    lemon)
3/4 cup canola or mild olive oil
Salt and fresh-ground black pepper to taste

1. In a small, dry skillet over medium heat, toast the coriander seeds until they are fragrant, shaking the pan constantly. This should take 2 to 3 minutes.

2. Grind the coriander in a spice mill. Then put the coriander into a medium bowl, and add the mustard, honey, garlic, and lemon juice. Place a damp, folded kitchen towel under the bowl to secure it in place. Begin whisking the mixture while slowly pouring in the olive oil, in a stream the width of a pencil. Season with salt and pepper. Store the dressing in a covered container in the refrigerator. It will keep for up to 1 week.

Makes about 1 cup dressing

# Miso Dressing

Miso dressings are endless in variety. This one is spiked with fresh ginger. With sour cream added, it makes a great dip for raw vegetables (see the Variations).

1 tablespoon minced fresh ginger
2 garlic cloves, minced
1 pinch fresh-ground Sichuan or black
    peppercorns
1/2 cup rice vinegar

## Hot Chile Sauces

I divide chile condiments into three main types: The first is chile paste, available in Asian stores, which you must stir with water before using. The chile peppers are ground, salted, and fermented, creating an enticing, pungent flavor. The second type is Asian bottled chile sauces, often labeled tuong or siracha. Usually consisting of chiles, vinegar, and sugar, these sauces resemble Western sauces but are thicker and sweeter. The third, Western hot sauces, ranges from traditional Tabasco to newer sauces that include fruit and other ingredients, with vinegar usually heading the list. I often use the latter two types interchangeably, especially in vinaigrettes, stir-fried dishes, and slaws.

1 tablespoon honey
1 tablespoon miso paste (any kind will do)
½ cup canola or corn oil
3 tablespoons toasted sesame seeds (optional)

**1.** In a bowl, whisk together the first six ingredients.

**2.** Place a damp, folded kitchen towel underneath the bowl to secure it in place. While whisking, slowly add the canola or corn oil, in a thin stream. Then whisk in the sesame seeds, if you're using them. Covered in the refrigerator, the dressing will keep for up to 2 weeks.

### Variations:

- In step 1, add any one of the following: 2 tablespoons minced onion, 1 teaspoon chile paste or ¼ teaspoon chile flakes, 1 teaspoon wasabi powder, or 1½ teaspoons ground coriander seeds.
- In step 2, after adding the oil, whisk in 2 tablespoons sour cream or 2 tablespoons chopped cilantro.
- Use sherry vinegar instead of the rice vinegar.
- Instead of ½ cup rice vinegar, use 1 teaspoon tamarind concentrate plus ⅓ cup rice vinegar.
- Use two shallots instead of two garlic cloves.

Makes 1⅓ cups dressing

# Fiery Sweet-and-Sour Dressing

I add chile pastes and hot sauces to foods the way other people add salt and pepper. In recipes like this one, though, chile paste or sauce takes center stage.

Among the many kinds of chile pastes and hot sauces available, I prefer Lan Chi "Chilli Paste with Garlic," Panda "Hot Chili Sauce" (both available in Asian markets) or "Cholula" hot sauce, imported from Mexico and available in an increasing number of supermarkets.

1 cup apple cider vinegar
½ cup sugar
2 large garlic cloves
1 teaspoon Dijon mustard
1 to 3 teaspoons chile paste, or 1 to 2
    tablespoons of your favorite hot sauce
½ teaspoon salt
1 cup canola or corn oil

**1.** In a small saucepan over high heat, heat the vinegar and sugar until the mixture boils. Stir well, then turn off the heat.

**2.** In a blender or food processor, blend the garlic, mustard, and 1 teaspoon chile paste or 1 tablespoon hot sauce. Add the sugar and vinegar mixture, and blend well.

**3.** With the machine still running, add the salt, then slowly add the oil in a stream the width of a pencil. Taste, add more chile paste or sauce if you like, then run the machine again for half a minute. Stored in a sealed container in the refrigerator, the dressing will keep for 2 weeks.

Makes 2¼ cups
dressing

# Roasted Shallot Dressing

This dressing has a sophisticated taste, but it's not difficult to make. Just allow some time for the shallots to roast, then purée all of the ingredients in a blender. The flavor of the dressing is sweet and mellow. Try it drizzled over a fresh spinach, walnut, and tomato salad.

6 shallots, cut in half, skins left on
1 garlic clove, cut in half
2 tablespoons smooth Dijon mustard
2 tablespoons balsamic vinegar
1 cup olive oil
Salt and fresh-ground black pepper to taste

**1.** Preheat the oven to 400°. Wrap the shallots in foil, and bake them for 30 minutes. Remove the package from the oven, open it, and let the shallots cool for 5 minutes.

**2.** In a blender or food processor, combine the garlic, mustard, and vinegar. With your hands, separate the shallot skins from the flesh, and add the flesh to the machine. Purée the mixture.

**3.** Slowly, with the machine running, add the olive oil in a stream the width of a pencil. Add salt and pepper to taste. If kept covered in the refrigerator, this dressing will keep well for over a week.

Makes 1¹/₂ cups dressing

# Shocking Beet Vinaigrette

I once worked as the pastry chef at Nosmo King, a restaurant in Manhattan (unfortunately now closed) where organic foods were transformed into stunning dishes. The chef, Alan Harding, created one showstopper of a salad. On a large white dinner plate, he would lay an assortment of greens in a small pile, and next to it a large wedge of goat cheese. He would then carefully spoon beet vinaigrette onto a vacant part of the plate, and, with a small whack with the back of the spoon, splatter the vinaigrette to decorate the entire plate as well as the salad. This is my version of the vinaigrette, but the inspiration comes from Alan.

1 small beet (about 3 ounces), trimmed but
    unpeeled
1 teaspoon minced fresh ginger
1 shallot, chopped
1 tablespoon Dijon mustard
3 tablespoons balsamic vinegar
3/4 cup mild olive oil, preferably extra-virgin
1/2 teaspoon salt
Fresh-ground black pepper to taste

**1.** Place the beet in a small saucepan, and add enough water to cover it. Simmer the beet until it is tender, about 30 minutes. Drain the beet, and cool it with cold running water. Press the beet between your fingers so the skin slides off. Cut the beet into 5 or 6 pieces.

**2.** In a food processor or blender, purée the beet, ginger, shallot, and mustard. Blend in the balsamic vinegar.

**3.** With the machine running, slowly add the olive oil, in a stream the width of a pencil. Add the salt and pepper. Store the dressing in a covered container in the refrigerator. It will keep well for 5 days.

Makes 1 1/2 cups dressing

# Goat Cheese Dressing

Here is a dressing that celebrates the sublime combination of olive oil, garlic, and goat cheese. My favorite way to eat this dressing is tossed with mesclun (young mixed greens) and frisée (or curly endive), topped with fresh bread crumbs that have been pan-fried in olive oil.

1 garlic clove, cut in half
1 teaspoon Dijon mustard
2 tablespoons lemon juice

## Extra-Virgin, Extra-Sensitive

Olive oils are graded by their acidity. Extra-virgin oil comes from the first pressing of the olives and is only 1 percent acid. Although extra-virgin oil tastes better than oil from subsequent pressings, the fine flavor of the oil breaks down when the oil is heated. So if you are watching your pennies, use less expensive olive oil for cooking. Reserve the pricey extra-virgin oil for drizzling onto salads and fully grilled or roasted vegetables, and perhaps into soups and sauces when they are finished cooking. My favorite way to enjoy extra-virgin olive oil is to pour some into a shallow bowl with fresh chopped rosemary, and serve the oil with fresh bread.

½ cup crumbled soft, mild chèvre (goat cheese)
5 tablespoons plain yogurt or silken tofu
⅔ cup mild olive oil
½ teaspoon salt
Fresh-ground black pepper to taste

**1.** In a blender or food processor, combine the garlic, mustard, lemon juice, goat cheese, and yogurt or silken tofu. Blend until the mixture is smooth.

**2.** With the machine running, slowly add the olive oil, in a stream the width of a pencil. Add the salt and pepper. Store the dressing in a covered container in the refrigerator. It will keep for 1 week.

Makes 1½ cups dressing

# Sweet Japanese Vinaigrette

Do you want a no-fat salad dressing without zillions of stabilizers and additives? Here's one—a sweet and perky dressing that puts the spotlight on ginger. This dressing is delicious tossed with julienned endive strips, cucumbers, or delicate greens.

½ cup water
1 cup sugar
3 tablespoons minced fresh ginger
1 cup rice vinegar
1 teaspoon salt
½ teaspoon chile paste (optional)

**1.** Bring the water, sugar, and ginger to a boil in a heavy saucepan. Let the mixture boil for 2 minutes, then take it off the heat, and let it stand for 5 minutes.

**2.** Strain the ginger out of the syrup, and add the vinegar, salt, and, if you like, the chile paste. Whisk well. The dressing will keep in the refrigerator, covered, for at least 2 weeks.

*Makes 2 cups dressing*

# Sesame-Ginger Dressing

I developed this recipe at the Delux Cafe. When the time came to change the menu and replace this salad dressing, I went through a short but painful mourning period. Somehow, this dressing can make anything taste good. Try it with mixed greens, or tossed with Chinese noodles and blanched broccoli. You can make this dressing in a food processor or blender, if you like.

1½ tablespoons minced fresh ginger
1 small garlic clove, minced
1 tablespoon smooth Dijon mustard
3 tablespoons apple cider vinegar
¼ teaspoon fresh-ground Sichuan or black pepper
½ teaspoon salt
2 tablespoons sugar
¼ cup dark sesame oil
½ cup canola or corn oil
½ to 1 teaspoon chile paste (optional)

**1.** In a bowl, whisk together the ginger, garlic, mustard, vinegar, pepper, salt, and sugar. Place a damp, folded towel underneath the bowl to secure it. Then, while whisking, slowly add the sesame oil. Add the canola or corn oil in a stream the width of a pencil, whisking constantly. Whisk in the chile paste, if you like.

**2.** Store the dressing in a covered container in the refrigerator. The dressing will keep for at least 2 weeks.

*Makes 1 cup dressing*

# Creamy Three-Herb Dressing

No one will guess that silken tofu is the secret to this creamy, rich-tasting dressing. Tofu not only reduces the amount of oil needed, but it is also a good source of protein. Try this as a dressing for green salads, or as a dip for carrot sticks, green beans, and other vegetables.

1 garlic clove
2 teaspoons Dijon mustard
2 tablespoons chopped oregano or mint
1 cup loose basil leaves, coarsely chopped
1 cup cilantro leaves
12 ounces silken tofu
1/3 cup lime juice (from about 3 limes)
1/3 cup extra-virgin olive oil
1/2 cup plain yogurt
1/2 teaspoon salt, or more, to taste
Fresh-ground black pepper to taste

**1.** In a blender or food processor, blend the garlic, mustard, and herbs. Add the tofu and the lime juice, and blend until smooth.

**2.** With the machine running, add the olive oil in a stream the width of a pencil. Blend in the yogurt and salt and pepper. You can store this dressing in a covered container in the refrigerator for up to 5 days, although, because of the fresh herbs, the dressing is better if eaten sooner.

Makes 1 1/2 cups dressing

# CHAPTER 7

# Simple Sides

# Asparagus with Curry Butter

Asparagus is great simply with melted butter and fresh-ground pepper. But curry butter takes the vegetable one step further. Take note that only half of this curry butter is used for the asparagus. You can freeze the other half to use later, with steamed brown rice or another grain or with vegetables.

1/2 teaspoon ground cumin seeds
1/2 teaspoon ground coriander seeds
2 teaspoons curry powder, store-bought or
    homemade (page 36)
1/2 cup butter (1 stick), softened
1 teaspoon lemon juice
2 tablespoons minced shallots
Salt and fresh-ground black pepper to taste
1 pound asparagus

**1.** In a dry skillet, combine the cumin, coriander, and curry. Over medium heat, toast the spices, stirring constantly, until they become aromatic. Let them cool.

**2.** In a bowl, combine the butter, toasted spices, lemon juice, and shallots with a spoon until the flavorings are well incorporated. Mix in salt and pepper. Spoon the butter onto a large piece of plastic wrap, and roll and shape the butter into a 4-inch log. Twist the ends of the plastic wrap to help shape the log. Chill the butter for at least 30 minutes (freeze it if you're in a hurry).

**3.** Break off and discard the tough end of each asparagus spear. Steam or boil the asparagus for 3 to 4 minutes, until it is tender.

**4.** Slice half of the chilled butter log into four rounds. Lay one round on each serving of asparagus. Freeze the remainder of the butter for future use.

Serves 4

# Brown-Buttered Broccoli

I don't know why broccoli tastes so good with butter. But it tastes even better when the butter is browned. This is a quick dish to make, with no special ingredients besides the broccoli. The other ingredients are probably already in your kitchen.

1 small bunch broccoli, cut into long-stemmed florets
1/4 cup butter
2 tablespoons lemon juice (from about 1/2 lemon)
Salt and fresh-ground black pepper to taste

**1.** Steam the broccoli until it is just tender, about 7 to 9 minutes.

**2.** While the broccoli steams, heat the butter in a small skillet over medium heat. Let the butter bubble until it turns a dark golden color, then promptly take it off the heat and add the lemon juice.

**3.** When the broccoli is tender, transfer it to a bowl, and add the butter-lemon mixture. Toss the broccoli, and season it with salt and pepper. Serve it right away.

Serves 4

# Little-Cabbage Hash

I prefer to call brussels sprouts "little cabbages." This way people don't run away so fast; besides, brussels sprouts are indeed part of the cabbage family. Here the brussels sprouts are "hashed"—that is, minced—along with carrot and red pepper. This quick side dish can enhance many an entrée.

*" In America only cheap restaurants moisten mashed potatoes with their cooking water rather than with milk and cream. In France no self-respecting peasant would think of doing otherwise… The potatoes, halved or quartered if large, should be only just cooked (cooking water saved), and gently pushed through a sieve…, a generous quantity of butter stirred, but not beaten in, and enough cooking liquid added to bring them to a barely pourable consistency, tasted for salt, and generously peppered. Try them on the family (guests might suspect that you had made a mistake, or that you had never read a cookbook). I love them. "*

—RICHARD OLNEY,
SIMPLE FRENCH FOOD

1 tablespoon olive oil
1½ cups minced onions
2 garlic cloves, minced
1 pound brussels sprouts, trimmed of stems and
  minced
1 large carrot, chopped fine
½ cup water
1 red bell pepper, seeded and minced
½ teaspoon salt
Fresh-ground black pepper to taste

**1.** In a large skillet, heat the olive oil over medium heat. Add the onions, and sauté them, stirring frequently, for 5 minutes or until they have softened.

**2.** Add the garlic, brussels sprouts, and carrot to the onions. Add the water, and simmer the vegetables, stirring occasionally, about 5 to 8 minutes, or until the water has completely evaporated. Then stir in the bell pepper, salt, and black pepper to taste. Sauté the hash another minute, and serve.

Variation: At the end of the cooking, stir in 2 tablespoons toasted chopped cashews or almonds.

Serves 4

# Sautéed Cherry Tomatoes and Eggplant

Here is a way to sauté eggplant without using huge amounts of oil. First you salt the eggplant rounds, then you press them dry with paper towels. This way, the eggplant doesn't soak up a lot of oil. The cooked eggplant pieces are tender but don't fall apart. The cherry tomatoes in this dish add sweetness, juiciness, and a big splash of color.

1 small eggplant (about 1 pound)
2 teaspoons kosher salt, or 1 teaspoon table salt
2 tablespoons olive oil
2 large garlic cloves, minced
1 cup cherry tomatoes
Salt and fresh-ground black pepper to taste
1/4 cup basil leaves, lightly packed, cut into thin
    strips

**1.** Slice the eggplant into ½-inch-thick rounds. Place them in a colander, and salt the slices. Let the eggplant sit for 30 minutes.

**2.** Rinse the eggplant with cold water. Then fold 7 or 8 paper towels into quarters to make small squares. Lay a slice of eggplant on one square, and with another square press hard to extract as much liquid from the eggplant as possible. Continue with the other slices, moving on to fresh paper towels as the used ones become saturated. Cut the eggplant slices into ½-inch cubes.

**3.** In a large non-stick skillet, heat the olive oil over medium heat. Add the eggplant, and cook it for 10 minutes, stirring frequently. Add the garlic and the cherry tomatoes, and cook 2 minutes more or until the raw garlic flavor has dissipated. Add the salt, pepper, and fresh basil. Toss the eggplant well, and serve.

Serves 4 to 6

# Fava Bean Succotash

Succotash comes from the Narragansett Indian word *msikquatash,* which simply means "boiled cut corn." This gives people who aren't big fans of lima beans (me, for one) a valid reason to exclude them from the dish. I use tender fresh

## Quick Sides

*S ide dishes should be easy to make, although this doesn't mean you have to settle for steamed broccoli or green beans. There are other choices—perhaps a steamed artichoke with a lemon and olive oil vinaigrette? Or some lima or fava beans quickly sautéed with brown butter? You might try steamed brussels sprouts, or maybe a purée of sweet potatoes. How about roasted beets or new potatoes, a roasted or grilled red onion, or baked acorn squash halves? Perhaps you'd like braised endive or celery, or seared kale or mustard greens with garlic and a splash of red wine vinegar. Or steamed snap peas or green beans with sautéed cherry tomatoes? The choices are nearly endless.*

fava beans instead (although dried favas can be used, too). Corn cut fresh from the cob provides much better flavor and texture than the traditional hominy.

½ cup shelled young fresh fava beans (about
   8 ounces before shelling), or ½ cup cooked
   dried fava beans
2 tablespoons olive oil
1 cup fresh corn kernels
1 ripe tomato, cut into ½-inch pieces
Salt and fresh-ground black pepper to taste

**1.** If you are using mature fresh fava beans—that is, if your beans are ¾ to 1 inch in length—peel off the skin of each bean with your thumbnail. If your beans are young—about ½ inch long—the skin will be tender enough to leave intact. Cooked dried beans need no peeling.

**2.** In a skillet, heat the olive oil over medium heat. Add the fava beans, and sauté them for 2 minutes. Add the corn, and sauté 2 minutes more. Then add the tomato, salt, and pepper, and toss well. Serve the succotash right away.

**Variation:** Add 1 tablespoon of chopped fresh dill just before serving.

Serves 2

# Roasted Fennel with Green Apples

M any years ago, my mom used to nibble on raw fennel instead of carrot sticks or crackers. My sisters and I thought perhaps she was part witch, ritually chewing on this strange vegetable. Now fennel is the darling of chefs and home cooks nationwide, and I, at least, acknowledge my dear mother as the daring, unappreciated pioneer she has been for all these years.

1 large or 2 smaller fennel bulbs (about 1$\frac{1}{2}$
    pounds)
6 shallots, peeled and sliced
1 large green apple, peeled, cored, and sliced thin
Salt and fresh-ground black pepper to taste
2$\frac{1}{2}$ tablespoons olive oil

**1.** Preheat the oven to 400°. Remove the outer layers of the fennel bulbs if they seem old or tough. Cut the bulbs in half, and cut them crosswise into ¼-inch slices. Put them into a large casserole dish.

**2.** Add the shallots and apple to the casserole dish, and toss them with the fennel. Salt and pepper the mixture, then drizzle in the olive oil. Roast the dish, uncovered, for 20 to 25 minutes, or until the fennel is very tender. Serve right away.

Variation: This dish can be made into a gratin by adding 4 ounces of grated white cheddar cheese 5 minutes before the end of the baking time.

Serves 4

# Sesame-Glazed
# Green Beans

These Asian-style beans are sweet, sour, and slightly spicy. Combine them with Shiitake Spring Rolls (page 72) for a light supper or Rice Noodles with Shiitakes, Choy, and Chiles (page 283) for a heartier meal. Sugar snap peas, snow peas, and bok choy (in large slices) are just a few of the other vegetables that can be prepared the same way.

½ pound green beans, trimmed
½ cup water

## Simplicity: A Roasted Apple

I once enjoyed a simple meal in the third arrondissement of Paris. Among other things on the plate was a whole roasted apple. It was delicious and pretty, and I had fun deciding which other foods to eat it with. Here is my recipe for roasted apples for two: Place two small Granny Smith or Cortland apples in a small baking dish. Mix 2 tablespoons honey with a teaspoon of Dijon mustard and 3 tablespoons water, and pour this over the apples. Roast the apples at 400° for 30 minutes, basting once or twice with the juices. These apples are delicious alongside a dish of grains and seared leafy greens.

½ red bell pepper, seeded and cut into julienne strips
1 tablespoon soy sauce
½ teaspoon cornstarch
1 teaspoon dry mustard
1 tablespoon honey
1 tablespoon dark sesame oil
1 tablespoon toasted sesame seeds (optional)

**1.** Put the green beans and water into a saucepan, and bring the water to a boil. Simmer the beans, uncovered, until they are almost tender and there is just a bit of water left, then stir in the red pepper strips. Simmer a little longer, until the beans are tender and all of the water has evaporated. Take the pan off the heat.

**2.** While the beans cook, combine the soy sauce, cornstarch, dry mustard, and honey in a small bowl. Put the green beans back over medium-high heat, and add the soy mixture. Toss until the vegetables are well coated, letting the sauce boil and thicken a bit.

**3.** Take the pan off the heat. Drizzle in the sesame oil, and sprinkle on the toasted sesame seeds, if you are using them. Serve the beans immediately.

Variation: For a kick, add ¼ teaspoon chile flakes to the soy mixture.

Serves 4

# Roasted Acorn Squash

The blend of nutmeg and coriander here produces a fragrant and flavor-filled side dish that is perfect with freshly cooked brown rice.

2 acorn squashes
3 tablespoons butter
2 medium onions, sliced thin
3 garlic cloves, minced
1 teaspoon ground coriander seeds
½ teaspoon freshly grated nutmeg
½ teaspoon salt
Fresh-ground black pepper to taste

**1.** Preheat the oven to 375°. Cut the squashes in half. Roast them cut side up on a baking sheet for 50 minutes or until the flesh is just tender. Let the squash cool for 20 minutes.

**2.** In a large skillet over medium heat, melt the butter, then add the onions. Stirring occasionally, cook the onions for 10 minutes, or until they begin to brown at the edges. Add the garlic, coriander, and nutmeg. Cook the mixture 2 minutes more, then remove the pan from the heat.

**3.** Spoon the seeds and stringy middle out of the squash, and discard these. Spoon out the flesh, chop it, and add it to the onion mixture. Discard the skins.

**4.** Heat and stir the squash-onion mixture, then season it with salt and pepper. Serve the squash hot.

Serves 4

# Spanish Swiss Chard with Raisins and Hazelnuts

Inspired by a Spanish dish of sautéed spinach, raisins, and pine nuts, this dish makes a meal when coupled with brown rice or a grain such as quinoa. Swiss chard is increasingly available in supermarket produce sections, and I think it's one of the tastiest leaf vegetables around.

## Squashed

*Roasted and mashed butternut squash has become a favorite side dish in my house. Here's how to prepare the squash: Split it in half, then roast it in a hot oven until the squash is tender. Let it cool for 5 minutes. Spoon out and discard the seeds, then spoon the flesh into a bowl. Add a couple of tablespoons butter, salt and pepper, two or three pinches of cinnamon, freshly grated nutmeg, and a bit of chopped canned chipotles or minced fresh ginger. Use a potato masher, or just stir vigorously, to incorporate the butter and the spices. Reheat the squash before serving, if necessary.*

3 tablespoons raisins
1 pound Swiss chard, washed well
2 tablespoons olive oil
2 garlic cloves, minced
3 tablespoons toasted hazelnuts, chopped
Salt and fresh-ground black pepper to taste

**1.** Place the raisins in a small pan with water to cover. When the water begins to boil, take the pan off the heat, and let the raisins sit for at least 5 minutes.

**2.** While the raisins are soaking, cut each Swiss chard leaf away from the stem and central rib. Cut the leaves into ¼-inch crosswise slices. Dice the stems and central ribs.

**3.** In a large pot, heat the olive oil over medium heat. Add the Swiss chard and the garlic, and sauté, stirring frequently, for 6 to 8 minutes or until the chard is tender. Drain the raisins, and toss them and the hazelnuts into the Swiss chard. Add salt and pepper, and serve.

Serves 4

# Rabe-Stuffed Tomatoes

Here broccoli rabe (or broccoli raab, or rapini) is first blanched to cut the bitterness, and then chopped and sautéed in olive oil with garlic. Gorgonzola cheese and silken tofu are stirred in, and the mixture is spooned into the tomatoes, which are then baked. The baked tomatoes hold their shape well and have a sweet, delicate flavor. This is a nice accompaniment to rice and grain dishes.

# Leafy Greens

More than three hundred varieties of edible leafy greens are grown in this country alone. They include hearty greens like broccoli rabe and collard as well as all kinds of lettuce. Dark leafy greens are especially nutritious, because they contain a lot of vitamins C and E and beta carotene, all of which are antioxidants, which help prevent cancer. Recently, it has been discovered that most leafy greens, whether pale or dark green, contain lesser-known nutrients that also fight cancer, and possibly heart disease as well.

**TO WASH GREENS:** The best way is to fill a sink with cool water, add the greens, and swish them gently in the water. Dry them in a salad spinner, or drain them in a colander.

**TO COOK GREENS:** I often add chopped leafy greens directly to a stew or vegetable medley, letting them cook until tender with the accompanying vegetables. This method is especially good with hearty greens such as kale and collard, which are also delicious steamed. The more tender greens, such as watercress, arugula, and spinach, are often eaten raw, in salads. When I cook them, I usually sauté them very briefly. Boiling seems too harsh a method, since some of their flavor and texture is lost the moment they hit the water.

## HERE ARE SOME OF MY FAVORITE LEAFY GREENS AND THE WAYS I LIKE TO COOK AND EAT THEM:

**ARUGULA**—Arugula has a hot, horseradish-like taste. Most often used as a salad green, it is also delicious when quickly sautéed. Heat some olive oil in a pan, add the arugula, and sauté it for only 5 seconds; the peppery flavor will be lost if it cooks longer. Sautéed arugula is very nice tossed with pasta or as a bed for risotto or grain cakes. Try raw arugula in burritos.

**BEET GREENS**—I cut off the stems (and the beets, which I cook separately), and cook only the leaves. Slightly sweet in flavor, beet greens are good steamed with a little water and butter or olive oil.

**BELGIAN ENDIVE**—Its leaves looking like long, thin flower petals, endive is the sophisticate of leafy greens. When braised, it loses its bitter edge. Braise endive whole in one part white wine to two parts water for 20 minutes. To fully enjoy endive's flavor, use it as a salad green.

**BOK CHOY, NAPPA (CHINESE) CABBAGE, AND OTHER ASIAN GREENS**—Asians enjoy many greens in the cabbage family, including Chinese broccoli, tat soi, and choy sum. Most of these are mild in flavor and therefore versatile. Try them stir-fried; cook them only for a minute or two so they retain their crunch. I also use them in slaws and kimchi.

**BROCCOLI RABE (OR BROCCOLI RAAB, OR RAPINI, OR CIME DE RAPA)**—This small-headed form of broccoli is delicious when it is first steamed to reduce its bitterness, then sautéed in olive oil with plenty of garlic. Italians do not steam broccoli rabe; they simply sauté it in olive oil with garlic.

**CABBAGE**—In season, this is often the cheapest vegetable around. Green cabbage is delicious braised with a bit of butter, water, and onion, with plenty of salt and fresh pepper. Red cabbage is good cooked in this way, too, with a spoonful each of red wine vinegar and sugar added. I find red cabbage to be too tough for slaw (unless I use a mandoline, or vegetable slicer), but I use hand-sliced green cabbage in all kinds of slaws. It needs to sit in a salted dressing for a few hours to soften. Savoy cabbage is slightly more expensive than regular cabbage, but many people prefer its milder flavor and softer texture.

**COLLARD GREENS**—High in calcium, collard greens need longer cooking because of their thick, tough leaves. I like first to remove the stems and then chop the leaves before adding the leaves to stews or boiling them for a side dish. Although Southerners may boil collard greens for hours, boil them just until they are tender, usually no more than 15 minutes. Once they are drained, I mix the greens with balsamic vinegar, salt and pepper, and extra-virgin olive oil. Setting a risotto cake on top of a mound of boiled collard makes for some really good eating. If collard greens are very fresh and young, I roll the leaves, slice them fine, and add them to slaws.

**DANDELION GREENS**—High in calcium and especially in beta carotene, these greens should be as expensive as vitamins. Sauté them with a bit of olive oil and garlic, or use young dandelion greens in a salad.

**ESCAROLE**—Looking a lot like bibb or Boston lettuce but actually a kind of endive (or chicory), escarole tastes slightly bitter and nutty. It is delicious added to minestrone-style soups; cook it in the soup for 15 to 20 minutes. Try adding some chopped escarole to Lima Minestrone (page 109) in step 1, when you add the stock. Or add braised escarole to white beans and garlic, perhaps in a stew.

**KALE**—Once told I had to use purple kale as a garnish on *every* dish at one restaurant, I have since made a remarkable psychological comeback, and can now really enjoy kale. It's best steamed (the large stems removed) for 4 to 5 minutes, then quickly sautéed with olive oil and vinegar. Or chop it, then add it to minestrone-style soups. Kale has high levels of antioxidants—cancer fighters—and is therefore a valuable addition to any diet.

**MUSTARD GREENS**—Sliced thin, mustard greens stand up in stir-fried dishes against strong flavors such as ginger, sesame oil, and vinegar. Mustard greens have a pungency similar to that of horseradish, a relative. Unlike arugula, mustard does not lose pungency when cooked.

**SPINACH**—This ever-popular leafy green is one of my favorites. I like it in just about anything—clear soups, hearty stews, and stir-fried dishes are only a few examples. I often sear spinach in a wok or skillet with olive oil and garlic just until the spinach wilts, then I quickly remove it.

**SWISS CHARD**—A beet without the swollen root, Swiss chard comes in two kinds, red and white. The red is stronger in flavor, but both are good sources of vitamins A and C, and iron. Wash chard in a tub of cool (not cold) water twice to remove the dirt from the crevices. Some people remove the stems and cook them separately to avoid overcooking the leaves. I like to chop chard and cook it with olive oil and garlic, stirring often, until it is tender.

**WATERCRESS**—I enjoy this peppery green tossed in salads, especially with mild greens such as Boston or red-leaf lettuce and with balsamic vinegar–based vinaigrettes.

1 bunch broccoli rabe (about 1 pound)
1 tablespoon olive oil
2 garlic cloves, minced
2 tablespoons crumbled Gorgonzola or other
    blue cheese
1/4 cup crumbled silken tofu
Salt and fresh-ground black pepper to taste
4 large plum tomatoes

**1.** Preheat the oven to 350°. Bring a large pot of salted water to a boil. Trim off the thick lower parts of the broccoli rabe stems. Boil the broccoli rabe for 3 minutes, then drain it, and rinse it well with cold water. Chop it fine.

**2.** In a large skillet, heat the olive oil, and add the garlic. Add the broccoli rabe, and sauté it over medium heat for 3 minutes. Take the pan off the heat.

Add the blue cheese and tofu. Mix well with a spoon, and season with salt and pepper.

**3.** With a sharp paring knife, cut a small circle around the stem end of each tomato, as you would cut the top off a jack-o'-lantern, and remove the tomato top. Slice ⅛ inch off the other end of the tomato, so that the tomato can stand upright. With a spoon, take out from the open end the seeds and the inner meat of the tomato (don't dig too deep; you don't want to pierce the closed end of the tomato). Stuff the hollowed tomatoes with the broccoli rabe mixture.

**4.** Stand the tomatoes in a buttered muffin pan. (At this point, you can refrigerate the tomatoes for up to 3 days, if you like.)

**5.** Bake the tomatoes for 30 minutes. Serve them hot from the oven.

**Variation:** Simmer 2 tablespoons raisins with 1 tablespoon Madeira and a splash of water in a small saucepan until the liquid is evaporated. Add the raisins to the stuffing in step 2, before seasoning with salt and pepper.

Serves 4

## Broccoli Rabe

*Americans have been slow to warm up to this vegetable, but it has been loved in Italy for many, many years. It has flavor similar to that of conventional broccoli but with an intriguing bitter edge. First-time rabe eaters should probably blanch the vegetable briefly before pan-frying it (or steaming it) to lessen the bitterness. A little olive oil and garlic and a touch of salt and pepper are all the extras needed in the skillet. Before serving, you might add grated Parmesan cheese and a squeeze of lemon. Broccoli rabe is available from fall to spring in many produce markets and whole-foods stores.*

# Crumbed Zucchini

Is every food better with pan-fried bread crumbs? Sometimes I think so. Tossed in a salad, thrown into fettuccine, or sprinkled atop shepherd's pie, pan-fried bread crumbs stay crunchy while absorbing and transporting the flavors of many of my favorite dishes. Here the bread crumbs liven up sautéed zucchini.

2 tablespoons olive oil
2 slices sandwich bread (white or whole-wheat), lightly toasted, then chopped fine (crusts included)
3 garlic cloves, minced
1 medium zucchini (about 1 pound), quartered lengthwise, then cut crosswise into 1/2-inch pieces
1/2 teaspoon salt
Fresh-ground black pepper to taste

**1.** Over medium-high heat, heat 1 tablespoon olive oil in a large skillet. Add the bread crumbs and half the garlic. Pan-fry for 2 to 3 minutes or until the crumbs become golden brown and crunchy. Transfer them to a plate.

**2.** Heat the remaining 1 tablespoon olive oil in the same skillet over medium-high heat, and add the zucchini. Sauté the zucchini for 2 to 3 minutes, stirring occasionally, until it begins to brown a bit. Add the remaining minced garlic, and cook another minute. Add the bread crumbs, and season with the salt and pepper. Toss the mixture, and serve it immediately.

Variation: Make this a dinner for two by adding cooked pasta (I like penne) to the skillet once the zucchini is cooked (step 2). You'll need to start with about 8 ounces dried pasta.

Serves 4

# Stuffed Zucchini

Here is yet another recipe to help you use up your stale bread. Perhaps because this dish has a Mediterranean feel, I like to eat it with White Bean and Fresh Mozzarella Salad (page 135). Together, they make quite a lovely meal.

1 medium zucchini (about 1 pound)
1½ tablespoons olive oil
1 cup chopped onion
1 garlic clove, minced
1 medium tomato, chopped
2 slices sandwich bread, chopped fine
1 tablespoon drained capers
½ cup chopped basil
2 ounces soft, mild chèvre (goat cheese; optional)
Salt and fresh-ground black pepper to taste

**1.** Preheat the oven to 400°. Cut the zucchini in half lengthwise, and trim the ends. With a teaspoon, carve out the center of each half, leaving a ½-inch-thick shell and reserving the spooned-out flesh. Put the zucchini shells into a small casserole dish, and add ½ cup water. Cover the dish with foil. Bake the zucchini for 10 minutes. Remove the dish from the oven, and reduce the heat to 350°.

**2.** Make the stuffing: Heat the olive oil in a large skillet over medium-high heat, and add the onion. Cook, stirring occasionally, until it softens, about 5 minutes. Chop the reserved zucchini flesh, and add it to the pan with the garlic and tomato. Cook 5 minutes more. Take the skillet off the heat, and add the bread bits, capers, basil, and, if you like, goat cheese. Mix well, and season with salt and pepper.

**3.** Drain the water from the casserole dish, and fill the zucchini halves with the stuffing. Bake the stuffed zucchini for 15 minutes, and serve it hot.

Serves 2

# Celery Root and Potato Mash

Celery root's mild yet intriguing flavor combines well with that of potato. For a simple dinner, serve this mash on a bed of sautéed greens such as watercress or spinach, sprinkled with grated Parmesan or Asiago cheese and accompanied by grilled bread brushed with olive oil.

1 pound (2 to 3) russet, Yellow Finn,
    Yukon Gold, or any boiling potato
2 pounds (about 2 medium) celery roots
2 garlic cloves, peeled
2 to 3 tablespoons extra-virgin olive oil
3/4 teaspoon or more salt
Fresh-ground black pepper to taste
1 to 2 teaspoons lemon juice
2 tablespoons chopped parsley or chives

**1.** Bring a large pot of salted water to a boil. While the water heats, peel the potatoes, and cut them in half. Peel the celery roots with a sharp chef's knife, cutting away all the brown skin and rootlets. Cut the celery roots into 1-inch cubes. Put the potatoes, celery root, and garlic into the boiling water, and gently boil for 25 minutes or so, or until the vegetables are very tender when tested with a fork.

**2.** Drain the vegetables, and return them to the pot. Add the olive oil, salt, pepper, and lemon juice. Mash the vegetables with a potato masher, and adjust the seasonings, if you like. Stir in the parsley or chives. Serve the mashed vegetables immediately, or refrigerate them, and later reheat them slowly in a skillet, stirring frequently.

Serves 4 to 6

---

## Do the Mash

In every restaurant I've worked in, I've noticed that any entrée will sell well if it comes with mashed potatoes. I've eaten mashed potatoes in many variations, and not one has been bad. Here's how to make a few of them:

Sauté sliced shallots in butter until they begin to caramelize, then add a splash of vinegar. Mix the shallots into potatoes mashed with milk, salt, and pepper.

Mash together equal amounts of boiled sweet potatoes and white potatoes, adding a pinch of nutmeg as well as milk, salt, and pepper.

Mash the potatoes with extra-virgin olive oil, water (instead of milk), and some minced garlic.

# Crispy Rosemary Potatoes

Fresh potatoes are essential here. Yellow Finns or new potatoes are a good choice. The potato slices develop a crisp crust when they are seared in the olive oil. A small amount of rosemary, added at the end of the cooking, makes the dish altogether enticing. These potatoes are delicious alongside a veggie burger or other sandwich, or even with eggs in the morning.

1 pound Yellow Finn, Yukon Gold, or new
    potatoes
2 tablespoons olive oil
1 garlic clove, minced
1/2 teaspoon fresh or dried rosemary
1/2 teaspoon salt
Fresh-ground black pepper to taste

**1.** Bring a large kettle of salted water to a boil. While the water heats, cut the potatoes in half (do not peel them). Put them into the boiling water, and simmer them just until they are tender (check them often; they must not overcook, or they will break into pieces).

**2.** When the potatoes are done, immediately drain them, and put them into a large bowl filled with water and ice. Let them sit in the water for at least 5 minutes, then drain them. Cut them into large crosswise slices, about ½ inch thick, and place the slices on a kitchen towel to absorb any excess water.

**3.** Heat a large, heavy skillet over medium-high heat. Add the olive oil, then quickly add the potatoes. Salt and pepper the potatoes well. Cook the potatoes for about 5 minutes, until they are a deep golden color on their undersides. Turn the potatoes over, either by shaking the pan or by using a spatula; try not to break them. Cook the potatoes for 5 minutes more.

Then sprinkle them with the garlic and rosemary. Shake the skillet or use a spatula to turn the potatoes again, and cook them another 2 minutes. Serve the potatoes hot.

Serves 2

# Roasted Garlic Mashers

If you have roasted garlic on hand, by all means try this dish. If you don't have any roasted garlic, glance at the Variation that follows this recipe.

1 pound (2 to 3) potatoes, such as russet,
    Yellow Finn, Yukon Gold, or new potatoes
1 tablespoon or more roasted garlic purée (see
    page 32)
1 tablespoon unsalted butter
2 to 4 tablespoons milk
Salt and fresh-ground black pepper to taste

**1.** Bring a large kettle of salted water to a boil. Meanwhile, peel the potatoes and cut them in half. Add them to the water, and boil the potatoes gently for 25 minutes or until they start falling apart.

**2.** Drain the potatoes, and then return them to the pot. Place the pot over very low heat. With a potato masher or a fork, mash in the roasted garlic, butter, and milk. Mash until the potatoes are as smooth as you like (I like some lumps in my potatoes, but this is a personal matter). Add salt and pepper, taste, and adjust the seasonings, if you like.

**3.** Serve the potatoes immediately, or refrigerate them, and later reheat them slowly in a skillet while whipping them with a fork (add a bit more milk if necessary).

## The Many Ways of Mashed

Plain mashed potatoes are wonderful just as they are, but for special occasions it's fun to jazz them up. Here are some suggestions: After mashing the potatoes with either olive oil or butter, add shallots that have been cooked slowly in olive oil until they are brown and caramelized. Or add to the mashed potatoes a few spoonfuls of onion confit (see page 393) or a handful of fresh herbs (my favorite melange is thyme, sage, and parsley). Ray Gillespie, a remarkable chef at Mama Maria in Boston, likes to make red beet mashed potatoes, a mixture of mashed potatoes, reduced red wine, and cooked and puréed beets.

*Variation:* If you don't have roasted garlic on hand, you can simply make garlic mashed potatoes: Cook and drain the potatoes as directed, and return them to their pot. Melt the butter over low heat in a small skillet. Mince two cloves of garlic, and add the garlic to the butter. Sauté the minced garlic, stirring frequently; be careful not to brown it. Add the softened garlic to the potatoes. Add the milk, and mash.

Serves 2

# Persian Basmati Rice with Cinnamon and Pistachios

Sautéing the uncooked rice in a little butter until the rice turns golden is part of the secret of this pleasing side dish. If you don't have basmati rice, you can use jasmine or regular long-grain white rice.

1 tablespoon butter
1 cup uncooked white basmati rice
1/2 teaspoon salt
1 pinch fresh-ground black pepper
1 garlic clove, minced
2 2-inch strips orange peel
1/2 teaspoon ground cinnamon
1 pinch curry powder
2 cups water
2 tablespoons toasted pistachios
2 tablespoons yellow raisins (sultanas)

**1.** In a heavy saucepan, heat the butter over medium heat. Add the rice, and sauté it for 3 minutes, stirring constantly, until the grains become slightly golden. Add the salt, pepper, garlic, orange peel, cinnamon, and curry powder. Sauté another minute, stirring. Add the water, turn down the heat, and cover the pan.

**2.** Let the rice cook over low heat for 25 minutes. Then stir in the pistachios and raisins, remove the 2 orange peels, and serve.

Serves 4

# Split Pea-laf

Split peas are an integral part of this pilaf. The two other components are long-grain brown rice and a *tadka,* a flavorful Indian spice mixture that is cooked in butter. The *tadka* is stirred into a dish at the end of its cooking to boost the flavor. You could make this pilaf the center of your meal by serving it with some steamed spinach or Swiss chard and some steamed carrots.

1 cup uncooked long-grain brown rice
3¼ cups water
1 cup dried green or yellow split peas
1 teaspoon salt, or a bit more, to taste
2 tablespoons butter
½ cup minced onion
2 teaspoons minced fresh ginger
½ teaspoon ground cardamom
½ teaspoon ground cloves
¼ teaspoon ground cinnamon

**1.** In a saucepan, combine the rice and 2 cups water. Let them come to a simmer, then cover the pan, and turn the heat to low. Continue to simmer the rice for 10 minutes.

**2.** Add to the saucepan the split peas, 1¼ cups water, and 1 teaspoon salt. Bring the ingredients to a simmer over high heat, then cover the pan, and turn the heat to low. Let the contents simmer gently for 35 to 40 minutes, or until the split peas and rice are tender. Take the pan off the heat, but keep it covered.

**3.** Make the *tadka:* In a skillet, heat the butter over medium heat. Add the onions, and sauté them for 2 minutes, stirring frequently. Add the ginger and ground spices. Sauté, stirring constantly, for 1 minute. Then, using a plastic spatula, transfer the *tadka* to the pilaf. Stir the pilaf well, taste it, and add a little more salt, if you like. Serve the pilaf right away, or chill it, and reheat it later in a microwave or in a large pan over low heat with ¼ cup water.

*Serves 4*

# Smokin' Beans

Black beans cooked with onion, garlic, chipotles, and cilantro make for good comfort food. Cilantro stems, often thrown out, impart their savory flavor to these beans; you can save the leaves for another purpose. Chipotles provide smokiness as well as a bit of fire. Smokin' Beans are good in a burrito, and also make a great brunch dish when spooned over cornbread, topped with a fried egg, then topped with salsa.

1 pound dried black beans

10 cups or more water

2 to 3 chipotle peppers, dried and soaked in hot water for 30 minutes, or canned in adobo sauce

2 teaspoons ground cumin seeds

1 cup chopped onion

2 large garlic cloves, minced

1 cup minced cilantro stems

1 to 2 teaspoons salt

## How to Eat Beans

*Whether you make Smokin' Beans or a facsimile using canned beans and a drop or two of liquid smoke, there are many ways to use smoky black beans. Eat them along with some rice and roasted vegetables, in a taco or quesadilla, or in Chilaquiles (page 410). Or ladle the beans into a shallow bowl, spread some spicy salsa on top, and serve them with tortilla chips for dipping. Or make a four-layer dip: Put the beans into a shallow casserole dish, then add layers of grated cheddar cheese, guacamole, and sour cream. Serve the dip either cold or hot. You can also turn the beans into a soup by thinning them with Roasted Vegetable Stock (page 80).*

**1.** Soak the beans overnight in at least 3 quarts of water, or use the quick-soak method: Bring a large pot of water to a boil, and add the beans. Boil them for 5 minutes, then let them soak in the water for 1 hour. After soaking the beans according to either method, drain them and rinse them well.

**2.** In a large pot, combine the beans, 10 cups water, and the chipotles, cumin, onion, and garlic. Bring the mixture to a boil, then turn down the heat, and simmer for 60 minutes. Add the cilantro stems and salt, and continue to cook the beans, adding water if they become too dry, for 30 minutes or until they are very tender.

**3.** If you used dried chipotles, retrieve them from the beans, and split them open. Remove the seeds. Mince the chipotles, and return them to the beans. Add some of the seeds if you'd like more heat. Serve the beans hot. They will keep for 4 days, covered, in the refrigerator.

**Variation:** If you're really daring, add some liquid smoke to the black beans instead of the chipotles. The beans won't be hot, just smoky—but, boy will they be smoky! A restaurant near my house cooks black beans this way, and the flavor (and aroma) is delicious, especially when the beans are served in burritos. Add the liquid smoke when the beans are fully cooked. Start with just ¼ teaspoon, and taste the beans before adding more. My favorite brand of liquid smoke—and the flavor does vary among brands—is Gerwer Tex-Mex Mesquite Liquid Smoke, an all-natural product available in health-food stores and some supermarkets.

Serves 6

# Main Dishes

# Rice—
## White, Black, Brown, & Wild

# Indian Spiced Rice

This simple rice dish doesn't take much longer to prepare than the rice itself. It is also one of those dishes that can often be made without any grocery shopping, because the ingredients are likely to be in the kitchen already. A simple salad of bibb lettuce, red onion, and orange, with a balsamic vinegar and olive oil dressing, would go nicely with this dish.

1 tablespoon canola or corn oil

1 cup chopped onion

1 tablespoon minced fresh ginger

1 garlic clove, minced

1/2 teaspoon ground coriander seeds

1/2 teaspoon ground cardamom

1/4 teaspoon fresh-ground nutmeg

1/2 teaspoon ground or whole cumin seeds

1 1/4 cups uncooked jasmine or other long-grain white rice

3/4 teaspoon salt

1/2 cup dried lentils (optional)

2 1/2 or 3 cups water

1 russet potato, peeled and cut into 1/2-inch cubes

1 small yellow or red bell pepper, seeded and minced

1/2 cup peas

3 tablespoons raisins

1 tablespoon butter (optional)

**1.** In a large skillet or saucepan, heat the oil over medium heat. Add the onions, and cook, stirring frequently, until they have softened. Add the ginger, garlic, coriander, cardamom, nutmeg, and cumin. Cook for 3 minutes more, stirring frequently.

**2.** Add the rice, and sauté for 2 minutes, stirring constantly. Add the salt and, if you like, the lentils. Add 3 cups water if you're using the lentils, or 2½ cups water if you're not. Add the potato, and cover the pan. Bring the mixture to a boil, then turn the heat to the lowest setting. After 10 minutes, lift the lid and add the bell pepper, peas, and raisins. Stir well, then cover the rice again. Cook 10 minutes more, or until the rice, potatoes, and lentils (if you're using them) are tender.

**3.** Stir in the butter, if you like. Serve immediately.

Serves 4

# Home-style Brown Rice Pilaf

My friend Amy grew up on this dish, and she still eats it regularly. I myself could eat it twice a week, and not get tired of it. It's comfort food at its best, with flavors mild and enjoyable. It's simple to make, and it's quite nutritious. The kind of rice you use is up to you—long- or short-grain brown rice, brown basmati rice, wehani rice—any of these will do. You can even use leftover rice; add 2 cups of it in step 3, and heat it thoroughly in the pilaf.

1½ cups water
½ teaspoon salt
3/4 cup uncooked brown rice
3 tablespoons butter
1½ cups chopped onions
1 garlic clove, minced
2 medium carrots, sliced into ¼-inch-thick
    rounds
2 cups sliced fresh mushrooms
1 cup cooked chickpeas (garbanzo beans)
2 eggs, beaten
Fresh-ground black pepper to taste
¼ cup chopped parsley or cilantro
20 toasted cashews or almonds, coarsely chopped
Soy sauce

**1.** In a saucepan, bring the water and salt to a boil, and add the rice. Bring the contents back to a boil, cover the pan, and turn the heat to the lowest setting. Simmer for 45 to 50 minutes, or until the rice is tender.

**2.** About 20 minutes before the rice is done, heat the butter in a large skillet over medium heat. Add the onions, and sauté, stirring frequently, until they soften, about 5 minutes. Add the garlic and the carrots, and continue to sauté, stirring often, for 5 more minutes. Add the mushrooms, and cook for another 10 minutes, stirring often, until the mushrooms are beginning to brown. Add the chickpeas, and cook, stirring, for 1 minute. When the rice is ready and you are ready to eat, pour the eggs into the skillet, and cook the mixture, stirring constantly, until the eggs are just set, about 2 minutes.

**3.** Take the egg-mushroom mixture off the heat, and stir in the pepper, the parsley or cilantro, and the cashews or almonds. Add the cooked hot rice, and stir well. Serve the pilaf along with soy sauce for adding at the table.

Serves 4

# Dirty Rice

This no-fuss dish is popular along the Texas-Mexico border. For an accompaniment, I suggest fried plantains. Peel and slice yellow (medium-ripe) plantains, and pan-fry them in olive oil with a touch of salt and pepper. If you want to get fancier, try Sweet Fried Plantains, page 57.

◾▪◾▪◾▪◾▪◾

2 tablespoons olive oil
3 garlic cloves, minced
1 cup chopped onion
1 green bell pepper, seeded and chopped
1 tablespoon chili powder
2 teaspoons ground annatto seeds (optional; see the Note)

1/4 teaspoon chile flakes or ground chiltepin
   peppers
1 teaspoon ground cumin seeds
1/4 teaspoon ground cinnamon
1 1/3 cups uncooked long-grain white rice
2 3/4 cups water
1 teaspoon salt, plus more to taste
3 plum tomatoes, chopped fine
1 1/3 cups blanched corn kernels (from about
   2 ears)
1 cup cooked and rinsed black beans
1/4 cup toasted pine nuts
Fresh-ground black pepper to taste
1 small red onion, sliced thin
1 tablespoon lime juice (from about 1/2 lime)
2 tablespoons chopped cilantro (optional)
1 lime, cut into 8 wedges

**1.** In a heavy saucepan, heat 1 tablespoon of the olive oil over medium heat. Add the garlic and the chopped onions. Sauté for 5 minutes, stirring frequently, then add the bell pepper, chili powder, ground annatto if you like, chile flakes or ground chiltepíns, cumin, and cinnamon. Sauté, stirring, for 2 minutes. Add the rice, and stir well. Add the water and 1 teaspoon salt. Bring the rice to a boil over high heat, then cover the pan, and turn the heat to low. Simmer the rice for 25 minutes.

**2.** When the rice is cooked, add the tomatoes, corn, black beans, and pine nuts. Stir well, add the salt, pepper, and lime juice, and turn up the heat. When the mixture is heated through, spoon it onto plates, and top with the sliced red onion and cilantro. Serve a wedge or two of lime with each plate, for squeezing over the rice.

Variations: Feel free to improvise on this recipe. Add chunks of roasted yam, sweet potato, or russet potato. Use a poblano pepper instead of the green bell pepper if you want more kick. Roasted fennel or carrot would also be nice. Try adding a chopped canned chipotle pepper in step 2, along with the tomatoes.

**Note:** Annatto seeds, also called achiote seeds, can be found in Latin American markets. They add a slight musky flavor and, more importantly, an attractive rusty red color. Because the seeds are quite hard, you'll need to grind them in a spice mill for about 1 minute.

Serves 4 to 6

# Basmati Rice with Chard, Olives, and Beans

The flavors of celery seed and garlic perfume this healthful meal. Whole unpitted olives enhance the appearance of this dish, but you can use pitted olives if you prefer.

2 tablespoons olive oil
1½ cups sliced onions
¼ teaspoon celery seeds
1½ cups uncooked basmati rice
3 cups water
1 teaspoon salt
1 pound Swiss chard
2 large garlic cloves, minced
2 tablespoons white wine or sherry
20 Kalamata olives
1 15-ounce can cannellini or navy beans, undrained, or 1½ cups cooked beans plus ½ cup water
Fresh-ground black pepper to taste
2 tablespoons chopped parsley

**1.** In a heavy saucepan, heat 1 tablespoon of the olive oil over medium heat. Add the sliced onions, and sauté them, stirring frequently, for 5 minutes or until they have softened. Add the celery seeds and the rice. Stir constantly for 1 minute, then add

# Rice: The Long and Short of It

**ARBORIO RICE.** Imported from Italy, this rice is so short-grained it is almost round. It's also extra starchy, so that the cooked rice seems creamy. This is the classic rice used in risotto. It is also wonderful in rice pudding.

*To cook:* To serve four, start with 1¼ cups uncooked rice. Sauté the rice in butter or olive oil. Stirring frequently, add a glass of white wine, and then add some hot broth or water in small amounts until the risotto is al dente (you'll need about four parts liquid to one part rice). For more precise instructions, see the risotto recipes in this chapter.

**BASMATI RICE, WHITE.** Named after a fragrant flower that grows in Southeast Asia, this long-grain rice has a luscious floral aroma. Available in many supermarkets, Asian markets, and specialty food stores as well as Indian groceries, basmati rice is a perfect match for most curries (Thai or Indian) as well as various pilafs.

*To cook:* Rinse basmati rice with water to prevent the grains from sticking together. Bring 1½ cups salted water to a boil, and add 1 cup rice. Cover the pan, reduce the heat to the lowest setting, and simmer the rice for 20 minutes. You should have 2½ cups cooked rice.

**BASMATI RICE, WHOLE-GRAIN.** This doesn't have nearly the flavor or aroma of white basmati rice, but it contains more fiber and nutrients. Look for brown basmati rice in whole-foods stores; some supermarkets carry it, too.

*To cook:* Use 2 cups water for every 1 cup rice. Simmer the rice over low heat for 45 minutes. One cup raw rice makes 3 cups cooked rice.

**BLACK SWEET RICE.** Black rice is a staple of Southeast Asia and India. Available in some Asian markets, it is indeed black on the outside (that is, the bran is black), and when cooked the rice turns a racy purplish-black. Black rice has a strong woodsy flavor; I find it best mixed with an equal volume of long-grain white rice (the unusual color is retained, but the flavor is better this way). Serve black rice with stir-fried vegetables or any Asian-inspired dish.

*To cook:* Bring 3 cups salted water to a boil, add ½ cup black rice, cover the pan, and reduce the heat. Cook for 20 minutes, then add ½ cup white rice, and stir. Cook the rice over low heat, covered, 30 minutes more, or until it is tender. You should have 2½ cups cooked rice.

**BROWN RICE, SHORT-GRAIN.** Slightly sticky, rich in fiber, and a bit sweeter than long-grain brown rice, short-grain brown rice has a pleasing nutty flavor that is perfect for winter meals. Serve it with stir-fried dishes, or stuff vegetables such as acorn squash or peppers with a short-grain brown rice pilaf. Short-grain brown rice is available in whole-foods stores.

*To cook:* Bring 2 cups salted water to a boil, and add 1 cup rice. Reduce the heat, and cover the pan. Cook for 45 to 50 minutes over low heat. You should have 3 cups cooked rice.

**BROWN RICE, LONG-GRAIN.** One of my favorites, this rice is rich in fiber and has a buttery, nutty flavor. Serve it with roasted vegetables and stir-fried dishes; use it in pilafs and rice salads. Sold in supermarkets, this rice is delicious plain, but it's also good with flavor enhancers such as cumin, nutmeg, fresh ginger, pecans, ground coriander, and caramelized onion.
*To cook:* Bring 2 cups salted water to a boil. Add 1 cup rice, reduce the heat, and cover the pan. Cook the rice over low heat for 45 minutes. You should have 3 cups cooked rice.

**GLUTINOUS (SWEET) RICE.** This white rice, sold in Asian markets, is very, very sticky. It is used to make sweets in tropical Asia, and in China it is used in poultry stuffings. In Japan, sweet rice is steamed, mashed, then dried to form *mochi,* rice cakes.
*To cook:* Soak 1 cup rice in water overnight, then drain the rice. Bring 1 cup salted water to a boil, add the drained rice, reduce the heat, and cover the pan. Cook the rice for 15 minutes over low heat. You should have 2 cups cooked rice.

**JASMINE RICE.** Thailand is the major producer of this subtly fragrant long-grain rice. I use it quite often because it is so wonderfully versatile. It can absorb many flavors, during or after cooking. Look for jasmine rice in Asian markets. Some supermarkets carry it, too.
*To cook:* Bring 1¾ cups salted water to a boil. Add 1 cup rice, reduce the heat, and cover the pan. Cook the rice for 20 minutes over low heat. You should have 2¾ cups cooked rice. Jasmine rice also makes super rice pudding.

**TEX-MATI RICE.** This Texas variety was developed as a less expensive alternative to basmati rice. Tex-mati rice is less floral in flavor and aroma than basmati, and therefore more versatile but also less interesting.
*To cook:* Rinse Tex-mati rice with water to prevent the grains from sticking together. Bring 1½ cups salted water to a boil, and add 1 cup rice. Cover the pan, reduce the heat to the lowest setting, and simmer the rice for 20 minutes. You should have 2½ cups cooked rice.

**WEHANI RICE.** Grown in California, this is a basmati hybrid sold in whole-grain form, that is, with its bran intact. Its particular bran gives wehani a rust color. Mix wehani with other rice varieties in pilafs (with dried fruits) and in rice cakes. Wehani is also nice in rice salads.
*To cook:* Bring 2 cups salted water to a boil. Add 1 cup rice, reduce the heat, and cover the pan. Cook the rice over low heat for 45 minutes. You should have 3 cups cooked rice.

**WHITE RICE, SHORT-GRAIN (SUSHI-STYLE RICE).** Grown in California as well as Japan, this is the favorite rice of the Japanese, and the only kind used for authentic sushi. Short-grain white rice is sold in supermarkets as well as Asian markets. I prefer Kokuho brand, but other chefs rely on Nishiki brand.
*To cook:* Rinse 1 cup rice in a colander for 5 minutes. Let the rice drain for 30 minutes. Bring the rice with 1 cup water to a boil. Turn the heat to low, cover the pan, and cook for 15 minutes. Remove the rice from the heat, and let it stand 10 minutes, covered. You should have 2 cups cooked rice.

the 3 cups water and the salt. Cover the pan, bring the rice to a boil, and then turn the heat to low. Simmer the rice for 20 minutes.

**2.** While the rice cooks, use a paring knife to cut out any Swiss chard stems wider than 1 inch (see page 458 for ideas on using these separately). Slice the rest of the chard into ½-inch crosswise strips.

**3.** About 10 minutes before the rice is ready, heat the remaining 1 tablespoon olive oil in a large skillet over medium-high heat. Add the garlic and the chard, and cook them, stirring frequently, for 5 minutes. Transfer the chard to a plate, then add to the skillet the wine or sherry, the olives, and the beans with their liquid or ½ cup water. Bring the mixture to a simmer, and cook it until the beans are heated through. Season with pepper. Return the chard to the pan, add the rice, and mix well. Garnish with the parsley, and serve.

Serves 4

# Jamaican Rice Mix-Up

The same interplay of crunchy and soft textures that you find in Chinese fried rice are also at work in this Jamaican rice pilaf. The flavors of the Caribbean—curry, pumpkin, ginger, and allspice—are unmistakable.

1 small sugar pumpkin or pie pumpkin, about
    2 pounds, or 1 small butternut squash
2 cups water
1 cup uncooked long-grain rice
1 teaspoon salt
2 tablespoons canola or corn oil, plus a little
    more for pan-frying the plantains

## Collard Greens

*W*ondering what to do with left-over collard greens? I like to slice the greens thin (I usually roll them first) and pan-fry them with olive oil and garlic over high heat, stirring constantly. After a minute or so, I add a teaspoon or two of balsamic vinegar, then I continue to cook the greens for another minute. Sometimes I add pine nuts as well. This method is much quicker and, to my palate, tastier than the long, slow braising that is done in the South.

*The tastiest collard greens are available during the fall and winter months. Like many leafy greens, collard is not only high in vitamins and fiber, but it also contains enzymes that protect against cancer.*

2 medium onions, minced
1 tablespoon minced fresh ginger
2 garlic cloves, minced
½ teaspoon allspice
1 tablespoon curry powder, store-bought or homemade (page 36)
1 jalapeño pepper, minced (optional)
2 cups thinly sliced collard greens, beet greens, or mustard greens
1 cup cooked black beans
Salt and fresh-ground black pepper to taste
2 ripe plantains or large ripe bananas (optional)
1 tomato, cut into ½-inch cubes

**1.** Preheat the oven to 400°. Cut the pumpkin or squash in half. Scoop out the seeds with a metal spoon, and discard them. Place the halves face down on a baking sheet. Bake the pumpkin or squash for 1 hour or until it is easily pierced with a sharp knife. Remove it from the pan and let it cool slightly.

**2.** While the pumpkin or squash cools, bring the water to a boil in a medium saucepan. Add the rice and salt, and bring the rice to a boil. Cover the pan, and reduce the heat to low. Steam the rice for 20 minutes.

**3.** While the rice cooks, heat the oil in a large skillet. Add the onions, and cook them, stirring occasionally, for about 10 minutes, until they begin to brown. Add the ginger, the garlic, the allspice, the curry powder, and, if you like, the jalapeño. Cook for 2 to 3 minutes more. Remove the pan from the heat.

**4.** When the pumpkin has cooled slightly, scoop out the flesh, and discard the skin. Chop the flesh into large pieces.

**5.** When the rice is ready, reheat the onion mixture over medium heat. Add the rice, and cook, stirring occasionally, for 5 minutes. Add the greens, toss well, and continue to cook for 5 minutes more. Add the pumpkin or squash and the black beans, and toss again. Season with salt and pepper.

**6.** If you'd like to garnish the dish with plantains or bananas, slice them in half lengthwise. Lightly coat a non-stick skillet with canola or corn oil, and set it over medium high heat. Pan-fry the plantains or bananas until they are golden, about 1 to 2 minutes per side, turning them carefully with a spatula. Transfer them to a paper towel.

**7.** Spoon the rice mixture onto plates. Top it with a little chopped tomato for color, and serve the plantain or banana slices alongside the rice.

Serves 4 to 6

# Basmati Spinach Ragout

Combining basmati rice, spinach, and the provocative spices of southern India, this stew is fast, filling, and good to the very last grain. If you're seeking additional protein, note the Variation at the end of the recipe. This is a perfect accompaniment for Naan (Indian bread, page 16).

1½ teaspoons coriander seeds
1 teaspoon brown mustard seeds
1 teaspoon cumin seeds
½ teaspoon black peppercorns
¼ cup unsweetened flaked coconut
1 tablespoon canola or corn oil
1 tablespoon minced fresh ginger
1 jalapeño pepper, seeded and minced
1 14-ounce can coconut milk
1 cup uncooked white basmati rice
4½ cups water
½ teaspoon salt
2 carrots, peeled and sliced into ½-inch-thick
    half-rounds

10 ounces spinach, large stems removed
Salt and fresh-ground black pepper to taste

**1.** In a small skillet over medium heat, toast the coriander, mustard, cumin, and peppercorns, stirring constantly, until the spices become fragrant. Grind them fine in a blender or spice mill. Add the flaked coconut to the spices, and grind again. Set the mixture aside.

**2.** In a stockpot or large saucepan, heat the oil over medium heat. Add the ginger and jalapeño, and cook for 1 minute. Add the coconut milk, rice, water, and salt. Over high heat, bring the mixture to a boil, stirring constantly. Then cover the pan, and turn the heat to low.

**3.** When the stew has simmered for 10 minutes, add the carrots. Cover the pan again, and cook for 8 minutes, stirring once or twice to keep the rice from sticking to the bottom of the pan. Stir in the spice-coconut mixture. If the carrots and rice are not yet tender, cook the stew a few more minutes. When they are tender, stir in the spinach (you may need to do this in two batches, waiting a minute or so for the first batch to wilt). Let the stew cook, covered, for another minute, then stir it, season it to taste with salt and pepper, and serve it in large bowls with crusty bread on the side.

**Variation:** For a more protein-rich meal, tofu works very well in this dish. Use half of a 16-ounce package of firm tofu, and cut it into ½-inch cubes. Add the tofu to the stew along with the spices. A bit of extra salt will be needed, too.

**Note:** If you're curious about asafetida, as I am, this is a good dish in which to try a bit. Found in Indian markets, asafetida powder is the earthy-smelling ground resin of a fennel-like plant. Add ½ to 1 teaspoon to the stew along with the spice-coconut mixture.

Serves 4

## Basmati Rice

With a fragrance reminiscent of toasted nuts and spring roses, basmati rice is delectable. It works well with stews, chili, and Southeast Asian dishes as well as Indian curries. Grown in Northern India and Pakistan, as it has been for thousands of years, basmati rice is aged after harvest for a year to develop its flavor fully. Texmati rice, a strain of basmati now grown in Texas, is less intensely perfumed and less nutty. Whole-grain or brown basmati, available in many whole-foods stores, is also less aromatic than white basmati, but it is richer in nutrients and fiber.

# Braised Cabbage and Basmati Rice

I learned to love butter-braised cabbage while working at La Varenne, a cooking school in France. Chambrette, the head chef, would let the cabbage stew for an hour or so with no other liquid but melted butter (and a lot of it). The cabbage would then be so tender that it would practically dissolve in your mouth. Here I've revised the concept to use much less butter. This hearty pilaf contains basmati rice, tarragon, and lentils as well as braised cabbage. Serve it along with a simple salad.

**BRAISED CABBAGE:**

2 tablespoons butter

1 cup finely chopped onions

1 large garlic clove, minced

4 cups thinly sliced green cabbage, about 2/3 of
     a small head

1/2 cup water

Salt and fresh-ground black pepper to taste

**PILAF:**

2 cups water

2/3 cup white wine

1 1/3 cups uncooked basmati rice

1/2 cup dried *lentilles du Puy* (French lentils) or
     brown lentils

1/2 teaspoon salt, plus more to taste

1 teaspoon chopped fresh tarragon, or
     1/2 teaspoon dried tarragon

1 cup cherry tomato halves

Fresh-ground black pepper to taste

**1.** In a large, heavy skillet, melt the butter over medium heat. Sauté the onions, stirring frequently, for 5 minutes or until they have softened. Add the garlic, the cabbage, ½ cup water, and salt and pepper. Cover the skillet, and let the cabbage cook for 10 minutes, checking periodically to make sure that it's not scorching. Remove the lid, and let the cabbage cook for 20 minutes more over medium-low heat, stirring every 5 minutes or so.

**2.** While the cabbage cooks, start the pilaf: In a saucepan, bring the 2 cups water to a boil with the wine. Add the rice, the lentils, the ½ teaspoon salt, and the tarragon. Cover the pan, and turn the heat to low. Cook for 20 to 25 minutes or until the rice and lentils are tender.

**3.** Stir the braised cabbage into the rice. Add the cherry tomatoes, season with salt and pepper, and stir gently. Serve hot.

Serves 4

# Thai Tofu with Red Curry Sauce over Coconut-Scallion Rice

Even if tofu turns you off, try this dish. The flavors will win you over. The fragrance of the ground cilantro and lime leaves, the richness of the toasted ground peanuts, and the heat of the red chile together create a sauce that makes tofu taste great.

The coconut rice is hearty enough to be the centerpiece of a meal (try the rice topped with grilled or pan-fried vegetables). I use canned coconut milk, and I reduce the fat by taking out a lot of the solids in the milk. If you'd like to do this, a 14-ounce can of coconut milk will be just the amount you need.

For the heat in this dish, I like to use Panda Hot Chili Sauce, which comes in a squeeze bottle, or Lan Chi Chilli Paste with Garlic. Both are available in Asian markets.

10 dried kaffir lime leaves (available in Asian
    markets), or 1½ teaspoons grated
    lime rind
1¼ cups (10 ounces) coconut milk
2¾ cups water
1 teaspoon salt
1½ cups jasmine, basmati, or regular long-grain
    white rice
1 bunch cilantro, coarsely chopped (you'll need
    ⅔ cup for the sauce and 2 tablespoons for
    garnish)
2 large garlic cloves, cut in half
¼ cup dry-roasted, unsalted peanuts
1 tablespoon Thai or Vietnamese fish sauce, or
    ½ teaspoon salt
¼ cup canola or corn oil
3 tablespoons hot chile sauce, or 2 tablespoons
    chile paste
1 16-ounce package firm tofu, patted dry and cut
    into ½-inch cubes
½ bunch broccoli, cut into small pieces (about
    4 cups)
1 cup minced scallions, both green and white
    parts

**1.** Soak the kaffir lime leaves in 1 quart very hot water for 30 minutes.

**2.** While the leaves soak, bring the coconut milk, 2¼ cups of the water, and the 1 teaspoon salt to a boil, then add the rice. Cover the pan, and reduce the heat to the lowest setting. Let the rice cook, covered, for 25 minutes.

**3.** Drain the lime leaves, and, with a very sharp knife, chop them into pea-sized pieces. In a food processor or blender, combine the lime leaves (or lime rind), ⅔ cup chopped cilantro, the garlic cloves, and the peanuts. Run the machine in spurts until the lime leaves are pulverized, pushing them down with a rubber spatula if necessary. Slowly, with the machine running, add the fish sauce (or ½ teaspoon salt) and 3 tablespoons of the oil, then add the chile sauce or paste. Transfer the mixture to a small bowl.

**4.** Into a wok or a non-stick skillet, over high heat, pour the remaining 1 tablespoon oil. Add the tofu, and cook until the pieces form a golden crust on the bottom. Then turn them with a spatula, and let the tofu form more golden crust on the other side. Transfer the tofu to a plate.

**5.** Into the same wok or skillet, put the broccoli and the remaining ½ cup water. Cover, and steam the broccoli for 2 minutes. Stir in the lime leaf–peanut paste, and cook, stirring, for 1 minute more. Add the tofu, and toss.

**6.** Stir the scallions into the rice. Mound the rice on plates, and spoon the tofu and sauce around it. Sprinkle with 2 tablespoons chopped cilantro, and serve.

Serves 4

# Fennel Risotto

Bulb fennel, or finocchio, is a sensual vegetable, with a curvaceous shape and a subtle and alluring licorice flavor. When fennel is combined with Arborio rice and Barsac wine, I'll take it over a good-looking man any day (excluding Harrison Ford).

5 cups water, Basic Vegetable Stock (page 79), or Carrot-Fennel Broth (page 83)
3/4 cup Barsac wine (or Riesling, Gewürztraminer, or any sweet or semi-sweet white wine)
2 cups minced fennel bulb, and 3 tablespoons chopped fennel leaves
1 large garlic clove, minced
1/4 cup heavy cream

2 small plum tomatoes, seeded and chopped fine
1/2 teaspoon salt
1 1/2 tablespoons olive oil
1 cup minced onion
1 teaspoon dried thyme
1 1/4 cups uncooked Arborio rice
1/3 cup grated Parmesan cheese, or a bit more, to taste
Salt and fresh-ground black pepper to taste
2 tablespoons chopped parsley

**1.** Make the sauce: In a heavy saucepan, place ½ cup of the water or stock, ½ cup of the wine, 1 cup of the minced fennel bulb, the garlic, and the cream, and stir to combine. Bring the sauce to a boil, and let it boil hard for 10 minutes. Reduce the heat, add the tomatoes and the chopped fennel leaves, and simmer for another 5 minutes. Remove the pan from the heat. There should be about 1¼ cups sauce.

**2.** Heat the remaining 4½ cups water or stock with the salt in a saucepan until the liquid is very hot, then turn the heat to low.

**3.** Heat the olive oil in a heavy saucepan over medium-high heat. Add the onions and the remaining 1 cup minced fennel. Cook for 5 minutes. Add the thyme and the rice, and stir to coat the rice with the oil. Add the remaining ¼ cup of the wine and ½ cup of the hot water or stock. Wait until the liquid is absorbed, then add another ½ cup of the liquid. Continue adding the stock or water in this fashion; do not make the next addition until the liquid from the previous one is absorbed. Stir often to keep the rice from sticking. After about 18 to 20 minutes, most of the liquid should be used, and the rice should be tender but still slightly chewy. Stir in ⅓ cup Parmesan cheese, and add salt, pepper, and, if you like, a bit more Parmesan.

**4.** Reheat the sauce, and spoon the risotto onto four plates. Drizzle the sauce around each mound, or make a well in the middle of the mound and spoon the sauce into it. Sprinkle with the chopped parsley, and serve.

Serves 4

## Fennel—or Is It Anise?

*A*lthough most cookbooks and magazines refer to this vegetable as fennel, many supermarkets label it anise. Fennel grown as a vegetable—finocchio *to Italians—has a large, white, bulbous base and long green stalks adorned with leaves like those of dill. The flavor of fennel is reminiscent of licorice, but if you don't like licorice you'll probably still like fennel when it is roasted, braised, grilled, or cooked in any way, because its flavor becomes sweet and subtle. The stalks as well as the bulb can be cooked and eaten, and the feathery leaves can be chopped and used as a fresh herb. I add chopped fennel leaves to sour cream and minced onion to create a quick dip for raw vegetables.*

# Wild Risotto

The word *wild* in the title refers not only to the wild rice in this dish, but also to my wildly experimental sous-chef Loretta. One day, during her tarragon phase, she combined tarragon and coconut milk in an Italian-style risotto without thinking twice about it. I didn't think the flavors would mesh. But the dish was so good that I ate it until my stomach hurt. I knew then that I had to include the recipe in this book.

If you open a can of coconut milk to make this dish, freeze the remainder for later use.

1 cup water
¼ cup uncooked wild rice
4 cups water or Basic Vegetable Stock (page 79)
2 teaspoons olive oil
6 scallions, both white and green parts, chopped fine
2 garlic cloves, minced
1½ cups uncooked Arborio rice
½ cup dry white wine
1 teaspoon chopped fresh tarragon, or
   ½ teaspoon dried tarragon
2 plum tomatoes, chopped
⅔ cup coconut milk
1 cup fresh, or frozen and thawed, peas

**1.** In a saucepan, bring the 1 cup water to a boil. Add the wild rice, cover the pan, and reduce the heat. Simmer 25 minutes. Drain the rice.

**2.** In a saucepan, bring the 4 cups water or stock to a simmer, and keep it hot.

**3.** In a large skillet, heat the olive oil. Sauté the scallions and garlic over medium-high heat for 1 minute. Add the Arborio rice, and stir it for 2 minutes. Add the wine, the wild rice, and the tarragon. Cook, stirring frequently, for 2 minutes, then add

½ cup of the heated stock or water. Stir frequently until the liquid is absorbed, then add ½ cup more water or stock. Continue adding the water or stock in this manner, waiting between additions until the liquid is absorbed and stirring frequently. After about 18 to 20 minutes, most of the liquid should be used, and the rice should be tender but still slightly chewy.

**4.** When all of the stock or water is used, add the tomatoes, coconut milk, and peas. Stir the mixture, and simmer it, stirring often, until most of the liquid is absorbed. Serve at once.

Serves 4

# Herbed Risotto
# with Pipérade

A dish from Basque country, pipérade is a combination of cooked tomatoes, bell peppers, onions, and olive oil. Here, on each plate, pipérade is ladled into a well in a mound of herbed risotto, and fresh herbs are sprinkled over. With a grilled slice of a sourdough baguette at the edge of the plate, the dinner becomes quite special.

**PIPÉRADE:**
2 large ripe tomatoes, cored
2 quarts boiling water
1 tablespoon olive oil
2 cups sliced onions
1 garlic clove, minced
2 red bell peppers, seeded and cut into thin
   julienne strips
2 green bell peppers, seeded and cut into thin
   julienne strips
Salt and fresh-ground black pepper to taste
½ teaspoon chile flakes (optional)

**RISOTTO:**

4½ cups water or Basic Vegetable Stock
   (page 79)
2 teaspoons olive oil
4 shallots, minced
1½ cups uncooked Arborio rice
½ cup white wine
1 teaspoon salt
Fresh-ground black pepper to taste
½ cup grated Parmesan cheese
½ cup combined chopped basil and parsley

**1.** Prepare the pipérade: Put the cored tomatoes into a nonreactive bowl. Pour the boiling water over them and let them sit for 1 minute. Drain the tomatoes, rinse them under cold water, and skin them. Chop the tomatoes, and set them aside.

**2.** In a large skillet over medium heat, heat the oil. Add the onions, and cook, stirring frequently, until they soften. Add the garlic and bell peppers. Cook for 15 minutes over medium-low heat, stirring occasionally. Add the tomatoes, salt, and pepper, and, if you like, the chile flakes, and cook for 5 more minutes, stirring often. Remove the pan from the heat.

**3.** Prepare the risotto: Bring the water or stock to a simmer, and keep it hot. In a heavy saucepan, heat the olive oil over medium-high heat, and add the shallots. Cook for 2 minutes, stirring, then add the rice, and stir it over the heat for 1 minute. Add the wine, the salt, and ½ cup of the water or stock. Stir frequently until the liquid is absorbed, then add ½ cup more water or stock, and stir until it is absorbed. Continue adding the water or stock in this manner until all of it is used, about 18 to 20 minutes.

**4.** When all of the liquid is absorbed and the rice grains are tender but still slightly chewy, stir in the pepper and grated Parmesan. Then stir in all but 2 tablespoons of the herbs. Reheat the pipérade. Spoon the risotto onto plates, and make a depression in the middle of each mound. Spoon the pipérade into the wells, sprinkle with the remaining chopped herbs, and serve.

Serves 4

# Saffron Risotto
# with Mushrooms

The unique fragrance and flavor of saffron can render a risotto irresistible. But golden, saffron-scented risotto is even more heavenly when surrounded by a moat of garlicky sherried mushrooms, as in this recipe.

**RISOTTO:**
1 tablespoon olive oil
1 cup minced onion
1 garlic clove, minced
1/2 cup dry white wine
1 cup uncooked Arborio rice
1/2 teaspoon salt
1 large pinch saffron threads
2²/₃ to 3 cups water, Basic Vegetable Stock
    (page 79), or Roasted Vegetable Stock
    (page 80), kept at a slow simmer on the
    stove
1/2 cup grated Parmesan or Asiago cheese
Salt and fresh-ground black pepper to taste

**MUSHROOM MOAT:**
1 tablespoon butter
1 tablespoon olive, canola, or corn oil
2 large garlic cloves, minced
4 cups chopped white button, portobello, or
    shiitake mushrooms
1 red bell pepper, seeded and chopped fine
1/4 cup sherry
Salt and fresh-ground black pepper to taste

**GARNISH:**
3 tablespoons finely chopped parsley

## Missing the Meat

❀

*I*f you ever crave the flavor and heartiness of meat but don't want to eat it, try satisfying your craving with one of these richly flavored foods: mushrooms, winter squash, roasted garlic, caramelized onions, smoked cheese, truffle or shiitake oil, or chipotle peppers. Or turn to one of these recipes: Roasted Squash Soup (page 118), Roasted Garlic Mashers (page 191), Penne with Ancho Peppers, Tomatoes, and Corn (page 291), Mushroom Blinchiki (page 339), Portobello Burgers (page 367), Squash and Potato Enchiladas with Mole Sauce (page 403), or Smoky Mexican Lasagna (page 421).

**1.** Heat 1 tablespoon olive oil in a large saucepan over medium-high heat. Add the onion and garlic, and cook, stirring occasionally, until they have softened, about 5 minutes. Add the Arborio rice and the salt, and stir for 1 minute. Add the wine, the saffron, and ½ cup of the simmering water or stock. Cook, stirring often, until the liquid is completely absorbed, then add ½ cup more water or stock. Continue adding liquid in this manner, waiting for it to be absorbed (but continuing to stir often) before adding more, until all of the water or stock is used. Continue cooking the rice until it is tender but still slightly chewy, about 18 to 20 minutes, then stir in the Parmesan or Asiago cheese and salt and pepper.

**2.** If possible, prepare the mushrooms while the rice is cooking: Melt the butter and oil in a large skillet over medium heat. Add the garlic, and let the butter and oil bubble for 15 seconds. Add the mushrooms and red pepper, and stir. Cook the mushrooms for 7 minutes, stirring frequently. (The mushrooms will seem dry after a few minutes, but will release more moisture toward the end of this time.) Add the sherry, and let the mixture boil until the sherry is reduced by half. Season with salt and pepper.

**3.** Divide the risotto among four plates, and spoon the mushrooms around each mound. Sprinkle with chopped parsley, and serve.

Serves 4

# Risotto with Tomato, Corn, and Basil

**T**his is a risotto dish well suited for the end of summer, when the tomatoes and corn are at their best. Using milk in the risotto gives the dish a lovely richness and creaminess.

2¹/₂ cups water

2 cups whole or low-fat milk

2 tablespoons butter

1 cup minced onion

1 garlic clove, minced

3/4 cup uncooked Arborio rice

3 tablespoons sherry or white wine

1 ripe tomato, seeded and drained of juice,
    chopped fine

Kernels from 2 ears corn (about 1¹/₃ cups)

¹/₂ cup grated Parmesan cheese

¹/₂ cup basil leaves, thinly sliced

¹/₂ teaspoon salt

Fresh-ground black pepper to taste

**1.** In a saucepan, heat the water and milk to a simmer. Keep the pan over low heat.

**2.** Melt the butter in a large casserole or skillet over medium-high heat. Add the onion, and cook for 3 to 4 minutes, stirring occasionally. Add the garlic and the rice, and stir constantly for 1 minute. Add the sherry or wine, and stir until completely absorbed. Begin to add the heated milk-water mixture ½ cup at a time, stirring frequently. Wait until each addition is almost completely absorbed (but continuing to stir often) before adding the next.

**3.** When the rice has cooked for 15 minutes and most of the liquid has been incorporated, add the corn kernels and tomatoes along with the end of the milk-water mixture. Cook, stirring frequently, until the rice is tender but still slightly chewy. The risotto should take 18 to 20 minutes of cooking in all.

**4.** Stir in the Parmesan cheese, most of the basil, and the salt and pepper. Spoon the risotto immediately onto plates, top with the remaining basil strands, and serve.

Serves 4

# Zucchini Risotto Cakes
# with Provençal Sauce

These risotto cakes are a perfect entrée when your garden is overflowing with tomatoes and zucchini. The zucchini is grated and added to the risotto as it cooks. For the compote, the chopped tomatoes and onion are quickly cooked, then combined with olives and basil. This is simple food that speaks of the earth.

**RISOTTO CAKES:**

3 tablespoons olive oil

1 cup chopped onion

2 large garlic cloves, minced

3/4 cup uncooked Arborio or sushi-style white rice (I prefer Kokuho sushi rice from California)

1/2 cup white wine

1/2 teaspoon salt

2 to 2 1/2 cups water, kept at a slow simmer on the stove

1 medium zucchini, grated (about 1 1/2 cups)

2/3 cup grated Parmesan cheese

Fresh-ground black pepper to taste

**TOMATO COMPOTE:**

3 ripe medium tomatoes, chopped

1/2 cup minced onion

25 imported black olives, such as Kalamata, pitted

1/4 cup basil leaves, sliced thin

Salt and fresh-ground black pepper to taste

**GARNISH:**

Grated Parmesan cheese

1/4 cup basil leaves, sliced thin

**1.** In a large skillet, heat 1 tablespoon olive oil over medium-high heat. Add the onions, and sauté them, stirring frequently, until they soften, about 5 minutes. Add the garlic and rice, and sauté, stirring, for 2 minutes. Add the wine and salt, and cook and stir until the wine has almost evaporated. Add ½ cup of the simmering water. Let the rice cook, stirring frequently, until the water has been absorbed, then add ½ cup more water, and continue stirring. Keep adding the water, waiting for it to be absorbed (but continuing to stir often) before adding more, until all of the water is used. As you are adding the water, note when about 10 minutes have elapsed since you began adding it; at that time, stir in the grated zucchini.

When the risotto is done (after about 18 to 20 minutes), the rice will be tender but still a little chewy, and the risotto creamy but not too wet. Take the risotto off the heat, and stir in the Parmesan cheese and pepper. Transfer the risotto to a bowl, and chill it for at least ½ hour.

**2.** Make the compote: Heat the tomatoes in a skillet over medium heat. Once they are hot, add the onion. Cook, stirring frequently, for 1 minute. Then promptly take the pan off the heat. Stir in the olives, the basil, and the salt and pepper.

**3.** Make the risotto cakes: Heat the remaining 2 tablespoons oil in a heavy skillet over high heat. Form the risotto into four cakes about 1½ inches thick. When the oil is very hot, place the cakes in the skillet. Turn the heat down a bit, and sear the cakes on one side for 3 to 4 minutes, or until they are golden brown on the undersides. Flip the cakes with a spatula, and sear them on the other side for 3 minutes.

**4.** Divide the tomato-olive compote among four plates. Place a risotto cake on each plate, then garnish with some additional Parmesan cheese and basil slivers.

*Serves 4*

## Japanese Risotto?

*Some people may wonder what Japanese-style short-grain rice is doing in my risotto cake recipes when it is normally used for sushi. Here's the answer in a nutshell: at the Delux, where the entrées are all under nine dollars, I need to watch the bottom line. I wanted to try my hand at risotto cakes because I had fallen in love with them at other restaurants. But the Italian Arborio rice was definitely over my budget. So I started experimenting with less expensive rice. I knew that Japanese style short-grain rice didn't work well for classic risotto, but I happily discovered that it is more than acceptable for risotto cakes, especially if the rice is kept 'al dente.'*

# Wehani Cakes with Curried Spinach Sauce

Wehani is a red rice grown in California and available in well-stocked supermarkets and whole-foods stores. A handsome grain, it can be used like wild rice but isn't nearly as expensive. Here wehani is combined with short-grain brown rice in pan-fried cakes; the starch in the brown rice (and a sprinkling of flour) holds the cakes together. For best results, begin cooking the rice at least 2 hours before serving time. The curried spinach sauce, which takes only 15 minutes to prepare, turns the rice cakes into a tantalizing entrée.

**RICE:**
1 cup minced onion
3 small garlic cloves, minced
2¹/₂ cups water
¹/₂ teaspoon salt
¹/₂ cup uncooked wehani rice
3/4 cup uncooked short-grain brown rice

**CURRIED SPINACH SAUCE:**
1 tablespoon olive oil
1 cup minced onion
2 garlic cloves, minced
1 tablespoon minced fresh ginger
1 teaspoon ground cumin seeds
1 teaspoon ground coriander seeds
¹/₂ teaspoon ground cardamom
¹/₄ teaspoon ground white or black pepper
1 large ripe tomato, minced
10 ounces fresh spinach, coarsely chopped
    (7 to 8 cups)
¹/₃ cup water
1 to 2 pinches cayenne
¹/₂ teaspoon salt
Fresh-ground black pepper to taste

**RICE CAKES:**

1 egg, beaten

2 tablespoons flour, plus a bit more for flouring
     your hands

1 tablespoon olive oil

**1.** In a heavy saucepan, combine the onion, garlic, water, and salt. Bring the mixture to a boil, and add the wehani and brown rice. Turn the heat to low, cover the pan, and simmer the rice for 55 minutes or until it is tender but slightly chewy. Turn the cooked rice out into a bowl, and let the rice cool, uncovered, for at least 1 hour.

**2.** Make the sauce: In a large skillet, heat the olive oil over medium heat. Add the onion, garlic, and ginger, and sauté, stirring occasionally, for 5 minutes or until the onion softens. Add the cumin, coriander, cardamom, and pepper, and sauté for 2 minutes more. Add the tomato, spinach, and water, and cook for 3 minutes. Add cayenne, salt, and pepper. Remove the pan from the heat.

**3.** Make the rice cakes: In a small bowl, combine the egg and 2 tablespoons flour. Whisk well. Incorporate this mixture into the chilled rice. With well-floured hands, form four large patties from the mixture. In a large, heavy skillet, heat the olive oil over medium-high heat. When the oil is very hot, add two or more of the rice cakes, depending on the size of your skillet. Sear the cakes for about 3 to 4 minutes per side, until the surface of each cake is golden.

**4.** Reheat the sauce, and spoon some of it onto each of four plates. Place a hot patty on each plate, and serve.

**Variation:** If you can't get wehani rice, you can make the rice cakes entirely from brown rice. You'll need to start with 1¼ cups uncooked rice.

Serves 4

# Twice Wild

**W**ild rice has a wonderful, nutty flavor and is high in protein. Here I've combined wild rice and long-grain rice in a cake and served it with a sauce of mushrooms, thyme, and caramelized onions. This is an elegant dish, worthy of a special occasion. To break the cooking time into two manageable parts, cook the rice in the morning or on the day before serving.

**RICE:**
2$\frac{1}{2}$ cups water, or a bit more
$\frac{1}{2}$ teaspoon salt
$\frac{1}{3}$ cup uncooked wild rice
$\frac{2}{3}$ cup long-grain white rice

**SAUCE:**
1$\frac{1}{2}$ tablespoons butter or olive oil
2 cups thinly sliced onions
1 tablespoon fresh thyme or 1 teaspoon dried thyme
1 large carrot, peeled and chopped fine
2 garlic cloves, minced
1$\frac{1}{2}$ cups chopped portobello mushrooms
$\frac{1}{2}$ cup white wine
$\frac{3}{4}$ cup water or Basic Vegetable Stock (page 79)
3 tablespoons whole, low-fat, or nonfat sour cream
Salt and fresh-ground black pepper to taste

2 tablespoons unbleached white flour
2 eggs, beaten
$\frac{1}{4}$ cup grated Parmesan cheese (optional)
1 tablespoon olive oil, or a bit more
Thyme sprigs

**1.** In a large saucepan, bring 1½ cups water to a boil with the salt. Add the wild rice, turn the heat to low, and cover the pan. Cook the wild rice for 30 minutes. Add the white rice to the pan, stir well, and add the remaining 1 cup water. Cover the pan again, and let the rice mixture cook for 20 minutes over low heat.

Check whether both kinds of rice are tender. If not, and if all the water has been absorbed, add a bit more water, and cook the rice, covered, for 5 to 10 more minutes. Transfer the cooked rice to a large bowl, and let it cool.

**2.** While the rice is cooling, make the sauce: Heat the butter in a heavy large saucepan over medium heat. Add the onions, and cook them about 15 minutes, stirring occasionally, until they reach a mustard-brown color. Add the thyme, carrot, and garlic, and cook for 5 minutes more, stirring often. Then add the mushrooms, and cook and stir for 1 minute. Add the white wine and the water or stock, and let the sauce simmer for 5 minutes, until the liquid is reduced by about one-third. Take the pan off the heat, and stir in the sour cream, salt, and pepper. Then set the sauce aside.

**3.** When the rice is no longer hot, stir the flour, beaten eggs, and Parmesan cheese into it. Heat the olive oil in a large skillet over medium-high heat. When the oil is very hot, drop ⅓ cup of the rice mixture gently into the skillet. Flatten the rice mixture with a spatula. Add as many rice cakes as the skillet will hold without crowding. Let the cakes cook for 2 minutes per side, then transfer the cooked cakes to a paper towel–lined plate in a warm oven. Add a bit more oil to the skillet, if necessary, and cook the remaining cakes in the same fashion.

**4.** Reheat the sauce until it is hot, but do not let it boil. Ladle the sauce onto plates, lay the rice cakes in the sauce, garnish with thyme sprigs, and serve.

*Serves 4*

# Golden Rice Cakes
# with
# Sweet Potato–Ginger Sauce

Jasmine rice, a traditional crop in Thailand, has been grown in the United States since 1989. Its flavor is subtly sweet, and the grains become slightly sticky once cooked. Here jasmine rice is formed into cakes with crunchy crusts and light, moist interiors. Ginger, coconut milk, and sweet potatoes harmonize in the sauce.

**RICE:**
3 tablespoons canola or corn oil
2 garlic cloves, minced
2 cups uncooked jasmine rice
2¹/₂ cups water
1 teaspoon salt

**SWEET POTATO–GINGER SAUCE:**
1 medium sweet potato (about 3/4 pound)
14 ounces coconut milk
¹/₂ cup water or orange juice
1 tablespoon minced fresh ginger
Salt and fresh-ground black pepper to taste

1 carrot, coarsely chopped
¹/₂ red bell pepper, seeded and coarsely chopped
4 scallions, both green and white parts, coarsely chopped, and 2 scallions, finely chopped
2 eggs, beaten

**1.** In a saucepan with a tight-fitting lid, heat 1 tablespoon of the canola or corn oil with the garlic over medium heat for 1 minute, stirring constantly. Add the jasmine rice, and stir constantly for 1 minute more. Add the water and salt. Bring the rice to a boil, then reduce the heat to low, cover the pan, and cook the rice for 15 minutes. Transfer the rice to a large bowl, and let it cool for 15 minutes.

**2.** While the rice cooks, cut the sweet potato into thirds. Place the pieces in a pot, and cover them with cold water. Bring the potatoes to a boil, and cook them until they are tender, about 20 minutes. Drain them, and let them cool.

**3.** In a saucepan, bring the coconut milk, the water or orange juice, and the minced ginger almost to a boil, then turn the heat to low, and cook for 5 minutes. Remove the pan from the heat.

**4.** Slip the skin off the cooled sweet potato, and purée the flesh with the coconut-ginger liquid in a blender or food processor. Pour the sweet-potato purée back into the saucepan, and add salt and pepper. Keep the sauce warm.

**5.** Mince the carrot, the red pepper, and the coarsely chopped scallions in a food processor. Add half of the jasmine rice and the 2 beaten eggs, and run the machine in spurts until the mixture has a mealy consistency. Put this mixture back into the bowl with the rest of the jasmine rice, and mix well. Put half of this mixture into a clean bowl.

**6.** Heat two skillets or a large griddle over medium-high heat. Divide the remaining canola or corn oil between the skillets, or spread it all on the griddle. Divide the rice mixture in each bowl into thirds. Form each of the six parts into a ball, then place each ball in a skillet or on the griddle, and pat the ball down to form a cake about 1½ inches thick. Fry the cakes for 3 to 4 minutes per side, or until they are golden brown.

**7.** Reheat the sauce, and ladle it onto plates. Place a rice cake on each plate, and top with the finely chopped scallions.

**Variations:** To make this entrée heartier, embellish it with some pan-fried tofu. Or rest the rice cake on some spinach that has been pan-fried in olive oil and formed into a round slightly larger than the rice cake, and ladle the sauce around the spinach.

Serves 6

# Black Rice Cakes with Zucchini and Lemongrass

Here black-rice patties sit boldly in a zesty sauce of shredded zucchini, lemongrass, cilantro, and rice wine. The spirited flavor of lemongrass marries well with the low-keyed zucchini. Black rice, which is indeed black, is sold in many Chinese markets. If you can't find it, however, you can leave it out, and double the amount of sushi-style rice or short-grain brown rice.

**RICE CAKES:**

2 3/4 cups water

3 tablespoons chopped shallots

1 teaspoon salt

2/3 cup uncooked black rice

2/3 cup uncooked sushi-style white rice (I prefer Kokuho sushi rice from California) or short-grain brown rice

**SAUCE:**

1 thick lemongrass stalk

2 tablespoons canola or corn oil

2 garlic cloves, minced

1 medium zucchini (about 3/4 pound), grated

1/3 cup Chinese rice wine, or sherry or sake

1 to 2 tablespoons Thai or Vietnamese fish sauce, or 1 to 2 tablespoons soy sauce

1 1/2 teaspoons cornstarch

2/3 cup water or Basic Vegetable Stock (page 79)

3 tablespoons lemon juice (from about 1/2 lemon)

3 tablespoons finely chopped fresh cilantro

**1.** Bring the 2¾ cups water, the shallots, and the salt to a boil in a large saucepan. Add the two kinds of rice, turn the heat to low, and cover the pan. Cook the rice for 40 minutes if your nonblack rice is white, or 50 minutes if it's brown.

Check to make sure the rice is tender. If it's not, add a bit of water, and continue to cook it for 5 to 10 minutes more. Transfer the rice to a large bowl, and chill it at least 30 minutes.

**2.** While the rice chills, prepare the lemongrass: Cut off the bulbous bottom third of the stalk. Remove the tough outer leaves, and, with a sharp chef's knife, cut this piece into thin slices, then mince it. You should have about 3 tablespoons. (Save the top part of the stalk for stocks, soups, stews, or even tea.)

**3.** In a large skillet, heat 1 tablespoon of the canola or corn oil over medium-high heat. Add the garlic and the minced lemongrass, and sauté them for 2 minutes. Add the zucchini, the wine, and the fish or soy sauce. Bring the mixture to a boil, and boil it for 1 minute. Dissolve the cornstarch in the ⅔ cup water or stock, and add this and the lemon juice to the sauce. Boil the sauce for 20 to 30 seconds, then taste it, and adjust the seasonings, if you like. Take the pan off of the heat.

**4.** Form four 1½-inch-thick patties from the cooled rice. In another large skillet, heat the remaining 1 tablespoon canola or corn oil over high heat. When the oil is very hot, add the rice cakes. Fry the cakes for 3 to 4 minutes per side, until a brown crust develops. Reheat the sauce, pool it on plates, and place the cakes on top. Garnish with the cilantro, and serve.

*Serves 4*

# Hijiki Rice Salad

For those who get nervous at the thought of eating seaweed, hijiki is a safe "sea vegetable" with which to start. Looking like short strands of pasta, hijiki has a likable texture and a sweet, mild flavor. Mixed here with rice, ginger, toasted sesame seeds, and a slightly sweet vinaigrette, hijiki will refresh the body and rejuvenate the spirit. It is available at wholefoods stores and at Japanese markets.

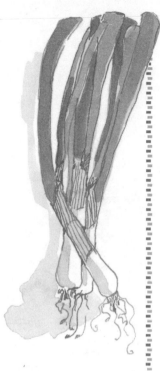

1 ounce dried hijiki (about 1 cup)
2¼ cups water
¾ teaspoon salt
1 cup uncooked long-grain rice
2 tablespoons toasted hulled sesame seeds
4 scallions, minced
1½ cups snow peas, cut into thin julienne strips
1 small carrot, minced
1 teaspoon grated fresh ginger
¼ cup rice vinegar
2 teaspoons sugar
2 tablespoons canola or corn oil
Fresh-ground black pepper to taste

**1.** Soak the hijiki in cool water for 1 hour, then drain it.

**2.** Bring the water and ½ teaspoon salt to a boil in a medium saucepan, and add the rice. Turn the heat to low, and cover the pan. Simmer the rice for 20 minutes.

**3.** While the rice simmers, cook the hijiki: In a saucepan, cover the hijiki generously with water. Simmer it over medium-low heat for about 15 to 20 minutes, or until the hijiki is tender. Drain the hijiki, and rinse it in cold water.

**4.** Toast the sesame seeds in a small, dry skillet over medium heat, shaking the pan periodically, until they brown lightly. Transfer the seeds to a small plate to cool.

**5.** Combine the scallions, snow peas, and carrot in a large bowl. In a smaller bowl, combine the ginger, vinegar, sugar, and oil.

**6.** Add the warm cooked rice to the vegetables. Add the cool hijiki and the vinaigrette, too. Toss well, add the sesame seeds, the remaining ¼ teaspoon salt, and the pepper, and toss again. Serve the salad warm, or chill it for 1 hour first. It will keep in the refrigerator, covered, for 3 days.

Serves 4

# Malay
# Rice Salad

The cuisine of Malaysia is based on rice, intricate curries, and wonderfully sour and spicy condiments called sambals. The dishes include many Indian spices as well as Southeast Asian ingredients such as kaffir lime leaves, dried shrimp, galangal, lemongrass, and candlenuts. This rice salad, served at room temperature, includes pineapple, cilantro roots or stems, shredded coconut, cashews, and kaffir lime leaves. But you don't need to use every one of the recipe's fourteen ingredients. If you don't have, say, the kaffir lime leaves, pineapple, and shredded coconut, the salad will still taste great.

4 cups water

1½ teaspoons salt

2 cups uncooked jasmine, basmati, or other long-grain white rice

12 cilantro roots (include the lower 3 inches of the stems—or just use the stems)

2 garlic cloves, minced

2 teaspoons minced fresh ginger

1 to 2 small hot red chile peppers (such as bird peppers), minced

2 dried or fresh kaffir lime leaves, ground in a mortar or spice mill, or ½ teaspoon grated lime rind

2 tablespoons canola or corn oil

½ cup lemon juice (from about 2 lemons)

2 to 3 tablespoons Thai or Vietnamese fish sauce, or 1 teaspoon salt

⅓ cup shredded coconut (fresh or dried, but not sweetened)

⅓ cup chopped dry-roasted, unsalted cashews or peanuts

## Kaffir Lime Leaves

*Picked from the kaffir lime trees of Asia, kaffir lime leaves possess an intense lemony and floral aroma. The fragrance is so strong that I wouldn't want to use these leaves every day, but once in a while they are a delight. Available in Asian markets, they are best fresh, but they are easier to find dried or preserved in brine. If you use the brined lime leaves, be sure to rinse them well. Soak dried lime leaves in warm water, or add them directly to soups or stews, especially those with Thai flavors. Kaffir lime leaves are also delicious when ground in a spice mill and used in Thai curry pastes.*

2 carrots, peeled and minced
1½ cups chopped fresh pineapple (from about
   ⅓ of a pineapple)

**1.** In a large saucepan, bring the water and salt to a boil. Add the rice, and stir. Cover the pan, and bring the rice to a boil. Then turn the heat to the lowest setting, and cook the rice for 20 minutes. Uncover the pan, and set it aside until you're ready to mix the salad.

**2.** While the rice is cooking, prepare the dressing: Soak the cilantro roots and stems in lukewarm water for 5 minutes. Then trim off the stringy rootlets on the ends, and mince the stems and main roots. In a bowl, combine the chopped cilantro, garlic, ginger, chiles, kaffir lime leaves or lime rind, oil, lemon juice, and fish sauce or salt. Mix well.

**3.** Transfer the warm rice to a large bowl. Add the shredded coconut, the nuts, the carrots, and the pineapple. Toss well, add the dressing, and season with salt and pepper, if you like. Serve. (You can make the salad ahead and refrigerate it, but let it sit at room temperature 15 to 20 minutes before serving.)

Serves 6

# CHAPTER 9

# Grain Central Station

# Soft Polenta with Spicy Tomato Sauce

I'll bet anyone that a tomato sauce on soft polenta tastes better than a tomato sauce on spaghetti. Okay, so polenta takes longer to cook than spaghetti. But, like polenta, this tomato sauce takes 40 minutes, so you might as well cook the two together, especially since polenta takes very little effort.

In this polenta, quinoa is added because of its nutty flavor and its high protein content (it has four times as much protein as cornmeal does). You can make this a vegan entrée simply by omitting the cheese.

1 quart water
1/2 cup coarse-ground yellow cornmeal,
    preferably labeled organic or stone-ground
1/2 cup quinoa (or more cornmeal)
1/2 teaspoon salt
2 tablespoons olive oil
2 cups minced onions
1 large portobello mushroom, including stem,
    chopped
3 large garlic cloves, minced
3 1/2 cups (1 28-ounce can) peeled plum tomatoes
1/4 cup sherry
About 1/2 teaspoon chile flakes, to taste
1 teaspoon dried oregano
Salt and fresh-ground black pepper to taste
2 cups finely chopped scallions
1/2 cup grated Parmesan cheese
1/4 cup shaved Parmesan or Ricotta Salata cheese

**1.** In a small bowl, whisk together 2 cups water with the cornmeal, quinoa, and salt. Bring the remaining 2 cups water to a boil in a heavy saucepan. Stir the cornmeal mixture into the boiling water, and continue stirring. Be careful—the polenta may spit and sputter, and the hot bits of polenta can really burn. Turn the heat to very low, and cook the polenta for 40 minutes, stirring with a wooden spoon every ten minutes or so.

**2.** While the polenta is cooking, make the tomato sauce: In a large saucepan, heat the olive oil over medium heat, and add the onions. Cook them for about 5 minutes, stirring often, until they have softened. Stir in the chopped mushrooms and the garlic, and sauté, stirring, for about 5 minutes. Then add the tomatoes, sherry, chile flakes, and oregano. When the sauce comes to a boil, turn the heat to low. Simmer the sauce for 30 minutes, then season it with salt and pepper.

**3.** When the polenta has cooked for 40 minutes, add the scallions and grated cheese. Stir well. Mound the polenta on plates, make a well in the center of each mound, and ladle in the tomato sauce. Garnish with the shaved cheese.

**Variation:** Pan-fry the polenta: After adding the scallions and cheese, pour the polenta into an oiled 9-by-11-inch casserole pan, and smooth the top with a rubber spatula. Chill the polenta, then cut it into twelve triangles. Place them in a very hot skillet coated with olive oil. Fry the polenta on both sides until it is golden. Serve it with the spicy tomato sauce, and sprinkle it with Parmesan cheese.

Serves 4

# Pan-fried Polenta with Corn, Kale, and Goat Cheese

Most Italians make their polenta from a cornmeal coarser than that generally available in U.S. supermarkets. Yellow corn grits are an adequate substitute, but I prefer to use cornmeals labeled organic or stone-ground; they are coarser and make polenta with excellent texture and flavor. In this dish, I love the delicate crunch of the fresh corn kernels against the smooth texture of the polenta.

▪▪▪▪▪▪▪▪▪▪

1 tablespoon butter
2 garlic cloves, minced
4$^1/_3$ cups water
1 cup coarse-ground yellow cornmeal, preferably
    labeled organic or stone-ground
$^1/_2$ teaspoon salt
Kernels from 2 ears corn (about 1$^1/_3$ cups)
Fresh-ground black pepper to taste
2 tablespoons grated Parmesan cheese
$^1/_2$ bunch kale
1 tablespoon olive oil
1 ripe tomato, sliced into $^1/_2$-inch-thick rounds
3 ounces soft chèvre (goat cheese)

▪▪▪▪▪▪▪▪▪▪

**1.** In a medium saucepan, heat the butter over medium heat. Add the garlic, and stir constantly for about 1 minute; don't let the garlic brown. Add 3 cups of the water, and bring it to a boil.

**2.** While the water heats, quickly whisk together in a bowl the cornmeal, the salt, and 1 cup water to make a smooth slurry. When the water in the saucepan comes to a boil, pour the slurry into it, whisking constantly for 3 minutes to prevent lumps from forming. Turn the heat to low. Cook the polenta for 40 minutes, stirring it with a wooden spoon every 10 minutes or so.

**3.** Stir in the corn kernels, and cook the polenta 5 minutes more. Add the pepper and the Parmesan cheese. Pour the polenta into a lightly oiled 8-by-8-inch pan, and smooth the top with a plastic spatula. Let the polenta chill in the refrigerator for at least 1 hour.

**4.** Cut away the stems and center stalks of the kale, and cut the leaves into 3-inch pieces. Using a butter knife, cut the chilled polenta into four large triangles. Heat the olive oil in a large non-stick skillet over medium-high heat. When the oil begins to smoke, carefully add the polenta triangles. Pan-fry the polenta until it is golden brown on the underside, about 3 minutes, then turn the polenta over with a spatula, and cook it until it is golden brown on the other side. Transfer the polenta to a baking sheet.

**5.** Into the skillet in which you cooked the polenta, put the kale and the remaining ⅓ cup water. Cover the skillet, and cook the kale over medium-high heat for 4 minutes. Keep the kale warm.

**6.** Preheat the broiler. Place the tomato slices on the polenta triangles, then top with the goat cheese. Place the polenta under the broiler until the cheese melts and the tomatoes begin to cook. Serve the polenta immediately, on top of the cooked kale.

Serves 2

# Quinoa-Sorrel Salad

If you find yourself thinking about pasta salad, why not think quinoa salad? It's quite nutritious, it takes no more than 15 minutes to cook, and it has a delicate consistency that takes well to vinaigrettes. In this salad, quinoa joins up with fresh sorrel, red onion, tomato, and feta cheese, and is then tossed in a light balsamic dressing. If you're wary about eating uncooked sorrel, you may be glad to know that it has been enjoyed as a salad green for many years in England. But use arugula instead, if you prefer.

1½ cups quinoa
¼ to ⅓ cup olive oil, to taste

3 cups water
½ teaspoon salt
3 tablespoons balsamic vinegar
1 small bunch sorrel (or arugula), stemmed
    and cut into julienne strips
1 cup thinly sliced red onion
1 ripe tomato, chopped
Salt and fresh-ground black pepper
    to taste
⅓ cup crumbled feta cheese or any tangy
    goat cheese
Mixed salad greens (I like to combine sorrel,
    watercress, Italian parsley, and red-leaf
    lettuce)

**1.** Put the quinoa into a fine-meshed sieve, and rinse the grain well under cold water for 1 minute to extract the bitter saponins. Let the quinoa drain for 2 minutes.

**2.** Heat a skillet with a lid over medium-high heat. Add 1 tablespoon olive oil. When the oil is hot, add the quinoa. Cook it, stirring often with a wooden spoon, for 2 minutes or until the quinoa smells toasted. Add the water and ½ teaspoon salt. Bring the mixture to a boil, cover the pan, and reduce the heat to low. Let the quinoa cook for 15 minutes.

**3.** While the quinoa cooks, combine the balsamic vinegar and remaining oil in a large bowl. Add the sorrel or arugula, the red onion, and the tomato. Season the vegetables with salt and pepper.

**4.** When the quinoa is cooked, add it to the vegetables and vinaigrette. Toss well, add the feta, and add more salt and pepper, if you like. Chill the salad, or serve it warm. Either way, serve it on a bed of mixed salad greens.

*Serves 4*

## Grain Quiz

*Do you know which grain is higher in protein than any other? Do you know which grain contains the most amino acids? And do you know which grain contains the most complete protein? The answers are quinoa, quinoa, and quinoa. And the surprising thing is that quinoa actually tastes good. Quinoa, pronounced "KEY-nwa," is the seedlike fruit of a broad-leafed plant, Chenopodium quinoa, that can reach 5 feet high. A traditional food of the Andes, cooked quinoa has a nutty flavor and fluffy texture. It is a splendid foil for curries, tagines, and pilafs. Rinse the quinoa grains before cooking them to remove the outer wall, which contains bitter saponin.*

# Lemongrass Quinoa Pilaf

Quinoa plays a part here that might more traditionally be assigned to rice. But the nutty flavor of quinoa marries well with lemongrass, ginger, and Sichuan pepper.

2 cups quinoa

4 3/4 cups water

1 teaspoon salt, plus more to taste

1 lemongrass stalk

2 tablespoons canola or corn oil

1 tablespoon minced fresh ginger

2 large garlic cloves, minced

1 teaspoon ground Sichuan pepper (or 1/4 teaspoon ground ginger, 1 pinch ground cloves, and 1/2 teaspoon ground black pepper)

12 ounces firm tofu, cut into 1/2-inch cubes

3/4 bunch broccoli, cut into small florets and thin-sliced stems (about 6 cups)

1/2 red bell pepper, seeded and minced

**1.** Rinse the quinoa in a fine-meshed sieve under cold running water for 1 minute to extract the bitter saponins. Let the quinoa drain for 2 minutes.

**2.** Bring 4½ cups water to a boil in a saucepan, then add 1 teaspoon salt and the quinoa. Cover the pan, and turn the heat to low. Cook the quinoa for 15 minutes.

**3.** While the quinoa cooks, prepare the lemongrass: Cut off the bulbous bottom third of the stalk. Remove the tough outer leaves, and, with a large, sharp chef's knife, cut this piece into thin slices, then mince it. (Save the rest of the stalk for stocks, soups, stews, or even tea.)

**4.** In a large skillet, heat the oil with the ginger and garlic over medium heat, stirring constantly. After a minute or two, add the minced lemongrass, Sichuan pepper, and tofu. Add salt to taste. Stir-fry the mixture over medium-high heat for 2 or 3 minutes. Add the broccoli and the remaining ¼ cup water. Cover the skillet, and let the mixture steam over low heat for 5 minutes.

**5.** Uncover the skillet, and add the quinoa, red pepper, and salt to taste. Stir gently until all the contents are hot, then serve.

*Serves 4*

# Asparagus and Mushroom Stew over Quinoa

Here, exotic mushrooms are cooked in butter, combined with a porcini broth and asparagus, and served over quinoa. Healthful and easy, although a bit more expensive to make than most of the dishes in this book, this is a very special meal when served with fresh, warm bread to soak up the juices.

¹/₃ ounce dried porcini mushrooms (also called cepes)
2 cups quinoa
2 tablespoons olive oil
1¹/₂ cups chopped onions
3 garlic cloves, minced
¹/₂ teaspoon dried sage or thyme or 1 teaspoon chopped fresh sage or thyme
1 teaspoon salt
¹/₂ pound fresh chanterelle, shiitake, portobello, or other flavorful mushrooms
²/₃ pound asparagus
¹/₂ cup plus 1 tablespoon sherry

1 red bell pepper, seeded and cut into thin
    julienne strips
1 teaspoon cornstarch dissolved in 1 tablespoon
    water
1 teaspoon red or white wine vinegar
Salt and fresh-ground black pepper to taste

**1.** In a small bowl, cover the dried mushrooms with boiling water. Let them soak 15 minutes. (Do not discard the soaking liquid.)

**2.** Rinse the quinoa in a fine-meshed sieve under cold running water for 1 minute to extract the bitter saponins. Let the quinoa drain for 2 minutes.

**3.** Bring 4 cups water to a boil. In a saucepan, heat 1 tablespoon olive oil over medium heat. Add the onions and 1 minced garlic clove, and sauté, stirring frequently, until they soften, about 5 minutes. Add the sage or thyme and the quinoa, and cook 1 minute more, stirring constantly. Add ½ teaspoon of the salt and the 4 cups water, turn the heat to low, and cover the pan. Let the mixture cook for 15 minutes.

**4.** While the quinoa cooks, drain the dried mushrooms, saving the soaking liquid. Remove the stems of the fresh mushrooms if they are shiitakes. Chop the fresh and the dried mushrooms into bite-size pieces; keep the fresh and dried mushrooms separate. Break off the tough ends of the asparagus, and cut the rest of the stalks into 2-inch lengths.

**5.** Heat the remaining 1 tablespoon oil in a large skillet. Add the fresh mushrooms and the remaining minced garlic, and cook over medium heat 2 to 3 minutes, stirring frequently. Then add the ½ cup sherry, the remaining ½ teaspoon salt, and the mushroom soaking liquid. Add the asparagus, red pepper, and dried porcini, and simmer the mixture 6 to 7 minutes, until the asparagus is just tender. Add the dissolved cornstarch and the vinegar, let the sauce come to a boil, and simmer it until it thickens slightly, about 30 seconds. Remove the pan from the heat, and add 1 tablespoon sherry. Stir, and add salt, if you like, and pepper.

> " *With fresh asparagus, the higher your income, the higher up the stalk you cut off the tips.* "
>
> —BILL RATHJE

**6.** Spoon the quinoa onto plates. Spoon the mushroom and asparagus mixture over, and serve.

*Serves 4*

# Barley Pilaf
# with Lentil Confetti

Here barley and brown rice form the foundation of a hearty meal. The confetti-like French lentils, also known as *lentilles du Puy,* are interspersed throughout, and portobellos and potatoes provide earthy flavor. All you need for a meal is to add a salad or some bread. This pilaf is particularly delicious with Banana-Ginger Chutney (page 44).

2 tablespoons olive oil
1 cup chopped onion
2 teaspoons minced fresh ginger
2 cups chopped portobello mushrooms
1 garlic clove, minced
1½ teaspoons ground coriander seeds
1 cup pearled or hulled barley (see the Note)
½ cup uncooked brown rice (I like to use brown
    basmati rice)
1 teaspoon salt, plus more, to taste
Fresh-ground black pepper to taste
3¼ cups water
⅓ cup dried French lentils (available at specialty
    food stores and some supermarkets) or
    brown lentils
1 small potato, peeled and chopped into ½-inch
    cubes
⅓ cup chopped parsley

# Cooking with Grains

When cooking grains in water, it's important to lightly salt the water. Use approximately 1 teaspoon salt to 4 cups water.

## Non-wheat grains

**AMARANTH.** Once considered just a weed, amaranth is very rich in protein. Cooked amaranth is wonderful mixed with other grains, such as bulgur or quinoa, in pilafs, and with oatmeal for porridge.

*To cook:* To make 2 cups cooked amaranth, bring 1 cup amaranth and 2½ cups water to a boil. Simmer the amaranth for 20 minutes, covered. Since amaranth cooks in about the same time as coarse bulgur and quinoa, it can be cooked along with either.

**BARLEY, HULLED.** The husk is removed; the bran is not. Hulled barley is good in soups, breads, and as a side dish mixed with herbs.

*To cook:* Bring 3 cups water and 1 cup hulled barley to a boil. Simmer the barley, covered, for 45 minutes to 1 hour. Drain it, if necessary. You should have 3½ cups cooked barley.

**BARLEY, PEARLED.** The husk and bran are removed. Pearled barley is more delicate-tasting than hulled barley. Combine pearled barley with olive oil and other flavorings in grain salads.

*To cook:* Bring 3 cups water and 1 cup barley to a boil. Simmer the barley, covered, for 45 minutes. Drain it, if necessary. You should have 3½ cups barley.

**BUCKWHEAT GROATS, OR KASHA.** Hulled, crushed, and toasted buckwheat kernels, these groats are rich in protein and have an unmistakable nutty, hearty flavor. They are combined with bow-tie pasta in a traditional Jewish dish. Try them also in pilafs with nuts and raisins or currants.

*To cook:* To make 2 cups cooked kasha, bring 2 cups water and 1 cup kasha to a boil. Simmer the kasha, covered, for 15 to 20 minutes.

**MILLET (HULLED).** This high-protein grain is good with roasted vegetables and roasted garlic; mixed with Indian spices, dried fruit, and nuts; and as a tabouli-style salad (try it with cilantro). Millet is also good as a hot breakfast cereal.

*To cook:* To make 3 cups cooked millet, bring 3 cups water and 1 cup millet to a boil. Simmer the millet, covered, for 45 minutes.

**ROLLED OATS.** It's great to start the day with a bowl of oatmeal, a little milk, and perhaps some maple syrup or brown sugar. Some people like cinnamon sprinkled on top, too. I prefer thick (old-fashioned) rolled oats to the quick-cooking, thin kind.

*To cook:* Bring 2 cups water to a boil. Add 1 cup old-fashioned rolled oats, turn the heat to low, and simmer the oats 5 minutes, stirring often. You'll have enough for 3 or 4 people.

**STEEL-CUT OATS.** This is the grain used in traditional Scottish porridge. Cooked steel-cut oats are delicious with a bit of butter and a spoonful of brown sugar.
*To cook:* Bring to a boil 1 cup steel-cut oats and 4 cups water. Cook the oats over low heat for 20 minutes, stirring often. You'll have enough for 3 or 4 people.

**POLENTA (COARSE CORNMEAL).** If you have no Italian grocery nearby, use cornmeal labeled organic or stone-ground, with grains the size of kosher salt crystals. Serve polenta soft from the pot, or chilled and then pan-fried. Wild mushrooms, fresh herbs, and olives are good additions.
*To cook:* For 2½ cups polenta, mix 1 cup cold water with 1 cup cornmeal. Bring 3 cups water to a boil, then whisk in the cornmeal-water slurry. Add salt and fresh-ground black pepper to taste, and cook the polenta over low heat for 40 minutes, stirring often with a wooden spoon. At the very end, stir in 2 tablespoons of butter, and some grated Parmesan cheese if you like.

**QUINOA.** This traditional food of the Andes cooks in only 15 minutes and contains more protein than any other grain. Lighter in flavor than most grains, it works well in pilafs, salads, stuffings, and even puddings.
*To cook:* To make 4 cups cooked quinoa, sauté 1 cup quinoa in 1 tablespoon olive oil for 2 minutes, stirring. Add 2 cups water, bring the mixture to a boil, then turn the heat to low. Cook the quinoa, covered, for 15 minutes.

**RYE BERRIES.** These are strong-flavored on their own, better mixed with other grains, and nice in soups and breads.
*To cook:* To make 2 cups cooked rye berries, bring to a boil 1 cup rye berries and 2½ cups water. Simmer the berries, covered, for 1½ hours.

**RYE FLAKES.** These are good in granola, muesli, and muffins, and as a breakfast porridge. Ground coarse or fine in a food processor, they are tasty in pancakes and bread.
*To cook:* Toast the flakes, if you like, before adding them to the cereals and baked goods. For porridge, bring 1 cup flakes and 1 cup water to a boil, then lower the heat. Simmer, covered, for 10 minutes. Serve the porridge with a touch of butter and brown sugar. You'll have enough for 2 or 3 people.

**TRITICALE.** Triticale is a rye-wheat hybrid. The berries are fabulous in pilafs with beans, nuts, or veggies, and in breads. Try the berries also as a salad, with tomatoes, olives, and a simple vinaigrette.
*To cook:* To make 2 cups cooked triticale, bring to a boil 1 cup triticale berries and 1½ cups water. Simmer, covered, for 1 hour, or until the berries are tender. For porridge, cook 20 minutes more, adding extra water if necessary.

*Continued on next page*

# Cooking with Grains

## Wheat grains

**BULGUR.** Parboiled, dried, and cracked wheat, bulgur is good in tabouli and other salads, in pilafs, and in stuffings.

*To cook:* Since bulgur is precooked, it's very quick to prepare. To make 3 cups cooked bulgur, just pour 2½ cups boiling water over 1 cup bulgur, and wait for the grain to absorb the liquid. For pilafs and stuffings, sauté the bulgur in olive oil before adding the liquid.

**COUSCOUS.** A granular form of semolina (coarse-ground durum wheat), couscous is a staple in North African cuisine. It is delicious with sautéed vegetables, especially if they create their own sauce (if they include tomatoes, for example). Chickpeas and raisins are often added to couscous sauces. A light seasoning of spices such as ground coriander, paprika, and cumin is also nice. Almost all couscous sold in the U.S. is a precooked variety that needs only to soak in hot water to be ready.

*To cook:* To make 3 cups cooked couscous, bring to a boil 2 cups water and 1 cup couscous. Simmer the couscous for 2 minutes, then take it off the heat. Let it sit, covered, for 10 minutes. Flake it with a fork before serving.

**CRACKED WHEAT.** Cracked wheat looks like bulgur, but it is not precooked. It is good in pilafs, stuffings, breakfast porridge, breads, and muffins.

*To cook:* To make 3 cups cooked cracked wheat, bring to a boil 1 cup cracked wheat and 2½ cups water. Simmer the cracked wheat, covered, for about 30 minutes.

**WHEAT BERRIES.** Wheat berries are fabulous in pilafs with beans, nuts, or veggies, in soups, and in breads. Try the berries also as a salad, with tomatoes, olives, and a simple vinaigrette.

*To cook:* Soak 1 cup wheat berries in 3 cups water overnight. Bring the soaked berries to a boil with 2 quarts water. Simmer them, uncovered, for 45 to 60 minutes, until they are agreeably chewy. You'll have 2 cups wheat berries.

**WHEAT FLAKES.** These are good in granola, muesli, and muffins, and as breakfast porridge. Ground coarse or fine in a food processor, they are tasty in pancakes and bread.

*To cook:* Toast the flakes, if you like, before adding them to the cereals and baked goods. For porridge, bring 1 cup flakes and 1 cup water to a boil, then lower the heat. Simmer, covered, for 10 minutes. Serve the porridge with a touch of butter and brown sugar. You'll have enough for 2 or 3 people.

**1.** In a heavy saucepan, heat the olive oil over medium heat. Add the onion and the ginger, and sauté for 5 minutes, stirring often. Add the portobellos, garlic, and coriander, and cook, stirring often, for another 2 minutes. Then add the barley and rice. Add the 1 teaspoon salt, the pepper, and the water. Cover the pan, and bring the mixture to a boil. Turn the heat to low, and let the mixture cook for 20 minutes.

**2.** Stir in the lentils and cover the pan again. After 5 minutes, add the potato. Cook the mixture, covered, for about 20 minutes more or until the lentils are tender, adding additional water if the mixture is dry. Stir in the parsley and additional salt and pepper to taste. Serve the pilaf hot.

Note: Some people claim that hulled barley, a less refined form, takes 20 to 30 minutes longer to cook than pearled barley. I have found, however, that it takes nearly the same amount of time (about 45 minutes). Barley varieties may vary, however, so you may have to experiment to get your barley just as tender as you want.

Serves 4

# Barley, Kale, and Kidney Bean Stew

Gordon Hamersley, a Boston chef I once worked for, told me that salting kale is a very delicate matter; kale can taste intensely salty after only a pinch of salt is added. I know this is true, since I had to season an entrée of kale and cod tail every night at Gordon's restaurant. More than once I had to replace the kale in the stew because it became too salty. So keep the brakes on when salting this dish.

1½ tablespoons olive oil

2 cups sliced onions

3 garlic cloves, minced

1 cup pearled or hulled barley

2 teaspoons chopped fresh sage, or 1 teaspoon
   dried sage

½ teaspoon salt, or more, to taste

10 cups water or Basic Vegetable Stock (page
   79), or more as needed

1 large russet potato, peeled and chopped into
   1-inch cubes

2 cups ½-inch-thick carrot rounds

1 small bunch kale

1¼ cups cooked and rinsed kidney beans

2 tablespoons lemon juice (from about ½ lemon)

Fresh-ground black pepper to taste

⅓ cup grated Parmesan cheese

4 teaspoons extra-virgin olive oil

**1.** In a large saucepan, heat the olive oil over medium heat, and add the onions. Cook the onions for 5 to 6 minutes, stirring occasionally, then add the garlic, barley, sage, ½ teaspoon salt, and 7 cups of the water or stock. Cover the pan, bring the stew to a boil, then turn the heat to low. Let the stew simmer for 25 minutes, then add the potato, carrots, and 2 cups more water or stock. Cover the pan again, and let the stew simmer for 10 minutes more.

**2.** Cut the stem and inner stalk from the kale. Coarsely chop the leaves (there should be about 6 cups), and add them to the stew with 1 cup water or stock. Simmer for 10 minutes more, adding more water or stock if the stew seems too dry.

**3.** Add the kidney beans, stir well, then add the lemon juice. The stew should be similar to a pilaf, but slightly less dry. Taste the stew, and add salt and pepper, keeping in mind that you'll also be adding Parmesan cheese. Ladle the stew into bowls, sprinkle the Parmesan cheese over, then dribble 1 teaspoon extra-virgin olive oil over each bowl. Serve the stew hot.

**Variation:** Substitute mustard greens or blanched broccoli rabe for the more mildly flavored kale, and simmer the greens for 5 instead of 10 minutes.

Serves 4

# Barley-Shiitake "Risotto"

I don't know how people managed to live happily without the shiitake mushroom, which was unavailable in U.S. supermarkets until the late 1980s. Combining shiitakes with barley, garlic, and parsley, this dish, cooked in the style of risotto, is a meal I couldn't turn down.

5 to 6 cups water or Basic Vegetable Stock (page 79)
1 tablespoon butter
4 shallots, minced
2 garlic cloves, minced
1 1/2 cups shiitake mushroom caps, sliced thin
1 large carrot, diced fine
1 1/2 cups pearled or hulled barley
1 teaspoon salt, or more, to taste
1/2 cup grated Parmesan cheese
1/4 cup chopped parsley
Fresh-ground black pepper to taste
1 lemon wedge

**1.** Bring the water or stock to a boil, then turn the heat to low. Heat the butter in a large skillet over medium heat. Add the shallots, and cook them, stirring frequently, for 5 minutes. Add the garlic, the shiitakes, and the carrot. Sauté for 5 more minutes, stirring often, then add the barley. Sauté the mixture for 2 minutes more, stirring frequently.

**2.** Add 1 cup of the simmering water or stock and the 1 teaspoon salt, and stir. Turn the heat to low, and add the remaining water or stock ½ cup at a time, stirring occasionally and waiting until the liquid is almost completely absorbed before adding more. The barley should cook for about 45 minutes, or until it is tender but slightly chewy.

**3.** When the barley is done, stir in the Parmesan cheese and 3 tablespoons of the parsley. Season to taste with salt (if necessary), pepper, and a squeeze or 2 of lemon.

**4.** Spoon the risotto onto plates, sprinkle the remaining 1 tablespoon parsley over, and serve.

*Variation:* Add 2 teaspoons chopped fresh sage with the 1 cup water or stock in step 2.

Serves 4

# Couscous with Red Pepper, Chickpea, and Almond Stew

Paprika, cinnamon, red wine, and tomatoes give this stew its aromatic earthiness. Carrots, onions, and red peppers are gently stewed together, then slivered almonds and chopped cilantro are added just at the end. The whole ragout is then spooned over hot couscous.

STEW:
2 tablespoons olive oil
1 cup sliced shallots or onion
2 large garlic cloves, minced
2 carrots, sliced thin diagonally
2 large red bell peppers, seeded and cut into
    ½-inch squares

## Leftover Beans or Chickpeas

*If you have leftover beans or chickpeas, whether they came from a can or were cooked from scratch, here are two quick and tasty ways to use them:*

- *Make a bean or chickpea salad with minced onion, chopped mint or parsley, garlic, extra-virgin olive oil, lemon juice, and finely chopped carrots.*

- *Mash either white beans or chickpeas with a potato masher, add some garlic, and mash further. Add a few tablespoons of extra-virgin olive oil and some water to create a coarse but creamy purée. Season it with salt and fresh pepper, and use it as a dip for pita toast or crudités.*

2 large ripe tomatoes, chopped
$1/2$ teaspoon salt
Fresh-ground black pepper to taste
$1/2$ cup red wine (or sherry)
2 teaspoons paprika (I like to use a spicy Hungarian paprika)
$1/4$ teaspoon ground cinnamon
1 cup cooked chickpeas
$1/4$ cup slivered almonds, lightly toasted
1 tablespoon lemon juice
3 tablespoons chopped cilantro

### COUSCOUS:
$2^{1}/_{3}$ cups water
$1^{1}/_{3}$ cups couscous
$1/2$ teaspoon salt

**1.** In a large saucepan or skillet, heat the oil over medium-high heat. Add the shallots or onion, and cook for 5 minutes, stirring often. Add the garlic, and cook another minute. Stir in the carrots, red peppers, tomatoes, salt, pepper, and wine. Then add the paprika and cinnamon. Stir, and bring the stew to a boil. Turn the heat to low, and cover the pan tightly. Simmer the stew for 15 minutes or until the carrots are tender. Stir in the chickpeas.

**2.** Meanwhile, make the couscous: In a saucepan, bring the water to a boil, and add the couscous and salt. Remove the pan from the heat, cover the pan, and let the couscous stand for 5 minutes. Fluff the couscous by lightly running a fork or a whisk back and forth in the pan, starting with the very top layer of granules and gradually working your way down.

**3.** Stir the almonds, lemon juice, and cilantro into the stew. Spoon the couscous onto plates, and make a well in the middle of each mound. Spoon in the stew, and serve.

Serves 4

# Couscous Cakes with a Tomato-Garlic Ragout

With their crusty outsides and delicate, cheesy insides these couscous cakes rival the delicious Zucchini Risotto Cakes (page 223). But these are easier to make, because couscous takes almost no time to cook. A little blue cheese gives the cakes a cheesy flavor without adding a lot of fat. Make sure the tomatoes you buy are ripe, because tasteless tomatoes have nowhere to hide in the accompanying ragout.

**COUSCOUS CAKES:**

3 cups water
1 teaspoon salt
Fresh-ground black pepper to taste
$1^2/_3$ cups couscous
3 eggs
1/2 cup unbleached white flour
1/2 cup chopped parsley
1/4 cup crumbled blue cheese, such as Danish blue
    or Wisconsin Gorgonzola
1 tablespoon olive oil

**TOMATO-GARLIC RAGOUT:**

1 tablespoon olive oil
1 cup chopped onion
3 to 4 garlic cloves, minced
10 plum tomatoes, chopped
1/2 cup white wine
1/4 cup water
Salt and fresh-ground black pepper to taste

**GARNISH:**

6 parsley sprigs

**1.** Put the water into a saucepan over high heat. When the water comes to a boil, add the salt, pepper, and couscous. Remove the pan from the heat, cover it, and let it sit undisturbed for 5 minutes. Fluff the couscous by lightly running a fork or a whisk back and forth in the pan, starting with the top layer and gradually working your way down.

**2.** In a large bowl, whisk the eggs, then slowly whisk in the flour. Then, with a spoon, stir in the parsley and the blue cheese. Add the couscous, and chill the batter for 30 minutes.

**3.** In a medium saucepan, heat 1 tablespoon olive oil, and add the onion. Sauté over medium heat for 5 minutes, stirring occasionally. Add the garlic, and sauté for 5 minutes more. Then add the tomatoes, white wine, and water. Let the ragout simmer for 10 to 15 minutes, until it has the consistency of a thick sauce. Season it with salt and pepper, and keep it warm.

**4.** When the couscous mixture has cooled, heat a large skillet with 1 tablespoon olive oil over medium-high heat. When the oil is hot, drop couscous batter onto the skillet to form 3-inch cakes. Sear them on one side for about 3 minutes, or until the undersides are golden brown. Then flip them with a spatula, and sear them on the other side, for about 3 minutes. Remove the cakes to a plate, and add more batter to the pan. Continue making cakes until all the couscous batter is used. You should have three cakes per person.

**5.** Serve the cakes hot atop the warmed tomato-garlic ragout, garnished with the parsley sprigs.

*Serves 6*

# Tomatoes and Eggplant over Couscous with Caper Sauce

This dish makes me momentarily feel as if I am in an old Moroccan village sitting in a cafe overlooking the thrashing Mediterranean. The sun, a little red ball, is falling into the ocean. A dashing waiter who resembles a young Marlon Brando is pouring me a glass of Chianti. This is all much more fun than looking out of my kitchen window, which faces another building.

* * * * *

1/4 cup olive oil
1 large eggplant (about 1 1/2 pounds), sliced into
    1/2-inch-thick rounds, and each round cut
    in half
1 teaspoon salt, plus more to taste
Fresh-ground black pepper to taste
2 medium round tomatoes, cut into eighths, or
    4 plum tomatoes, cut into quarters
2 1/2 cups minced onions
1 teaspoon cumin seeds
1/2 teaspoon ground coriander seeds
3 garlic cloves, minced
1 teaspoon grated lemon rind
1/4 cup lemon juice (from about 1 lemon)
1/3 cup sherry
5 cups water or Basic Vegetable Stock
   (page 79)
2 tablespoons drained capers
1 cup cooked chickpeas
2 cups couscous
2 tablespoons chopped cilantro

* * * * *

**1.** Preheat the oven to 400°. Brush a large baking sheet with 1 tablespoon of the olive oil. Lay the eggplant slices on the baking sheet, and salt and pepper them. Place the tomatoes in a casserole dish, drizzle them with 1 tablespoon of the olive oil, and salt and pepper them. Bake both the eggplant and the tomatoes. The tomatoes will be done in 15 minutes; the eggplant will take about 15 to 20 minutes (when it's done, the flesh will be soft). Remove the tomatoes and the eggplant from the oven. When the eggplant has cooled, cut it into bite-size pieces.

## Capers

*If you stumbled across a caper plant (which wouldn't be likely unless you were in Europe), you probably wouldn't connect it with the caper we know and love. A trailing shrub, the caper plant sports small, light green flower buds in early summer; these are capers in their fresh form. If capers are left on the shrub, they open into delicate white flowers, resembling small, long-stemmed roses. If you tried a raw caper you'd see why they need to be pickled. The bitter, acrid bud becomes piquant, sweet, and peppery when tamed by salt and vinegar. I enjoy capers of all sizes; the larger ones make nice garnishes. Many consider the capers from the island Pantelleria, which lies south of Sicily, to be the finest of all.*

**2.** Pour the remaining olive oil into a saucepan. Add the onions, cumin, and coriander. Sauté over medium heat, stirring occasionally, until the onions are soft, about 5 minutes. Add the garlic. Sauté 3 to 4 minutes more, stirring often. Add the lemon rind and juice, the sherry, and 1 cup of the water or stock. Let the mixture boil for 3 minutes. Then add the capers, chickpeas, eggplant, tomatoes, ¼ teaspoon salt, and pepper to taste, and remove the pan from the heat.

**3.** Bring the remaining 4 cups water or stock to a boil in a large saucepan with ¾ teaspoon salt. Add the couscous, bring to a boil, then take the pan off of the heat. Let the couscous stand, covered, for 5 minutes.

**4.** Reheat the eggplant-tomato mixture, and season it with more salt and pepper, if you like. Fluff the couscous by lightly running a fork or a whisk back and forth in the pan, starting with the top layer and gradually working your way down. Spoon the vegetables and sauce onto the couscous. Garnish with the chopped cilantro, and serve.

*Serves 4*

# Planet Moussaka

I'm in the Greek moussaka camp, where a béchamel cream sauce is poured over the top of the casserole; Turkish moussaka leaves this out. In my version, I've lightened the traditional cream sauce a bit and added a handful of fresh herbs. All you need to round out this dinner is a lightly dressed salad and some hearty whole-grain bread.

5 cups water
1 teaspoon salt
2½ cups bulgur
1 large eggplant (about 1½ pounds), sliced into
    ½-inch-thick rounds
2 tablespoons butter

2 garlic cloves, minced
3 tablespoons unbleached white flour
3 cups whole or low-fat milk, warmed
½ cup chopped basil, cilantro, parsley, or dill, or
    a combination
1 pinch ground nutmeg or ground cinnamon
Salt and fresh-ground black pepper to taste
3½ cups (1 28-ounce can) peeled plum tomatoes
1 egg, beaten

**1.** Preheat the oven to 400°. In a large saucepan, bring the water and the 1 teaspoon salt to a boil. Add the bulgur, and cover the pan. Let the bulgur sit for 10 minutes.

**2.** Lay the eggplant slices on one or two lightly greased baking sheets. Bake them in the oven for 15 minutes or until the eggplant has softened but is not browned. Remove the eggplant from the oven, and lower the temperature to 350°.

**3.** While the eggplant bakes, make the béchamel: Melt the butter in a saucepan over medium heat. Add the garlic, and cook it, stirring, for 1 minute. Add the flour, and stir constantly for 1 minute. Slowly add the milk, ½ cup at a time, whisking well after each addition. Simmer the mixture, stirring frequently, for 5 minutes, then take the pan off the heat. Add the herbs, the nutmeg or cinnamon, and salt and pepper.

**4.** Spoon the bulgur into a 9-by-11-inch casserole dish, and pat the bulgur down well. Then lay the eggplant slices on the bulgur, overlapping them in rows. Squeeze the tomatoes through your hands to break them up, and spread the broken tomatoes and their juice over the eggplant.

**5.** When the béchamel has cooled a bit, whisk the egg into it. Pour the sauce over the tomatoes. (At this point you can cover the dish with plastic wrap and refrigerate the moussaka for up to 2 days, if you'd like to bake it later.)

**6.** Bake the moussaka, uncovered, at 350° for 45 minutes (or 55 minutes if it has been chilled). Slice it as you would lasagna, and serve.

**Variation:** For the ultimate moussaka, slice 3 cups onions, and sauté them with 1 tablespoon olive oil and salt and pepper. Cook them well, about 20 minutes over low heat, stirring occasionally. Spoon the onions over the bulgur before adding the eggplant.

*Serves 8*

# Farro "Risotto" with Shiitakes in Roasted Acorn Squash

This dish is a favorite of mine. Every diner gets a baked acorn squash stuffed with shiitake mushrooms and cracked farro cooked in the style of risotto. Farro, the Italian term for spelt, is closely related to common wheat but has 30 percent more protein. Cracked, it looks like bulgur, and can be found in some Italian markets. If you can't find farro, cracked wheat or Arborio rice makes a good substitute (see the Variations following the recipe).

Serve this dish with a tossed salad and some fresh bread. In Boston, many markets sell a wonderful pecan-raisin loaf that seems to be made just for this meal.

2 large acorn squashes, halved and seeded
3 tablespoons butter
1 cup minced onion
1½ cups minced fennel bulb or celery stalks
1 large garlic clove, minced
1½ cups cracked farro (or cracked spelt)
⅓ cup sherry or white wine
4½ cups water or Basic Vegetable Stock (page 79)
1 teaspoon salt
¼ cup grated Parmesan cheese
Salt and fresh-ground black pepper to tast
2 cups chopped shiitake mushroom caps

**1.** Preheat the oven to 400°. Slice a bit off the outside of each squash half so that the halves won't wobble on plates. Bake the squash flesh side down on a baking sheet for 1 hour or until the flesh is tender.

**2.** Meanwhile, heat 1½ tablespoons butter in a large skillet over medium heat. Add the onion and the fennel or celery. Sauté the vegetables, stirring occasionally, for about 8 minutes, or until they have softened.

**3.** Add the garlic, and sauté 2 minutes more. Add the farro, and sauté, stirring, for 1 minute. Add the sherry or wine, and continue stirring. When the wine is absorbed, add ½ cup of the water or stock and the 1 teaspoon salt, and stir as the mixture simmers. Add another ½ cup water or stock once the first is absorbed, and stir occasionally. Continue adding liquid in this manner until it is all added and absorbed, about 30 minutes. When the farro is tender but slightly chewy, stir in the Parmesan cheese and salt and pepper to taste. Take the skillet off the heat.

**4.** In a smaller skillet, melt the remaining 1½ tablespoons butter. Sauté the shiitakes over medium heat, stirring often, for 5 minutes. Add salt and pepper to taste. Fold half of the shiitakes into the farro, and reserve the rest.

**5.** Assemble the dish: If the squash has cooled, reheat it in the oven. Then place the squash halves cut side up on plates, and fill them with the warm risotto. Mound the risotto so that one-quarter of it fits in each half. Top the risotto with the remaining sautéed shiitakes, and serve right away.

**Variations:** If you can't find farro, you can use cracked wheat or Arborio rice. Cracked wheat, found in well-stocked supermarkets and whole-foods stores, shouldn't be confused with bulgur, which is precooked. For cracked wheat, use the same quantities of grain and water as for farro, and cook the cracked wheat about the same amount of time (30 minutes). For Arborio rice, use only 1¼ cups rice and 3¾ cups water or stock. The rice will be done in about 20 minutes, when it is tender but still slightly chewy.

*Serves 4*

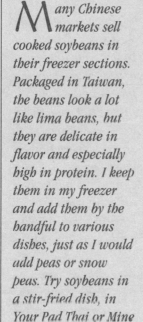
# Whole Spelt with Choy and Sesame

Spelt is a tasty as well as protein-rich grain. It can be eaten whole, as in this recipe, or broken into pieces and cooked like rice, as in the Farro "Risotto" with Shiitakes in Roasted Acorn Squash (page 261). Finding spelt may be a challenge; look for it in whole-foods stores. If searching out spelt is too much trouble, just use short-grain brown rice instead. It will work very well without any adjustments in measurements or cooking times.

If you can get to an Asian market, do look for the soybeans in the freezer section. They are pretty and delicious as well as full of protein.

2 tablespoons canola or corn oil
1 cup chopped onion
3 cups plus 3 tablespoons water
Pinch of salt
1½ cups whole spelt
1½ pounds bok choy, joy choy, or any choy you choose
1½ tablespoons sugar
2 tablespoons soy sauce
2 tablespoons apple cider vinegar
2 tablespoons Chinese rice wine, sherry, or sake
1 teaspoon cornstarch
3 garlic cloves, minced
1½ cups frozen soybeans (optional)
1 red bell pepper, seeded and cut into thin julienne strips
8 ounces firm tofu, cut into ½-inch cubes
2 teaspoons dark sesame oil
¼ cup chopped toasted cashews

1. In a saucepan, heat 1 tablespoon of the canola or corn oil over medium heat. Add the onion, and sauté for 5 minutes or until the onion softens. Add the 3 cups water and a pinch of salt, and bring the water to a boil. Add the spelt, turn the heat to low, and cover the pan. Simmer for 45 minutes.

2. While the spelt is cooking, soak the choy greens in a tub of cold water for 5 minutes, then drain them in a colander for 15 minutes. In a small bowl, stir together the sugar, soy sauce, vinegar, 3 tablespoons water, wine, and cornstarch.

3. About 10 minutes before the spelt is done, heat a wok or large skillet (preferably non-stick) with the remaining 1 table-spoon canola or corn oil over medium heat. Add the minced garlic, then the drained choy greens (stand back—the pan may spit oil), and turn the heat to high. Stir with a wooden spoon for 2 to 3 minutes, then add the soybeans if you like, the red pepper, and the soy-cornstarch mixture. Cover the pan, turn the heat back down to medium, and simmer the vegetables for 8 minutes.

4. Stir the vegetables, and add the tofu and the sesame oil. Toss gently. Spoon the spelt onto the plates, then spoon the choy-tofu mixture over the grain. Sprinkle the plates with the chopped cashews, and serve.

*Serves 4*

# Giant Stuffed Mushrooms

Don't try passing these around as hors d'oeuvres; they're too big to fit in anyone's mouth. The large portobello mush-rooms are stuffed with kasha, mushroom stems, carrot, celery, and parsley. Kasha is the Russian name for toasted buckwheat groats, whose distinct nutty and woodsy flavor is a natural part-ner for the portobello mushroom. Just one of these enormous stuffed mushrooms can be dinner for a hungry person.

## Complementary Proteins

*Back in the Wood-stock era, a lot of people were talking about "complemen-tary proteins." In the influential book* Diet for a Small Planet, *Frances Moore Lappé described meals that carefully combined different plant pro-teins to create a high-quality protein simi-lar to animal protein. For instance, beans were to be eaten with grains because beans and grains are rich in different plant pro-teins, thus "comple-menting" each other. But recent studies have shown that you don't need to eat two protein-rich foods to-gether; they will com-plement each other so long as you eat them within the same day. It is much easier than previously thought to get complete proteins on a vegetarian diet.*

4 large portobello mushrooms (each at least
   6 inches in diameter)
2 tablespoons olive oil
1/2 teaspoon salt, plus more to taste
Fresh-ground black pepper to taste
1 to 2 garlic cloves, minced
1 cup chopped onion
1 large carrot, chopped fine
1 celery stalk, chopped fine
2/3 cup kasha (toasted buckwheat groats)
1 1/4 cups water
3 tablespoons chopped parsley

**1.** Preheat the oven to 400°. Remove the mushroom stems from the caps, and set the stems aside. Place the caps gill side up on a baking sheet. Drizzle them with 1 tablespoon of the olive oil, and sprinkle them with salt and pepper. Roast them in the oven for 25 minutes. Keep them warm.

**2.** While the mushroom caps roast, make the pilaf: Cut off the dirty base from each mushroom stem, and chop the stems fine. In a large skillet, heat the remaining 1 tablespoon olive oil over medium heat. Add the garlic and onion, and sauté them, stirring often, until they are softened, about 5 minutes. Then stir in the carrot, celery, and kasha, and cook 2 minutes more. Add the water and 1/2 teaspoon salt, bring the mixture to a boil, then turn the heat to low. Simmer, covered, for 15 to 20 minutes or until the kasha is tender, then take the pan off the heat. Stir in the chopped parsley, and season to taste with salt and pepper.

**3.** Stuff the warm caps with the hot pilaf, and serve.

Variation: In the summertime, I like one of these stuffed mushrooms on a bed of fresh arugula dressed with balsamic vinegar and olive oil.

Serves 4

# Lambless
# Shepherd's Pie

When one of my friends asked me to devise a vegetarian version of shepherd's pie, I gladly accepted the challenge. I've always liked the notion of a savory pie topped with mashed potatoes. This dish takes some time to prepare (about 1¼ hours to assemble, and 30 minutes more to bake), but it is worth the effort.

5 medium russet potatoes, peeled
4 tablespoons butter
1½ teaspoons salt
Fresh-ground black pepper to taste
2 cups warm whole or low-fat milk
½ cup kasha (toasted buckwheat groats)
⅔ cup bulgur
2 cups minced onions
2 garlic cloves, minced
2 carrots, chopped fine
2 cups sliced mushrooms (any variety)
1½ tablespoons unbleached white flour
1 cup frozen or fresh and blanched corn kernels
3 tablespoons chopped parsley

**1.** Bring 2½ quarts of water to a boil in a large pot. Cut the potatoes into thirds, and drop them into the water. Gently boil the potatoes for 20 minutes or until they are tender. Drain them, and return the potatoes to the pot. Add 2 tablespoons of the butter, ¾ teaspoon salt, and pepper. Mash the potatoes with a potato masher, incorporating ½ cup of the warm milk, until they are fairly smooth. Set the pot aside.

**2.** In a saucepan, bring 1½ cups water to a boil with ½ teaspoon salt, and add the kasha. Reduce the heat, and simmer the kasha, uncovered, for 15 minutes. Add 1½ cups more water, and bring the mixture to a boil. Then add the bulgur, cover the pan, and take it off the heat. Let the grain stand undisturbed for 10 minutes. Transfer the contents to a large bowl.

**3.** In a large saucepan, heat the remaining 2 tablespoons butter. Add the onions, garlic, and carrots, and sauté them over medium heat, stirring frequently, until the onions soften. Add the mushrooms, and continue cooking for 3 to 4 minutes, stirring frequently. Sprinkle the flour over the vegetables, and stir constantly for 2 minutes, until the flour begins to brown. Pour the remaining 1½ cups milk over the vegetables, and turn the heat to high. While the sauce boils, stir with a whisk until it is smooth. Turn the heat down, and simmer the sauce for 5 minutes. Add the corn, ¼ teaspooon salt, and black pepper to taste.

**4.** Add the vegetable-gravy mixture to the bowl of kasha and bulgur. Stir well. Butter a 10-inch pie pan or casserole dish, and spoon the vegetable-grain mixture into it. Smooth the mixture with a plastic spatula. Then spoon on the mashed potatoes, leaving an uneven top surface. (At this point you can refrigerate the dish for up to 2 days, if you like.)

**5.** Preheat the oven to 350°. Bake the pie uncovered for 30 minutes, or 45 minutes if the pie was chilled. Garnish with the chopped parsley, cut the pie into pieces, and serve.

Serves 6 to 8

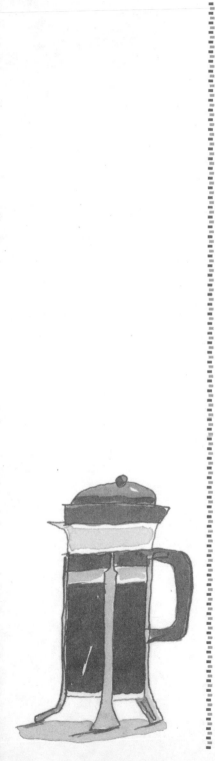

# Peanut Millet with Grilled Curried Vegetables

High in protein, millet is the staple food for one-third of humanity. It is a mild-tasting and inexpensive grain that takes well to many flavors. Although I call for grilling the vegetables in this dish, they are just as good when roasted (see the Variation at the end of the recipe). Millet is available in whole-foods stores and well-stocked supermarkets.

2²/₃ cups water

1¹/₂ teaspoons salt, plus more to taste

1 cup hulled millet

6 tablespoons olive oil

3 tablespoons balsamic vinegar

2 tablespoons orange juice

4 garlic cloves, minced

1 tablespoon minced fresh ginger

2 tablespoons curry powder, store-bought or homemade (page 36)

¹/₂ teaspoon ground cinnamon

¹/₂ teaspoon fresh-ground black pepper, plus more to taste

1 tablespoon honey

3 of the following vegetables: 1 red onion, quartered; 2 carrots, peeled and sliced in half lengthwise; ¹/₂ of a 1-pound eggplant, sliced in ¹/₂-inch-thick rounds; 1 red bell pepper, seeded and cut into narrow strips; 8 large white button mushrooms, cut in half, or 1 large portobello mushroom, sliced into ¹/₂-inch-thick strips

¹/₂ cup chopped dry-roasted, unsalted peanuts

2 tablespoons minced cilantro

1. In a large skillet over medium heat, heat the water with 1 teaspoon salt until the water comes to a boil. Add the millet, and bring to a boil again. Cover the pan, and turn down the heat. Cook the millet for 30 minutes over low heat, then turn off the heat and keep the pan covered.

2. While the millet is cooking, heat a grill over a medium-hot fire. (If you can hold your hand 5 inches away from the fire for 3 seconds and no longer, it is medium-hot, says Chris Schlesinger, co-author of *The Thrill of the Grill*. But, please, blame Chris, not me, if you get burned.)

3. In a small bowl, combine the olive oil, vinegar, orange juice, garlic, ginger, curry powder, cinnamon, black pepper, honey,

and ½ teaspoon salt. Place all of the vegetables in a large bowl, and pour the marinade over them. Toss well with your hands. (The vegetables can sit for up to 24 hours in this marinade; just cover and refrigerate them.)

**4.** Place the vegetables on the grill, and salt and pepper them well. Grill the carrots and onion on the coolest part of the grill for 10 minutes or so, turning them periodically. Grill the eggplant, pepper, and mushrooms for about 3 minutes per side.

**5.** Stir the peanuts into the warm millet. Spoon the millet onto plates, then distribute the grilled vegetables on top. Spoon the remaining marinade over the vegetables, sprinkle with cilantro, and serve.

**Variation:** If you'd like to roast the marinated vegetables instead of grilling them, place them in a large baking dish, and roast them in a preheated 400° oven until the vegetables are tender, about ½ hour.

*Serves 4*

# Fragrant Millet Pilaf

With the flavors of saffron, orange rind, coriander seed, and cardamom infusing each grain, plain millet is plain no more. Tofu, corn kernels, and tomatoes are interspersed throughout this pilaf, providing enough substance and variety to make the dish a meal in itself.

1 tablespoon olive oil
1 cup minced onion
1 cup hulled millet
1 teaspoon ground coriander seeds
¼ teaspoon ground cardamom
1 pinch saffron threads
1 teaspoon salt, plus more to taste
Fresh-ground black pepper to taste

## Millet

There are a lot of ways to eat millet. For a nutty flavor, sauté the millet for a few minutes in olive oil before adding water or stock (whether you sauté the millet or not, you'll need 3 cups liquid for each cup of millet) You can add cooked millet to burger mixes, stuff vegetables with it, or make a side dish of millet and dried fruits. Chilled cooked millet is good tossed with vinaigrette. Millet is sold in health-food and whole-foods stores. Besides having high levels of phosphorus, B vitamins, and iron, millet is rich in lysine, making it a high-quality protein.

2³/₄ cups water or Basic Vegetable Stock
    (page 79)
8 ounces firm tofu
²/₃ cup white wine
¹/₃ cup minced shallots
2 garlic cloves, minced
Kernels from 2 ears corn, or 1¹/₃ cups frozen
    corn kernels
1 teaspoon grated orange rind
1¹/₂ cups chopped tomatoes
2 tablespoons chopped chives or scallions

**1.** In a heavy saucepan, heat the olive oil over medium heat. Add the onion, and sauté for 5 minutes, stirring frequently. Add the millet, coriander, and cardamom, and sauté for another minute or two, stirring constantly. Add the saffron threads, salt, pepper, and water or stock. Bring the mixture to a boil over high heat, then cover the pan, and simmer for 30 minutes.

**2.** While the millet simmers, prepare the tofu: Cut the tofu into small cubes, about the size of peas. Place the tofu in a saucepan, and cover it with the white wine. Add the shallots and the garlic. Place the pan over medium-high heat until the wine comes to a simmer, then turn the heat to low. Simmer the tofu for 10 minutes or until the wine is reduced by half.

**3.** When the millet has simmered for 30 minutes, add to it the tofu, its cooking liquid, the corn, and the orange rind. Stir well, then cover the pan again, and continue cooking for 5 more minutes.

**4.** Stir the tomatoes into the millet. Season with salt and pepper, then spoon the millet pilaf onto plates. Garnish with the chopped chives or scallions, and serve.

Serves 4

# CHAPTER 10

# The Global Noodle

# Soba with Toasted Sesame Seed Sauce

S oba are Japanese noodles usually made from both wheat and buckwheat flours. Available in Asian markets, whole-foods stores, and some supermarkets, they can be fairly expensive. In this recipe, you can substitute Asian wheat noodles or even Italian vermicelli, if you like. But soba's silken texture is irresistible, so do splurge if you can spare an extra dollar or two.

This sesame-flavored noodle dish is best served at room temperature.

½ cup hulled white sesame seeds

8 ounces dried soba noodles

2 tablespoons Chinese black vinegar (available in Chinese markets; I recommend Gold Plum's Chinkiang) or balsamic vinegar

1 tablespoon sugar

2 to 3 tablespoons soy sauce

1 to 2 teaspoons minced fresh ginger

1 garlic clove, minced

1 teaspoon dark sesame oil

5 scallions, both white and green parts, chopped fine

3 cups small broccoli pieces or 2-inch asparagus pieces, blanched

**1.** Preheat the oven to 375°. Pour the sesame seeds onto a rimmed baking sheet. Toast the seeds in the oven for 10 to 12 minutes, until they are a rich brown around the edges.

**2.** Meanwhile, bring a large pot of salted water to a boil. Add the noodles, and cook them for 5 to 6 minutes, or until they are just tender. Drain them, rinse them well with cold water, and drain them again.

**3.** In a large bowl, mix together the vinegar, sugar, soy sauce, ginger, garlic, sesame oil, and scallions. Add the noodles and the toasted sesame seeds. Stir well, then stir in the broccoli or asparagus. Let the dish sit for 30 minutes at room temperature before serving.

**Variation:** I've also made this dish with the dark gray Korean noodles made from sweet-potato starch. The flavor and textures are sensational. These noodles can be found at Korean and Japanese markets. Like the soba, they take 5 to 6 minutes to cook.

Serves 2 to 3

# Wakame and Soba Noodle Soup

Wakame, a sea vegetable (the politically correct term for seaweed), gives this dish the aroma of a Japanese seafood stew. Combining the wakame with soba (Japanese buckwheat noodles), carrots, tofu, and scallions, this hearty soup makes an easy one-dish dinner, though you might add a salad or dessert.

Wakame and soba are available in whole-foods stores and Japanese markets; you may even find soba in your supermarket.

7 cups water
1 ounce wakame sea vegetable
2 cups sliced onions
1 1-inch piece fresh ginger, sliced into 6 thin
    rounds
6 ounces dried soba noodles
2 cups chopped carrots
1 tablespoon dark sesame oil
8 ounces silken tofu, cut into ½-inch cubes
½ cup finely chopped scallions

### Seaweed Scoop

Don't think you can escape eating seaweed! Sea vegetables, to use the current term, are in commercial ice creams, baked goods, and even hot dogs; they serve as stabilizers, thickeners, and emulsifiers. But whole sea vegetables are much better for you; they are loaded with iodine, iron, magnesium, calcium, and phosphorus. Vegetarians like to use sea vegetables in miso soups, Asian-style stews, and sushi. Some of the mildest and best-liked seaweeds include nori (used in sushi), arame, kombu (kelp), hijiki (flaked kelp), and dulse. Look for seaweeds in health-food or whole-foods stores and in Japanese markets. Dried seaweeds keep indefinitely if they are stored in airtight containers.

1 tablespoon rice vinegar, or a bit more, to taste
2 tablespoons miso, or a bit more, to taste
Salt to taste (optional)

**1.** In a large pot, combine the water, wakame, onions, and ginger. Over medium heat, let the mixture simmer for 20 minutes.

**2.** Meanwhile, bring a large pot of salted water to a boil. Add the soba noodles, boil them for 4 to 5 minutes, then drain them and rinse them with cool water. Set the rinsed soba aside.

**3.** Add the carrots to the simmering wakame liquid, and continue to simmer for 10 more minutes. Add the noodles, sesame oil, tofu, scallions, vinegar, and miso. Taste the soup, and add a little salt, vinegar, or miso, if you like. Ladle the soup into large soup bowls (discarding the ginger or leaving it in the bowls), and eat it with spoons.

Variation: Peel and halve lengthwise 4 inches of daikon radish, then slice the halves crosswise into thin half-moons. Add the daikon to the soup with the carrots in step 3.

Serves 4

# Vietnamese Rice-Noodle Salad

Based on a terrific Vietnamese sauce called *nuoc nam ngo,* the dressing for this salad consists of cilantro, garlic, sugar, lime juice, and fish sauce (strict vegetarians can use salt instead of the fish sauce). *Nuoc nam ngo* is traditionally made in a mortar, so that the pounding of the coriander leaves releases their aromatic oils, helping to emulsify the sauce. But a food processor or blender does the job nearly as well. Tossed with cold rice noodles, grated carrot, cucumber, and tender nappa cabbage leaves, this light salad makes for a satisfying meal on a warm day.

4 to 6 garlic cloves

1 cup chopped and loosely packed cilantro

1/2 jalapeño or other fresh hot pepper, chopped (optional)

3 tablespoons sugar

1/4 cup lime juice (from about 2 limes)

3 tablespoons Thai or Vietnamese fish sauce, or 1 teaspoon salt

12 ounces dried rice vermicelli

2 carrots, peeled and cut into very thin julienne strips or grated

1 cucumber, peeled if it looks waxed, then halved lengthwise, seeded, and sliced into thin half-rounds

1/4 cup coarsely chopped fresh mint

4 leaves from a nappa cabbage, sliced thin (optional)

1/4 cup chopped dry-roasted, unsalted peanuts

4 mint sprigs

**1.** To make the sauce by hand, mince the garlic with the cilantro and the hot pepper. Transfer the mixture to a bowl, add the lime juice, fish sauce or salt, and sugar, and stir well. To make the sauce in a food processor or blender, briefly blend the garlic with the cilantro, hot pepper, and sugar, until the vegetables are coarsely chopped. Then blend in the lime juice and fish sauce or salt. Let the sauce sit for 5 minutes.

**2.** Bring a large pot of salted water to a boil. Add the rice noodles, and boil them for 2 minutes (but no more). Drain the noodles, and rinse them well with cold water until they have cooled. Let them drain again for a few minutes.

**3.** In a large bowl, combine the sauce, noodles, carrots, cucumber, mint, and, if you're using it, nappa cabbage. Toss well, and serve the salad garnished with the peanuts and mint sprigs.

Serves 4

# Your Pad Thai or Mine

One of my favorite meals, Pad Thai is a brilliant combination of ingredients and flavors. I love the chewy, almost sticky texture of the sautéed rice noodles. In this version, I've omitted the traditional dried shrimp, but I've retained the fish sauce. Those who want 100-percent vegetarian Pad Thai can use salt instead. (Don't use soy sauce; its flavor and color would overwhelm this delicate noodle dish.)

3/4 pound dried rice noodles (the width of
    fettuccine or linguine)
1/4 cup lime juice, or more, to taste (from 2 to 3
    limes)
3 tablespoons Thai or Vietnamese fish sauce, or
    1 teaspoon salt
2 tablespoons brown sugar
1 to 2 teaspoons hot chile sauce
3 tablespoons canola or corn oil
2 eggs, beaten
2 garlic cloves, minced
1 teaspoon minced fresh ginger (optional)
1 carrot, peeled and cut into thin julienne strips
8 to 10 scallions, halved lengthwise, then cut into
    2-inch lengths
1 cup mung bean sprouts
1/4 cup chopped dry-roasted, unsalted peanuts
1/4 cup chopped cilantro
1 lime, sliced into 1/8-inch rounds (optional)

**1.** Soak the noodles in 3 quarts hot water for 30 minutes, then drain them. (At this point you can store them, covered, for up to 24 hours in the refrigerator.)

**2.** In a small bowl, combine the lime juice, fish sauce or salt, sugar, chile sauce, and 1 tablespoon water.

**3.** Pour 1 tablespoon of the oil into a large non-stick skillet, and cook the eggs over low heat, stirring with a wooden spoon. Once the eggs are barely cooked, transfer them to a plate.

**4.** In the same skillet (rinsed if necessary), add the remaining 2 tablespoons oil. Over medium heat, add the garlic and ginger. Sauté for about 30 seconds, then add the carrot and scallions. Sauté for 1 minute more, stirring frequently. Add the lime juice mixture, then the drained noodles. Cook the noodles, stirring constantly, until they are tender but still chewy, about 1 minute. Add a bit more lime juice if you'd like a perkier Pad Thai, and add the sprouts and the scrambled eggs, stirring well. Quickly divide the mixture among plates, sprinkle with the peanuts and cilantro, garnish with the lime slices, if you like, and serve.

Note: Do not try to reheat this dish in the microwave. A friend of mine did, and it became a large and scary gelatinous glob of noodles that was absolutely inedible.

Serves 4

# Crispy Chinese Noodles with Eggplant and Peanuts

People who try this dish always want to know what kind of noodles they're eating. They are fresh Chinese noodles, the best bargain around. Although fresh Italian pasta is quite expensive, fresh Chinese noodles are usually under a dollar a pound. In this dish they form a crunchy crust over eggplant and peanuts in a Vietnamese-inspired sauce of ginger, sherry, vinegar, and onions.

1 eggplant (about 1 pound), cut into ½-inch
    cubes
1 teaspoon salt

1 pound fresh Chinese wheat noodles (available
    in Chinese markets and in the produce
    sections of many supermarkets)
2 tablespoons sherry
1 tablespoon cornstarch
1/4 cup red wine vinegar
1/3 cup water or Basic Vegetable Stock (page 79)
1 tablespoon minced fresh ginger
1 tablespoon sugar
2 tablespoons Thai or Vietnamese fish sauce, or
    1 teaspoon salt
2 cups sliced onions
3 tablespoons canola or corn oil
4 garlic cloves, minced
1 red bell pepper, seeded and cut into thin
    julienne strips
4 tablespoons chopped dry-roasted, unsalted
    peanuts
1 tablespoon chopped fresh mint (optional)

**1.** Put the eggplant cubes into a colander. Add the salt, and toss well. Let the eggplant drain for 15 minutes, then rinse it lightly with water. Let it drain again in the colander.

**2.** Bring a large pot of water to a boil. Add the noodles, and boil them for about 5 minutes, until they are tender. Drain them, and rinse them well with cold water. Let them drain in a colander for at least 10 minutes.

**3.** Combine the sherry with the cornstarch in a small bowl, and set the bowl aside. In a saucepan, combine the red wine vinegar, water or stock, ginger, sugar, fish sauce or salt, and onions. Bring the mixture to a boil, turn the heat to low, and let the mixture simmer for 5 minutes.

**4.** In a large skillet, preferably non-stick, heat 1½ tablespoons oil over medium-high heat. Add the eggplant, and cook it for 5 minutes, stirring frequently. Add the garlic and red pepper, and cook, stirring occasionally, for 5 minutes more or until the eggplant softens. Add both the onion-vinegar mixture and the

# Asian Noodles

**RICE VERMICELLI, OR RICE STICKS.** These very thin noodles are sold dry, often divided into skeins, in clear plastic packages in Asian markets and many supermarkets.
*To cook:* Soak the noodles in warm water until soft, about 30 minutes, before adding to soups, stir-fried dishes, and sauces. To serve cold or in rice-paper rolls, boil for 1 minute, then rinse well. They can also be deep-fried; drop them into hot oil, and they will immediately puff up. Drain the fried noodles, and use them in salads and stir-fried dishes.

**DRIED RICE NOODLES (THE WIDER ONES).** These noodles, used in pad Thai and other pan-fried dishes, vary in width from 1/16 to 1/3 inch. They are sold in Asian markets.
*To cook:* Pour a lot of very hot water over the noodles, and let them stand until soft (about 30 minutes). Strain the noodles, and lightly coat them with oil. Add them to a pan-fried dish such as pad Thai, to soup, or to stew.

**BEAN THREAD OR CELLOPHANE ("TRANSPARENT") NOODLES.** Made from mung-bean starch, these thin, dry noodles are sold in Asian markets and some supermarkets.
*To cook:* Soak the noodles in warm water until they are soft, about 15 minutes, then add them to soup or a stir-fried dish.

**FRESH RICE NOODLES (SHA HE FEN OR HU TIEU).** These are sold in folded sheets in larger Asian markets. When cooked, the noodles have a wonderful slippery, satiny texture.
*To cook:* The sheets are cut into thin strips and stir-fried, or cut into wide strips, rolled around a filling, and steamed or pan-fried. Best used the day they are purchased, but will keep for up to 5 days in the refrigerator. After refrigeration, they need to be resoftened: Drop them into boiling water, and boil for about 2 minutes.

**FRESH CHINESE WHEAT NOODLES, OR MEIN.** Typically sold in 1-pound packages, these noodles vary in width. They are sold in most supermarkets as well as Asian markets.
*To cook:* Boil these in plenty of unsalted water until they are tender, about 4 to 6 minutes. Rinse the cooked noodles before adding them to a pan-fried dish or soup.

**DRIED CHINESE WHEAT NOODLES.** These are sold in swirled nests and straight lengths.
*To cook:* Ignore any directions on the package. Boil the noodles in unsalted water until they are tender; the time will vary depending on the width of the noodles. Use the noodles as you would fresh wheat noodles: pan-fried, in soups, or in stews.

**DRIED UDON.** These medium-size Japanese wheat noodles are sold in 12-ounce and 16-ounce packages in Asian markets and whole-foods stores. If unavailable, substitute soba.
*To cook:* Typically served in broth, udon noodles are first boiled in water until tender.

**DRIED SOBA.** These Japanese buckwheat noodles may also contain wheat flour. They are traditionally served with *dashi* (a stock of bonito and kelp). Sold in Asian markets and whole-foods stores, they are rather expensive. Udon noodles can be substituted.
*To cook:* Boil soba noodles in water until they are tender. Serve them cold or pan-fried.

cornstarch-sherry mixture. Cook for 2 to 3 minutes, stirring occasionally. Keep the mixture warm.

**5.** In a large non-stick or well-seasoned skillet, heat the remaining 1½ tablespoons oil over medium-high heat. When the oil begins to smoke, add the noodles, then place two or three plates on top of them so that more surface area will brown. Let the noodles sit over medium-high heat for 5 minutes. When the noodles have developed a golden brown crust on the underside, remove the plates, turn the noodles over with a spatula, and cook them 5 minutes on the other side. Then take the pan off the heat.

**6.** Add the peanuts to the eggplant mixture, and spoon it onto plates. Divide the noodles into four parts, and place them atop the vegetables and sauce. Sprinkle with mint, if you like, and serve.

*Serves 4*

# Chinese Noodle Pancakes with Asparagus

A deep-brown crust develops on these noodle cakes, and every bite brings a splendid crunch against the soft noodles inside. The vegetables swim in a simple sauce of soy and sherry or rice wine, accented with fresh ginger, sesame oil, and a sprinkling of fermented black beans.

1 pound fresh Chinese wheat noodles (available
    in Chinese markets and in the produce
    sections of many supermarkets)
½ pound fresh asparagus
2 tablespoons canola or corn oil
2 garlic cloves, minced
1 teaspoon minced fresh ginger

1 cup water or Basic Vegetable Stock (page 79)
1 tablespoon cornstarch
2 tablespoons Chinese rice wine, sherry, or sake
2 tablespoons soy sauce
1 tablespoon unrinsed fermented black beans
    (available in Chinese markets; optional)
8 ounces fresh spinach, with stems
2 teaspoons dark sesame oil or hot chile
    sesame oil
Salt and fresh-ground black pepper to taste

**1.** Bring at least 3 quarts water to a boil. Add the noodles, and boil them for about 5 minutes, until they are tender. Drain the noodles, and rinse well with cold water until they are cool.

**2.** Break off the tough ends of the asparagus, and cut the rest of the spears into 2-inch lengths. In a large skillet, heat 1 tablespoon of the oil over medium heat. Add the garlic and ginger, and sauté for 1 minute, making sure not to brown the garlic. Add the asparagus and ½ cup of the water or stock. Simmer for 2 minutes. Put the cornstarch into a bowl, and stir in the remaining ½ cup water or stock and the rice wine or sherry. Stir well. Add this mixture, the soy sauce, and the fermented black beans, if you're using them, to the simmering vegetables. Let the sauce boil for a few seconds, then add the spinach, and stir until it wilts. Remove the skillet from the heat.

**3.** Fry the noodle cakes: Heat the remaining oil in your largest skillet over high heat. Divide the noodles into four mounds, and place the mounds of noodles in the hot skillet. (If there isn't enough space, fry two mounds at a time, adding a little more oil for the second two. Keep the first two warm in a slow oven while you cook the second two.) Place 2 or 3 plates on top of the mounds, so that more surface area will brown, reduce the heat to medium-high, and fry the cakes for at least 5 minutes, until they develop a golden-brown crust on the bottom. Turn the cakes over, and fry them for 3 minutes.

**4.** While the noodle cakes cook, reheat the vegetables and the sauce slightly. Add the sesame oil, salt, and pepper.

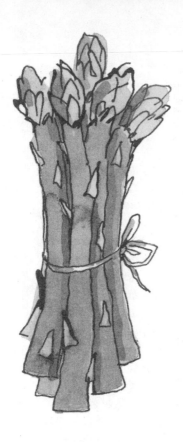

**5.** Place the noodle cakes on plates, spoon the sauce and vegetables over and around the cakes, and serve.

**Variations:** Substitute broccoli for the asparagus. Cut the broccoli into small florets and stem pieces; use about 2 cups. Cook the broccoli in the same way as the asparagus.

If you don't mind one more step, try fried shallots on this dish; they are wonderful. Fry 1 cup thinly sliced shallots in ¼ cup hot canola or corn oil until they brown, then remove them with a slotted spoon, and drain them on paper towels. Sprinkle them over the fried noodle cakes and vegetables before serving.

Serves 4

# Rice Noodles with Shiitakes, Choy, and Chiles

Fresh rice noodles, also called *sha he fen* or *hu tieu*, have a luscious soft, silky texture. They are delicious pan-fried, as in this recipe. Here I've combined them with shiitakes and choy and seasoned the mixture with a peppy sauce of ginger, sesame oil, black vinegar, and chiles. If you can't find fresh rice noodles, cooked dried rice noodles will work just fine. Dried rice noodles can be found in many supermarkets as well as in Asian markets. Fresh rice noodles and black vinegar can be found in Asian markets.

2½ tablespoons soy sauce
3 tablespoons Chinese rice wine, sherry, or sake
2 tablespoons Chinese black vinegar
  (I recommend Gold Plum's Chinkiang)
  or balsamic vinegar
2 teaspoons sugar
3 tablespoons water

2 teaspoons cornstarch

1 tablespoon canola or corn oil

2 tablespoons dark sesame oil

2 garlic cloves, sliced very thin

6 small dried red chile peppers, cut into ¼-inch
  pieces and seeded

1 tablespoon minced fresh ginger

1 small bunch bok choy, joy choy, or Shanghai
  bok choy, cut into 1½-inch strips

20 fresh shiitake mushroom caps, quartered

8 scallions, halved lengthwise

2 9-ounce packages fresh rice noodles (or
  8 ounces fettuccine-width dried rice noodles
  that have been soaked in hot water for 30
  minutes)

2 tablespoons toasted sesame seeds

**1.** Make the sauce: In a small bowl, whisk together the soy sauce, rice wine or sherry, vinegar, sugar, water, and cornstarch.

**2.** In a large skillet or wok, heat the oils over high heat. When the oil is nearly smoking, add the garlic and hot peppers. Take the skillet or wok off the heat after 10 seconds.

**3.** Reduce the heat to medium-high, and return the skillet or wok to the heat. Add the ginger, choy, shiitakes, and scallions, and cook for 3 minutes over high heat, stirring constantly. Add the fresh or soaked rice noodles and the soy mixture, and cook 2 minutes more or until the noodles are hot and tender. Serve the noodles immediately, topped with the toasted sesame seeds.

Note: If you won't be using fresh rice noodles the same day you buy them, refrigerate them. If you do so, however, you'll need to soften them before using them: Drop them in their sealed plastic bags into boiling water for a few minutes, and remove the bags with a slotted spoon. Then use the noodles as instructed in step 3.

Serves 4

## Choy-ville

*I*t takes just one stroll through the produce section of an Asian market to learn that bok choy is only one of many choys. Most stores sell four or five kinds; don't be afraid to try them. Shanghai bok choy, for example, is usually smaller than regular bok choy, with delicious, light green leaves and stems. Bok choy sum looks and tastes a lot like bok choy but is eaten in the flowering stage; it has little yellow flowers and narrower stalks. Yow choy has long thin stalks with large green leaves and tiny yellow flowers. Its flavor is more bitter than the others'.

Larger choy stalks are best split down the middle lengthwise (so the stems cook faster and the leaves don't overcook) and steamed or stir-fried.

# Pasta with Arugula Pesto

The unique flavor of arugula makes this pesto peppery and robust. Substitute a grain such as barley or millet for the pasta, if you like (check the chart on page 248 for cooking instructions).

¼ cup walnut pieces
2 to 3 large garlic cloves, cut in half
2 cups coarsely chopped arugula (stems included), firmly packed (about 1 bunch)
¼ cup coarsely chopped cilantro or basil
½ cup plus 1 tablespoon olive oil (preferably extra-virgin)
⅓ cup grated Parmesan cheese
Salt to taste
1 pinch cayenne
1 pound dried pasta (any kind, but I like spaghettini)
More Parmesan cheese, for garnish (optional)

**1.** Combine the walnuts, garlic, arugula, and cilantro or basil in a food processor or blender. Whirl them just until they are coarsely chopped. While the machine is running, add the olive oil in a thin stream. Transfer the pesto to a bowl. (At this point the pesto can be frozen. Thaw it before proceeding.)

**2.** Stir the Parmesan cheese, salt, and cayenne into the pesto.

**3.** Bring a large pot of salted water to a boil. Add the pasta, and cook it, stirring occasionally, until it is just tender.

**4.** Drain the pasta, return it to the empty pot, and toss it with the pesto, adding a tablespoon or two of water if necessary to distribute the pesto evenly. Transfer the pasta to a serving bowl or to individual plates, garnish with additional Parmesan cheese, if you like, and serve.

Serves 4

# Pasta with Jalapeño Pesto

This recipe came about one day when I had tons of jalapeños around the restaurant. Since some jalapeños are hotter than others, I always taste each pepper before deciding how many seeds I'd like to keep in my dish. If you have a low heat tolerance, you should definitely remove all the jalapeño seeds.

2 green bell peppers
3 large jalapeño peppers
5 tablespoons unsalted hulled raw pumpkin seeds,
    toasted 6 to 8 minutes in a 350° oven
1/4 cup coarsely chopped cilantro
2 to 3 large garlic cloves
1/4 cup olive oil
2 tablespoons lime juice (from about 1 lime)
1/2 teaspoon salt, or more, to taste
Fresh-ground black pepper to taste
1 pound dried pasta, such as fettuccine or
    linguine
1 1/2 cups cherry tomato halves
1/2 lime, cut into wedges

**1.** Preheat the oven to 450°. Place the bell and jalapeño peppers on a baking sheet. Roast the peppers for 15 to 20 minutes, until the skin blisters. (Or pierce each pepper with a fork, and char it lightly and evenly over a gas flame.) Let the peppers cool a bit, then pull the skin away from the flesh, and discard the skin.

**2.** In a food processor or blender, combine 4 tablespoons of the pumpkin seeds, the cilantro, the garlic, and the peppers (jalapeño seeds included, if you'd like more heat). Blend until the contents are coarsely chopped. With the machine running, slowly add the oil and the lime juice. Blend in the salt and pepper. (At this point the pesto can be refrigerated for up to 1 week.)

3. Bring a large pot of salted water to a boil. Cook the pasta, stirring occasionally, until it is just tender, drain it, and return it to the empty pot. Set it over medium heat, and add the tomatoes and the pesto. Stir well. Add more salt and pepper, if you'd like, and spoon the pasta onto plates. Serve it garnished with the remaining pumpkin seeds and the lime wedges.

Serves 4

# Pasta with Vietnamese Pesto

I like pasta with pesto because it is a one-bowl, one-pot deal. (The one bowl is the food processor or blender bowl, and the one pot is for boiling the noodles in.) Lately I have been experimenting with pesto-like sauces made with Vietnamese ingredients. Here cilantro, basil, peanuts, and chiles are ground together as a sauce for either rice or wheat noodles. To control the amount of heat in the pesto, begin with one chile pepper, and add more according to your taste. Consider doubling this recipe; it freezes beautifully.

1 pound dried rice noodles (I like them the width
    of vermicelli or fettuccine) or any dried
    pasta
1 1/2 cups coarsely chopped cilantro
1/2 cup lightly packed sweet, Thai, or lemon
    basil leaves
2 large garlic cloves, cut in half
1/2 teaspoon minced lemongrass bulb or grated
    lemon rind
1 to 2 jalapeños or other fresh chile peppers,
    seeded and chopped
1 tablespoon Thai or Vietnamese fish sauce, or
    1/2 teaspoon salt
4 tablespoons chopped dry-roasted, unsalted
    peanuts

7 tablespoons canola or corn oil
½ lime, cut into wedges
Salt and fresh-ground black pepper to taste

**1.** If you are using rice noodles, soak them in a large bowl of cold water for 30 minutes. Drain the noodles, and set them aside.

**2.** Make the pesto: In a blender or food processor, combine the chopped cilantro, basil, garlic cloves, lemongrass or lemon rind, chile peppers, fish sauce or salt, and 2 tablespoons of the peanuts. Whirl just until the herbs and peanuts are coarsely chopped.

**3.** While the machine is running, add the oil in a thin stream. Then add the remaining peanuts, and run the machine in short spurts until the peanuts are coarsely chopped. (At this point you can transfer the pesto to a container with a tight-fitting lid for later use. Store the pesto in the refrigerator for up to 1 week, or in the freezer for up to 3 months.)

**4.** If you are using dried wheat pasta, bring a large pot of salted water to a boil, and add the pasta. Cook the pasta, stirring occasionally, until it is just tender. Drain it, and return it to the pot. Add almost all of the pesto, and stir well, adding a few tablespoons of water if the pesto is clumping.

If you are using rice noodles, put them into a large skillet with ½ cup water over medium-high heat. Stir until most of the water has been absorbed and the noodles are tender. Then add almost all of the pesto, and stir constantly until the pesto is well incorporated.

**5.** Taste the pasta, and add more pesto, lime juice, fish sauce, salt, or pepper, if you like. Garnish the pasta with the remaining 2 tablespoons peanuts, and serve it right away.

**Variation:** Try this pesto with mint instead of or in addition to the basil. Mint is often used in Vietnamese salads, and it goes well with both cilantro and basil.

Serves 4

# Pasta with Baby Red Lentils and Ginger

Don't thumb past this recipe; the dish is "magically delicious," as Kelly, our super-waitress at the Delux, says, and it's easy to boot. The ginger flavor is mild, and the butter gives the pasta a lustrous finish. Red lentils (as they are usually called, although they are actually orange) are found in many whole-foods stores, supermarkets, and Indian markets. If you have a choice among lentil sizes, choose the smallest (for their appearance—they taste the same as bigger ones).

1 pound dried penne or other pasta
8 tablespoons butter
2 large garlic cloves, sliced very thin
1 2-inch piece of ginger, cut into thin julienne strips
1 teaspoon minced fresh sage, or 1/2 teaspoon crumbled dried sage
3/4 cup red lentils
1 cup water
2 cups fresh spinach, firmly packed
1 teaspoon salt
Fresh-ground black pepper to taste

**1.** Bring a large pot of salted water to a boil. Drop the pasta into the water, stir, and cook the pasta, stirring occasionally, until it is just tender. Drain it, and rinse it well.

**2.** Melt the butter in a large saucepan or skillet over medium heat. When the butter begins to turn golden with some brown specks, add the garlic and ginger. Cook for 1 minute, stirring constantly. Then add the sage, the lentils, and the 1 cup water. Bring the mixture to a boil, cover the pan, and reduce the heat to low.

**3.** Let the lentils simmer for 10 minutes or until they are tender but still slightly chewy (if the lentils are large they may need more time and more water). Stir the spinach and salt into the lentils, and turn the heat up a bit. Stir often until the spinach wilts, about 1 minute. Then add the cooked pasta and pepper to taste, and heat the mixture through. Serve immediately.

Serves 4 to 6

# Penne with Red Pepper Sauce and Broccoli

In this quick and easy recipe, sautéed red bell peppers and onions are puréed with almonds, for texture, and balsamic vinegar, which brings out the sweetness in the peppers. There's no need to roast and peel the peppers, since the skins also contribute to the pleasing texture of the sauce.

4 tablespoons olive oil
1½ cups chopped onions
2 large garlic cloves, minced
2 red bell peppers, seeded and chopped
¼ cup whole almonds
2 teaspoons balsamic vinegar
½ teaspoon salt, or a bit more, to taste
Fresh-ground black pepper to taste
1 or 2 pinches cayenne
4 cups broccoli florets
1 pound dried penne pasta
⅓ cup grated Parmesan cheese
½ cup basil leaves cut into thin strips

**1.** Heat 2 tablespoons of the olive oil over medium heat in a large skillet. Add the onions, and sauté them for about 5 minutes, stirring occasionally, until they soften. Lower the heat a bit, and add the garlic and red pepper. Continue to cook the vegetables, stirring often, for 15 minutes.

**2.** In a food processor or blender, chop the almonds fine. Add the pepper-onion mixture, the vinegar, and the remaining olive oil, and blend all to a purée. Add the salt, black pepper, and cayenne, and blend briefly to incorporate them.

**3.** Arrange a vegetable steamer over water in a saucepan. Bring the water to a boil, and add the broccoli. Cover the pan, and cook the broccoli over medium heat for 5 minutes or a bit longer, until it is as tender as you like. Keep it warm.

**4.** Cook the pasta in a large pot of salted boiling water until it is just tender. Drain the pasta, and return it to the pot. Add the red pepper sauce, the Parmesan cheese, the broccoli, and the basil. Heat the contents over medium heat until the pasta is very hot, and add more salt and pepper to taste, if necessary. Serve the pasta immediately.

*Serves 4 to 6*

# Penne with Ancho Peppers, Tomatoes, and Corn

Although rooted in Italian cuisine, pasta marries well with Mexican flavors. Corn, tomatillos, pumpkin seeds, and anchos create a sauce that is tart, sweet, smoky, and very delicious. Ancho peppers, which are poblano peppers in dried form, can be found in many supermarkets as well as Latin American markets. If you can't find anchos, use fresh poblanos cut into thin strips.

2 ancho peppers or 2 poblano peppers
12 whole tomatillos, husked
2 tablespoons olive oil

## Color-Coding Bell Peppers

*So little time, so many colors! Although bell peppers are never hot, their flavors do vary along with their colors. Green bell peppers are bittersweet and juicy. Red, yellow, and orange bell peppers are ripe, and therefore much sweeter than green peppers. Purple bell peppers are green under their skins, but they are often thinner-fleshed and less juicy than green bell peppers.*

2 cups chopped onions
1 teaspoon cumin seeds
2 large garlic cloves, minced
1 large tomato, chopped
1 cup fresh or frozen corn kernels
1 pound dried penne (or rotini)
1/3 cup heavy cream
3/4 teaspoon salt, or more, to taste
Fresh-ground black pepper to taste
3 tablespoons unsalted hulled raw pumpkin seeds,
    toasted 6 to 8 minutes in a 350° oven
2 tablespoons chopped fresh cilantro (optional)

**1.** In a saucepan, simmer the anchos in barely boiling water for 5 minutes. Remove the peppers with a slotted spoon, and set them aside to cool. (If you are using poblanos, you do not need to boil them.) Plunge the tomatillos into the boiling water. Let them cook for 1 minute. Drain the tomatillos, and let them cool.

**2.** Slice the ancho peppers thin, and remove the seeds unless you like your pasta spicy-hot. Chop the tomatillos well, and put them and their juice into a small bowl.

**3.** In a large skillet, heat the olive oil, and sauté the onions over medium heat, stirring occasionally. When the onions have softened, add the cumin seeds and the garlic. Sauté for 5 minutes more, stirring often. Add the chopped tomatillos, the tomato, the corn kernels, and the anchos. Sauté, stirring often, for 5 minutes.

**4.** Bring a large pot of salted water to a boil. Add the penne or rotini, and cook it, stirring occasionally, until it is just tender. Drain the pasta.

**5.** Add the heavy cream to the ancho sauce, and cook over medium heat until the cream is just heated through. Season with salt and pepper. Add the pasta and the pumpkin seeds, and stir well until all the ingredients are hot. Garnish each plate with chopped cilantro, if you like, and serve.

*Serves 4*

# Baked Rigatoni with Broccoli and Gorgonzola

You don't have to make lasagna to enjoy the combination of ricotta cheese and pasta. This baked pasta dish combines ricotta, rigatoni, Gorgonzola cheese, tomatoes, and broccoli. It's just as good as lasagna, but it takes a lot less work.

8 ounces dried rigatoni
2 tablespoons olive oil
3 garlic cloves, minced
1/2 bunch broccoli, cut into florets (about 4 cups)
1 1/3 cups ricotta cheese, whole-milk or part-skim
3 ounces Italian or Wisconsin Gorgonzola (or
    Stilton or Blue D'Auvergne) cheese,
    crumbled (about 1/2 cup)
Salt and fresh-ground black pepper to taste
2 tomatoes, each cut into 8 wedges each
1 cup grated Parmesan or Asiago cheese

**1.** Bring a large pot of salted water to a boil. Add the pasta, and boil it, stirring occasionally, until it is just tender. Drain the pasta, and rinse it well with cold water.

**2.** In a large skillet, combine the olive oil and garlic over low heat. Sauté the garlic for 2 minutes or until the garlic releases its aroma (do not let it brown). Turn up the heat, and add the broccoli and 1 cup water. Cook the broccoli, uncovered, for 3 minutes or until most of the water is evaporated. Add the ricotta cheese and the Gorgonzola. Stir the sauce until it is nearly smooth, and season it with salt and pepper.

**3.** In a bowl, combine the pasta, the cheese-broccoli sauce, the tomatoes, and 2/3 cup of the Parmesan or Asiago cheese. Add more salt and pepper to taste, if necessary. (At this point you can refrigerate the mixture for baking later.)

**4.** Preheat the oven to 400°. Spoon the mixture into a 9-by-13-

inch casserole dish. Sprinkle the remaining Parmesan cheese over the casserole. Bake the casserole, uncovered, for 10 to 15 minutes (or a little longer if the mixture has been refrigerated). Spoon the contents onto plates, and serve.

*Serves 4*

# Orzo with Olives, Broccoli, and Basil

Looking like large aerodynamic grains of rice, orzo slithers down my throat as if each piece were coated with satin. I have come to adore this little pasta, not just because of its silkiness, but also because it is so easy to pick up with my fork. Unlike spaghetti, orzo is a breeze to eat while I am at work or at a party. Serve this dish warm or cold, with fresh, crusty bread and good extra-virgin olive oil.

⅓ cup olive oil
¼ cup minced shallots
2 garlic cloves, minced
3 cups small broccoli florets
1½ cups sliced fresh shiitake mushroom caps
10 ounces orzo
1 large ripe tomato, chopped
20 Kalamata olives, pitted and chopped coarsely
1 cup basil leaves, lightly packed
1 tablespoon fresh thyme leaves
1 tablespoon lemon juice
½ teaspoon salt, or more, to taste
Fresh-ground black pepper to taste

**1.** In a large skillet, heat 2 tablespoons olive oil over medium heat, and add the shallots. Sauté them for a few minutes, until they soften. Add the garlic, broccoli, and shiitakes. Cook the mixture, stirring, for 1 minute, being careful not to burn the garlic. Then add ⅔ cup water, and let the vegetables simmer for about 3 minutes or until the broccoli softens slightly and most of the water is evaporated. Transfer the mixture to a large bowl.

**2.** Meanwhile, bring a large pot of salted water to a boil. Add the orzo, and boil the pasta, stirring occasionally, until it is just tender. Drain it, and keep it hot.

**3.** Add the tomato, olives, basil, thyme, and remaining olive oil to the bowl of broccoli. Add the orzo, and combine well. Stir in the lemon juice, and add the salt and pepper to taste. Spoon the mixture onto plates, and serve.

**Variations:** This dish is very versatile. You can use cauliflower florets, sliced zucchini, or green beans instead of broccoli, or conventional mushrooms instead of shiitakes. Small cloves of roasted garlic (page 32) would be a nice addition. Instead of the tomato and broccoli, you could use orange sections and crumbled goat cheese. Or try using fresh mint and oregano instead of the basil and thyme. These are just a few ideas—you can take it from here.

Serves 4

# Basil and Its Relatives

*ny basil is delicious, and in most circumstances different basil varieties can be used interchangeably. Sweet basil, the kind most commonly available, has a sweet anise-like flavor with undertones of clove, mint, and tarragon. Thai basil, available in Asian markets and also known as holy basil and licorice basil, has a similar flavor, but with a noticeably stronger anise component. Thai basil is therefore best suited for dishes with other strong flavors. Purple basil is favored for bold color contrasts with greens and other vegetables. Also nice is lemon basil, grown in many home gardens for its strong lemony aroma.*

# Stuffed Shells Puttanesca

his is one of the few dishes that I enjoy the second day as much as the first. Because I work in a restaurant and deal with a large variety of foods, I never need to eat the same food two days in a row. But these stuffed shells are always so good on the second day that I'm glad to eat them two days in a row.

If you don't want to break up the tomatoes with your hands, you can use canned crushed tomatoes instead.

**STUFFING:**

1 fennel bulb, or 3 celery stalks
1 tablespoon olive oil
2 cups minced onions
2 garlic cloves, minced
1/2 cup ricotta cheese, whole-milk or part-skim
1/4 cup Parmesan cheese
Salt and fresh-ground pepper to taste

At least 16 large pasta shells

**SAUCE:**

2 tablespoons olive oil
3 garlic cloves, minced
3 1/2 cups (1 28-ounce can) peeled plum tomatoes
1/2 cup water, or 1/4 cup red wine and 1/4 cup
    water
1 teaspoon dried oregano
2 tablespoons drained capers
1/4 cup tiny Niçoise olives (the smaller the
    better), pitted
3 tablespoons chopped fresh basil
Salt and fresh-ground black pepper to taste

> *" Pasta and olive oil… you never know how good it is until you make a meal of it, all alone—that is, all by itself and all by yourself. "*
>
> —JOHN THORNE,
> *OUTLAW COOK*

**1.** If you are using fennel, remove the green stalks, and cut the bulb in half. Core it as you would a cabbage head, then chop the remaining fennel fine. There should be about 2 cups. If you are using celery, just cut each stalk in half lengthwise, then chop the stalks fine.

**2.** Make the stuffing: In a large skillet, heat the olive oil over medium heat. Sauté the onions for 5 minutes or until they soften, stirring occasionally. Add the garlic and fennel or celery. Sauté for 3 minutes, stirring often. Add 1/2 cup water, and let the vegetables cook for 10 minutes or until the fennel or celery is tender. Take the pan off the heat, and add the ricotta, Parmesan, and salt and pepper.

**3.** Meanwhile, begin the sauce: In a large saucepan, heat the olive oil over medium heat, and add the garlic. Sauté it for a minute or so (do not let it brown). Then break apart the tomatoes by squeezing them in your hand, one by one, and drop them into the sauce. Add the water, or red wine and water, and oregano, and simmer the sauce for 25 minutes. Take the sauce off the heat, and add the capers, olives, basil, and salt and pepper to taste.

**4.** Bring a large pot of salted water to a boil. Add the pasta shells, and cook them, stirring occasionally, until they are cooked al dente, about 8 minutes. Remove the shells with a sieve, and drop them into a big bowl of cold water. Then take out one shell, stuff it with a spoonful of the ricotta mixture, and place it in a lightly oiled casserole pan (a 9-by-9-inch pan works well). Stuff more shells until all the filling is used. You should have at least sixteen stuffed shells, snugly fitted in the pan. Pour the tomato sauce over the shells, and cover the pan with foil. (At this point you can refrigerate the shells, to be baked up to 3 days later.)

**5.** Preheat the oven to 350°. Bake the shells until they are hot, about 25 minutes (or about 35 minutes if the casserole was chilled). Serve the shells hot.

Serves 4

# Pappardelle with Asparagus and Herbed Cream

This is a perfect dish to show off your homemade pasta, or an easy dish if you can buy the pasta ready-made. The pasta is cooked in large ribbons, then tossed with a comforting herb cream sauce, asparagus, and cannellini beans.

If you want to use ready-made fresh pasta sheets, buy one pound, cut them into 1½-inch-wide strips, and begin at step 3.

PASTA:

1 pound fresh pasta sheets, cut into 1½-inch-
    wide strips, or the following 3 ingredients:
    2 cups unbleached white flour
    2 fresh eggs, beaten
    About 3 tablespoons water


½ pound asparagus
3 tablespoons butter
2 cups sliced onions
2 garlic cloves, minced
3 tablespoons unbleached white flour
3 cups whole or low-fat milk
1 tablespoon fresh thyme leaves, or 1 teaspoon
    dried thyme
½ teaspoon salt, or more, to taste
Fresh-ground black pepper to taste
1 squeeze lemon
1½ cups (1 15-ounce can) cooked and rinsed
    cannellini beans
2 tablespoons chopped dill
1 cup grated Parmesan cheese
Shaved Parmesan cheese (optional)

·ı·ı·ı·ı·ı·ı·

**1.** If you are making your own pasta: Put the flour into a large bowl, and make a well in the center. Add the beaten eggs, and, stirring with a sturdy wooden spoon, gradually blend the surrounding flour into the eggs. Stirring continuously, add enough water to form a dough that is stiff, not sticky, but not too hard, either. Put the dough onto a floured work surface, and knead the dough for at least 5 minutes. Transfer it to a plate, and refrigerate the dough for at least 30 minutes.

**2.** Roll the pasta very thin, by hand or by machine. I roll mine with an Atlas machine set to number 6. Cut the pasta into long strips about 1½ inches wide.

**3.** Break the tough ends off the asparagus, and cut the spears diagonally into 1½-inch lengths.

### Asparagus

I really don't believe in peeling asparagus, although I've peeled my fair share over the years as a prep cook in classical French restaurants and catering houses. I do believe in buying asparagus only in early spring, and only when it's fresh. Fresh asparagus usually is not tough, and therefore doesn't need peeling. Never choose asparagus that is flowering at the head or shriveled at the base. Pass by asparagus flown in from South America; it is usually weary and wilted by the time it reaches the supermarket.

Many people insist that white asparagus is more desirable than green. I find the opposite to be true, even if the white is fresh. The green just has more flavor.

**4.** Bring a large pot of salted water to a boil. Fill a large bowl with cold water. Add the pasta to the pot, and cook it about 1½ minutes, until it is tender. Lift the pasta from the water with a sieve, and put the hot pasta into the bowl of cold water. Keep the water in the pot boiling. Blanch the asparagus for 1 minute, then drain it and rinse it with cold water.

**5.** Make the cream sauce: Heat the butter in a heavy saucepan. Add the onions, and sauté them, stirring occasionally, until they have softened, about 5 minutes. Add the garlic, and sauté, stirring often, for 5 minutes more. Add the flour, and cook, stirring often, for 1 minute. Whisking constantly to avoid lumps, slowly add the milk, ½ cup at a time. Add the thyme, and simmer the sauce for 10 minutes, stirring every now and then. Add the salt and pepper and a squeeze of lemon. Take the pan off the heat. (At this point you can transfer the sauce to an airtight container and refrigerate it for up to 2 days.)

**6.** Just before serving, reheat the sauce gently in a large pot, and add the pasta, the asparagus, and the cannellini beans. Heat the contents thoroughly, tossing them once or twice, then add the dill and the grated Parmesan cheese. Taste, and add more salt or pepper, if you wish. Garnish with shaved Parmesan cheese, if you like, and serve.

*Serves 6*

# Spaghetti with Spaghetti Squash

Spaghetti squash is like a bundle of spaghetti contained in a yellow football. The savory long strands of squash meat make for a double play when combined with real spaghetti.

1 spaghetti squash (about 2 pounds)
6 tablespoons olive oil
Fresh-ground black pepper to taste

8 ounces dried spaghetti

3 to 4 garlic cloves, minced

6 stale or toasted bread slices, chopped or ground
  in a blender or food processor into crumbs

¼ cup walnut pieces

½ cup chopped Italian parsley

2 tablespoons lemon juice (from about ½ lemon)

½ teaspoon salt, plus a bit more, to taste

½ cup grated Parmesan cheese

½ red bell pepper, seeded and chopped fine

2 tablespoons drained capers

**1.** Preheat the oven to 375°. With a knife, carefully split the squash in half, and pull out the seeds with your fingers. Place the squash cut side up in a roasting pan. Spoon 2 tablespoons of the olive oil over the squash, and season it liberally with salt and pepper. Cover the two halves with foil, and bake the squash for 1 hour or until the flesh is soft. Let it cool 10 minutes.

**2.** Bring a large pot of salted water to a boil. Add the spaghetti, and cook it, stirring occasionally, until it is just tender. Drain it well. Return the spaghetti to the empty pot.

**3.** While the pasta is cooking, heat the remaining ¼ cup olive oil in a large skillet over medium heat. Add the garlic, bread crumbs, and walnuts. Cook, stirring constantly, until the crumbs are golden and the walnuts a bit toasted. Remove the mixture from the heat and add it to the spaghetti.

**4.** With a fork, scrape out the flesh from the spaghetti squash. Add to the spaghetti the squash flesh, the parsley, the lemon juice, and the ½ teaspoon salt. Heat the mixture, and stir in the Parmesan cheese. Mix well, adding salt and pepper to taste.

**5.** Serve the pasta on plates, garnished with the chopped red pepper and capers.

Serves 4 to 6

## Parsley Power

*P*oor parsley, always a bridesmaid, never a bride," says Rosina Tinari Wilson. Although parsley is our most widely used herb it is often taken for granted. I like to showcase it in mild-flavored dishes such as omelets, creamy soups, and pasta (with olive oil and garlic). Flat-leaf or Italian parsley has a more intense flavor than curly parsley and is generally preferred for chopping. Curly parsley is used for deep-frying and as a green in a mixed salad.

To deep-fry curly parsley, cut the stems off, and make sure the parsley is completely dry. Fry it briefly in hot peanut or other vegetable oil. Blot the parsley on paper towels.

# Ziti with Acorn Squash and Roasted Garlic

This dish is simple, inexpensive, and delicious from the first bite to the last. But the best thing about it is that both humans and cats love it. At least, *my* cat loves it. I was eating it one night when Henry, my cat, poked his cute little nose into my plate of ziti. So of course I got him his own plate and spooned him out a good amount. Henry ate those ziti tubes with wild abandon, and finished his plate in seconds. I must admit that Henry weighs seventeen pounds and loves to eat, but this was unusual. So try this dish out on your cat, or your dog. It may be something your whole household can enjoy.

1 acorn squash
6 tablespoons olive oil
15 large garlic cloves, peeled
1 pound dried ziti tubes (or penne)
1/3 cup white wine
1/2 teaspoon salt, or more, to taste
Fresh-ground black pepper to taste
2/3 cup grated Parmesan cheese, plus more for
    garnish
1/4 cup chopped walnuts, lightly toasted

**1.** Preheat the oven to 375°. Cut the acorn squash in half, remove the seeds, and place the halves on a baking sheet, cut side down. Bake the squash for 1 hour or until the flesh is soft. Let the squash cool, then spoon out the flesh from the shells, and chop it fine.

**2.** About ½ hour after the squash has begun baking, roast the garlic: Toss together the oil and the garlic, and place them in an oven-proof dish. Bake the garlic, uncovered, alongside the squash for 30 minutes or until the garlic is lightly golden.

**3.** Bring a large pot of salted water to a boil, and cook the ziti until it is just tender. Drain it, reserving ¾ cup of the drained pasta water.

**4.** While the pasta cooks, spoon the roasted garlic with its oil into a large skillet. Add the wine and the reserved pasta water, and bring the mixture to a boil. Let it boil for about 2 minutes. Add the chopped squash flesh, and boil the sauce 3 minutes more. Take the skillet off the heat.

**5.** Add the ziti to the sauce, and stir well. Add the salt, pepper, and Parmesan cheese, and toss. Divide the pasta among plates, sprinkle the walnuts over, and serve along with the additional Parmesan.

Serves 4

# Dumplings for Dinner

# Crispy Stuffed Foon

This is a special-occasion knockout of an entrée to make when you can spare an hour or two. Fresh rice noodles, also called *sha he fen* or *hu tieu,* come as sheets of dough folded in 8-ounce packages; you cut the dough into noodles the width of your choice. Fresh rice noodles have a silky texture that makes this meal quite an event. Unfortunately, there is no real substitute for them, so making this dish requires access to a well-stocked Asian market.

I like to serve this dish with slices of fresh mango or plum and long strands of chive.

1 lemongrass stalk
2 tablespoons canola or corn oil
1½ cups minced onions
1 garlic clove, minced
12 medium mushrooms, stems trimmed, the
    remainder sliced thin
2 carrots, cut into 3-inch-long julienne strips
3 scallions, both green and white parts, chopped
8 ounces firm tofu
1 tablespoon lime juice
2 teaspoons soy sauce
4 large sheets fresh rice noodles
Toasted Sesame Sauce (page 306)

**1.** Prepare the lemongrass: Cut off the bulbous bottom third of the stalk. Remove the tough outer leaves, and, with a large, sharp chef's knife, cut this piece into thin slices, then mince it. You should have 2 to 3 tablespoons minced lemongrass. (Save the rest of the stalk for stocks, soups, stews, or even tea.)

**2.** Heat 1 tablespoon oil in a wok or large skillet over medium-high heat. Sauté the onion, lemongrass, and garlic for 2 minutes, stirring often. Add the mushrooms, and cook, stirring frequently, for 5 minutes. Add the carrots and scallions, and sauté 3 minutes more. Add the tofu, and break it up with a spoon. Add the lime and soy sauce. Cook, stirring constantly, for 1 minute, then take the wok or skillet off the heat.

**3.** On a clean work surface, lay out one noodle sheet with a long side facing you. With a butter knife, cut the sheet into 3 wide strips (each strip will be 5 to 6 inches wide) from one long side to the other. Lay 3 tablespoons stuffing at one end of each strip. Fold up each strip into triangles, as you would fold a flag.

**4.** Heat a skillet with the remaining 1 tablespoon oil. When the oil is hot, add as many stuffed triangles as you can without crowding them. Pan-fry them for about 5 minutes over medium heat, until they are slightly browned on the undersides, then turn them over. Fry them for 5 minutes more. Serve them hot in small pools of Toasted Sesame Sauce.

Note: If you aren't using the noodles the same day you purchased them, refrigerate them, then, before stuffing them, immerse them in their original plastic package into boiling water for 2 minutes so that they become pliable again.

*Serves 4*

## Toasted Sesame Sauce

Don't stop at Crispy Stuffed Foon in finding uses for this sauce. Serve it as a dip with raw vegetables, or as a sauce for Asian noodles or ravioli.

½ cup white sesame seeds (about 3 ounces)
2 tablespoons dark sesame oil
2 tablespoons tahini (optional)
1 large garlic clove, minced
1 teaspoon minced fresh ginger
3 tablespoons rice vinegar
2 tablespoons honey
5 tablespoons soy sauce
¼ cup water

## Fun Dippers

*When you feel like dipping something other than carrot and celery sticks, try one of these alternatives:*

- *Sliced fennel (store it in ice water until you're ready to serve it)*
- *Blanched green beans*
- *Blanched asparagus*
- *Endive leaves*
- *Sliced sweet peppers in various colors*
- *Sliced jicama (store it in ice water until you're ready to serve it)*
- *Sliced daikon radish*
- *Diagonally sliced bok choy*
- *Yellow pear tomatoes*
- *Boiled, chilled, and halved new potatoes*
- *Sliced Asian pear*
- *Snap peas*
- *Grilled bread brushed with olive oil*

**1.** Preheat the oven to 350°. Toast the sesame seeds on a baking sheet for 10 to 15 minutes, until most of the seeds have turned a rich brown (but be careful not to burn them). Let them cool.

**2.** In a spice grinder or food processor, grind about half the sesame seeds, in batches. Combine the ground and whole sesame seeds in a bowl. Add the remaining ingredients, and whisk well. Put the sauce into a jar, and seal it. Let the sauce sit for 1 hour so the flavors mix and mellow. You can store the sauce in the refrigerator for up to 2 weeks.

# Daikon Pot-Stickers with Ginger-Sesame Sauce

These refreshing dumplings sport a filling of sautéed daikon, carrots, and tofu. The sauce, really just a vinaigrette, is rather addictive. Serve the pot-stickers with a tossed green salad or Tame Kimchi (page 125) for a satisfying meal.

Daikon radishes, which look like gigantic white carrots, are used a great deal in Japanese, Korean, and Chinese cooking. They are now commonly available in well-stocked supermarkets as well as in Asian markets.

**POT-STICKERS:**
3 tablespoons canola or corn oil
2 teaspoons minced fresh ginger
2 garlic cloves, minced
1¹/₂ cups minced daikon radish
1 cup grated carrot
¹/₃ cup crumbled firm or extra-firm tofu
2 tablespoons soy sauce
20 3¹/₄-inch square or round wonton skins or
   gyoza skins (the thinnest ones you can find)

**GINGER-SESAME SAUCE:**

2 tablespoons balsamic vinegar

3 tablespoons soy sauce

1 tablespoon honey or sugar

2 tablespoons water

2 teaspoons Dijon mustard

1 garlic clove, minced

1 tablespoon minced fresh ginger

1/2 teaspoon or more wasabi powder (available in
    whole-foods stores and Japanese markets;
    optional)

2 tablespoons dark sesame oil

2 teaspoons toasted sesame seeds (optional)

1. Make the pot-stickers: In a large skillet, heat 1 tablespoon of the oil over medium-high heat. Add the ginger and garlic, and let them sizzle for 10 seconds or so. Quickly add the daikon, and stir constantly for 2 minutes. Then add the grated carrot. Stir constantly for 1 minute. Add the tofu and soy sauce, and cook for 1 minute more. Take the skillet off the heat, and let the mixture cool.

2. Lay four or five of the wonton skins on a work surface. Place a tablespoon of the filling in the center of each wrapper. Wet the rim of the wonton skin. Fold one corner to the opposite one to form a triangle, and pinch the edges tight. On the long side of the triangle, turn the two ends up like two small dog ears. Continue in the same manner for the remaining dumplings, to make twenty in all. (At this point you can place the dumplings on a large plate, cover them with plastic wrap, and store them in the refrigerator for up to 48 hours.)

3. Make the sauce: In a bowl, whisk together the balsamic vinegar, soy sauce, honey or sugar, water, mustard, garlic, and ginger. Whisk in the wasabi powder, if you like. Slowly pour in the sesame oil while whisking constantly. Ladle the sauce into small dipping bowls, and sprinkle in the sesame seeds, if you wish.

4. Heat 1 tablespoon canola or corn oil in a large skillet over medium heat. Add half of the dumplings, and fry them for about 2 minutes per side, until they become golden brown. Transfer the dumplings to a plate lined with paper towels. Add the remaining 1 tablespoon oil to the skillet, if necessary, and fry the remaining dumplings. Divide the hot dumplings among plates, and place the bowls of dipping sauce close by.

Serves 2

# Carrot Dumplings in Lemongrass Broth

Inspired by the many different Vietnamese noodle soups that I love, this dish is light, yet substantial enough to be a dinner. Silken tofu and frothed egg white make the dumplings extra light.

**DUMPLINGS:**
1¹/₂ cups finely grated carrots
3 tablespoons minced scallions or chives
2 eggs, separated
¹/₂ teaspoon salt
6 tablespoons silken tofu
1 cup unbleached white flour

**BROTH:**
1 tablespoon canola or corn oil
1¹/₂ cups sliced onions
2 lemongrass stalks
3 garlic cloves, minced
1¹/₂ cups shiitake or white button mushrooms,
    sliced thin (discard the shiitake stems)
8 cups water or Basic Vegetable Stock
    (page 79)

1 cup sherry

3 tablespoons Thai or Vietnamese fish sauce, or
   1 teaspoon salt

1/2 lime, plus additional lime juice to taste

4 plum tomatoes, halved lengthwise, then sliced
   into 1/4-inch half-rounds

1 to 3 teaspoons hot chile sauce, or 1/2 teaspoon
   or more chile flakes, to taste

1/4 cup chopped cilantro

**1.** Mix the carrots, scallions or chives, egg yolks, and salt together in a large bowl. Add the tofu, and use a potato masher to incorporate the tofu into the mixture. In another bowl, whisk the egg whites for about 1 minute, until they are frothy and tripled in volume but form no peaks. Add the tofu mixture to the whites, and beat with a whisk for 10 seconds. Then add the flour to the mixture, in three batches, folding it in with a plastic spatula until it is all incorporated. Chill the mixture for 20 minutes.

**2.** Make the broth: Heat the oil over medium-high heat in a large pot. Add the onions, and sauté them for 5 minutes or until they have softened. While they cook, remove the tough outer leaves from the stalks of lemongrass, then cut each stalk into three pieces about 4 inches long. Crush the lemongrass pieces by smashing them with a heavy pan. Add the lemongrass, the garlic, and the mushrooms to the onions. Cook for 3 minutes more, stirring often. Add the stock or water, the sherry, the fish sauce or salt, and the lime half to the pot, and bring the mixture to a boil. Let the broth simmer for 15 minutes.

**3.** Using a soup spoon, drop spoonfuls of the dumpling batter into the simmering broth, and cook the dumplings for 5 to 7 minutes. Add the tomatoes, and cook for 2 to 3 minutes more. Season to taste with the chile sauce or flakes and salt, if you like. Remove the lime half, and squeeze out the juice into the stew. Taste, and add more lime juice to taste, if needed. Serve the broth in large bowls with the chopped cilantro sprinkled on top. Let the diners remove the lemongrass pieces as they eat.

Serves 4

# Chickpea-flour Dumplings in Spinach-Tomato Sauce

These Indian-inspired dumplings, which are akin to pakoras but have no vegetable or cheese filling, are among the tastiest I've eaten. Because they are hearty, they are accompanied by a light sauce, made of spinach, tomatoes, and yogurt.

▪▫▪▫▪▫▪▫▪

**SAUCE:**
10 ounces fresh spinach, or 10 ounces thawed
    and drained frozen spinach
1 tablespoon canola or corn oil
1½ cups chopped onions
1 tablespoon minced fresh ginger
1 large garlic clove, minced
¼ teaspoon ground allspice
½ teaspoon ground cardamom
2 medium tomatoes, chopped
1 cup cooked peas (optional)
½ cup whole, low-fat, or nonfat plain yogurt
½ cup water
Salt and fresh-ground black pepper to taste

**DUMPLINGS:**
2 cups chickpea flour (available in Indian
    markets and many whole-foods stores)
½ teaspoon salt
1 teaspoon baking powder
1 pinch cayenne
1 teaspoon ground coriander seeds
2 tablespoons butter, melted
3/4 cup very cold water
1 cup canola or corn oil, for frying

▪▫▪▫▪▫▪▫▪

**1.** Make the sauce: Bring a pot of salted water to a boil. Add the spinach, and cook it for 30 seconds. Drain the spinach, rinse it with cold water, then squeeze out the water. Place the spinach on a cutting board, and chop it well.

**2.** Heat the oil in a large saucepan over medium heat. Cook the onions, stirring often. After 2 to 3 minutes, add the ginger, garlic, allspice, and cardamom. Cook another 2 minutes, stirring often. Add the tomatoes, and cook 5 minutes more, stirring often. Add the spinach and the peas, if you're using them, and cook until the mixture is thoroughly heated. Take the pan off the heat, and stir in the yogurt, ½ cup water, and salt and pepper to taste.

**3.** Make the dumplings: In a large bowl, combine the first five dumpling ingredients. Add the butter, stir a few times with a spoon, then add the cold water, and mix well.

**4.** In a small saucepan, heat the 1 cup canola or corn oil over medium heat. When a teaspoonful of batter dropped in the oil quickly sizzles and cooks, the oil is ready. Take up some of the dough with a soup spoon, and, using another spoon to dislodge the dough, drop it into the hot oil. Add spoonfuls of dough in this way until the pan is full but not crowded (I cook five dumplings at once). After about 2 minutes, turn the dumplings over. Cook them for 2 minutes more, then transfer them to paper towels. Continue cooking dumplings until all of the batter is used. (If you're not yet ready to serve them, you can reheat them later in a moderate oven.)

**5.** Reheat the sauce, and spoon it onto plates. Place the dumplings on the sauce, and serve.

Serves 4

# Spinach-Ricotta Dumplings in Portobello Tomato Sauce

Sautéed mushrooms add an incomparable depth of flavor to many dishes. Here, fresh basil, tomatoes, and sautéed portobello mushrooms make a flavorful sauce for the spinach dumpling. Watercress (stems trimmed) can be substituted for the spinach with equally good results.

**DUMPLINGS:**
1 tablespoon olive oil
1 garlic clove, minced
10 ounces fresh spinach, long stems trimmed off, or 10 ounces thawed and drained frozen spinach
3 tablespoons water
1 cup ricotta cheese, whole-milk or part-skim
1 egg, beaten
1 teaspoon baking powder
$2/3$ cup unbleached white flour
$1/2$ cup grated Parmesan cheese
$1/2$ teaspoon salt
Fresh-ground black pepper to taste

**PORTOBELLO TOMATO SAUCE:**
4 medium portobello mushrooms
2 tablespoons olive oil
2 garlic cloves, minced
$3 1/2$ cups (1 28-ounce can) peeled plum tomatoes, chopped fine
2 tablespoons chopped fresh basil
Salt and fresh-ground pepper to taste

**GARNISH:**
2 tablespoons grated Parmesan cheese

1. If you are using fresh spinach, heat the olive oil in a large stockpot over medium heat, and sauté the garlic until it is soft but not brown. Add the spinach and the water. Stir constantly until all of the spinach is wilted, about 1 minute or so. Take the stockpot off the heat. Spoon the spinach onto a cutting board, and chop it fine. Gently squeeze the spinach to remove excess liquid, then transfer the spinach and the garlic to a large bowl.

If you are using frozen spinach, put it into a large bowl with the raw garlic. Omit the 1 tablespoon olive oil.

**2.** Stir the ricotta cheese and the beaten egg into the spinach mixture. Mix the baking powder into the flour. Add to the spinach mixture the flour mixture, the Parmesan cheese, the salt, and the pepper. Stir well until the mixture is smooth. Chill the dumpling mixture in the refrigerator for 30 minutes.

**3.** Make the tomato sauce: Trim the dirty bases from the mushroom stems. Chop the mushrooms, including the stems. Heat the olive oil over medium heat in a large saucepan. Add the mushrooms, and sauté them for 3 to 4 minutes or until they soften. They will quickly absorb the oil, but continue to cook them without adding more oil. Add the garlic, and cook 1 minute more, stirring. Add the tomatoes, and simmer for 15 minutes. Take the saucepan off the heat, and add the basil, salt, and pepper.

**4.** Bring a large pot of salted water to a boil. Keeping your hands well floured, form the dumpling dough into balls, about 1 inch in diameter or a bit larger. When the dumplings are all formed, drop them into the boiling water all at once. Cook the dumplings at a rolling boil for 4 to 5 minutes. About halfway through the cooking, they should rise to the top of the water. Remove the cooked dumplings with a slotted spoon or a small sieve.

**5.** Reheat the tomato sauce, if necessary. Spoon the warm sauce onto plates, and top with the dumplings. Sprinkle with the 2 tablespoons Parmesan cheese, and serve.

*Serves 4*

# Potato and Kale Stew with Corn Dumplings

This delicious stew is easy to make, despite its many ingredients. It is inspired by two traditional dishes. The first is the Indian dish *karhi,* which combines chickpea-flour dumplings in a sauce thickened by more chickpea flour. Here, similarly, cornmeal both binds the dumplings and thickens the broth. My second source of inspiration is *aïgo bouido,* a simple Provençal soup in which garlic, pepper, and a bay leaf are steeped in water, which is then thickened with egg yolk. In this recipe, the broth is heavily flavored with garlic, bay leaf, sherry, and chiles. There is no need for egg yolk, since the cornmeal thickens the stew.

**DUMPLINGS:**

1 cup cornmeal

1/2 cup unbleached white flour

1 teaspoon baking powder

1/2 teaspoon salt

5 tablespoons cold butter

1/3 cup whole or low-fat milk

1 egg, beaten

**STEW:**

8 cups water or Basic Vegetable Stock (page 79)

12 large garlic cloves

1/2 cup sherry

2 bay leaves

1 teaspoon ground coriander seeds

1 jalapeño pepper, cut into thin rings and, if you like less heat, seeded

2 large potatoes (about 1 pound), peeled and cut into 1/2-inch cubes

3 large carrots, peeled and cut crosswise into 1/2-inch pieces

3 cups kale, large stems removed, cut into 1-inch
   strips
3 tablespoons cornmeal
1/4 cup heavy cream or light cream
1 medium tomato, chopped
1/4 cup chopped cilantro
1/2 teaspoon salt, or more, to taste
Fresh-ground black pepper to taste
1 tablespoon lime juice (from about 1/2 lime)

**1.** Make the dumplings: In a large bowl or in a food processor, stir together the cornmeal, flour, baking powder, and salt. With a pastry blender or fork, cut in the butter until the mixture has a sand-like consistency. Add the milk and the egg, and stir well with a large spoon, or run the processor in spurts, just until the dough comes together. Chill the dough, covered, for 30 minutes to 24 hours.

**2.** With well-floured hands, form the dough into 1-inch balls.

**3.** Make the stew: In a stockpot, combine the water or stock, garlic, sherry, bay leaves, coriander, and jalapeño. Bring the ingredients to a simmer, and simmer them for 10 minutes, uncovered. Drop the dumplings into the broth, and simmer them until they rise to the surface and a bit longer, 5 to 7 minutes in all. Remove the dumplings with a slotted spoon to a plate (if you spoon up some garlic cloves with the dumplings, return them to the pot). Add the potatoes, carrots, and kale to the pot, and simmer the mixture, partly covered, for 15 minutes or until the potatoes are almost tender. Then sprinkle the cornmeal over the mixture, and stir in the cream. Cook for another minute, stirring.

**4.** Add the tomato to the pot, and return the cornmeal dumplings to it. Simmer the stew for a minute or two, then add the cilantro, salt, pepper, and lime juice. Serve the stew in large bowls, discarding the garlic cloves, if you like.

Variation: Fresh corn kernels are a nice addition to this stew. Add them along with the dumplings and tomatoes in step 4.

Serves 4

## Think Small

❀

Smaller is better with many vegetables. Zucchini, cucumbers, and eggplant, for instance, all taste better when they are young. As these vegetables grow older, they develop thicker cell walls, which don't always soften with cooking. Also, fully mature vegetables have larger seeds than young vegetables. The problem is that agribusiness works for profit, not for flavor. It is more profitable to let small vegetables grow large, since vegetables are sold by the pound. So if you see small vegetables, grab them. You'll find that the vegetables are more tender—and cuter, too.

# Ratatouille with Soft Basil Dumplings

When I lived in France, I was taught that ratatouille should never, ever be stirred, because any movement would break down the vegetable shapes. I have found this rule nearly impossible to follow, at least in the beginning of the cooking. Still, the less stirring, the better.

Use good, fresh vegetables for this dish—shiny, taut-skinned eggplant; small, firm zucchini; and vine-ripened tomatoes. If you don't have a lot of time, you can skip the dumplings; just serve the ratatouille over steamed rice.

**RATATOUILLE:**
2 tablespoons olive oil
2 cups chopped onions
1 large green bell pepper, seeded and cut into 3/4-inch squares
1 small zucchini, cut into 3/4-inch cubes
3/4 pound eggplant (half of a large one, or a whole smaller one), peeled and cut into 3/4-inch cubes
2 large garlic cloves, minced
2 ripe tomatoes, diced small
1/2 teaspoon fennel seeds
1/2 cup water
1/2 teaspoon salt
Fresh-ground black pepper to taste

**DUMPLINGS:**
1/2 cup lightly packed basil leaves
1/4 cup grated Parmesan cheese
2 eggs, separated
1/2 cup ricotta cheese, whole-milk or part-skim
2 tablespoons whole or low-fat milk
1 cup plus 2 tablespoons unbleached white flour

1 teaspoon baking powder
1 teaspoon salt

1 tablespoon butter
3 tablespoons chopped chives

**1.** In a large skillet, heat the olive oil over medium heat. Add the chopped onions, and sauté them for 5 minutes or until they have softened, stirring occasionally. Add the bell pepper, zucchini, eggplant, garlic, tomatoes, fennel seeds, and ½ cup water, and stir well. Cover the stew, turn the heat to low, and simmer for 30 minutes, stirring gently once or twice to make sure the vegetables aren't scorching on the bottom. Season the ratatouille with salt and pepper.

**2.** While the ratatouille cooks, make the dumplings: Chop the basil fine, and put it into a large bowl. Add the Parmesan cheese, the egg yolks, the ricotta cheese, and the milk. In another bowl, mix together the flour, baking powder, and salt. In a third bowl, whip the egg whites with a pinch of salt until soft peaks form. Gently fold the egg whites into the ricotta mixture with a plastic spatula. Then fold in the flour mixture a little at a time until it is all incorporated. Chill the batter for at least 15 minutes.

**3.** Bring a large pot of water to a boil. Using a soup spoon, drop batter by the spoonful into the simmering water, being careful not to crowd the dumplings, which will expand quite a bit. (If your pot is on the small side, cook the dumplings in two batches.) Simmer the dumplings for 10 to 12 minutes. Remove them with a slotted spoon or small sieve, and place them on a kitchen towel to dry.

**4.** In a large skillet, heat the butter over medium heat, and add the dumplings. Sauté the dumplings, tossing them often, until they become golden, about 10 minutes.

**5.** Spoon the ratatouille into shallow bowls, and divide the dumplings among the bowls. Sprinkle the chives over the bowls, and serve.

Serves 4

# Wild Mushroom Stew
# with Herbed Dumplings

Old-fashioned dumplings studded with fresh herbs and black pepper float in a flavorful stew composed of fresh mushrooms and a dried porcini–infused broth. Serve the stew with crusty bread for a very satisfying meal.

This recipe includes directions for a quick vegetable stock. If you have 8 cups of vegetable stock on hand, you can save time by using it instead; just start at step 2.

**QUICK STOCK:**
2 carrots, cut into large chunks
1 tomato, cut into large chunks
1 fennel bulb, cut into large chunks
1 large onion, cut into large chunks
8 garlic cloves, crushed
10 cups water

1/2 cup Madeira
1/3 ounce dried porcini mushrooms

**DUMPLINGS:**
2 cups unbleached white flour
1 teaspoon baking powder
1 teaspoon salt
1 teaspoon fresh-ground black pepper
2 tablespoons chopped fresh herbs (any combination of rosemary, sage, oregano, thyme, or tarragon)
3 tablespoons butter
2 eggs, beaten
1/2 cup whole or low-fat milk

2 tablespoons olive oil

1 pound mushrooms (any combination of
 shiitakes, portobellos, hen-of-the-woods,
 cremini, chanterelle, or white button
 mushrooms), sliced
1 large carrot, cut into small rounds
1 garlic clove, minced
2 teaspoons fresh thyme leaves or chopped fresh
 sage
Salt and fresh-ground black pepper to taste
1 tablespoon truffle oil (available in specialty
 foods stores; optional)

**1.** Make the quick stock: In a large pot, combine all of the ingredients. Bring them to a boil over high heat, then turn the heat to low. Simmer the stock for 30 minutes.

Strain out the vegetables, and save the stock. You should have about 8 cups.

**2.** While the stock simmers, heat the Madeira with ½ cup water in a small pan until the liquid begins to simmer. Add the porcini, turn off the heat, and cover the pan. Let the mushrooms steep for at least 15 minutes.

**3.** Make the dumplings: In a large bowl, combine the flour, baking powder, salt, pepper, and herbs. Add the butter in small pieces, and, with a pastry cutter or fork, incorporate the butter into the flour mixture. Add the eggs, then the milk. Stir the mixture with a spoon until it just comes together. Add a bit more milk if there are dry spots.

**4.** In a 4-quart saucepan, heat the olive oil. Add the sliced mushrooms and carrot, and sauté them over medium-high heat, stirring frequently. The mushrooms will quickly absorb all of the oil, but continue to cook them for 2 minutes more, stirring constantly. Add the garlic, and sauté 30 seconds more, stirring. Then add the 8 cups stock and the soaking liquid from the porcini mushrooms. Bring the stew to a gentle boil, add the thyme or sage, and season the stew with salt and pepper. (At this point you can cover and chill both the dumpling batter and the mushroom stew for later use.)

**5.** Using a soup spoon, drop dumpling batter by the spoonful into the simmering stew. If the dumplings seem crowded, don't worry; just poke them with a spoon from time to time to make sure they aren't sticking together. Roll the dumplings over after 4 to 5 minutes. When the dumplings have cooked for at least 10 minutes, ladle the stew into large bowls. If you have some truffle oil, drizzle it over each bowl of stew just before serving.

*Serves 4*

# Mashed-Potato Pierogi

When I put pierogi on the menu at the Delux, they became a smash hit. But pierogi are labor-intensive, so as they became more and more popular we had to come into work earlier and earlier to get everything done.

I wouldn't suggest starting a pierogi fast food restaurant, but making enough for four people isn't an overwhelming task. Stuffed with mashed potatoes and mushrooms, these dumplings are rolled in hot butter and brown onions. Since this is a filling dish, you might serve it with just a simple salad, perhaps some greens tossed with Pomegranate-Poppy Dressing (page 162).

2 large or 3 medium baking potatoes, peeled and
   cut in half
6 tablespoons unsalted butter
1/2 cup whole or low-fat milk
1 teaspoon salt, plus more to taste
Fresh-ground black pepper to taste
1 garlic clove, minced
3 cups sliced white button or shiitake
   mushrooms

# Mushroom Breakdown

Many once-exotic mushrooms, such as shiitakes, portobellos, and creminis, are now farmed in the United States. Other mushrooms, collected in the wild, are even more prized by cooks, if only because they are rare.

Many fungi are best cooked before eating, because they contain proteins that are difficult to digest otherwise. Besides white button mushrooms, exceptions are fresh porcini, cremini, portobello, and enoki mushrooms, and truffles.

The best way to clean a mushroom is first to trim off the base of the stem, because this is where most of the dirt lies. Then wipe the mushroom with a clean damp cloth. If you must rinse mushrooms, do it quickly, then immediately cook them. Otherwise they will absorb water and lose flavor.

Dried mushrooms are generally soaked in hot water until they are plump, about 30 minutes. Because of their intensified flavor, dried mushrooms make a great addition to pasta sauces, risotto, cream soups, and grain dishes. They are usually chopped once plumped, then added to a dish and further cooked, although further cooking isn't necessary.

Mushrooms are high in nutrients. They provide B vitamins and potassium, and some are rich in protein. In fact, porcini mushrooms contain more protein per ounce of dry weight than any other vegetables except soybeans.

## THESE ARE SOME OF THE MUSHROOMS CURRENTLY AVAILABLE:

**SHIITAKES**—Sold fresh in most supermarkets, they are worth their price. Sauté the caps in butter or olive oil (discard the stems). Rich and almost steak-like in flavor, they make a succulent contribution to soups, pastas, pizzas, risottos, and warm salads. Dried shiitakes, available in Asian markets, have an intensified flavor.

**PORTOBELLOS**—These oversized cremini mushrooms can span 6 inches across the cap. Both the cap and the stem are good to eat. Portobellos have a woodsy flavor and meaty texture; some say they are the best meat substitute around. They are good grilled whole or sliced and sautéed, or quartered and roasted with olive oil and garlic.

**CREMINIS**—These brown mushrooms have a slightly heavier flavor than their cousin, the white button mushroom. Roast them whole with olive oil, slice and sauté them for pilafs, or use them in any way you might use white mushrooms.

**ENOKIS**—With their spaghetti-like white stems and tiny, pushpin-like caps, these mushrooms look as if they belong in a fairyland. Mild in flavor, they are usually served raw, in salad or as a garnish for soup or a stir-fried dish. They are expensive.

**MORELS**—In the spring, morels are gathered in the Pacific Northwest and are flown to many cities, where they are sold at high prices in specialty markets and gourmet supermarkets. Usually dark brown, morels have a conical shape with a honeycomb exterior. They taste meaty, earthy, and nutty, and they combine well with many spring vegetables, such as peas, asparagus, and new potatoes.

**WOOD EARS**—Also known as tree ears, these mushrooms grow on logs and look similar to human ears. They are slightly crunchy in texture and somewhat bland in flavor. They tend to soak up the flavors of foods with which they are combined. Looking like dark chips, they are sold dried in Asian markets. Wood ears add good texture and flavor to soups, stir-fry dishes, pasta, and pilafs.

**TRUFFLES**—These fungi (they aren't considered mushrooms) grow underground in France and Italy. Both the white and black truffles are increasingly difficult to find (and therefore increasingly expensive) because of overharvesting, shrinking habitat, and unknown causes. Pigs or dogs are needed to find truffles, and a truffle will begin to rot if touched by human hands.

White truffles are delicious raw, shaved over a creamy pasta dish or risotto. The black truffle is more pungent in flavor. Because fresh truffles are so quick to rot, prohibitively expensive, and difficult to find fresh, I suggest substituting truffle oil, which is made in Italy by infusing olive oil with white truffles. Use only a few drops in salads (especially salads containing cheese or warm foods), or in pasta, risotto, gnocchi, or even grain dishes.

**PORCINI**—Also called cepes and king boletes, these mushrooms are available dried in packages and sometimes fresh. Slice fresh porcini paper thin, add them to salads, and dress with lemon and olive oil. Dried porcini have an intensely woodsy aroma and an intoxicating flavor. Reconstitute them in a hot liquid such as Madeira, wine, or stock, and add them and their soaking liquid to sauces, risotto, pilafs, and pasta dishes.

**CHANTERELLES**—These golden mushrooms have a distinctive flavor that some compare to that of apricots. Chanterelles are expensive, so showcase them, if you get some, but prepare them simply. I like them best lightly cooked in butter and garlic, then tossed with fresh pasta, a handful of chopped herbs (parsley, chopped fennel tops, thyme, chives), a squeeze of lemon juice, and a touch of grated Parmesan cheese. Chanterelles are gathered in the wild in the summer and fall.

2 tablespoons water
3 cups thinly sliced onions
1 batch (4 balls) Pizza Dough (page 443)
4 teaspoons sour cream (optional)

**1.** In a large saucepan, cover the potatoes with salted water, and bring the water to a boil. Boil the potatoes until they are very tender, then drain them, and return them to the dry pan. Add 1 tablespoon of the butter and all of the milk, and mash the potatoes until they are as creamy as you like. Add the 1 teaspoon salt and some pepper, and set the pan aside.

**2.** Melt 1 tablespoon butter in a large skillet over medium heat. Add the garlic, and sauté it for a few seconds. Add the mushrooms, and cook them, stirring occasionally. When they have absorbed the butter, add the 2 tablespoons water, and stir. Cook the mushrooms for 5 minutes more, stirring often. Season them with salt and pepper, and set the skillet aside.

**3.** In another skillet, melt 2 tablespoons of the butter over medium-high heat. Add the onions, and cook them, stirring occasionally, for 15 to 20 minutes or until they are brown (but not burnt). Season them with salt and pepper, and set the skillet aside.

**4.** Make the dumplings: Cut each ball of pizza dough in half, to form 8 balls in all. On a floured surface, roll each ball into a 5-inch circle. Put a portion of the mashed potatoes in the center of each round, then top with a portion of the mushrooms. Moisten the outer ½ inch of the circle with water, and fold the dough into a semicircle. Seal each dumpling by pinching the edge with your fingers. (At this point you can place the dumplings on a floured baking sheet, cover them with plastic wrap, and refrigerate them for up to 24 hours.)

**5.** Bring a large pot of water to a boil. Gently drop the dumplings into the water, and let them cook in the simmering water for 5 minutes. Remove them with a slotted spoon onto a plate lined with paper towels.

**6.** Reheat the onions, and add the remaining 2 tablespoons butter. Add the dumplings, and gently toss them in this mixture. Serve 2 dumplings on each plate, hot, with the onions and some of the buttery sauce spooned over them, and, if you like, small dollops of sour cream.

*Serves 4*

# Sweet-Potato Gnocchi with Leafy Greens and Madeira

Made from a mixture of sweet and white potatoes, these gnocchi are mildly sweet. They rest in a rich Madeira sauce with toasted pecans and Swiss chard, mustard greens, or beet greens. A light soup such as Lima Minestrone, or, perhaps, an endive and watercress salad with your favorite dressing, could precede this hearty dish.

**GNOCCHI DOUGH:**

1/2 pound (about 1 medium) sweet potato

1 pound Yellow Finn or russet potatoes

1 egg yolk

2 tablespoons whole or low-fat milk

1 1/2 cups unbleached white flour, plus a bit more

1 teaspoon salt

2 pinches freshly grated nutmeg

1 or 2 pinches cayenne

**SAUCE:**

2/3 cup dry Madeira (such as Sercial) or dry Marsala

1 tablespoon plus 1 teaspoon cornstarch

1 tablespoon honey

2 tablespoons butter

3 shallots, chopped fine

1 large garlic clove, minced
1½ cups water or Basic Vegetable Stock
    (page 79)
1 teaspoon fresh thyme leaves
4 cups chopped leafy greens (Swiss chard,
    mustard greens, or beet greens)
Salt and fresh-ground black pepper to taste

5 tablespoons coarsely chopped pecans, lightly
    toasted
⅓ cup grated Parmesan cheese
4 thyme sprigs

1. Preheat the oven to 400°. Bake the whole sweet and white potatoes until they are soft; the sweet potatoes should take about 40 minutes, the Yellow Finns or russets about 55 minutes. Cut the potatoes in half, and let them cool for at least 15 minutes (do not refrigerate them).

2. Spoon the cooled sweet potato and white potato flesh into a sieve. With your fingers, push the flesh through the sieve into a medium bowl. Make a small well in the center, and add the egg yolk and milk. With a fork, mix the yolk and the milk. Then, with a large spoon, gently mix the egg mixture into the potatoes. Stir in the flour, salt, nutmeg, and cayenne. Turn the dough out onto a floured work surface, and knead the dough lightly for 2 to 3 minutes, adding a bit more flour if the dough gets sticky.

3. Bring a large pot of water to a boil. Meanwhile, with a sharp knife, cut the dough into three pieces on a floured surface, and roll each piece into a long roll about ½ inch in diameter. Cut each roll into 1-inch pieces. Press the back of a fork onto each gnocchi to create ridges. Lightly flour the gnocchi.

4. Add all the gnocchi to the boiling water, and boil them for 5 minutes. Drain them and rinse them briefly with cool water.

5. Mix 3 tablespoons of the Madeira with the cornstarch and honey in a small bowl, and set the bowl aside. Melt the butter in a medium saucepan, and sauté the shallots and garlic over

## About Canned Stock

*Most of the dishes I cook have flavors bold enough to stand on their own without stock. But the other day I tried College Inn's Garden Vegetable Broth in the sauce for Sweet-Potato Gnocchi, and I must admit that the stock improved the sauce. The stock had an appealing albeit salty taste, with a pronounced red-pepper flavor. I also tried Hain Pure Foods Vegetable Broth, which was almost three times the price. The flavor of this stock was dull and the texture too mealy, probably because of the high proportion of potatoes.*

*If you are using canned stock, or broth from a dry cube, just be sure you add the salt after the broth, not before, and add only enough to taste.*

medium heat, stirring, for 2 to 3 minutes (don't let the garlic brown). Whisk in the remaining Madeira, the water or stock, the thyme, and the leafy greens, and simmer for 5 minutes, stirring often. Stir in the cornstarch-Madeira mixture, and simmer the sauce about 1 minute more, stirring frequently, until it thickens slightly. Take the pan off the heat, and add the salt and pepper.

**6.** When you're ready to serve, reheat the sauce, if necessary, and add the gnocchi. Heat and stir the sauce until the gnocchi are heated through. Divide the sauce and gnocchi among plates or shallow bowls, and sprinkle each serving with pecans and Parmesan cheese. Garnish with the thyme sprigs, and serve.

**Variation:** Substitute ½ teaspoon ground Sichuan peppercorns for the nutmeg in the gnocchi. Sichuan peppers are similar to nutmeg in flavor and aroma, but a bit more complex, with hints of clove and ginger.

Serves 4

# Semolina Gnocchi with Stilton and Mustard Greens

Semolina is coarse-ground durum wheat, the hard wheat from which factory pasta is made. Semolina can be found in some supermarkets as well as in Italian and specialty food shops. Because it is difficult to find in some areas, however, I've listed cornmeal as a substitute, although the two grains aren't related.

Containing two kinds of cheese (Stilton and Parmesan), four egg yolks, and 6 tablespoons of butter, this dish is quite rich by most standards, but the indulgence is well worth it. I suggest serving the gnocchi with a light salad of baby greens and Three-Citrus Vinaigrette (page 155).

**GNOCCHI:**

2 tablespoons butter, melted

4 egg yolks

²/₃ cup yogurt or buttermilk

¹/₂ cup semolina or cornmeal

2 cups unbleached white flour

¹/₂ teaspoon salt

¹/₂ cup grated Parmesan cheese


5 tablespoons butter

1 cup minced onion

2 garlic cloves, minced

4 cups chopped mustard greens

2 tablespoons sherry, white wine, or water

4 tablespoons (about 2 ounces) crumbled Stilton
    cheese (or Roquefort or Gorgonzola cheese)

3 tablespoons grated Parmesan cheese

**1.** Make the dumplings: In a bowl, combine the butter, egg yolks, and yogurt or buttermilk. Stir well. Add the semolina or cornmeal, 1 cup of the flour, the salt, and the Parmesan cheese. Stir the mixture until it is well blended. Chill the dough for at least ¹/₂ hour.

**2.** Heat at least 4 quarts of salted water in a large pot. While the water heats, put the remaining 1 cup flour into a large, shallow bowl. Using a teaspoon, scoop up a small amount of gnocchi dough. Flour your hands, and form the dough into a ball about the size of an olive. Drop the ball into the bowl of flour. Continue forming gnocchi in this manner until about one-third of the batter is used. Then pick the gnocchi out of the flour, place them in a sieve, and shake off the excess flour. Place the gnocchi on a plate. Repeat this procedure with the second third of the dough, and then with the remainder.

**3.** When the water comes to a boil, gently drop the gnocchi into the boiling water, and keep the water at a simmer for 6 to 8 minutes. Remove the gnocchi from the water with a sieve or a slotted spoon, and drain them on a kitchen towel.

**4.** In a large skillet, melt the butter over medium heat. Add the onion and the garlic, and sauté them, stirring occasionally, until the onion has softened, about 5 minutes. Add the mustard greens, and sauté for about 5 minutes more, until the stems have softened. Add the sherry, wine, or water.

**5.** Preheat the oven to 400°. Spoon the mustard greens and the butter sauce into a small casserole dish (about 9 inches round or square). Then lay the gnocchi on top. Sprinkle with the crumbled Stilton and Parmesan cheese. Bake the gnocchi and greens for 10 to 12 minutes in the middle of the oven and serve them hot.

*Variations:* Substitute chopped beet greens or kale, or whole watercress or arugula leaves, for the chopped mustard greens. If you use watercress or arugula, sauté it for only 30 seconds instead of 5 minutes.

Serves 4

# Chèvre Quenelles in Fennel and Tomato Sauce

Quenelles are delicate French dumplings made from ground fish, chicken, or red meat, with a binding agent such as a panade (bread crumbs or flour, milk, and egg) or choux pastry. Here chèvre, better known as goat cheese, takes the place of meat or fish. Quenelles are not as fast to make as some of the other dumplings in this chapter, but they're worth the trouble. They come out so soft and lovely that your friends may think little angels came down to make them. Grilled or warm bread is the natural accompaniment to this dish.

**QUENELLES:**

1/2 cup water

3 tablespoons butter

1/2 cup plus 2 tablespoons unbleached white flour

2 eggs

6 tablespoons crumbled chèvre (goat cheese),
    about 2 ounces

Salt and fresh-ground black pepper to taste

2 egg whites

**FENNEL AND TOMATO SAUCE:**

1 1/2 tablespoons olive oil

1 cup chopped onion

1 garlic clove, minced

1 medium fennel bulb, chopped fine (about
    2 cups)

3 medium tomatoes (about 1 pound), chopped

3/4 cup water

1/2 teaspoon salt

Fresh-ground black pepper to taste

2 tablespoons chopped parsley

**1.** Make the quenelles: In a heavy saucepan, heat the water with the butter. When the mixture begins to simmer, take the pan off the heat, immediately add all of the flour, and stir vigorously with a wooden spoon. Replace the pan over medium heat, and stir constantly until the dough comes away from the side of the pan and begins to form a ball. Remove the pan from the heat again, and add the eggs one at a time, beating hard until the dough is smooth. Add the goat cheese and salt and pepper, and again beat until the dough is smooth. Let it cool for 10 minutes.

**2.** Beat the egg whites to soft peaks with a pinch of salt, and fold them gently into the goat-cheese mixture. Chill the dough for 1/2 hour to 24 hours, so that it will be easier to handle.

**3.** Make the sauce: Heat the oil in a large skillet over medium heat. Add the onion, garlic, and fennel, and sauté until the onion and fennel soften, about 10 minutes. Add the tomatoes and water, and simmer for 10 minutes, stirring from time to time. Add the salt and pepper, and remove the skillet from the heat.

**4.** Bring at least 4 quarts of salted water to a boil in a large saucepan or pot. Spoon the dough, about 1 tablespoon at a time, into the simmering water, fitting as many quenelles into the pot as you can without crowding them. Simmer them for 10 minutes, turning them over after 5 minutes. Remove the quenelles with a slotted spoon, and transfer them to paper towels.

**5.** Warm the fennel and tomato sauce, divide it among plates, then place the quenelles on top. Garnish with the chopped parsley, and serve.

Serves 4

# Zucchini Pakoras with Scallion Raita

Here slices of zucchini are enrobed in a chickpea batter, then quickly fried. (Strictly speaking, pakoras, from northern India, are fritters—not dumplings—but I've reckoned they fit better in this chapter than anywhere else.)

Chickpea flour can be found in many whole-foods and Middle Eastern markets as well as in Indian food stores.

**SCALLION RAITA:**

1 cup plain whole, low-fat, or nonfat yogurt

4 scallions, both white and green parts, minced

1½ teaspoons sugar

¼ teaspoon salt

**PAKORAS:**
1/2 teaspoon cumin seeds
1/2 teaspoon brown mustard seeds
1 cup chickpea flour
1/2 teaspoon salt
1/2 teaspoon fresh-ground black pepper
Large pinch cayenne (optional)
1/2 cup plain whole, low-fat, or nonfat yogurt
About 1 cup peanut, canola, or corn oil
1/2 teaspoon baking soda
2 medium zucchini (about 1 pound total), cut into
    1/4-inch diagonal slices

**1.** Make the raita: Combine the yogurt, chopped scallions, sugar, and salt in a bowl, and stir well. (The raita can be stored for up to 24 hours in a covered container in the refrigerator.)

**2.** In a dry skillet over medium heat, toast the cumin and mustard seeds, shaking the pan, until the mustard seeds turn gray. In a bowl, combine the chickpea flour, the toasted cumin and mustard seeds, the salt, the pepper, and the cayenne, if you're using it. Add the yogurt and 1/3 cup water, and stir well. The batter should be about the consistency of yogurt; if it seems too thick, stir in more water. (The batter can be prepared to this point and refrigerated, covered, for up to 24 hours.)

**3.** Heat a large skillet with 1 inch of oil over medium-high heat. Add the baking soda to the batter, and stir well. Drop a tiny bit of the batter into the oil. If the batter fizzes immediately, the oil is ready. Dip one slice of zucchini in the batter to coat it evenly, and place it carefully in the hot oil. Continue with more slices until the skillet is full but not crowded. Turn the pakoras over after a minute or so, and cook them on the other side for another minute. Transfer them with a slotted spoon to paper towels. Continue this process until all the zucchini is fried. Serve the pakoras right away, with the raita.

**Variation:** For a fun and filling meal, sandwich a thin slice of mozzarella cheese between two slices of zucchini, then coat the zucchini sandwich with batter, and fry it.

Serves 4

## Mustard Seeds

❀

*There are generally two types of mustard seeds to choose from, white (also called yellow) or brown. I usually opt for the more pungent brown, available in Indian groceries and whole-foods stores. Before I add mustard seeds to a dish, I usually toast them in a dry skillet until they turn gray to bring out their flavor. I add them to vinaigrettes, to slaws, and to sour-cream dips (along with prepared mustard and honey) for crudités. Brown mustard seeds are used in Indian curries, for which they are either toasted in a dry skillet or cooked in hot oil with other spices before the liquid is added. Brown mustard seeds are also used in Chinese and European prepared mustards.*

# CHAPTER 12

# Savory Crepes & Cakes

# Thai Vegetable Crepes with Peanut Sauce

G lutinous rice flour gives these crepes a sponge-like texture, which makes them fun to eat. Although this dish takes some time to prepare, it is terrific for entertaining, since the sauce, the filling, and the crepes can all be made beforehand.

I use the peanut sauce (recipe follows) with many foods besides the crepes. It makes a sumptuous dip for raw vegetables, for instance, and I also love it tossed with pan-fried tofu and fresh Chinese wheat noodles.

1 recipe Peanut Sauce (recipe follows, page 336)

**FILLING:**
1 1-pound eggplant, peeled and cut into ¹/₂-inch cubes
1 tablespoon canola or corn oil
3 carrots, cut into 3-inch-long julienne strips
10 scallions, halved lengthwise, cut into 3-inch lengths, then cut into julienne strips
2 red bell peppers, seeded and cut into julienne strips
1 tablespoon soy sauce
2 cups cooked rice, or 4 cups chopped nappa cabbage

**CREPES:**
1³/₄ cups unbleached white flour
²/₃ cup glutinous rice flour (available in Asian markets)
1 teaspoon salt
4 eggs
1³/₄ cups water
About 1 tablespoon canola or corn oil (or some spray oil)

**GARNISH:**
*Whole chives*

**■■■■■■■■■**

**1.** Make the filling: Preheat the oven to 375°. Spread the egg-plant cubes on a baking sheet that has been lightly coated with oil. Bake the eggplant for 15 minutes or until it has softened.

While the eggplant bakes, heat the 1 tablespoon oil over medium heat in a large skillet. Add the carrots, scallions, and peppers. Sauté them for about 8 minutes, stirring frequently. Stir in the soy sauce, then the rice or nappa cabbage. Cook for 2 minutes more, stirring frequently. Take the pan off the heat, and stir in the baked eggplant.

**2.** Make the crepe batter: In a large bowl, mix the white flour, the rice flour, and the salt. In another bowl, combine the eggs and the water. Slowly add the liquid to the dry ingredients, whisking continuously. Whisk until the mixture is almost smooth.

**3.** Cook the crepes: Over medium-high heat, coat a griddle, a crepe pan, or a large skillet with oil. Ladle ⅓ cup of the batter onto the surface, and let the crepe cook for 1 minute. Flip the crepe over with a spatula, and cook it another minute. Transfer the crepe to a plate, and ladle another ⅓ cup batter onto the hot surface. Continue cooking the crepes in this fashion until you have twelve. Keep them warm by covering them with a kitchen towel.

**4.** Assemble the crepes: Warm the filling in the skillet. Warm the peanut sauce over low heat in another skillet. Then ladle some sauce (about ¼ cup) onto each large dinner plate. Spoon about 3 tablespoons filling onto each crepe, roll the crepes, and place two on each plate. Serve the crepes garnished with whole, crisscrossed chives.

Serves 6

## Peanut Sauce

¹/₄ cup smooth or chunky peanut butter
¹/₂ cup coconut milk (you can freeze the rest of
the milk in the can for later use)

1/4 cup finely chopped dry-roasted, unsalted
   peanuts
2 tablespoons Thai or Vietnamese fish sauce, or
   1 tablespoon soy sauce
3 tablespoons rice vinegar
2 teaspoons minced fresh ginger
2 garlic cloves, minced
2 tablespoons chopped cilantro (optional)
Hot chile sauce to taste (optional)

**1.** In a large bowl, whisk together the peanut butter and the coconut milk for a minute or two, until the mixture is smooth.

**2.** Add the peanuts, fish or soy sauce, rice vinegar, ginger, garlic, and, if you like, cilantro. If you want some heat, add a bit of chile sauce.

# Buckwheat Crepes Filled with Potatoes and Kale

*H*ere is a filling dinner for a cold winter's night. The characteristic buckwheat flavor pairs nicely with the hearty filling of kale and potato. The crepes sit in a sweet and slightly smoky sauce made from seared onions, tomato, and red bell peppers. This recipe includes several steps, but each step is simple, and the end result makes the effort well worthwhile.

**CREPES:**
1/3 cup unbleached white flour
1/2 cup buckwheat flour (available in whole-foods
   stores)
1/2 teaspoon salt
1 1/4 cups whole or low-fat milk
2 eggs, beaten
About 1 tablespoon olive oil (or some spray oil)

**SAUCE:**

1 tablespoon olive oil

2 cups sliced onions

2 garlic cloves, minced

1 large red bell pepper, chopped

1 small tomato, chopped

1 cup water or Basic Vegetable Stock (page 79)

Salt and fresh-ground black pepper to taste

**FILLING:**

1 tablespoon olive oil

2 cups chopped onions

2 to 3 garlic cloves, minced

1 cup water

2 russet potatoes, peeled and cut into ½-inch
  cubes

6 cups stemmed, chopped, and firmly packed kale

Salt and fresh-ground black pepper to taste

4 to 6 tablespoons sour cream (optional)

**1.** Make the crepe batter: In a large bowl, combine the two flours with the salt, and mix well. Make a well in the center, and add the milk and eggs. With a whisk, slowly incorporate the flour from the side of the bowl. Mix until all the ingredients are combined and the batter is smooth. Let the batter rest for 15 minutes.

**2.** Meanwhile, make the sauce: In a large skillet, heat the olive oil over medium heat, and add the onions. Cook them for at least 8 minutes, until they brown at the edges. Add the garlic and red pepper, and cook 3 minutes more, stirring often. Add the tomato and the water or stock, and simmer the mixture for 15 minutes, covered. Transfer the mixture to a food processor or blender. Purée the sauce well (if you're using a blender, remove the center of the lid to let air out; otherwise, the hot sauce may burst out). Season the sauce with salt and pepper and keep it warm.

**3.** Make the filling: In a large skillet, heat the olive oil over medium heat. Add the onions, and cook them until they soften, about 5 minutes. Add the garlic, water, potatoes, and kale. (You may need to add the kale in two batches to fit it all in the skillet. If so, add the first half with the potatoes, and the rest a few minutes later, once the first batch of kale becomes limp.) Cook, covered, until the potatoes soften, then season the mixture with salt and pepper. Keep it warm.

**4.** Cook the crepes: Heat a crepe pan or a non-stick skillet over medium-high heat. When the pan is hot, add 1 teaspoon olive oil, and swirl the oil around the pan (or use spray oil). Add about ¼ cup of the crepe batter so that the crepe is at least 7 inches in diameter. Cook the crepe over medium heat for 1 minute, then flip it with a spatula. Cook the crepe for 15 seconds more, then remove the crepe to a plate. Continue in this manner with the remaining batter, using additional olive oil only if the crepes begin to stick. Stack the crepes, and keep them warm in a slow oven. There should be at least eight crepes.

**5.** Assemble the crepes: Place a crepe on a clean work surface. Spoon about ½ cup of the kale-potato filling down the center, and roll the crepe neatly. Fill the rest of the crepes the same way. Ladle the sauce onto dinner plates, then place two of the crepes in the sauce on each plate. Garnish with sour cream, if you like, and serve.

Serves 4 to 6

# Mushroom Blinchiki

Here delicate whole-wheat blinis are stacked between layers of seasoned ricotta cheese, sautéed mushrooms, and onions. The torte, about 4 inches high, is cut into wedges like a cake. This is a variation on the classic Russian blini torte, blinchiki. Serve the blinchiki hot, accompanied by a simple green salad.

⅔ cup unbleached white flour
⅔ cup whole-wheat flour
1 teaspoon salt
1 cup whole or low-fat milk
2 eggs
1 tablespoon olive oil
3 cups thinly sliced onions
2 large garlic cloves, minced
1 pound white button mushrooms, sliced thin
½ cup white wine
Salt and fresh-ground black pepper to taste
2 cups ricotta cheese, whole-milk or part-skim
⅓ cup grated Parmesan cheese
⅔ cup club soda or carbonated water

**1.** Make the batter: In a large bowl, combine the two flours and the salt. In a smaller bowl, whisk together the milk and the eggs. Make a well in the center of the flour mixture, and pour the milk-egg mixture into the well. Stir the liquid with a whisk, gradually incorporating the flour. Continue stirring until the batter is smooth, then let it sit for 20 minutes while you prepare the mushrooms and the ricotta mixture.

**2.** Make the filling: Heat the olive oil in a large, preferably non-stick skillet. Add the onions, and sauté them over medium heat, stirring occasionally, for about 10 minutes or until they begin to brown slightly at the edges. Add the garlic, and sauté another minute. Transfer the mixture to a plate, and place the skillet back on the heat. Put the mushrooms and the wine into the empty skillet, cover the skillet, and simmer for 5 minutes. Remove the lid, and continue to cook until the wine has evaporated. Then return the onions and garlic to the pan, and season well with salt and pepper. Set the skillet aside.

**3.** In a small bowl, combine the ricotta and the Parmesan, and mix well. Add the salt and pepper to taste.

**4.** Preheat the oven to 375°. Add the soda or carbonated water to the crepe batter, and mix well. Heat a non-stick skillet over medium heat. Wipe the pan with olive oil, then ladle about 3

## Parmesan Alternatives

*A s I watched the price of Parmigiano Reggiano rocket into orbit a few years ago, I started to use hard grating cheeses that were less expensive. A good choice is Parmigiano Grana, also made in Italy but with fewer regulations; the quality can vary, but usually it is high. Another option is Asiago, whose flavor is similar to that of Parmesan. Another choice is aged Monterey Jack. Made in Monterey, California, this hard grating cheese comes dusted with cocoa, rubbed with olive oil, and sprinkled with cracked pepper. Pecorino Romano, made from sheep's milk, is too tangy and salty for many people, although some prefer it to Parmesan.*

tablespoons of the batter into the hot pan. Spread the batter by tilting the skillet in different directions. Let the blini cook for about 1 minute, then turn it over, and cook it 30 seconds more. Remove it to a plate, and cook more blinis until you've used all of the batter. (The blini making goes faster if you use two pans at once.) You should have at least seven crepes.

**5.** Place one blini on a baking sheet, and spread ¼ cup of the ricotta mixture fairly evenly over it. Top it with another blini. Spread ¼ cup of the mushroom mixture evenly over. Continue to add blinis and alternate fillings, ending with a crepe on the top.

**6.** Bake the blinchiki for 20 minutes, or until it is heated through. Slice the torte as you would cut a cake, and serve.

*Serves 4*

# Carrot Crepes Florentine

These crepes have a pretty yellow-orange color and a mildly sweet flavor because of the puréed carrots in the batter. Stuffed with spinach and onions, the crepes are served on a light cream sauce studded with white beans. Make this dish when you have plenty of time to prepare and enjoy the crepes. Since the unfilled crepes freeze well, you may want to make a double batch and freeze half for later use.

**CREPES:**
4 large carrots, cut into ½-inch cubes
1¾ cups whole or low-fat milk
⅓ to ½ cup water
4 eggs
1¾ cups unbleached white flour
1 teaspoon salt
About 1 tablespoon olive oil (or some spray oil)

**SPINACH FILLING:**
1 tablespoon olive oil
3 cups thinly sliced onions
1½ pounds fresh spinach, large stems removed
Salt and fresh-ground black pepper to taste

**WHITE CREAM SAUCE:**
2 tablespoons butter
2 shallots, cut in half
2 garlic cloves, cut in half
2 tablespoons unbleached white flour
2½ cups whole or low-fat milk
½ teaspoon salt
Fresh-ground black pepper taste
1 cup cooked lima beans, preferably baby white

**1.** Make the crepes: Bring 1 quart of water to a boil in a saucepan, and add the chopped carrots. Simmer them for 20 minutes or until they are tender. Drain the carrots, and rinse them in cold water in a colander to stop the cooking. Set them aside.

**2.** In a small bowl, whisk together the milk, ⅓ cup water, and the eggs. In a larger bowl, combine the flour and the salt. Make a well in the center, and add the milk-egg mixture. With a whisk, gradually blend the flour into the liquid. Mix until the batter is smooth.

**3.** In a blender or food processor, purée the carrots with about 1 cup of the crepe batter until the mixture is smooth. Add the mixture to the remaining crepe batter, and stir well. The batter should have the consistency of thin pancake batter. Add a little more water if it seems too thick. Let the batter rest for 15 minutes.

**4.** Heat a 9-inch skillet or crepe pan over medium-high heat. When the pan is hot, add 1 teaspoon olive oil, and swirl the pan to coat it with the oil (or use spray oil). Add about ¼ cup crepe batter, and immediately swirl the pan so the batter covers the entire base of the skillet. Cook the crepe for 1 minute, then, with a small spatula, flip the crepe, and cook 15 seconds more. Remove the crepe to a plate. Cook more crepes in this manner until all the batter is used, adding olive oil only if the crepes begin to stick. Stack the crepes on the plate; there should be at least eight. (If you have two skillets or crepe pans of the same size and are adept at crepe making, try using both at once. At the cafe, I use four crepe pans at once, but I've known chefs who can manage seven or eight!)

**5.** Make the filling: In a very large skillet, heat the olive oil over medium heat. Add the onions, and cook them, stirring frequently, until they have softened, about 5 minutes. Add the spinach, and turn the heat to high. Sauté the spinach, stirring, until it wilts, then season it with salt and pepper. Set the skillet aside.

**6.** Make the cream sauce: In a heavy-bottomed saucepan, melt the butter with the split shallots and garlic. Sauté them for 1 minute over medium heat. Add the flour, and stir with a whisk for 1 minute, making sure the flour doesn't brown. Add the milk ½ cup at a time, whisking well after each addition and letting the sauce begin to boil before adding more. When all of the milk is incorporated, the sauce should be smooth. Strain the sauce through a sieve into another saucepan, to remove the shallots and garlic, and add the salt and pepper. Stir in the beans. (At this point you can wrap or cover the crepes, the filling, and the sauce, and refrigerate them for up to 3 days before proceeding.)

**7.** Assemble the dish: Preheat the oven to 350°. Place one crepe on a clean work surface. Spoon some of the spinach down the center, and roll the crepe neatly. Fill the remaining crepes the same way. Place the filled crepes in an oiled casserole dish, and cover the dish with foil. Bake the crepes for 30 minutes. Meanwhile, reheat the sauce. Spoon some of the sauce onto each plate, then place two crepes in the sauce on each plate.

**Variation:** For a richer version, spread 1 tablespoon soft goat cheese on each crepe before adding the spinach.

**Note:** If you'd like to freeze this dish, place the stuffed crepes in a plastic storage container, and cover them with the sauce. Cover the container tightly, and freeze it for up to 3 months. Thaw the crepes overnight in the refrigerator, then bake them, covered, for 30 to 40 minutes, until they are heated through.

Serves 4

# Masa Cakes with Salsa Verde

Running my hands through masa harina, or limewater-treated cornmeal, feels exactly like playing with the sand on a Bermuda beach. The grains are a similar size, and they bunch together in the same way. Fortunately, they don't taste the same. These crispy masa cakes make a quick as well as hearty and delectable meal. The chopping, mixing, and blending of the ingredients take no more than 20 minutes, and the cakes cook in only 8 minutes.

Make the masa dough just before cooking the cakes, or else the dough will become stiff and dry in the meantime. If you must make the dough ahead, stir in more buttermilk at the last minute to bring the dough back to its original consistency.

**SALSA:**
¹/₂ pound tomatillos, husked and cut in half
1 garlic clove, cut in half
1 small onion, quartered
¹/₄ cup coarsely chopped cilantro
¹/₂ cup water
Salt and fresh-ground black pepper to taste
¹/₂ jalapeño pepper, quartered (seeds included if you like plenty of heat)
1 green apple, peeled, cored, and cut into small cubes

**MASA CAKES:**

2 eggs

1²/₃ cups buttermilk

3 tablespoons unsalted butter, or a
 bit more

1¹/₂ cups masa harina

1 cup unbleached white flour

1 teaspoon salt

¹/₂ teaspoon baking soda

³/₄ cup corn kernels, frozen and thawed or
 fresh and blanched

**1.** Make the salsa: In a blender or food processor, combine all of the salsa ingredients except the apple, and whirl until the onion and tomatillos are chopped. Transfer the mixture to a bowl, and add the apple. Keep the salsa at room temperature.

**2.** Make the masa dough: Melt 2 tablespoons of the butter. In a large bowl, beat the eggs. Add the buttermilk and melted butter. With a wooden spoon, gradually stir in the masa harina, flour, salt, and baking soda. Stir until the mixture forms a mass. Add the corn kernels, and stir again.

**3.** In a large skillet, melt 1 tablespoon butter over medium heat. With your hands, form a 5-inch patty from one-quarter of the masa dough. Place the patty in the skillet. Make three more patties with the remaining dough, and add them to the skillet as well (if you don't have enough room in the skillet, make two cakes at a time, adding a little more butter for the second batch). Cook the cakes until the undersides are golden brown, about 4 minutes, then flip them, and cook them 4 minutes more on the other side. Remove them from the pan, and serve each cake in a pool of the salsa verde.

Serves 4

# Reina's Pupusas

I first learned about pupusas (masa cakes stuffed with pork or cheese) from Reina, the cousin of Santos, our Salvadoran prep cook at the Delux. Soon after Reina came to help us in the kitchen for a few weeks, we discovered she made pupusas as a sideline. I have been indebted to her ever since.

Pupusas are quick to make. Here I've lightened the traditional masa mixture with roasted winter squash. I've also added smoked cheese for a richer flavor. The pupusas are served with hot sauce—use your favorite—and a spoonful of sour cream.

1 acorn squash, or 2 medium delicata squashes
2¹/₄ cups masa harina
1 teaspoon salt
¹/₂ teaspoon fresh-ground black pepper
3 ounces grated smoked cheese, such as Jack, cheddar, Gouda, or mozzarella (about ³/₄ cup)
1 cup water, at room temperature
2 tablespoons olive oil
4 tablespoons sour cream (optional)
Your favorite hot sauce

**1.** Preheat the oven to 400°. Cut the squash in half lengthwise, and spoon out the seeds. Put the squash halves cut side down into a casserole dish, and bake them 40 to 50 minutes, until they are tender. Let them cool. Spoon out the flesh, and put it into a large bowl (you can chop the skin and add it, too, if you like).

**2.** Add the masa harina to the bowl of squash. Mix in the salt and pepper. Add the cheese, and mix well again. Add the water, and mix with one hand until the dough is smooth.

**3.** On a lightly floured surface, form a 3-inch wide patty from a large spoonful of masa dough. Form seven more patties from the remaining dough. They will be rather soft and fragile.

## Delicata Squash: A New Favorite

Looking like a fat yellow cucumber with dark green racing stripes, delicata is one of the tastiest winter squashes. Often available in supermarkets, this squash has a bright orange interior, which becomes creamy, sweet, and custard-like when baked. After baking, the skin of the delicata is tender enough to eat.

To roast delicata squash, split it in half lengthwise, drop a teaspoon of butter or olive oil into each cavity, and add salt, pepper, and a teaspoon of brown sugar. Bake the squash at 400° for 40 to 50 minutes or until it is tender, brushing the cut surface once or twice with the juices.

**4.** Place a large skillet over medium heat. When it is very hot, add 1 tablespoon of the olive oil. Fry four of the pupusas for about 5 minutes per side, until they form a golden crust on both sides. Transfer them to a plate, and keep them warm in a slow oven. Heat the skillet again, add the remaining olive oil, and fry the four remaining pupusas in the same manner. Serve the pupusas with dollops of sour cream, if you like, and pass the hot sauce around the table.

Serves 4

# Spinach Patties with Cumin-Orange Raita

These cakes celebrate the flavor of spinach, a vegetable that I swore off for life as a child but relish as an adult. The spinach is bound with lentils, onion, and bread crumbs; chopped almonds provide a good crunch. The raita, an easily concocted condiment made primarily with yogurt, is refreshing against the hot spinach patties. Don't let the number of steps deter you from this recipe; each step is fast and easy. For an even faster version, see the Variation at the end of the recipe.

**SPINACH PATTIES:**
1/2 cup dried red or brown lentils
1 1/2 tablespoons olive oil
1 cup chopped onion
1 teaspoon apple cider vinegar
8 slices stale or lightly toasted sandwich bread
2 garlic cloves, minced
12 ounces fresh spinach, larger stems removed, rinsed and still damp
20 whole almonds, preferably toasted
1 red bell pepper, seeded and chopped fine
1/2 teaspoon salt, or more, to taste
Fresh-ground black pepper to taste

RAITA:

2 tablespoons finely chopped shallot or onion

1 teaspoon toasted cumin seeds, or 1 teaspoon
    ground cumin

1 teaspoon grated orange rind

3/4 cup plain whole, low-fat, or nonfat yogurt

Salt and fresh-ground black pepper to taste


3 tablespoons unbleached white flour

1½ teaspoons olive oil

**1.** In a small pan, cover the lentils with about 2 cups water. Bring them to a boil, then turn down the heat, cover the pan, and simmer the lentils until they are tender. This may take anywhere from 10 to 30 minutes, depending on the size and shape of the lentil (red lentils cook in 10 to 20 minutes, the brown ones in 25 to 30). Drain the lentils, and set them aside.

**2.** In a large skillet, heat 1½ teaspoons of the olive oil over medium heat, and add the onion. Sauté it for just 2 minutes, stirring occasionally. Add the cider vinegar, and stir for 10 seconds. Transfer the mixture to a large bowl. Wipe the skillet clean.

**3.** Tear the slices of bread into pieces, place them in a food processor, and run the machine until they form crumbs. (Don't clean the processor; you'll use it again shortly.) Place the wiped skillet over medium heat, and add the remaining 1 tablespoon olive oil. When the oil is hot, add the minced garlic and the bread crumbs. Cook them over medium heat, stirring occasionally, until the bread crumbs are crispy, about 5 to 8 minutes. Transfer the toasted crumbs to the large bowl of sautéed onion.

**4.** Place a large, dry skillet over medium-high heat, and add the damp spinach. Let it cook, stirring frequently, for 2 minutes or until it is wilted. Transfer the spinach to a cutting board, and chop it well. Then add it to the large bowl of onion and crumbs.

**5.** Add the lentils and almonds to the food processor, and run the machine in spurts until the lentils and almonds are chopped fine. Transfer the mixture to the bowl of onions. Add the chopped red pepper and the salt and black pepper to the bowl. Mix the ingredients well.

**6.** Make the raita: Combine all of the ingredients in a bowl.

**7.** Put the 3 tablespoons flour on a plate. Form eight patties from the spinach mixture, and dredge them well in the flour on both sides. In a large skillet, heat the 1½ teaspoons olive oil over medium-high heat. Pan-fry the patties well on both sides, about 3 minutes per side. Serve them hot, with the raita on the side.

Variation: To simplify this recipe, use frozen chopped spinach. Just thaw a 10-ounce package of spinach in a colander, press out the excess water, and add it to the bowl of sautéed onion and crumbs.

Serves 4

# Big Bammy

South Americans, Central Americans, and West Indians eat yuca (pronounced "you-ka" and also called yucca, manioc, and cassava) in a thousand different ways, just as Irish do potatoes. Santos, a Salvadoran who cooks in the Delux kitchen, likes his yuca boiled, then dressed with olive oil and lime juice. In Cuba, boiled yuca is often eaten with *mojo* sauce, a blend of olive oil, lime juice, and fried garlic. In Jamaica, along the northern coast, yuca is grated and cooked like a potato pancake. These pancakes, called bammies, are usually served with fried fish, but I serve my version with lime-marinated tomatoes. The process for making a bammy may appear complicated at first, but it's really quite simple.

**LIME-MARINATED TOMATOES:**
1/4 cup lime juice (from about 2 limes)
2 garlic cloves, sliced thin
1/2 jalapeño pepper, cut into thin rings (include
    the seeds if you like more heat)
1 tablespoon olive oil
2 ripe medium tomatoes
Salt and fresh-ground black pepper to taste

**BAMMY:**
1 1/2 pounds yuca (available in many
    supermarkets as well as in Latin American
    markets)
1 egg, beaten
1 1/2 cups chopped onions
1/2 teaspoon salt
Fresh-ground black pepper to taste

2 tablespoons olive oil

**1.** Marinate the tomatoes: In a bowl, combine the lime juice, garlic, jalapeño, and olive oil. Core the tomatoes, and cut them in half vertically. Place the tomatoes cut side down, slice them into half-rounds about ½ inch thick, and put them into the bowl with the marinade. Toss the tomatoes well, and season them with salt and pepper. Let the tomatoes sit at least 10 minutes.

**2.** Make the bammy: Whack the yuca hard with a chef's knife to cut it into 4-inch lengths. Stand each piece on the cutting board, and use the same knife to cut away the skin. Cut the peeled yuca into 1-inch cubes, and put half of them into a food processor. Run the machine until all the yuca has been pulverized. Transfer the yuca to the center of a clean kitchen towel. Lift all the sides of the towel, and squeeze the ball of yuca over the sink to extract as much liquid as possible. Put the drained yuca pulp (in Jamaica it is called the "yuca flour") into a bowl, and repeat the process with the remaining yuca.

## One Potato, Two, Three, Four, Five...

*Numerous potato varieties are sitting pretty in the produce section these days. Many can be used interchangeably. Here are the most popular. Brown-skinned, white-fleshed russet potatoes are ideal for baking, frying, mashing, latkes, gratins, and steak potatoes (see page 383). Yellow Finns are small yellow potatoes with a rich, creamy taste. They are good boiled, roasted, and in potato salads. Yukon Gold potatoes, also yellow-fleshed, come in many sizes. They have a delicious buttery flavor and are great mashed or roasted. Small, red new potatoes are excellent for potato salads, roasting, and boiling.*

**3.** Add to the yuca "flour" the beaten eggs, the chopped onions, and the salt and pepper, and mix well.

**4.** Heat 1 tablespoon olive oil over medium-high heat in a well-seasoned or non-stick 10- to 12-inch skillet. Add the yuca mixture, and pat it down well so that it covers the entire skillet. Turn the heat down to medium, and cook the bammy for 5 to 7 minutes, checking periodically to make sure the bottom isn't burning. When the bammy is golden brown on the bottom, carefully invert it onto a plate, and add the remaining 1 tablespoon olive oil to the skillet. Slide the bammy back into the skillet, brown side up, and cook it for 5 to 7 minutes more.

**5.** Slide the bammy onto a cutting board, and cut it into quarters. Serve it with the tomatoes and their marinade spooned on top.

**Variation:** Be adventurous—instead of tomatoes, use fruit such as halved grapes or sliced nectarines.

*Serves 4*

# Gruyère Potatoes Rösti

*R*östi means "crisp and golden," and in Switzerland it refers to grated potatoes that are flattened and sautéed until they are golden on both sides. In my version, Gruyère cheese provides a richness that makes this rösti work well as an entrée. Serve it with a bold salad of arugula and tomatoes, tossed with olive oil and a squeeze of lemon.

**YOGURT–SOUR CREAM SAUCE:**
2 tablespoons plain whole, low-fat, or nonfat yogurt
2 tablespoons plain whole, low-fat, or nonfat sour cream (or 2 tablespoons more yogurt)
2 tablespoons finely chopped scallions or chives

## RÖSTI:

1 egg
¼ cup unbleached white flour
2 medium russet potatoes (about 1 pound), peeled
    and grated
⅓ cup grated Swiss Gruyère cheese (or
    raclette; domestic Gruyère won't do)
⅓ cup chopped onion
¼ teaspoon caraway seeds (optional)
½ teaspoon salt
Fresh-ground black pepper to taste
1½ tablespoons unsalted butter

## GARNISH:

½ ripe medium tomato, chopped fine
1 tablespoon finely chopped scallions or chives

**1.** Make the sauce: In a bowl combine the yogurt, sour cream, and scallions or chives. Set the bowl aside.

**2.** Make the rösti: In a large bowl, whisk together the egg and the flour. With a wooden spoon, stir in the grated potatoes, Gruyère, onion, caraway seeds (if you're using them), and the salt and pepper.

**3.** Place a well-seasoned 9- to 11-inch skillet over medium-high heat. When it is hot, add the butter. When the butter has melted (but before it burns), add the rösti mixture, patting it to form one large cake in the pan. Reduce the heat to medium-low, and let the cake brown for 10 to 12 minutes, lifting it with a small knife after 8 or 9 minutes to check the color on the underside. When the underside is a dark golden brown, carefully invert the rösti onto a plate. Slide the rösti back into the skillet brown side up, and cook the rösti 10 to 12 minutes more over medium-low heat.

**4.** Slide the rösti onto a cutting board, and cut it into quarters. Serve two wedges per plate, topped with the yogurt–sour cream sauce and sprinkled with chopped tomato and scallions or chives.

Serves 2

# Golden Potato Cake with Fresh Herb Dressing

This is an easy dinner that looks impressive but doesn't take much time. Potatoes and carrots are sliced thin, then pan-fried until golden. The cooking is completed in the oven, and then the dish is inverted. Wedges of this warm cake are served on watercress and drizzled with a creamy fresh herb dressing.

You'll probably have more dressing than you need, but you can save the remainder for salads.

**POTATO CAKE:**
2 tablespoons olive oil
2 medium russet potatoes (about 1 pound), peeled and sliced as thin as possible
Salt and fresh-ground black pepper to taste
1 large carrot, peeled and sliced diagonally as thin as possible

**HERB DRESSING:**
2 tablespoons lemon juice (from about 1/2 lemon)
1 tablespoon chopped parsley
2 tablespoons chopped dill
1 garlic clove, minced
1 tablespoon mayonnaise
1 teaspoon Dijon mustard
2 tablespoons olive oil
Salt and fresh-ground black pepper to taste

1 small bunch watercress, large stems trimmed off

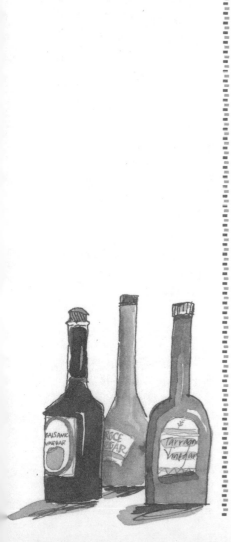

**1.** Make the potato cake: Preheat the oven to 400°. Heat an 8- or 9-inch well-seasoned oven-proof skillet (cast iron works well) over medium-high heat, and add the olive oil. When the oil is hot, add the potatoes. Generously salt and pepper them, then lay the carrot slices over them. Turn the heat to medium-low, and cook, without stirring, until the potatoes turn golden brown on the bottom, about 10 to 15 minutes (you can use a small knife to peek).

**2.** Cover the skillet tightly with foil, and place it in the oven. Bake the potatoes and carrot for 20 minutes, or until the potatoes yield no resistance when poked with a knife.

**3.** While the vegetables bake, make the dressing: Whisk together the lemon juice, parsley, dill, garlic, mayonnaise, and mustard in a small bowl. Then, whisking constantly, slowly pour in the oil. Season the dressing with salt and pepper.

**4.** Assemble the dish: When the potatoes are done, place a platter or a small cutting board over the skillet and invert it. Lift the skillet, using a knife to loosen any stuck potato slices. Cut the cake into wedges. Place each wedge on a bed of watercress, and drizzle the dressing over all. Serve immediately.

Serves 2 to 3

# Parsnip-Potato Cake with Horseradish Sour Cream

The crunch and flavor of these pancakes is so amazing that I sometimes forget to breathe while eating them. As with most latkes, the raw-potato mixture must be cooked

## Rising Star: The Parsnip

*Although the parsnip has been grown in the United States for over three hundred years, until now the vegetable has never gotten as much attention as it deserves.*

*Looking like a bleached carrot, the parsnip has a sweet, nut-like flavor. I especially like parsnips raw; try them grated or sliced thin in slaws, or tossed with thinly sliced red onion and julienned zucchini and dressed with lemon juice and olive oil. Roasted parsnips are delicious, too; cut parsnips into large chunks, toss them with salt, pepper, a bit of minced garlic, and a few spoonfuls of olive oil, then roast them in a 400° oven until tender.*

right away; if it sits it will discolor and leach water. Once cooked, latkes should also be eaten right away. They just aren't the same reheated.

∎∎∎∎∎∎∎∎∎∎

1 egg, beaten
3 tablespoons unbleached white flour
1 cup grated parsnip
1 large russet potato (about ½ pound), peeled and grated
½ teaspoon salt
Fresh-ground black pepper to taste
⅔ cup minced onion
1 garlic clove, minced
2 tablespoons prepared horseradish, or 1 tablespoon finely grated fresh horseradish
3 tablespoons sour cream
1 tablespoon butter

∎∎∎∎∎∎∎∎∎∎

**1.** Whisk together the egg and the flour in a large bowl. With a wooden spoon, stir in the parsnip, potato, salt, pepper, onion, and garlic.

**2.** In a small bowl, mix together the horseradish and the sour cream. Add fresh-ground pepper to taste. Set the bowl aside.

**3.** In a large well-seasoned skillet, heat the butter over medium-high heat. (Do not use a non-stick skillet, or else the latke crust will be too thin. Cast iron works well.) Form the latke mixture into two balls of equal size. When the butter begins to brown, add the balls to the skillet, and press each down with the palm of your hand to a cake 1½ inches thick and 5 to 6 inches wide. Turn the heat to medium, and brown the latkes for 4 to 6 minutes or until they are deep brown on the underside. Then turn the cakes over, and cook them for 4 to 5 minutes more. Serve them topped with dollops of the horseradish–sour cream mixture.

*Serves 2*

# Sweet-Potato Latkes

With a tossed salad to accompany it, this sweet-potato pancake makes a quick and delicious supper. Unlike regular potato latkes, these need no wringing to extract excess water; just grate the sweet potato, and mix it with the other ingredients. The sour-cream garnish is lightened with yogurt and enlivened with chile and lime.

**CHILE-LIME SOUR CREAM:**
2 tablespoons regular, low-fat, or nonfat sour cream
3 tablespoons plain whole, low-fat, or nonfat yogurt
1 small chile pepper, such as serrano, jalapeño, or Thai, seeded and chopped fine
2 tablespoons lime juice (from about 1 lime)
Salt and fresh-ground black pepper to taste

**LATKES:**
1 pound (about 1 large or 2 medium) sweet potatoes, peeled and grated
2/3 cup minced onion
1/2 teaspoon salt
Fresh-ground black pepper to taste
2 eggs, beaten
5 tablespoons unbleached white flour

2 tablespoons butter or olive oil
2 scallions, chopped

**1.** Make the chile-lime sour cream: In a small bowl, combine all of the ingredients, and stir well. Set the bowl aside.

**2.** Make the latke mixture: In a large bowl, combine the grated sweet potato with the onion, salt, pepper, and eggs. Mix well. Add the flour, and mix again. (Refrigerate the mixture, if you like, for up to 1 hour. The latke may be slightly less crispy if you refrigerate the mixture longer.)

**3.** In a large skillet, heat the butter or olive oil over medium-high heat. (Do not use a non-stick skillet, or else the latke crust will be too thin.) Divide the latke mixture in two, and drop the halves into the skillet to form two cakes. (If your skillet cannot hold both latkes, cook them one at a time.) Flatten the latkes with a large spoon until they are about 1 inch thick and about 5 inches in diameter. Fry the latkes about 4 to 5 minutes, until they are deep brown on the underside, then flip them, and cook them for 3 to 4 minutes more. Serve them right away, garnished with the chile-lime sour cream and the scallions.

*Serves 2*

# Zucchini-Jícama Cakes with Tomato Coulis

The combination of zucchini and jícama makes for a tasty vegetable cake. Jícama (pronounced "HEE-ca-ma") is a brown-skinned, white-fleshed root vegetable that is quite versatile; it's good both cooked and raw. It adds a surprising crunchiness to this cake and blends well with the flavors of zucchini, tomato, and red onion.

1 small jícama (about 1 pound)
1 medium zucchini, grated
½ red onion, sliced thin
1 teaspoon salt
2 tablespoons olive oil, or a bit more
½ cup chopped onion
2 garlic cloves, minced
3 tomatoes, chopped fine
½ cup water
1 tablespoon drained capers

## Introducing Jícama

*Looking like a beige, slightly flattened, grapefruit-sized Hershey's Kiss, jícama can be eaten either raw or cooked. Although jícama is sometimes called the Mexican potato, it does not have the potato's long shelf life, but lasts for about a week in the refrigerator. Jícama's bland flavor and terrifically crispy texture make for a versatile vegetable. Jícama is delicious grated in salads or slaws, or cut into tiny cubes and added to salsas and fruit salads. Also, try it roasted with olive oil as a side dish.*

Salt and fresh-ground black pepper to taste
2 eggs, beaten
½ cup unbleached white flour
1 dozen basil leaves, cut into thin slivers

**1.** Peel the jícama with a small paring knife. Cut the jícama in half, then cut it into thin slices. Cut the slices into matchstick pieces, then cut the matchsticks crosswise into tiny cubes (no bigger than the size of pencil erasers). Put the jícama into a large bowl, and mix in the zucchini and the red onion. Add the salt, and mix well. Transfer the vegetables to a colander and let them stand for 30 minutes.

**2.** Meanwhile, make the tomato coulis: Heat 1 tablespoon of the olive oil in a saucepan over medium-high heat. Add the chopped onion, and cook, stirring occasionally, for 5 minutes. Add one minced garlic clove, the tomatoes, and the water. When the mixture begins to simmer, turn the heat to low. Simmer the mixture for 5 minutes, then stir in the capers. Season the coulis to taste with salt and pepper, and set the pan aside.

**3.** Once the vegetables have drained for 30 minutes, shake the colander well, then put them into a clean bowl, and stir in the remaining garlic and the eggs. Then sprinkle in the flour and additional black pepper, and stir again.

**4.** Heat a large non-stick or well-seasoned skillet over medium heat. Add 1 tablespoon olive oil. Drop the batter, ½ cup at a time, into the skillet, trying not to let the cakes touch each other (you can probably cook three at a time). Cook the cakes for 3 minutes, or until they are golden brown on the bottom. Turn them with a spatula, and cook them 3 minutes more on the other side. Transfer the cakes to paper towels, and add a bit more olive oil to the skillet. Cook more cakes with the remaining batter; you should have six in all.

**5.** Reheat the tomato coulis, and spoon it onto plates. Set the hot cakes in the coulis, sprinkle with the slivered basil, and serve.

Serves 6

# Hearty Korean Pancakes

A substantial dinner, these pancakes are filled with brown rice, grated carrots, scallions, and tofu. Their crisp, crunchy outsides balance a soft, chewy inside. This is a great meal for novice tofu eaters.

Don't hesitate to substitute other vegetables—such as grated zucchini, daikon radish, or sweet potatoes, or chopped spinach—for the ones I've chosen here.

**PANCAKES:**

1 egg

1¹/₃ cups water

1 cup unbleached white flour

1 cup glutinous rice flour (available in Asian markets and many supermarkets), or an additional 1 cup white flour

¹/₂ teaspoon salt

1 cup cooked short-grain brown rice, or 1 cup glutinous (sweet) rice (available in Asian markets)

8 ounces firm tofu, cut into ¹/₂-inch cubes

2 large carrots, grated

6 scallions, both green and white parts, chopped fine

3 tablespoons canola or corn oil

**DIPPING SAUCE:**

3 tablespoons soy sauce

1 garlic clove, minced

1 teaspoon dark sesame oil

1 teaspoon apple cider vinegar

1 pinch chile flakes, or 1 dash hot chile sauce

1 pinch sugar (optional)

**1.** Make the pancake batter: In a small bowl, whisk together the egg and water. In a large bowl, stir together the flours and salt. Make a well in the center of the flour mixture, and add the egg-water mixture. Stirring slowly with a whisk, gradually incorporate the flour into the liquid. Stir until the batter is smooth. Add the cooked rice, tofu, carrots, and scallions to the batter, and stir well. Set the bowl aside.

**2.** Make the dipping sauce: In a small bowl, whisk together all of the sauce ingredients except the sugar. Taste the sauce, and add a pinch of suger, if you like.

**3.** In a well-seasoned skillet at least 10 inches in diameter (do not use a non-stick pan; the texture of the cakes would be quite different), heat 1 tablespoon oil over medium heat. Pour 1 generous cup of the batter into the middle of the pan. Turn the heat to medium-low, and spread the pancake with a spoon. Cook the pancake for about 5 minutes, or until it is lightly browned on the bottom. Turn the pancake with a spatula, and lightly brown the other side for 5 minutes. Slide the pancake onto a plate. Keep the pancake warm in a slow oven while you make the two more in the same way, using 1 tablespoon oil for each.

**4.** Pour the dipping sauce into small individual bowls, and serve the sauce with the hot pancakes.

**Variation:** For a wonderful texture and flavor, add 3 tablespoons toasted sesame seeds to the batter.

*Serves 3*

# Mu Shu Tofu

M u shu pork, a popular dish among Chinese-food aficionados, traditionally combines shredded pork with slivered mushrooms and scrambled eggs, with rice wine and soy for flavoring. The diners wrap the mixture in small pancakes at the table, and eat the filled pancakes with their hands.

# Cooking with Tofu

Tofu, or soybean curd, was invented in China over two thousand years ago. To make tofu, soybeans are soaked overnight, mashed, pressure-cooked, filtered, coagulated, left to settle and drain, then pressed into cakes. Although tofu is practically flavorless, it has an enticing soft texture that combines well with other foods and flavors.

With the exception of silken and very fresh tofu, tofu should always be cooked, to kill bacteria that may have developed during storage. To use tofu in a dip, lightly simmer it for 5 minutes, then drain it.

Be generous with spices and strong flavors when you're using tofu. In stir-fry dishes, use ingredients such as scallions, ginger, garlic, chile paste, bean paste, sesame oil, rice vinegar, peanuts, tamarind paste, and soy sauce. If you are stuffing enchiladas or burritos with tofu, pan-fry it over high heat (preferably in a non-stick skillet) in olive oil with some of the following: onions, garlic, hot peppers, cumin, coriander, lime juice, oregano, and cilantro. If you are making a tofu curry, add raisins, green apple, onion, cilantro, curry powder, and perhaps a touch of coconut milk. Tofu needs strong flavors to help it out, no matter if the dish is Italian, African, or Persian.

Is tofu better for you than meat? Both are good sources of protein. An ounce of tofu has only about one-third as much protein as an ounce of meat, but tofu is easier to digest and costs less per pound than most cuts of meat. (Besides, most Americans, vegetarians included, eat more protein than they need.) Tofu also has far less fat, especially saturated fat, than most meats. For example, whereas 3.5 ounces of pot roast contain 26 grams of fat, 10 of which are saturated, the same weight of tofu contains 6 grams of fat, less than 1 gram of which is saturated. Meat eaters as well as vegetarians would be wise to consider eating tofu often.

## TOFU CHOICES

**SILKEN TOFU**—Good for dressings, fruit shakes, and puddings, and for creaming soups and sauces.

**SOFT TOFU**—Use it cubed in soups, and puréed in dips, sauces, and salad dressings.

**FIRM TOFU**—Use it sliced or cubed in stir-fry dishes, and as filling for enchiladas or crepes.

**EXTRA-FIRM TOFU**—Good for pan-frying in large pieces, and roasting in cubes.

**LOW-FAT TOFU**—It should be labeled soft, firm, extra-firm, or silken. Use it accordingly.

**FRESH TOFU**—Available in Asian markets and whole-foods stores, this tofu sours after 2 to 3 days. Use it as you would soft or firm tofu.

In my version, tofu marinated in soy is combined with softly scrambled eggs and fresh portobello mushrooms, whose flavor and texture I prefer to that of the traditional dried mushrooms.

Mandarin pancakes are available in plastic packages (usually labeled "for Peking duck or mu-shu pork") in Chinese markets and some supermarkets (you'll probably find them next to the fresh noodles and wonton wrappers). If you can't get Mandarin pancakes, you can substitute warmed flour tortillas.

2 tablespoons soy sauce

1 teaspoon cornstarch

1 tablespoon rice vinegar

1 teaspoon sugar

1 16-ounce package firm tofu, drained and cut into 1/2-inch cubes

2 medium portobello mushrooms

2 tablespoons canola or corn oil

12 scallions, sliced in half lengthwise, then cut into 2-inch lengths

1 tablespoon minced fresh ginger

2 garlic cloves, minced

4 eggs, beaten

1/4 cup Chinese rice wine, or vermouth, or white wine

Soy sauce or salt (or both) to taste

1/2 cup mung bean or soy bean sprouts

16 Mandarin pancakes (or 12 small flour tortillas)

1/2 cup plum or hoisin sauce (available at Asian markets; optional)

**1.** In a small bowl, combine the soy sauce, cornstarch, rice vinegar, and sugar. Stir well. Add the tofu to the marinade, and stir to coat the tofu. Let the tofu marinate for 30 minutes.

**2.** Meanwhile, prepare the filling: Take the caps off the portobellos, and slice them as thin as possible. Cut off the dirt-laden end of the stem. Slice the stem into thin rounds.

## Ask the Pro

I asked Nina Simonds, who has written numerous books on Chinese cuisine (and speaks fluent Cantonese), whether dry sherry is an acceptable substitute for Chinese rice wine or sake. She was very clear: Sherry is just too strong in a subtly flavored dish. She suggested using vermouth or white wine if you don't have Chinese rice wine or sake. I list sherry as an option in many of my recipes, however, because I know that the other flavors are bold enough to balance it.

**3.** In a wok or large skillet over high heat, heat 1 tablespoon of the oil. Add the scallions and ginger, and stir-fry them for 10 seconds. Add the mushrooms and the garlic, and stir-fry for 1 minute. Remove all of the vegetables from the wok or skillet, and clean it with a paper towel.

**4.** Replace the wok over high heat. When the wok is hot, add the remaining 1 tablespoon oil. Add the tofu and its marinating liquid. Stir-fry the tofu over high heat for 1 minute, then reduce the heat to low. Add the beaten eggs to the tofu, and, stirring constantly, cook until the eggs begin to solidify. Return the vegetables to the wok or skillet, and add the wine and the soy sauce or salt. Stir over low heat for a minute or so, but be sure not to overcook the eggs. Transfer the filling, topped with the bean sprouts, to a serving dish. Keep it warm while you heat the pancakes.

**5.** Heat a non-stick or well-seasoned skillet over medium heat. Place a pancake in the skillet, and heat it for 5 to 10 seconds. Wrap the warm pancake in a clean towel. Warm the remaining pancakes the same way, and stack them in the towel. Place the pancakes in their towel in a basket, and place the basket on the table beside the dish of filling and a serving spoon. Provide small dipping bowls of plum or hoisin sauce, if you like.

Serves 4

# CHAPTER 13

# Burgers & Sandwiches

## The New Veggie Burgers

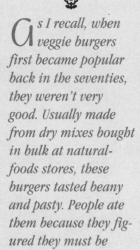

*As I recall, when veggie burgers first became popular back in the seventies, they weren't very good. Usually made from dry mixes bought in bulk at natural-foods stores, these burgers tasted beany and pasty. People ate them because they figured they must be good for you.*

*Lately, however, a new class of veggie burgers has arrived. Using fresh produce, unusual spices and herbs, and all kinds of grains and legumes, restaurant chefs and cookbook authors have been revamping the veggie burger. Their versions are low in fat and strut great flavor. Best of all, many hamburger-eaters fall in love with these newfangled veggie burgers.*

# Portobello Burgers

When I first added this burger to our menu at the Delux Cafe, I was a bit skeptical. I had never offered a veggie burger, and I predicted a lukewarm response. The response *was* lukewarm for the first couple of weeks, but then the sandwich took off. The Portobello Burger outsold all of our other dishes for the rest of the menu's duration.

Although I usually pan-fry them, try grilling these burgers over coals; they hold up surprisingly well on a grill. If you want to get fancy, wrap the burgers in fresh grape leaves before grilling them. The grape leaves darken and fall off when the burger is cooked, and they add a pleasant, citrusy flavor. Serve the burgers on bulky or kaiser rolls, with lettuce and tomato and some hot sauce, ketchup, or chutney.

You'll need a food processor for this recipe.

²/₃ cup dried lentils
6 ounces portobello mushrooms
2 tablespoons olive oil
1¹/₂ cups minced onions
2 large garlic cloves, minced
¹/₂ teaspoon ground cumin seeds
¹/₂ teaspoon salt, or more, to taste
Fresh-ground black pepper to taste
5 slices stale or toasted sandwich bread
¹/₂ cup chopped parsley

**1.** Bring 2 quarts water to a boil, and add the lentils. Simmer the lentils for 20 to 30 minutes or until they are tender. Drain the lentils, and let them cool.

**2.** Cut off the dirt-laden base of each mushroom stem, then chop the remainder of the stems and the caps fine.

**3.** Heat 1 tablespoon of the olive oil in a large skillet over medium heat, and add the onions. Cook them, stirring occasionally, for 5 minutes or until they soften. Add the garlic, and

# Cooking with Legumes

### ❋ ❋ ❋

Technically, legumes are plants whose seed pods split along both sides when ripe. There are thousands of species of legumes, and most of them are not consumed by humans. The most common legumes for culinary use are beans, lentils, peas, soybeans, and peanuts (yes, the peanut is a legume, not a nut). Legumes are all very rich in protein, which is one reason they are a staple food throughout the world.

All dry beans are best soaked in water overnight, then rinsed well before cooking. If you haven't planned ahead, boil the beans for 5 minutes, let them soak in the water for an hour, then rinse them before cooking them. Lentils, mung beans, and split peas don't need to be soaked.

Legumes can vary in cooking time depending on their age. If they are young, the cooking will be shorter (and the legume will taste better).

In general, salt should not be added until the last 10 minutes of cooking, since salt hardens the outer wall of the legume. Lima beans, however, should be salted at the beginning of the cooking; if they aren't salted, they tend to disintegrate.

Always cook legumes in plenty of gently boiling water. When cooking them, partially cover them with a lid. During the cooking process, add water as needed to keep the legumes submerged. After cooking, drain well. One cup dried legumes yields approximately 2 cups cooked.

| DRY LEGUMES | COOKING TIME |
| --- | --- |
| Adzuki beans | 1 to 1½ hours |
| Black beans | 1½ hours |
| Black-eyed peas | 1 hour |
| Chickpeas (garbanzo beans) | 2 to 2½ hours |
| Fava beans | Peel the skins after soaking, then cook 2 hours |

cook 2 minutes more, stirring constantly. Add the chopped mushrooms and the cumin to the skillet, and cook for 5 minutes, stirring occasionally. Season well with the salt and pepper, and take the pan off the heat.

**4.** Break the bread into pieces, and whirl them to crumbs in a food processor. Transfer 2 cups crumbs to a large bowl. Put the lentils into the processor, and run the machine in spurts until they are coarsely chopped and somewhat pasty. Add the chopped parsley and sautéed mushrooms and onions to the

| DRY LEGUMES (CONT.) | COOKING TIME |
| --- | --- |
| Great Northern beans | 1½ to 2½ hours |
| Kidney beans | 1½ to 2 hours |
| Lentils, brown | 20 to 25 minutes |
| Lentils, French (*lentilles du Puy*) | 20 to 25 minutes |
| Lentils, red (or Egyptian) | 15 minutes |
| Lima beans, baby | 1 to 1½ hours |
| Lima beans, large | 1 to 1½ hours |
| Mung beans | 1 hour |
| Navy beans | 1 to 1½ hours |
| Pigeon peas | 20 minutes |
| Pinto beans | 1 to 1½ hours |
| Red beans | 1½ to 2 hours |
| Soybeans | 3 hours or more |
| Split peas | 25 to 35 minutes |

## How to Eat Legumes

Legumes are truly versatile. They can be puréed into a spread (white beans and favas are especially good this way) or roughly mashed and used to fill tortillas (pinto beans, black beans, kidneys, and red beans are favorites for this purpose). Cooked beans can be dropped into minestrone-style soups, or added to stews for protein and richness. Bean, lentil, and pea salads are all delicious; add tomato, corn, chopped scallion, perhaps cut green beans, and fresh herbs along with your favorite dressing. Or combine legumes with grains or with vegetables in hot dishes. Put navy beans in a ratatouille, for instance, or add lentils to a quinoa and barley pilaf. All of the beans, lentils, and peas, finally, work beautifully in chilis.

bowl, and mix well with your hands or a sturdy spoon. Season with additional salt and pepper to taste. Add more bread crumbs if the mixture is too wet to form a patty. Chill the mixture from 1 hour to a week.

**5.** Form the burger mixture into four 4-inch patties. Heat the remaining oil in a large skillet (not non-stick) over medium heat. Pan-fry until the undersides are a deep golden brown, about 3 minutes. Flip the burgers, and cook them about 3 minutes more. Serve the burgers hot.

**Variation:** Try adding 3 ounces of soft goat cheese to the mixture before cooking it. The cheese adds a fine flavor and helps to bind the burger.

Makes 4 burgers

# Yellow Split-Pea Burgers

I am not a big fan of split peas, but I love the wholesome flavors in this burger. Besides, split peas are loaded with protein, inexpensive, and good for binding burgers together. Serve each burger on a bulky roll or kaiser roll with a slice of tomato and ketchup or chutney on the side.

If you don't have a food processor, see the alternative instructions following the recipe.

2 tablespoons canola or corn oil
2 cups chopped onions
1½ tablespoons minced fresh ginger
2 large garlic cloves, minced
1½ teaspoons ground cumin seeds
1 cup uncooked dried yellow split peas
3½ cups water
⅔ cup uncooked white or brown rice
1 teaspoon salt
Fresh-ground black pepper to taste
½ medium eggplant (about ½ pound), peeled and
    cut into 1-inch cubes
4 slices stale or toasted sandwich bread
1 red or green bell pepper, seeded and coarsely
    chopped

**1.** Heat 1 tablespoon of the oil in a large saucepan over medium heat. Add the onions, and sauté them for 5 minutes or until they soften, stirring often. Add the ginger, garlic, and cumin, and sauté 2 minutes more. Add the split peas and 1½ cups water. Bring the water to a boil, cover the saucepan, and lower the heat. Simmer the split peas for 30 minutes if you will be using white rice, and 10 minutes if you will be using brown rice. Stir the peas once or twice and adding a bit of water if they become dry.

**2.** Add the rice, the remaining 2 cups water, and ½ teaspoon salt to the split peas. Bring the mixture to a boil, then cover the pan, and turn the heat to low. Simmer until the rice is tender, about 25 minutes for white rice, 45 minutes for brown. Take the pan off the heat, remove the lid, and let the mixture cool for 5 minutes.

**3.** While the rice cooks, preheat the oven to 400°. Put the eggplant cubes on a baking sheet, and bake them for 15 to 20 minutes or until the cubes are soft to the touch.

**4.** Break the bread into pieces, and grind them to crumbs in a food processor. Transfer the crumbs to a large bowl. Put the eggplant and bell pepper into the empty food processor, and run the machine in short spurts until the pepper is chopped fine. Transfer the mixture to the bowl of crumbs. Add to the bowl the split pea–rice mixture, ½ teaspoon salt, and some black pepper, and mix well with a sturdy spoon or your hands.

**5.** Form the mixture into six burgers. Heat the remaining 1 tablespoon oil in a large skillet over medium heat. Pan-fry the burgers until the undersides are a deep golden brown, about 4 minutes, checking frequently so the burgers do not burn. Flip the burgers and cook them about 4 minutes more, checking frequently for burning. (If you cook the burgers in batches, keep the cooked ones in a warm oven, and add a bit more oil to the pan before cooking the second batch.) Serve the burgers hot.

**Variation:** You can make these burgers without a food processor by substituting 1¼ cups dry bread crumbs for the fresh, and chopping the bell pepper very fine by hand. Follow the recipe as instructed until step 4. Then mix together in a large bowl the bread crumbs, chopped pepper, eggplant, salt and pepper, and the split pea–rice mixture, and proceed to step 5.

Makes 6 large burgers

# Jamaican Burgers

Black beans, rice, allspice, ginger, and Scotch bonnet peppers come together to form a veggie burger that's bursting with flavor. Scotch bonnets (or habaneros, their Mexican cousins) can be found at Latin American grocery stores and at well-stocked supermarkets. If you can't find Scotch bonnets or habaneros, a jalapeño will substitute just fine. You might serve these burgers with a side dish of Sweet Fried Plantains (page 57) or Caribbean Sweet-Potato Salad (page 131).

4 slices stale or toasted sandwich bread
2 tablespoons canola or corn oil
1 1/2 cups chopped onions
2 garlic cloves, minced
1 tablespoon minced fresh ginger
1/2 teaspoon allspice (freshly ground, if possible)
1/2 teaspoon ground nutmeg
1 1/2 cups (1 15-ounce can) cooked, drained, and
    rinsed black beans
1 1/2 cups cooked rice
1/2 Scotch bonnet or habanero pepper, or 1
    jalapeño pepper, chopped (include the seeds if
    you want more heat)
1 teaspoon salt, or a bit more, to taste
Fresh-ground black pepper to taste
4 bulky or kaiser rolls or hamburger buns,
    toasted

**1.** Break the bread slices into pieces, and grind them to crumbs in a food processor. Transfer the crumbs to a large bowl.

**2.** In a large skillet, heat 1 tablespoon of the oil over medium heat. Add the onions, and sauté them, stirring occasionally, for 5 minutes or until they soften. Add the garlic, ginger, allspice, and nutmeg, and sauté for exactly 2 minutes more. Put the mixture into a food processor. Add the black beans, rice, and chopped chile pepper. Running the machine in quick spurts, chop the ingredients (do not purée them). Transfer the mixture to a bowl.

**3.** Add the salt, pepper, and bread crumbs to the bowl, and stir well with a large spoon. Taste, and adjust the seasonings, if you like. If the mixture is too wet to form patties, add more bread crumbs.

**4.** In a large skillet, preferably not non-stick, heat the remaining 1 tablespoon oil over medium heat. Form the burger mixture into four patties. Cook the burgers for about 4 minutes per side, until a dark brown crust forms. Serve the burgers in the toasted rolls, with tomato, lettuce, and your favorite ketchup or chutney.

*Makes 4 burgers*

# Curried Carrot-Walnut Burgers

Have you even seen a pretty burger? Once you rest your eyes on this one's delicate crust and soft orange interior, you'll be smitten.

Make the patties generous enough to stand up to bulky or kaiser rolls. Eat the burgers with tomato, onion, and homemade ketchup, if you have it. This recipe requires a food processor.

2 tablespoons canola or corn oil, or a bit more
1 medium onion, chopped
1 teaspoon ground coriander seeds
1 teaspoon curry powder, store-bought or homemade (page 36)
1 teaspoon fennel seeds

1½ cups (about 4 ounces) sliced white button
    mushrooms
1½ cups cooked and drained chickpeas (garbanzo
    beans; canned ones are fine)
4 medium carrots, grated
¼ cup chopped walnuts
3 tablespoons chopped cilantro
½ teaspoon salt
Fresh-ground black pepper to taste
Unbleached white flour (for dredging and
    forming the burgers)
5 to 6 slices cheddar cheese (optional)

**1.** In a large saucepan, heat 1 tablespoon of the oil over medium heat. Add the onion, and sauté it, stirring, for about 2 minutes. Add the spices, and continue cooking, stirring often, for 3 minutes more. Add the mushrooms, and sauté 5 minutes more, stirring frequently. Take the pan off the heat.

**2.** Transfer the contents of the pan to a food processor. Add the chickpeas. Run the machine in 1-second spurts until the mushrooms and chickpeas are well chopped (do not purée them).

**3.** Transfer the mixture to a large bowl, and mix in the carrots, walnuts, cilantro, salt, and pepper. Form the mixture into five patties, using plenty of flour to dust your hands and to prevent the patties from getting sticky.

**4.** In a large skillet (not non-stick), heat the remaining oil over medium heat. Cook the burgers without crowding them, until the undersides are a deep golden brown, about 4 minutes. Flip the burgers, and cook them about 4 minutes more. (If you need to do this in two batches, add a bit more oil once the first batch of burgers is done.) If you want to make cheeseburgers, place a slice of cheese over each burger after flipping it, and let the cheese melt while the burgers finish cooking. Serve the burgers hot.

Makes 5 burgers

# Felicia's Kasha Burgers

Felicia Sanchez runs the Centre Street Cafe, an adorable shoebox cafe with a large vegetarian clientele in Jamaica Plain, Massachusetts. Felicia's magical kasha burgers develop a crust on the outside rather like that of a char-grilled hamburger. The preparation takes about 30 minutes, and most of that time you're just waiting for the kasha to cook.

I suggest serving these burgers on bulky or kaiser rolls with tomato, lettuce, onion, and ketchup.

3 tablespoons margarine or canola or corn oil, or more, as needed

3 cups chopped onions

3 cups chopped flavorful mushrooms (one or more of the following varieties: portobello, oyster, shiitake, cremini, hen-of-the-woods)

2/3 cup white wine

2 cups water

1½ teaspoons dried thyme

½ teaspoon dried sage

3 tablespoons soy sauce

Fresh-ground black pepper to taste

1 cup kasha (toasted buckwheat groats)

3 tablespoons unbleached white flour, plus a bit more for forming the burgers

**1.** In a large saucepan, heat 1 tablespoon of the margarine or oil. Add the onions, and sauté them for 10 minutes over medium-high heat, stirring occasionally, until the onions begin to brown at the edges. Add the mushrooms to the onions, and add 1 tablespoon margarine or oil. Sauté for 2 minutes more, stirring frequently.

**2.** Add the wine, water, thyme, sage, soy sauce, black pepper, and kasha. Over high heat, bring the mixture to a boil. Cover the pan, and turn the heat to low. Simmer for 15 minutes.

## Kasha Kraze

Kasha is hulled, crushed, and roasted kernels of buckwheat. The unique, assertive woodsy flavor of kasha makes some people love it and others hate it. With its high proportion of essential amino acids, buckwheat groats contain nearly complete protein. One cup of kasha, in fact, will give you all the protein you need for a day.

Kasha is traditionally used in the Jewish dish varnishkas (bow-tie noodles, chicken fat, and kasha), but it is also delicious mixed with other grains, like rice or barley, or combined with vegetables such as parsnips, browned onions, and mushrooms.

When the kasha is ready, it should have absorbed almost all of the liquid, and the grains should be tender.

**3.** Transfer the mixture to a large bowl, and let the mixture cool for 10 minutes or so. Add the 3 tablespoons flour, and mix with a metal spoon or with your hands until the flour is well incorporated. The mixture should be sticky and like a thick porridge in consistency. (At this point, you can cover the mixture and refrigerate it for up to 3 days.) With well-floured hands, form four patties from the kasha mixture.

**4.** In a large non-stick skillet or on a griddle, heat the remaining 1 tablespoon margarine or oil over medium heat. Drop the kasha mixture 1 cup at a time into the skillet or onto the griddle, and pat each patty down with your hand until it is 1 inch thick. (You'll probably be able to cook only three burgers at a time.) Cook the burgers for about 3 minutes per side. They should develop a dark brown crust, but check the underside frequently, as they will be very prone to burning. (If you must cook the burgers in two batches, add a bit of oil or margarine to the pan before cooking the second batch.) Serve the burgers right away.

Note: Felicia likes to use 2 tablespoons margarine instead of oil for sautéing the onions in step 1. She says this gives the burgers a richer flavor.

Makes 6 burgers

# Tofu and Pumpkin-Seed Burgers

This is a high-protein burger that doesn't taste "good for you." The protein comes from four ingredients: tofu, adzuki beans (or black beans), pumpkin seeds, and miso paste. Adzuki beans are easier to digest (yes, they cause much less flatulence) and higher in protein than other beans. Fresh ginger, garlic, and toasted cumin give the burger zip. Eat it with homemade chutney, your favorite ketchup, or hot sauce on a toasted bulky or kaiser roll or hamburger bun. Adzuki beans can be found in whole-foods stores and some supermarkets. You can make these burgers without a food processor.

4 slices stale or toasted sandwich bread
1¹/₂ cups cooked, drained, and rinsed adzuki
    beans (or black beans; canned ones are fine)
¹/₃ cup hulled, unsalted pumpkin seeds, toasted 6
    to 8 minutes in a 350° oven
1 16-ounce package firm tofu
1 teaspoon cumin seeds
2 tablespoons grated fresh ginger
1 large garlic clove, minced
2 tablespoons miso paste
    (I like to use brown-rice miso)
3/4 cup minced onion
¹/₂ teaspoon salt, or more, to taste
Fresh-ground black pepper to taste
1 to 2 tablespoons canola or corn oil

**1.** Chop the bread fine, or break it into pieces and whirl it to crumbs in a food processor. In a food processor or with a potato masher in a bowl, coarsely chop or mash the beans. Coarsely chop the toasted pumpkin seeds. Combine the beans, bread crumbs, and pumpkin seeds in a large bowl.

**2.** Cut the tofu into four pieces, and squeeze each piece with your hand, letting the crumbled tofu fall into the bowl of mashed beans. Toast the cumin seeds in a small skillet over low heat, stirring, until they become fragrant. Add the ginger, garlic, cumin, miso, and onion to the bowl with the beans and tofu. Mix everything (this will be easiest to do with your hands). Mix in the salt and pepper. The mixture should be stiff enough to form a patty. If the mixture still seems a bit wet, add more bread crumbs. Form the mixture into patties.

**3.** Heat a large skillet, preferably cast-iron (non-stick skillets don't yield as crispy a crust), over medium-high heat. Add 1 tablespoon oil, and place as many burgers in the pan as you can without crowding them. Pan-fry the burgers, in batches, if necessary, until the undersides are a deep golden brown, about 3 to 4 minutes. Flip the burgers, and cook them about 3 to 4 minutes more. Serve the burgers right away.

Makes 6 burgers

# Speedy Burgers

Here black beans, chopped fennel or celery, and almonds are mixed together in minutes, thanks to the food processor. Chopped fresh cilantro adds a bright note, and the cloves and ground coriander provide some earthiness. From start to finish, you'll need no more than 20 minutes to make these burgers.

4 slices stale or toasted bread
1/2 cup whole or slivered almonds
1 teaspoon ground coriander seeds
1 garlic clove, minced
1/4 teaspoon ground cloves
1/2 cup chopped onion
1 cup coarsely chopped fennel bulb or celery
3/4 cup coarsely chopped cilantro stems and
    leaves
1 1/2 cups (1 15-ounce can) cooked, drained, and
    rinsed black beans
1/2 medium red bell pepper, seeded and chopped
    fine
2 tablespoons toasted wheat germ or untoasted
    rolled oats
1/2 teaspoon salt, or more, to taste
Fresh-ground black pepper to taste
1 1/2 tablespoons olive oil, or more, as needed

**1.** Break the bread into pieces, and whirl it to crumbs in a food processor. You should have 2 cups crumbs. Transfer them to a large bowl. Put the almonds into the processor, and run the machine until they are chopped fine.

**2.** In a dry skillet over medium-high heat, toast the chopped almonds with the coriander, shaking the pan constantly, for 1 minute or until the almonds taste lightly toasted. Transfer the coriander and the almonds to the bowl of bread crumbs. Add the cloves to the bowl.

**3.** Chop fine the onion, the fennel or celery, and the cilantro in the processor. Add the beans, and run the machine in 1-second spurts until the beans are mixed in and mostly chopped (not puréed). Transfer the mixture to a bowl. Add the bell pepper, wheat germ or rolled oats, salt, and pepper, and stir well (I use my hands). With well-floured hands, form six patties from this mixture.

**4.** Heat a large skillet or a griddle over medium-high heat, and add 1½ tablespoons olive oil. Cook the burgers about 3 minutes per side. (You may need to cook them in batches. If so, add a little oil to the pan before cooking the second batch.) Serve the burgers in bulky or kaiser rolls or in hamburger buns.

*Makes 6 burgers*

# Falafel Burgers

Falafel, although delicious, is high in fat. Chickpeas are ground, deep-fried, and sandwiched in pita bread with a sesame paste dressing. For a lighter sandwich, burgerize! Here chickpeas are mashed with carrot, cumin, garlic, parsley, and tahini, pan-fried in a little oil, and finished with a squeeze of lemon. The burger is great on a bulky or kaiser roll with nothing but mustard and fresh tomato. This recipe requires no food processor.

---

## How to Accessorize a Burger

To enjoy a good veggie burger, you won't need much except a good roll and some lettuce and tomato. But there are some occasions—such as not getting any bills in the mail, or not having snacked since lunch—that require something special on the burger. You can buy a good ketchup (I like the jalapeño ketchup from Gerwer Tex-Mex), or make a chutney or ketchup yourself (see chapter 2). Other fun toppings are relishes and pickles, thinly sliced red onion, arugula instead of lettuce, mustard mayonnaise, avocado slices, roasted red pepper, or a roasted or grilled portobello mushroom cap.

2 tablespoons olive oil

1¹/₂ cups minced onions

3 garlic cloves, minced

1 teaspoon ground cumin seeds

1 cup finely chopped carrot

1³/₄ cups (1 15-ounce can) cooked and drained
    chickpeas (garbanzo beans)

1¹/₂ tablespoons tahini (sesame paste) or peanut
    butter

¹/₄ cup minced fresh parsley

¹/₃ cup chickpea flour or unbleached white flour

¹/₂ teaspoon baking soda

1 teaspoon salt

¹/₂ lemon

**1.** In a skillet, combine 1 tablespoon of the olive oil with the onions over medium heat. Cook, stirring frequently, until the onions soften, about 5 minutes. Add the garlic, cumin, and carrot, and cook 2 minutes more. Transfer the mixture to a large bowl.

**2.** Add the drained chickpeas, and mash them with a potato masher or chop them in a food processor until they are broken down and unidentifiable. Add the tahini or peanut butter and the parsley. In a smaller bowl, combine the flour, baking soda, and salt. Add the mixture to the large bowl, and stir well.

**3.** With floured hands, form four patties from the chickpea mixture, then lightly dust the burgers with flour. Heat a skillet over medium-high heat, and add 1 tablespoon olive oil. Turn the heat to medium-low, and add the patties. After about 1 minute, or when they have just begun to brown, flip them. Cook them about 2 minutes more on the other side. Then flip them back onto the first side, and cook another minute. They should be a deep golden brown on both sides. (They burn easily, so watch them well.) Remove the burgers from the skillet, and squeeze a bit of lemon juice onto each. Serve immediately.

Makes 4 large burgers

# Apple Burgers

You are probably thinking, "A fruit burger? Dessert for dinner?" But before you turn the page in disgust, hear me out. With the green pepper and onion, the tart apples provide crunch and create a good balance of sweet and savory flavors. Because you need cooked rice for these burgers, they are a good way to use up the leftover rice from last night's Chinese take-out. And you can make these burgers without a food processor.

Eat the burgers naked (without buns, that is), maybe with Hot-and-Sour Slaw (page 142) on the side.

1 cup minced onion
2 tart apples (such as Granny Smith or
    Macoun), grated
8 slices stale or toasted sandwich bread
1 large green bell pepper, seeded and chopped
1 tablespoon minced fresh ginger
2 cups cooked white or brown rice
6 tablespoons rolled oats, ground in a blender or
    food processor
1/2 teaspoon salt, or more, to taste
Fresh-ground black pepper to taste
1 tablespoon canola or corn oil, or more, as
    needed

**1.** Put the onion into a large bowl. Squeeze the grated apples lightly to remove excess juice, then add them to the bowl. Chop the bread very fine, or break it into pieces and whirl it to crumbs in a food processor. Add the bread crumbs, bell pepper, ginger, cooked rice, and half of the ground oats to the apples and onion, and mix well. Season with salt and pepper.

**2.** Form four patties about 1½ inches thick. Place a large skillet over medium heat, and add the oil. Coat the patties with the remaining ground oats, then cook them for 2 to 3 minutes per side, or until they brown slightly. Add a little more oil to the pan if you need to cook a second batch. Serve the burgers with hot sauce, slaw, or both.

Makes 4 burgers

# All-Veggie Burgers

Here's a burger that is mainly composed of fresh vegetables instead of grains, lentils, split peas, or beans (or meat, of course). Grated carrot, tomatoes, onions, and eggplant form an unlikely but excellent union. The puréed eggplant helps bind the burger, and the dried tomatoes and carrots provide a sweet, mellow flavor. The sesame seeds give the burger a bit of crunch. I recommend serving these burgers between toasted bread slices.

Note that this recipe requires a food processor.

1 small or ½ large eggplant (about ¾ pound),
    peeled and cut into 1-inch cubes
1½ teaspoons salt
12 slices sundried or other dried tomato
1 tablespoon olive oil
2 cups chopped onions
1 large garlic clove, cut into four pieces
½ cup rolled oats
7 slices stale or toasted sandwich bread
2 tablespoons white sesame seeds
1½ cups grated carrots
Fresh-ground black pepper to taste
1 tablespoon canola or corn oil

## Steakless Steak Potatoes

❀

*S*teak potatoes are easy to make and are a perfect foil for veggie burgers. For four people, cut three large potatoes in half lengthwise, then cut each piece in half again lengthwise. Toss the potatoes with 3 tablespoons canola or corn oil, 1 teaspoon salt, and a lot of fresh-ground black pepper. Turn the potatoes onto a baking sheet (with any oil left in the bowl), and bake them at 400° for 20 minutes. Turn the potatoes with a spatula, return them to the oven, and cook them for 25 minutes more, or until they are browned and tender.

**1.** Preheat the oven to 400°. Put the eggplant cubes into a colander, and sprinkle 1 teaspoon salt over them. Toss the eggplant, and let it sit for 15 minutes. Meanwhile, put the dried tomatoes into a small saucepan, and cover them with water. Bring the water to a boil, and simmer the tomatoes for 5 minutes. Then remove the pan from the heat.

**2.** Rinse the eggplant cubes well with cold water. Put them onto a baking sheet, and drizzle the oil over them. Spread the onions and garlic on another baking sheet. Place both pans in the oven and bake the vegetables for 15 to 20 minutes until the eggplant is tender and the onions and garlic are lightly browned.

**3.** Pulverize the rolled oats in a food processor. Break the bread into pieces, and add them to the processor. Whirl until crumbs are formed. Transfer the mixture to a large bowl.

**4.** Drain the tomatoes. Put the cooked eggplant, onion, and garlic with the drained tomatoes into the processor. Process until the mixture is fairly smooth. Transfer it to the bowl of oats and bread crumbs.

**5.** Toast the sesame seeds in a heavy skillet over medium heat. When they start to brown, begin to shake the pan periodically. Toast the seeds until they are uniformly browned, adjusting the heat as necessary to prevent burning. Mix the sesame into the burger mixture with the grated carrots, ½ teaspoon salt, and pepper to taste. Chill the mixture, if possible, for an hour.

**6.** With well-floured hands, form four patties about 4 inches in diameter and 1½ inches thick. Pour the oil into a large skillet (not non-stick) over medium heat (not higher; these burgers burn easily). Add the burgers, and cook them until the undersides are a deep golden brown, about 3 minutes. Flip them, and cook them about 3 minutes more. Serve them hot.

**Variation:** If you like more of a crust on your burgers, coat them with additional ground oats before pan-frying them.

*Makes 4 burgers*

# Yucatán Burgers

This delicious burger features flavors from Mexico's Yucatán Peninsula. Red beans, about the same size as black beans, are more meaty and flavorful, but you can substitute either black beans or pinto beans, if you like. Serve the burgers on toasted bulky or kaiser rolls or hamburger buns.

1 small butternut squash (about 1½ pounds), cut in half

7 slices stale or toasted sandwich bread

2 tablespoons canola or corn oil

1½ cups chopped onions

2 garlic cloves, minced

1 teaspoon dried oregano

1 teaspoon ground coriander seeds

1½ cups (1 15-ounce can) cooked, drained, and rinsed red beans

½ cup chopped cilantro

1 tablespoon lime juice (from about ½ lime)

1 teaspoon salt, or more, to taste

½ teaspoon fresh-ground black pepper, or more, to taste

**1.** Preheat the oven to 400°. Place the squash cut side down on a baking sheet, and bake the squash for 45 minutes or until the flesh softens. Remove the squash from the oven, and let it cool.

**2.** While the squash cools, break the bread into pieces, and whirl them to crumbs in a food processor. Transfer the bread crumbs to a bowl.

**3.** In a large skillet, heat 1 tablespoon of the oil over medium heat. Add the onions, and sauté them, stirring occasionally, for 5 minutes or until they soften. Add the garlic, oregano, and ground coriander, and sauté for exactly 2 minutes more. Put the mixture into the food processor. Add the cooked beans

and the cilantro, and run the machine in spurts until the ingredients are chopped (not puréed). Transfer the mixture to a bowl.

**4.** When the squash is cool, spoon out and discard the seeds. Spoon out the flesh, chop it well, and add it to the bowl of beans and onions. Add the lime juice, the salt, the pepper, and 3 cups bread crumbs to the bowl, and mix well with your hands. If the mixture is too wet to form patties, add more bread crumbs.

**5.** In a large skillet (preferably not non-stick), heat the remaining 1 tablespoon oil over medium heat. Form the mixture into six patties. Pan-fry the burgers until the undersides are a deep golden brown, about 4 minutes. Flip the burgers, and cook them about 4 minutes more. Serve the burgers immediately.

*Makes 6 burgers*

# Havana Sandwiches

Although most of the sandwiches I've seen in Cuban cafes around Boston are composed of some sort of meat, they have another common trait—a very soft and chewy bread that looks like a French baguette split horizontally and flattened. It *is* flattened, in fact, by a large sandwich press called a *plancha*. This unique bread is then cut into pieces, filled, and pan-fried. In this meat-free sandwich, chipotle mayonnaise, charred onions and pepper, and tomato are a very satisfying combination. But you don't need a *plancha* or the authentic Cuban bread to enjoy this sandwich at home. A heavy pan, some elbow grease, and a loaf of French or Italian bread will work just fine.

1 very fresh baguette (the soft French or Italian
    bread sold in supermarkets is fine)
1 1/3 tablespoons olive oil
2 cups sliced onions
1 green bell pepper, seeded and cut into thin
    julienne strips
1 small garlic clove, minced
1 or 2 chipotle peppers, dried and soaked in hot
    water 30 minutes, or canned in adobo sauce
    (available in Latin American markets and
    some supermarkets), chopped
1/4 cup mayonnaise
1 large ripe tomato, sliced thin
Salt and fresh-ground black pepper to taste

**1.** Cut the bread crosswise into two pieces, each one about 7 inches long (use the leftover bread for another use). Split each piece horizontally, then press the pieces with a large stockpot or cast-iron skillet weighted with heavy cans or books. Press with your own weight on the skillet or pot for a few seconds, so that the bread flattens to a 1-inch thickness. Leave the weights in place.

**2.** Place a large skillet over medium-high heat, and coat it with 1 teaspoon olive oil. Sauté the onions and pepper, shaking the pan every 2 to 3 minutes, until they become somewhat blackened, about 20 minutes. Remove the pan from the heat.

**3.** While the vegetables are cooking, combine the garlic, chopped chipotles, and mayonnaise in a small bowl. Stir well.

**4.** Remove the weights from the bread. Spread the mayonnaise on all four halves. Lay the onions and peppers, topped by the tomato slices, over two halves. Top the tomatoes with salt and pepper to taste. Place the other two bread halves over these two to form sandwiches.

**5.** Heat the 1 tablespoon olive oil in a large skillet or on a griddle over medium heat. Place the sandwiches in the skillet or griddle, then place a skillet on top of them to weigh them down. Let them cook for 4 minutes, checking once or twice to make sure they aren't burning on the bottom. Turn the sandwiches over, and cook them 4 minutes more, checking the undersides frequently. Serve the sandwiches right away.

Note: This recipe is a good excuse to make *pan cubano,* the bread that is traditionally used to make Cuban sandwiches. Check out Steven Raichlen's cookbook *Miami Spice.* It includes a good recipe for this shortening-enriched bread as well as many other recipes for Cuban specialties.

Makes 2 sandwiches

# Green Apple and Brie Sandwiches with Quick Onion Chutney

This grilled cheese sandwich is always a big hit. The chutney takes about 2 minutes of preparation and 20 minutes of slow cooking. The tartness of the green apple (I use a Granny Smith) contrasts deliciously with the sweet onion chutney and the mild Brie cheese. Any of the slaws in chapter 5 would be a nice accompaniment.

2 tablespoons olive oil
2¹/₂ cups sliced onions
2 tablespoons brown sugar
1 tablespoon balsamic vinegar
1 tart green apple, such as Granny Smith or Crispin, sliced very thin
4 large slices white, whole-wheat, or pumpernickel bread
3 to 4 ounces Brie cheese, sliced thin

**1.** Make the chutney: In a heavy saucepan over medium-high heat, heat 1 tablespoon of the olive oil, and add the onions. Sauté them for about 10 minutes, stirring occasionally, until they begin to brown at the edges. Then stir in the brown sugar and the balsamic vinegar. Cook over medium heat, stirring frequently, until the onions turn deep brown, about 10 minutes. Take the pan off the heat, and let the chutney cool.

**2.** Spoon the chutney onto two pieces of bread, and layer apple slices on top (you'll probably need only about two-thirds of them). Layer the slices of Brie on top of the apple. Top each sandwich with the remaining pieces of bread.

**3.** Heat the remaining 1 tablespoon olive oil in a large skillet or on a griddle over medium heat. Place the sandwiches in the skillet or on the griddle. Place a skillet or a sandwich press on top of the sandwiches to weigh them down. Pan-fry them until they are golden brown on one side, about 3 minutes, then turn them over, and turn the heat to low. Lightly cook the sandwiches on the other side (watch carefully to be sure they don't burn). Take the sandwiches off the heat once the cheese has melted. Cut the sandwiches in half, and serve them immediately.

Makes 2 sandwiches

# Grilled Smoked-Gouda Sandwich with Mustard Dipping Sauce

*W*hen is it more fun to have the mustard on the outside of a sandwich? When the mustard is a dipping sauce, of course. It's fun, because you get to choose just how much mustard sauce you want with each bite.

1 teaspoon Dijon mustard
1 teaspoon honey
2 tablespoons plain whole, low-fat, or nonfat
   sour cream

*There are almost eight thousand varieties of apples in the world. Some people are satisfied with the Red or Golden Delicious apple, although many think that both these varieties are lackluster in flavor. The apples I enjoy most are the ones I eat while picking at a you-pick orchard near Boston. An apple fresh from the tree is just bursting with juiciness and flavor. And, as Edward Behr, author of* The Artful Eater, *comments, "A stolen apple always tastes better." During apple season I like the Cortlands, Northern Spies, Braeburns, and Macouns. After apple season I usually go for the long-keeping Granny Smiths, for both cooking and eating.*

3 ounces smoked Gouda cheese, sliced thin
4 slices bread (I like to use large slices of rye bread)
1 tomato, sliced thin
A small amount of thinly sliced onion
2 tablespoons olive oil

**1.** Make the dipping sauce: Stir together the mustard and the honey in a small bowl. Add the sour cream, and spoon the sauce into two dipping bowls.

**2.** Lay the cheese slices on two pieces of the bread, place the tomato slices on top of the cheese, and then top with as much onion as you'd like. Place the other two pieces of bread on top of the first two.

**3.** Heat the olive oil in a large skillet over medium heat. Place the two sandwiches in the skillet, and weigh down the sandwiches with either a sandwich press or another skillet. Reduce the heat to low. Pan-fry the sandwiches until they are golden on the bottom, about 3 minutes, then flip them. Continue to cook until the cheese is melting and the other side is golden. Cut the sandwiches in half, and serve them with the dipping sauce.

Makes 2 sandwiches

# Spinach and Mozzarella Grilled Cheese Sandwiches with Chile Dipping Sauce

This sandwich is great for parties because it looks so festive. The spinach, tomato, and mozzarella are rolled in lavash bread or a split pita, and then pan-fried. This is much easier than it may sound. The large, thin discs of lavash bread are available at Lebanese and Armenian markets and in many supermarkets, and they are delicious pan-fried, as for this sandwich. In case you can't find lavash, large pita pockets will work as well.

·•·•·•·•·•·

**CHILE DIPPING SAUCE:**
1 teaspoon hot chile sauce
2 tablespoons mayonnaise
2 tablespoons plain whole, low-fat, or nonfat yogurt, or nonfat sour cream
1 teaspoon Dijon mustard
2 teaspoons apple cider vinegar
1 small garlic clove, minced

**SANDWICHES:**
6 ounces fresh spinach (large stems removed)
2 fresh pieces of lavash bread, or 1 large split pita pocket
2 plum tomatoes, cut in half lengthwise, then sliced thin crosswise
2 ounces mozzarella cheese, grated (or sliced, if it's fresh mozzarella)
Salt and fresh-ground black pepper to taste
2 tablespoons olive oil

·•·•·•·•·•·

**1.** Make the dipping sauce: In a small bowl, combine the chile sauce with the mayonnaise, yogurt, mustard, cider vinegar, and garlic. Stir well.

**2.** Steam the spinach over high heat for 2 minutes. Let the spinach cool.

**3.** Lay one of the pieces of lavash or pita on your work surface, with a short side of the bread directly in front of you if you are using lavash. Lay half of the tomatoes across the bread, about 3 inches from the side closest to you. Squeeze any excess water from the spinach, then lay half of it on the tomatoes. Sprinkle or lay half of the mozzarella on top of the tomatoes and spinach. Sprinkle with salt and pepper to taste. Then roll the bread, starting with the side closest to you, as tightly as possible. Follow the same procedure for the second sandwich.

## Sources for Iron

*W*e often hear that it's important to have plenty of iron in the diet, especially for women, who require more iron than men. And it's better to get that iron from food rather than supplements. Here are some foods that have a high iron content:
◆ Beans and peas
◆ Whole-wheat bread
◆ Spinach
◆ Dried fruits
◆ Broccoli
◆ Kale
◆ Turnip and collard greens
◆ Tofu
◆ Prune juice
◆ Molasses
  You can also increase your iron intake by cooking in iron pots and pans.

**4.** Heat the olive oil in a large (preferably non-stick) skillet over medium heat. Place the two rolled sandwiches in the skillet, and place another skillet or sandwich press on top to weigh the sandwiches down. Cook the sandwiches for about 4 minutes or until they are golden brown, then turn them and cook them on the other side for 4 minutes more, checking the undersides frequently. Cut the sandwiches in half, and serve each with a small bowl of the dipping sauce.

*Makes 2 sandwiches*

# Eggplant, Tomato, and Mozzarella Sandwiches

I used to love the eggplant Parmesan at my neighborhood pizzeria. But because the eggplant was breaded and then deep-fried, and the dish was loaded with mozzarella cheese, I began to feel I was eating fat topped with more fat. So now I make my own version. The eggplant is baked with a bit of olive oil, then layered on bread with tomato, basil, and mozzarella and broiled in the oven as an open-face sandwich. I usually eat this for dinner, but it's nice for lunch, too.

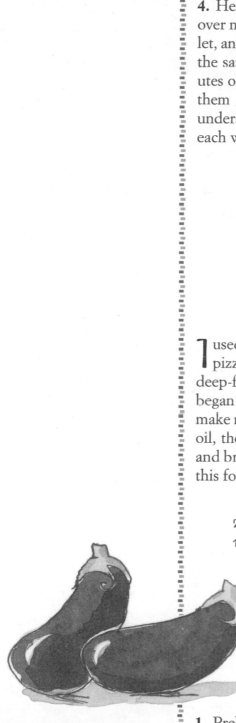

2 tablespoons olive oil
1 garlic clove
1 1-pound eggplant, peeled
   Salt and fresh-ground black pepper to taste
4 slices good sandwich bread
2 to 3 plum tomatoes, sliced thin crosswise
8 large basil leaves (optional)
4 ounces mozzarella cheese (preferably
   fresh), cut into 1/4-inch slices

**1.** Preheat the oven to 375°. Pour the olive oil into a small bowl. Crush the garlic with the broad side of a chef's knife.

Take off the skin, then stir the garlic into the olive oil. Let the garlic steep in the oil for about 5 minutes.

**2.** Slice the eggplant into ½-inch-thick rounds. Lay the rounds on a baking sheet. With a pastry brush or a spoon, distribute the olive oil on the eggplant rounds. Add salt and pepper to taste, and bake the eggplant for 20 minutes, or until it is soft. Remove the pan from the oven, but keep the oven on.

**3.** Lay the four slices of bread on the baking sheet. Return the baking sheet to the oven until the bread is lightly toasted, about 3 minutes, then remove the pan from the oven. Again, keep the oven on. Distribute the eggplant in a single layer on the bread. Lay the tomato slices on the eggplant, and salt and pepper the sandwiches. Place the basil leaves, if you're using them, on the tomatoes. Lay the mozzarella over the tomatoes. Bake the sandwiches for 7 to 10 minutes or until the cheese has melted thoroughly. Cut the sandwiches diagonally, and serve them at once.

### Variations:

- Substitute Brie cheese or goat cheese for the mozzarella.
- Substitute Mushroom Pesto (page 455) for the baked eggplant.
- Substitute sliced avocado for the baked eggplant.
- Instead of using whole basil leaves, spread some pesto on the bread before adding the eggplant to the sandwich.

*Makes 4 open-face sandwiches*

# Croque
# Mademoiselle

The croque monsieur, a ham-and-cheese sandwich dipped in egg batter, then pan-fried, is France's national sandwich. But when I lived in Paris I had a surprisingly difficult time finding a decent croque monsieur. I had daydreams of opening a croque monsieur cafe, where all of the most discriminating Parisian epicures would eat, and they'd say, "You American chefs are ze best!"

Here is a "Mademoiselle" of my own creation—a goat cheese, arugula, and tomato sandwich, dipped in egg, then pan-fried.

1 large egg
½ cup whole or low-fat milk
2 ounces soft, mild chèvre (goat cheese)
4 slices good white bread
1 ripe tomato, sliced thin
½ cup chopped arugula (remove the large stems before chopping)
Salt and fresh-ground black pepper to taste
2 tablespoons butter or olive oil

**1.** In a wide bowl, whisk together the egg and milk.

**2.** Divide the goat cheese in half, and spread it on two slices of the bread. Lay the tomato slices on top, then divide the chopped arugula between the two slices. Add salt and pepper to taste.

**3.** In a large skillet, melt the butter or olive oil over medium-low heat. Top the sandwiches with the two remaining bread slices. Press down well, then carefully dip one sandwich in the egg batter, and turn the sandwich over to soak both pieces of bread. Quickly place the sandwich in the skillet. Repeat this process for the second sandwich. Pan-fry the sandwiches for about 4 minutes per side, or until they are golden brown on both sides. Cut the sandwiches in half, and serve them right away.

Makes 2 sandwiches

## Onion Confit

*Salmon confit, blackberry confit, garlic confit—restaurants are producing confit of everything these days. Confit means "preserved" in French, and the word is most commonly associated with duck confit. Some of the newer confits, however, will have more interest for vegetarians.*

*Onion confit is easy to make: Cook 6 cups sliced onions in 2 tablespoons canola or corn oil over medium heat until the onions begin to caramelize (about 30 minutes). Add 1 tablespoon sugar and 2 tablespoons red wine vinegar, and cook 30 minutes more. Add 1 teaspoon salt. Add onion confit to pizza, pasta dishes, or grilled cheese sandwiches, or serve it with Indian curries.*

# Sprout, Carrot, and Quinoa Sandwiches

What could be better for you than a grated carrot, quinoa, and sprout salad stuffed in a pita? Quinoa is tossed with a lemon-dill dressing and combined with grated carrot, alfalfa sprouts, tomato, and red onion. Perfect stuff to pocket in a pita.

1 small garlic clove, minced
2 tablespoons fresh lemon juice (from about
    1/2 lemon)
2 tablespoons olive oil
3 tablespoons chopped dill
1 1/2 cups cooked quinoa (see page 248 for
    cooking directions)
1 large carrot, grated
1/2 small red onion, sliced thin
2 tablespoons crumbled feta cheese
1/2 cup alfalfa sprouts
1 plum tomato, chopped
Salt and fresh-ground black pepper to taste
2 large pita pockets

**1.** In a medium bowl, combine the garlic, lemon juice, olive oil, and dill. Stir well. Add the quinoa, carrot, onion, feta cheese, sprouts, and tomato. Toss well, then season the mixture well with salt and pepper.

**2.** Lightly toast or warm the pita pockets. Cut a small piece off the edge of each pocket, and fill the pocket with the salad. Eat this sandwich right away; it gets soggy after 10 or 15 minutes.

Makes 2 sandwiches

# Tomato Wonder Sandwich

Okay, so this one didn't require a *grand diplôme* in cuisine, but it tastes so good that I had to include it. I usually enjoy this sandwich on two pieces of toasted scali bread before I start my shift at the restaurant. Scali bread is the Italian version of Wonder Bread with a few sesame seeds around the edges. Don't use expensive bread; you need the cheap, light, fluffy stuff to create this great gastronomic experience. I think Hellmann's mayonnaise tastes better than any other kind in this sandwich.

1½ tablespoons Hellmann's mayonnaise
1 teaspoon Dijon mustard
4 slices light sandwich bread
1 ripe tomato, sliced
Salt and fresh-ground black pepper to taste
Very thinly sliced red onion

**1.** In a small bowl, mix together the mayonnaise and mustard. Toast the bread. Then spread the mustard-mayo onto all four pieces of toast. Lay the tomato slices onto two pieces of bread, then salt and pepper the tomatoes, and top with the red onion.

**2.** Put the sandwiches together, slice them in two, and serve.

Makes 2 sandwiches (enough for 1 hungry person,
or 2 if a slaw or tossed salad is served alongside)

# Pan Bagna

This simple marinated sandwich is the equivalent of our hamburger—a very popular, everyday food—in Nice, in the south of France. Pan bagna traditionally includes salted anchovies and tuna, but the bulk of the filling has always been vegetables. Here is my vegetarian version of pan bagna. Please feel free to add ingredients—roasted red peppers, sliced cucumbers, slices of hard-boiled egg, arugula, roasted eggplant, Toasty Hummus (page 55; instead of the mozzarella), Baba Ghanoush (page 54), or perhaps marinated mushrooms—you get the idea.

1 very fresh loaf French or Italian bread
4 tablespoons extra-virgin olive oil
1 teaspoon red wine vinegar
1 large garlic clove, minced
1/2 small red onion, sliced very thin
1 large ripe tomato, sliced
12 Niçoise or Kalamata olives, pitted and
    coarsely chopped
12 basil leaves
2 ounces mozzarella cheese (preferably fresh),
    sliced thin

**1.** Cut two 8-inch lengths from the loaf of bread (save any remaining bread for another use). Combine the olive oil, red wine vinegar, and garlic in a bowl. Add the sliced onion and tomato, and toss well. Add the olives and basil leaves, and toss again.

**2.** Split the two pieces of the loaf horizontally. Lay the marinated onion slices and tomato slices, and the mozzarella, on one side of each sandwich. Spoon over the vegetables the marinade, basil, and olives (the sandwich is supposed to be soggy). Top with the remaining bread halves, and lay a heavy plate over both sandwiches for 5 minutes. Serve these sandwiches right away, or wrap them in plastic and refrigerate them for later.

Makes 2 sandwiches

# Food for Flying

*Except for the time I was mistakenly put in first class, I have never enjoyed airplane food. So when I'm planning to fly I will often prepare a sandwich or snack to eat on the plane. An excellent sandwich to bring is Pan Bagna. It keeps well for up to two days, and the more the filling soaks into the bread, the better the sandwich gets. The Tomato Wonder Sandwich (page 395) is also a nice option for air travel. Vietnamese Rice-Paper Rolls (page 73) travel well, too, although a small container is needed for the dipping sauce. Creatively seasoned popcorn (see page 514) makes a good travel snack.*

# CHAPTER 14

# Tortilla Madness

# Enchiladas in Pumpkin Seed–Chile Sauce

This reliable enchilada recipe doesn't require any time-consuming procedures. The toasted pumpkin seeds give the sauce a delicious flavor as well as a boost in protein. Use the dark green, hulled pumpkin seeds that are available in whole-foods stores and some Latin American markets.

**SAUCE:**

1 green bell pepper

1 jalapeño pepper (or 2, if you'd like more heat)

2 teaspoons canola or corn oil

1 medium onion, coarsely chopped

2 garlic cloves, coarsely chopped

8 tomatillos, husked and chopped

1/2 teaspoon ground coriander seeds

1/2 cup hulled, unsalted pumpkin seeds, toasted
     6 to 8 minutes in a 350° oven

1/2 cup water

Salt and fresh-ground black pepper to taste

**FILLING:**

1 tablespoon canola or corn oil

2 medium onions, sliced thin

3 garlic cloves, minced

1 small green cabbage head, sliced

1 teaspoon ground cumin seeds

1 teaspoon ground coriander seeds

1/4 cup coarsely chopped cilantro

1/2 cup farmer's cheese, ricotta cheese, or mild,
     soft chèvre (goat cheese)

1/2 teaspoon salt

Fresh-ground black pepper to taste

8 large flour tortillas

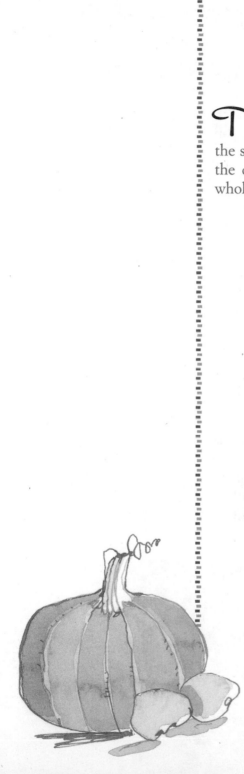

**1.** Preheat the oven to 450°. Place the bell and jalapeño peppers on a baking sheet, and bake them for 15 minutes or until they are blistered and soft. Let them cool.

**2.** Make the filling: Heat the oil in a large skillet over medium heat. Add the onions, and sauté them for 5 minutes, stirring occasionally. Add the garlic, cabbage, cumin, and coriander. Sauté, stirring frequently, for 20 minutes, then remove the pan from the heat. When the mixture has cooled, stir in the cilantro, farmer's cheese (or ricotta or goat cheese), and the salt and pepper.

**3.** When the peppers have cooled, remove the skins with your fingers. Chop the peppers coarsely.

**4.** Make the sauce: In a medium saucepan, heat the oil. Sauté the onion, garlic, and tomatillos until they are soft, about 5 minutes. Add the ground coriander, and sauté 2 minutes more. Transfer this mixture to a blender or food processor. Add the chopped peppers (jalapeño seeds included, if you want heat), all but 1 tablespoon of the pumpkin seeds, and the water. Blend the sauce until it is almost smooth. Add the salt and pepper.

**5.** Preheat the oven to 350°. Spread ⅓ cup filling down the middle of a flour tortilla. Roll the tortilla tightly, folding in the sides as you roll. Place the rolled tortilla in a 9-by-13-inch casserole pan. Do the same with the remaining seven tortillas, using all of the filling. Pour the sauce over the filled tortillas, and then cover the dish with foil. Bake the enchiladas for 25 minutes.

Serve the enchiladas garnished with the remaining pumpkin seeds.

*Serves 4*

## To Toast or Not to Toast

*Toasting spices such as cumin, coriander, mustard seeds, and fenugreek deepens their flavor and enhances the finished dish. To toast whole seeds, heat them in a dry skillet over low heat. Shake the pan constantly until the spices become fragrant (they will darken slightly). Remove them from the heat, and grind them or not as the recipe directs. Remember, though, that toasting won't do much for spices that have grown old and lost their flavor. To keep my spices fresh, I store them in airtight containers in a cool, dark spot. This way, they will usually keep well for over a year.*

# Nutty Enchiladas with Spicy Chile Sauce

B esides being really tasty, this dish is an excellent source of protein. Thanks to the almonds, black beans, and tofu, the enchiladas contain about 33 grams of protein per serving, or about two-thirds of the recommended daily amount for an adult (women need about 45 grams, men 55). With spinach included as well, this is just the kind of meal Popeye would eat.

**FILLING:**
1 tablespoon olive oil
2 carrots, chopped fine
1¹⁄₂ cups minced onions
1 garlic clove, minced
1 teaspoon chopped fresh oregano, or ¹⁄₂ teaspoon dried oregano
1 16-ounce package firm tofu
10 ounces fresh spinach, large stems removed (optional)
1¹⁄₂ cups (1 15-ounce can) cooked, rinsed, and drained black beans
1 cup low-fat or nonfat cottage cheese
¹⁄₂ teaspoon salt
Fresh-ground black pepper to taste

**SAUCE:**
1 tablespoon olive oil
1 large garlic clove, minced
2 teaspoons chili powder
1 teaspoon cumin seeds
3 cups (about 8) finely chopped plum tomatoes
¹⁄₄ cup sherry
1 tablespoon red or white wine vinegar
1¹⁄₃ cups water
1 pinch ground cloves

1 chipotle pepper (dried and soaked in hot water
    30 minutes, or canned in adobo sauce),
    or ¹/₄ teaspoon liquid smoke
¹/₄ cup chopped almonds, lightly toasted
¹/₂ teaspoon salt
Fresh-ground black pepper to taste

4 10-inch or 8 6- to 8-inch flour tortillas

**1.** Make the filling: In a large skillet, preferably non-stick, heat the olive oil over medium heat. Add the carrots, onions, garlic, and oregano. Sauté for about 8 minutes, stirring frequently. Meanwhile, take the tofu out of its water, and put it into a bowl. With your hands, break up the tofu by squeezing it through your fingers. Stir the spinach, if you're using it, into the onions and carrots, and cook until the spinach wilts. Stir in the black beans, and then the cottage cheese, tofu, salt, and pepper. Take the pan off the heat.

**2.** Make the sauce: In a medium-sized saucepan, heat the olive oil over medium heat. Add the garlic, chili powder, and cumin seeds. Stir constantly for 30 seconds, making sure the garlic does not brown. Add the tomatoes, then the sherry, vinegar, and water, and let the mixture simmer for 4 minutes. Add the cloves and chipotle pepper, and simmer 6 to 8 minutes more, stirring once or twice. Remove the pan from the heat.

**3.** Grind the almonds fine in a food processor or blender. If you used a dried chipotle, remove it from the sauce. Add half of the sauce to the blender or food processor, purée the mixture, and transfer it to a bowl. Purée the second half of the sauce, and add it to the first half. Season the sauce with salt and pepper. If you used a dried chipotle and you'd like a hotter sauce, chop the chipotle fine, and stir it in.

**4.** Assemble the dish: Preheat the oven to 350°. On your work surface, lay out 1 large tortilla or 2 small ones. Fill the tortilla(s) with one-quarter of the filling. Roll the tortilla(s) tight, folding in the sides as you roll. Fill the remaining tortillas the same way. Place the filled tortillas in a casserole dish large enough to hold them snugly. Pour the sauce over the enchiladas, then cover the dish with foil. Bake the enchiladas for 20 minutes. Serve the enchiladas hot.

Serves 4 (makes 4 large enchiladas or 8 smaller ones)

# Squash and Potato Enchiladas with Mole Sauce

Not all traditional mole sauces are heavy; nor do they all contain chocolate. This one is made from almonds, tomatoes, and plantains. It is so good that I once added a splash of water to some of the sauce and drank it as a soup (try it!). The enchilada filling is composed of butternut squash and potatoes, roasted in the oven with olive oil and oregano and Jack cheese. Don't worry that the vegetables will be oily; much of the olive oil remains in the roasting pan.

4 tablespoons olive oil
2 teaspoons chopped fresh oregano, or 1 teaspoon
   dried oregano
1 teaspoon salt, plus more, to taste
1/2 teaspoon fresh-ground black pepper
1 1/2 pounds medium potatoes (about 3), cut into
   1-inch cubes
1 small butternut squash (about 1 1/2 pounds),
   split in half and seeded
1 jalapeño pepper
1 cup chopped onion
1 teaspoon minced garlic
16 almonds
1/4 teaspoon ground cinnamon
1 pinch ground cloves
1/2 ripe plantain, or 1 ripe banana, cut into
   1/2-inch rounds

# Taco Party

Looking for a good time? Have a taco party! Create a taco bar, with bowls of various fillings and toppings, and soon your friends and family will be lining up. Taco shells can be stuffed with so many wonderful vegetable and legume concoctions that meat can take a back seat or no seat at all if you like. And you don't have to stop at fried-shell tacos. You can offer warm, fresh corn tortillas for those who want soft tacos, and warm flour tortillas for those who want to roll their own burritos. Here are some more ideas.

## Assemble your taco bar:

*Barbecued Tofu (below)*
*Smokin' Beans (page 194)*
*Dirty Rice (page 203)*
*Three-Chile Chili (page 462)*
*Avocado-Lime Dip (page 52)*
*Cilantro Vinaigrette (below)*
*Roasted Corn and Garlic Salsa (page 25)*
*Rasta Salsa (page 28)*
*Shredded nappa cabbage*
*Shredded romaine lettuce*

*Chopped tomatoes*
*Crumbled goat cheese*
*Thinly sliced red onion*
*Grated manchego cheese*
*Grated sharp cheddar cheese*
*Thinly sliced jalapeño peppers*
*Fried taco shells*
*Warm flour or corn tortillas*
*Sour cream*
*Hot sauces of all kinds*

## Set the scene:

Prepare a large table as festively Mexican as you can manage. A bright red or blue table-cloth would be nice, or, better yet, cover the table with an old Mexican shawl or throw. Buy some mangoes and bananas, and set a fruit bowl as your centerpiece (if you have a terrific Day-of-the-Dead doll, by all means use that instead). Then gather a bunch of bowls of varying sizes; terra cotta or wood is great, but use what you have. Fill the bowls with some or all of the foods listed above, adding your own inspirations. Make some margaritas, Ginger Iced Tea (page 513), or batidos (pages 519–20). Finally, throw on Linda Ronstadt's recording *Las Canciones de Mis Padres,* get your friends together, and enjoy.

# Barbecued Tofu

Although it is baked in the oven, this tofu cooks slowly, like real barbecue. Barbecued tofu is great in tacos, with brown rice, or with Ten-Minute Cornbread (page 18).

> 2 pounds (2 16-ounce blocks) extra-firm tofu
> 2 teaspoons salt
> 2 tablespoons sugar
> 2 teaspoons fresh-ground black pepper
> 1/2 teaspoon cayenne
> 1 tablespoon chili powder
> 2 tablespoons paprika
> 1 cup apple cider vinegar
> 2 large garlic cloves, minced

**1.** Preheat the oven to 300°. Cut the tofu into 1/4-inch cubes.

**2.** Combine the tofu with the rest of the ingredients in a bowl, and stir well. Place the tofu and its marinade in a large low-sided roasting pan, and bake it in the oven for 1 hour. Toss the tofu once or twice during the baking. Serve it hot.

Serves 8

# Cilantro Vinaigrette

Put this into a bottle, label it, and put it on your taco bar. This vinaigrette is heavy on the vinegar and low on oil, and every drop bursts with cilantro flavor. Drizzle the vinaigrette over tacos or shredded vegetables, or even try it spooned onto bread. It's also terrific over thinly sliced romaine lettuce and chopped tomatoes.

> 2 cups coarsely chopped cilantro
> 1 tablespoon sugar
> 2 garlic cloves, cut in half
> 1 1/2 cups apple cider vinegar or red wine vinegar
> 1/2 cup olive oil
> 1/2 teaspoon salt
> 1/2 teaspoon fresh-ground black pepper

**1.** In a blender or food processor, combine the cilantro, the sugar, the garlic, and 1/2 cup of the vinegar. Blend until the cilantro and garlic are chopped fine. Add the remaining vinegar, and blend again.

**2.** With the machine running, pour in the olive oil in a slow, thin stream. Then add the salt and pepper. Transfer the dressing to a squeeze bottle or salad-dressing bottle, and chill it until you're ready to use it. The dressing will keep well for 3 days.

Makes 2 cups

3 tomatoes, cut into 1-inch cubes

1/2 cup water

1/2 teaspoon salt

Fresh-ground black pepper to taste

8 10-inch flour tortillas

5 ounces Monterey Jack cheese, grated (about
     1 1/2 cups)

4 tablespoons whole, low-fat, or nonfat sour
     cream

**1.** Preheat the oven to 400°. In a bowl, combine 2 tablespoons olive oil, the oregano, and ½ teaspoon each salt and pepper. Add the potatoes, and toss them so they are well coated with the mixture. Put the potatoes and the squash, flesh side up, into a large roasting pan. Drizzle 1 tablespoon olive oil over the squash, and sprinkle it with salt and pepper. Bake the vegetables for 45 minutes or until they are tender. Remove the vegetables from the oven (but leave the oven on), and let them cool. Spoon out the flesh of the squash, and discard the skin.

**2.** While the vegetables bake, roast the jalapeño: If you are using an electric stove, place the jalapeño directly on a burner set on medium-high heat. Char the pepper, turning it frequently; it should become black in spots, but not all over.

If you are using a gas stove, insert a fork or skewer into the pepper and turn it over a medium flame until black spots develop.

When the jalapeño is cool enough to handle, peel off its skin. Stem and chop the jalapeño, removing some of the seeds if you want less heat. (You can add them later, if you like, when finishing the sauce.)

**3.** Make the sauce: In a medium skillet, heat the remaining 1 tablespoon olive oil. Sauté the onion, garlic, and almonds for about 5 minutes. Add the cinnamon and cloves, and sauté 2 minutes more. Add the plantain or banana and the tomatoes, and cook the mixture over medium heat for 5 minutes, stirring occasionally. Transfer the mixture to a blender or food processor. Add the water and the jalapeño and blend well. Season the sauce with ½ teaspoon salt, and pepper to taste.

**4.** Fill the tortillas: Spread about one-eighth of the potatoes and squash down the middle of one tortilla. Add a little of the grated cheese. Roll the tortilla tightly. Fill the remaining seven tortillas the same way, saving a small handful of cheese for the top of the casserole. Fit the tortillas snugly in a casserole dish.

**5.** Pour the mole sauce over the tortillas, and sprinkle with the remaining cheese. Cover the dish with foil, and bake the enchiladas for 35 minutes. Serve two enchiladas per person, with a dollop of sour cream on top.

*Serves 4*

# Sweet Potato–Tortilla Pie

If Mexicans had invented quiche, this is the way they might have made it. The crust of this pie is made of corn tortillas, and the custard is spiked with cumin, cilantro, and pepper Jack cheese. The roasted sweet potatoes in the custard provide a comforting, sweet flavor. I suggest serving this pie with Salsa Verde (page 29) or a good store-bought salsa.

1 large or 2 medium sweet potatoes (about 1
    pound), peeled and cut into 1/2-inch cubes
2 large garlic cloves, minced
1/2 teaspoon cumin seeds
1 tablespoon olive oil
5 corn tortillas
1 1/2 cups whole or low-fat milk
3 eggs
4 scallions, cut into 1/4-inch lengths
1 teaspoon salt
Fresh-ground black pepper to taste
3 tablespoons chopped cilantro
1 cup grated pepper Jack cheese (Monterey
    Jack with chopped jalapeños; about 3 ounces)

**1.** Preheat the oven to 400°. In a roasting pan, toss the sweet potatoes with the garlic, cumin, and olive oil. Bake the sweet potatoes for 20 minutes, stirring them once during the middle of the baking. Let them cool.

**2.** Butter a 10-inch quiche or cake pan (but not a springform pan). Layer the tortillas so that they cover the entire base and sides of the pan.

**3.** Set the oven to 375°. In a large bowl, beat together the milk, the eggs, the scallions, the salt and pepper, and 2 tablespoons of the cilantro. When the sweet potato mixture is no longer hot, spoon it evenly onto the tortillas. Then sprinkle the cheese over the sweet potatoes. Pour the beaten custard mixture over all; do not worry if some of the custard runs underneath the tortillas.

**4.** Bake the pie for 40 minutes or until the custard is set (when a knife inserted in the middle comes out clean). Slice the pie, and serve it hot, sprinkled with the remaining cilantro.

*Variation:* This pie would be equally good with roasted new potatoes in place of the sweet potatoes, and soft goat cheese rather than Jack cheese. Use about 3 ounces crumbled goat cheese and 1 pound quartered new potatoes. Roast the potatoes for 35 minutes; they will take a bit longer than the sweet potatoes.

*Serves 4*

# Stacked Tortillas

I make this quick dish for Jim, the bartender at our restaurant, who starts bellyaching if he hasn't eaten in the last thirty minutes. After I feed him I have to keep an eye on him, or else he'll throw out half of what I give him, and then in thirty minutes say he's starving again, just so he can try something else. But he never throws out this dish.

These stacked tortillas, filled with cheese and vegetables,

## Sweet Potatoes and Yams

Sweet potatoes and yams come from different plant species, and neither is related to the potato. The roots called yams in U.S. supermarkets aren't true yams at all, they are sweet-potato varieties with deep-orange flesh. True yams are grown in the tropics, in South and Central America and southern Asia. They are not widely available in the United States. They can be found, however, in some Latin American markets, where they are sold in big chunks.

are perfect to make on a busy weeknight because they're fast, satisfying, and filling.

1 tablespoon canola or corn oil
1 red onion, sliced thin
1 large portobello mushroom (both cap and
    stem), sliced thin
2 carrots, cut into thin julienne strips
1 medium zucchini, cut in half lengthwise, then
    sliced thin diagonally
1/2 teaspoon salt
Fresh-ground black pepper to taste
5 ounces grated Monterey Jack cheese (about
    1 1/2 cups)
12 corn tortillas
1 cup Apple-Chipotle Salsa (page 27) or spicy
    store-bought salsa
4 tablespoons whole, low-fat, or nonfat sour
    cream
1/2 cup chopped scallions

**1.** Preheat the oven to 400°. In a large saucepan, heat the oil. Add the onion, and sauté it over medium heat for 3 to 4 minutes, stirring frequently. Add the mushrooms, carrots, and zucchini, and cook, stirring occasionally, for 5 to 6 minutes more or until the vegetables are just tender. Take the pan off the heat, and stir in the salt and pepper.

**2.** Place the tortillas directly on the oven racks, fitting as many on as possible without overlapping them. Bake the tortillas for 2 to 3 minutes or until they have hardened. Remove them to a plate, but keep the oven on.

**3.** Place four tortillas on a large baking sheet. Arrange a spoonful or two of vegetables on each tortilla, then sprinkle a small amount of grated cheese over the vegetables. Place another tortilla on top of the cheese. Add another spoonful or two of vegetables, then some more grated cheese. Top each stack with a third tortilla.

**4.** Place the four tortilla stacks in the oven for 10 minutes, or until they are hot and the cheese is melted. Place one stack on each dinner plate, top with the salsa, sour cream, and scallions, and serve.

*Serves 4*

# Chilaquiles

This speedy dish, similar in theory to lasagna, is perfect for a weeknight dinner. Corn tortillas are cut into strips; crisped; tossed with summer squash, potatoes, red peppers, and ricotta cheese; and baked. Douse chilaquiles with a bit of hot sauce or salsa, and enjoy.

2 tablespoons olive oil
6 corn tortillas, cut into ¹/₂-inch-wide strips
1 medium potato, peeled and sliced into very thin
    rounds
1 large red bell pepper, seeded and cut into
    ¹/₂-inch-wide strips
1 small summer squash or zucchini, cut in half
    lengthwise, then cut crosswise into ¹/₂-inch
    half-moons
2 large garlic cloves, minced
²/₃ cup ricotta cheese, whole-milk or part-skim
¹/₂ teaspoon salt, or more, to taste
Fresh-ground black pepper to taste
Your favorite hot sauce or salsa

**1.** In a large skillet, heat 1 tablespoon of the oil over medium-high heat. Add the tortilla strips, and stir until the tortillas become stiff and spotted with brown. Transfer the strips to a plate.

**2.** Preheat the oven to 375°. In the skillet in which you cooked the tortilla strips, heat the remaining olive oil. Add the potato

## Homemade Tortilla Chips

✿

*Ever since I bought a large griddle I have been making these chips. I serve them with fresh salsa and sour cream. To feed 4 people as a snack, take 4 large (8-inch) flour tortillas. Stack them and cut them in half. Then cut each half into 3 wedges (there will be 24 chips). Heat a large griddle or two large skillets over medium-high heat. Coat with 1 tablespoon vegetable oil. Lay the tortillas down on the griddle or pans, then salt them generously. Let the chips sit for 5 minutes, adjusting the heat to make sure the tortillas don't burn. Once they are golden, remove them and let them dry on paper towels. Serve as soon as possible.*

slices, and cook them for 5 minutes, stirring frequently. Add the red pepper, squash, and garlic, and cook 5 minutes more, stirring frequently. Take the pan off the heat.

**3.** Mix in the ricotta cheese and tortilla strips with the vegetables, and add the salt and pepper. Put this mixture into a 9- or 10-inch round, oven-proof casserole dish. (At this point you can cover and chill the dish for up to 24 hours.)

**4.** Bake the chilaquiles for 15 minutes, or 25 minutes if it has been chilled. Divide it among plates, and serve it with hot sauce or salsa.

**Variation:** A nice addition to chilaquiles is avocado. When the dish is baked, slice an avocado thin, and place some slices on each serving.

*Serves 4*

# Good Goat Burritos

*B*urritos are casual food, yet these taste sophisticated enough to serve to Martha Stewart. A flour tortilla is wrapped around rice, sautéed scallions and tomatoes, black beans, and goat cheese. Just serve these with your favorite hot sauce and dollops of sour cream, and you've got dinner.

1 tablespoon olive oil
1¹/₂ cups chopped scallions, both white and green parts (about 1 bunch)
2 garlic cloves, minced
¹/₂ teaspoon ground cumin seeds
2 tomatoes, chopped into ¹/₂-inch cubes
2 cups cooked rice
Salt and fresh-ground black pepper to taste
1 cup cooked black beans, or more, to taste
4 tablespoons soft, mild chèvre (goat cheese)
2 10- or 12-inch flour tortillas (or 4 8-inch flour tortillas)

**1.** Heat the olive oil in a large skillet over medium heat. Add the chopped scallions, garlic, and cumin. Sauté, stirring frequently, for 5 minutes. Add the tomatoes and rice, and heat them well, stirring. Season the mixture with salt and pepper, and keep it warm.

**2.** In another skillet, heat the black beans with a bit of water to moisten them, stirring so they do not scorch. Keep them warm.

**3.** Sprinkle a bit of water on one tortilla, then place the tortilla in a large dry skillet over high heat. After a few seconds, turn the tortilla to heat the other side, again for only a few seconds. Place the hot tortilla on a work surface. Spread 2 tablespoons goat cheese across the center part of the tortilla. Place half of the rice mixture and half of the black beans over the cheese. Roll up the tortilla tightly, folding in the sides as you roll. Serve the burrito immediately, and make another just like it. (If you are using four 8-inch tortillas, use 1 tablespoon goat cheese and ¼ of the rice and beans per tortilla.)

*Serves 2*

# Potato and Cheddar Quesadillas

Potatoes give these quesadillas substance, and carrot provides color and a sweet flavor. Serve the quesadillas with Apple-Chipotle Salsa (page 27) or your favorite hot sauce.

2 tablespoons canola, corn, or olive oil
1 cup sliced onion
1 large carrot, chopped fine
1 large garlic clove, minced
3 cooked medium new potatoes, sliced into
    ¼-inch rounds (about 1½ cups)
2 8- or 10-inch flour tortillas

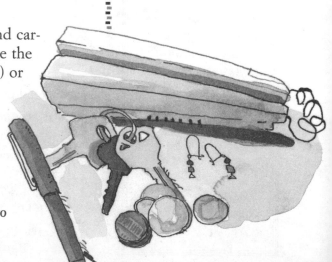

4 ounces sharp cheddar cheese, sliced thin or
grated
Salt and fresh-ground black pepper to taste

**1.** In a large skillet, heat 1 tablespoon oil over medium-high heat, and add the onions and carrot. Sauté them for 5 minutes, stirring frequently. Turn the heat to medium-low, add the garlic and sliced potatoes, and cook 5 minutes more, stirring occasionally. Season with salt and pepper.

**2.** In another skillet (at least 10 inches wide), heat ½ tablespoon oil over medium heat. Add one tortilla. On half of the tortilla, spread half of the cheese. Top with half of the onion-carrot-potato mixture. Let the quesadilla cook until the cheese is melted and the tortilla has browned on the bottom. Fold the empty half of the tortilla over the filled half, then transfer the tortilla to a baking sheet and keep the baking sheet in a warm oven until the other quesadilla is done.

Put the skillet back on the heat, and add the remaining ½ tablespoon oil. Make the second tortilla in the same manner as the first.

Cut both quesadillas into wedges, and serve them with hot sauce or salsa.

*Makes 2 quesadillas*

# Chile and Zucchini Quesadillas

I'm not sure why, but zucchini is splendid in quesadillas. This could be because the light vegetable balances an otherwise heavy dish, or because zucchini and cheese simply have an affinity for each other. Whatever the reason, these quesadillas are delicious. Just be sure to serve them the moment they are made; they can become soggy within minutes.

# Chile Breakdown

You see many kinds of peppers in the market these days, but what are you supposed to do with them? There are no rules, but here are some guidelines to help you to identify chiles and their heat levels, and to incorporate chiles into your cooking.

## Fresh Chiles

Buy firm chiles; the wrinkled ones have lost a lot of their flavor. If your chiles are fairly fresh, they should last at least one week in the refrigerator.

Most of the heat of a pepper is in the spongy internal ribs and the seeds. If you want to keep the heat down, remove the seeds, the ribs, or both. Here are some common fresh chile varieties:

**ANAHEIM**—Similar in flavor to bell peppers but mildly hot, Anaheims are usually sold green. They are long and narrow, with a pointed tip. Stuff them with cheese and bake them, or chop them and add them to salsas, sauces, stews, and cornbread batter.

**POBLANO**—These peppers are dark green (maturing to dark red-brown), large (about 5 inches long), boxy at the top, and pointed at the end. Named for the valley of Puebla, Mexico, where they are widely grown, they are moderately hot, tender, and richly flavored. They are perfect for stuffing (see the recipe for Poblanos Rellenos on page 424). Or try chopping grilled poblanos and adding them to salsa for a smoky, spicy flavor. The darker the color of the poblano, the richer its flavor will be.

**JALAPEÑO**—Two to three inches long, thick-fleshed, and glossy green (maturing to bright red), jalapeños are mildly to very hot, and quite versatile. They are named after Jalapa, the capital of the state of Veracruz, where they were first grown. You can lower their heat by removing their seeds. Jalapeños are good in salsas, stews, and cornbread. Or you can roast them, skin them, then either stuff them with goat cheese or slice them and use them in quesadillas.

**THAI (OR BIRD, OR SANTAKA)**—These are skinny little green or red peppers less than 1 inch long. They are very hot, slightly sweet, and perfect for Thai soups and stews and other Asian-inspired dishes. Use Thai peppers whole in pickles, or float them in sauces or soups. They are available in Asian markets and many supermarkets.

**SERRANO**—These pointed little peppers (about 2 inches long) are dark green to red in color. They are very hot, and a favorite with Mexican cooks. Chopped, they work well in salsas, beans, guacamole, and hot sauces.

**HABANERO**—Watch out! This orange, lantern-shaped pepper is the world's hottest. Developed in Yucatán, Mexico, it has a sweet floral aroma and flavor but a biting sting. When habaneros are used in moderation, their heat is pleasant, since it dissipates faster than that of other chiles. Along with their Caribbean cousins, Scotch bonnets, habaneros are great in salsas, guacamole, beans, and sauces. I like to mix habaneros with papayas or peaches cooked with onions, and purée the mixture for quesadillas and such.

When you cut and seed these peppers, wear rubber gloves or sandwich bags on your hands, and do not touch your eyes or other sensitive parts.

# Dried Chiles

There are many ways to treat dried chiles; the method of choice depends on the dish you are making. You can lightly toast them over a gas flame or directly on an electric burner, just until they start to blister, then grind them, seeds and all, to a powder, for use in rustic Mexican sauces. Or you can toast the chiles, seed them (or not), soak them in warm water until they are soft, then purée them and cook them in a sauce. Sometimes dried chiles aren't toasted at all, but just soaked in warm water or boiled for a few minutes, then chopped, simmered in a sauce, and puréed. In Yucatán and Oaxaca, dried chiles are sometimes burned to a crisp to make a black chile powder for certain moles (but while the chiles are burning, the house becomes filled with fumes that make the family gasp and cry for air).

Store dried chiles in a cool, dry place, or freeze them in a plastic bag. These chile varieties are commonly sold dry:

ANCHO—A dried poblano, the ancho is wrinkled, black, about 3½ to 5 inches long, and slightly bitter but raisin-like in flavor. Anchos are often used in moles. Mildly spicy, they are toasted or not, then soaked in warm water and puréed for sauces. I particularly like anchos in vegetarian chilis. They are available in some supermarkets and in Latin American markets.

CASCABEL—When fresh, this round, smooth pepper resembles an oversized black cherry. Cascabels are available dried in Latin American markets. Hot and nutty in flavor, cascabels are good in sauces, beans, and chilis. If you toast these chiles, do so lightly, since they burn easily. Whether you toast them or not, soak them in hot water before chopping or puréeing them.

CHIPOTLE—A jalapeño (or similar pepper) dried in wood smoke, this wrinkled brown pepper is often available canned in adobo sauce. (If you don't use the whole can at once, store the remainder in an airtight container in the refrigerator; the chipotles will keep indefinitely.) Chipotles impart a woodsy, smoky flavor to foods, as well as a considerable amount of heat. Soak dried chipotles in hot water for 30 minutes or until they are soft enough to chop. Add chopped chipotles to sauces, beans, salad dressings, soups, stews, and other dishes.

PASILLA—A dried chilaca pepper, the wrinkled, chocolate-colored medium-hot pasilla is about 6 inches long. Its flavor is rich yet sharp and slightly bitter. Pasillas are good in cooked sauces and rustic table sauces. For those who eat fish, these peppers are also good in seafood stews. They are available in Latin American markets.

CHILTEPÍN (OR CHILPEQUIN, PIQUÉN, OR PEQUÍN)—This very tiny red pepper (it is about the size of a fingernail) is also very, very hot. Ground in a spice mill, chiltepíns have a flavor similar to that of cayenne. They are good in chilis, sauces, beans, and soups. Add one or two to a cup of cocoa, in the tradition of seventeenth-century Spain.

2 ancho or pasilla peppers, or 1 teaspoon chili
    powder
2 tablespoons olive oil
1 large garlic clove, minced
1 small zucchini, sliced into 1/4-inch rounds
Salt and fresh-ground black pepper to taste
4 ounces Monterey Jack cheese, grated
2 12-inch flour tortillas
2 tablespoons whole, low-fat, or nonfat sour
    cream
Your favorite hot sauce

**1.** If you're using ancho or pasilla peppers, soak them in hot water for 30 minutes. Then drain them, seed them, and chop them fine.

**2.** Heat 1 tablespoon of the olive oil in a large skillet over medium heat. Add the garlic and the zucchini. Sprinkle with salt, pepper, and the chili powder, if you're using it. Sauté the zucchini, stirring often, until it softens, about 5 minutes. Transfer the zucchini to a plate.

**3.** In the same skillet over medium heat, heat 1/2 tablespoon oil. Add one tortilla. Sprinkle the cheese and chopped chiles, if you're using them, evenly over the tortilla. Cook until the tortilla crisps and the cheese melts, about 3 to 4 minutes. Place the zucchini rounds on the cheese, then top with the second tortilla. Slide the quesadilla from the skillet onto a plate, and invert it onto a second plate. Add the remaining oil to the skillet, then slide the flipped quesadilla back into the skillet. Let the quesadilla brown well on the flip side for 3 to 4 minutes.

**4.** Remove the quesadilla to a cutting board, and slice it into quarters. Place two pieces on each plate, top them with sour cream, and pass the hot sauce.

Serves 2

# Real Tamale Pie

The tamale pies I come across don't really taste like tamales. This is usually because cornmeal is used instead of fresh masa or masa harina. But in this Real Tamale Pie, the dough is the same one I use to make tamales. Fortunately, making tamale pie takes quite a bit less skill than making tamales. The pie is layered with the tamale dough, mashed beans, goat cheese, and roasted onions and peppers, and served with a spicy chile-tomato sauce.

4 cups sliced onions
2 large green bell peppers
2 cups masa harina
¼ pound butter (1 stick), softened
1 teaspoon salt
¾ cup water
1½ cups (1 15-ounce can) cooked and drained
    pinto beans or black beans
4 ounces soft, mild chèvre (goat cheese)
1 tablespoon chili powder
1 teaspoon cumin seeds
3½ cups (1 28-ounce can) crushed plum
    tomatoes
2 garlic cloves, minced
1 ancho pepper, soaked in hot water (optional)
1 pinch cayenne
1 pinch sugar
Salt and fresh-ground black pepper to taste
½ cup chopped scallions

**1.** Roast the onions and peppers: Preheat the oven to 450°. Spread the sliced onions on one ungreased baking sheet, and place the peppers on another. Put both baking sheets into the hot oven. Roast the onions, stirring once or twice, for 25 to 30 minutes, until they are browning and soft. Take out the pep-

## The Miracle of Masa

That a food like masa was ever invented is awe-inspiring to me. It would never have occurred to me to dry corn kernels in the sun, cook them in limewater, soak them overnight, grind them into a dough, then bake up a tortilla or two. I use masa for tamales, pancakes, pupusas, dumplings, and crepes, as well as for tortillas.

Finding fresh masa meal isn't easy, so I always call for masa in its dried form, masa harina. The flavor of both masa and masa harina—the flavor of corn tortillas—is unique, quite unlike that of ordinary cornmeal. Masa harina can be found in many supermarkets as well as in Latin American markets.

pers after 20 to 25 minutes, when the skin is blistering and swelling. Let the vegetables cool. Lower the oven temperature to 375°.

**2.** Make the masa dough: In a large bowl, combine the masa harina, butter, and 1 teaspoon salt. With your hand, incorporate the butter by squeezing the dough through your fingers. Add the water slowly, stirring and squeezing with your hand. Mix until the ingredients are blended.

**3.** Assemble the pie: Remove the skin from the peppers, split them open, and discard the seeds. Cut them into strips, if you like, or leave them in one piece. Mash the beans with a potato masher, or blend them in a food processor, leaving a bit of texture. Press the dough into a 9-by-9-inch baking pan. Spread the beans evenly over the dough. Lay the peppers on the beans. Dot with goat cheese, then cover the cheese with the onions. Cover the pan with foil. Bake the tamale pie for 40 minutes.

**4.** While the pie is baking, make the sauce: In a dry saucepan, heat the chili powder and cumin seeds over medium heat, shaking the pan constantly. After about 1 minute, when the seeds have begun to release their aroma, add the tomatoes and the garlic. If you are using the ancho chile, remove it from the water, chop it fine, and add it to the tomato sauce. Simmer the tomato sauce for 25 minutes, stirring once or twice. Toward the end of the simmering, add the cayenne, sugar, and salt and pepper to taste.

**5.** When the pie has finished baking, cut it into 4 pieces. Spoon a little of the tomato sauce on each of 4 plates, and place each piece on the sauce. Garnish with the scallions, and serve.

**Variations:** This dish can be dressed up with other garnishes—dollops of sour cream, chopped cilantro, toasted pumpkin seeds, and lime wedges.

Serves 4

# Things That Get Baked

# Smoky Mexican Lasagna

This lasagna is slightly unconventional, but not so much that traditional lasagna lovers won't love it. The smokiness comes from chipotle chiles, which are jalapeños dried in wood smoke. If you'd like an even smokier flavor, try using smoked mozzarella cheese instead of the regular kind.

1 tablespoon olive oil

3 garlic cloves, minced

2 cups chopped onions

1 teaspoon ground cumin seeds

1 teaspoon dried oregano

3½ cups (1 28-ounce can) peeled plum tomatoes, chopped

3 tablespoons sherry

2 chipotle peppers, dried or canned in adobo sauce (available in Latin American markets and some supermarkets)

1 pound dried lasagna noodles

1 small bunch cilantro, chopped (about ½ cup)

2 tablespoons tomato paste

½ to 1 teaspoon salt

Fresh-ground black pepper to taste

2 cups (1 pound) ricotta cheese, whole-milk or part-skim

2 cups blanched fresh corn or thawed and drained frozen corn

10 ounces fresh spinach (large stems removed), steamed 1 minute, or 10 ounces frozen spinach, thawed and drained

2 cups (about 4 ounces) grated mozzarella cheese

4 corn tortillas, cut into matchstick-size pieces (optional)

**1.** Heat a large saucepan over medium heat. Add 1 tablespoon olive oil, the garlic, and the onions. Sauté for 5 minutes. Add the cumin and oregano, and sauté, stirring, for 1 minute more. Add the chopped tomatoes, the sherry, and the chipotles. Cook the mixture over low heat for 30 minutes.

**2.** While the sauce simmers, bring a large kettle of salted water to a boil. Boil the noodles for 9 minutes, then drain them, and rinse them well.

**3.** Add to the tomato sauce the cilantro, tomato paste, and salt and pepper to taste. Stir well. Fish out the chipotles if you used dried ones, and chop them fine. Return them to the tomato sauce. Remove the saucepan from the heat.

**4.** Preheat the oven to 350°. Spread a thin layer of tomato sauce on the bottom of a 9-by-13-inch casserole pan, then add a layer of noodles. Distribute all of the ricotta evenly over the noodles. Sprinkle the corn over the ricotta, and distribute the spinach over the corn. Spoon some tomato sauce over the vegetables. Lay down more noodles, then more tomato sauce, then half of the mozzarella cheese. Add a final layer of noodles, then tomato sauce, then the rest of the mozzarella cheese.

**5.** Bake the lasagna, uncovered, for 40 minutes. If you'd like, garnish the lasagna with the tortilla strips: Bake them on a baking sheet along with the lasagna for 15 minutes. Sprinkle the strips with salt. When the lasagna is baked, sprinkle it with the tortilla strips. Serve immediately.

*Serves 6*

# Adrienne's Vegan Lasagna

**M**y friend Adrienne has worked as a waitress and a manager at some of Boston's top restaurants for years. Not only does she know how to serve great dishes, but she cooks her own at home. Here she shares her vegan lasagna. The tofu, mashed and mixed with garlic and fresh herbs, substitutes well for the traditional ricotta layer.

## Getting Enough B₁₂?

*Although a vegan diet (free of all animal products) can be very healthful otherwise, getting enough vitamin $B_{12}$ as a vegan may be tough. The foods that are richest in vitamin $B_{12}$ are red meat, fish, eggs, and dairy products. Vegans can obtain $B_{12}$ only from sea vegetables and tempeh. If you're a vegan, taking a $B_{12}$ supplement is a good idea, especially if you're pregnant or breastfeeding.*

**SAUCE:**

2 tablespoons olive oil

1 1/2 cups chopped onions

3 tablespoons minced garlic

7 cups (2 28-ounce cans) peeled plum tomatoes

1/3 cup tomato paste

1/2 cup chopped basil

1/2 cup chopped parsley

1 teaspoon each salt and fresh-ground black
   pepper

1 pound dry lasagna noodles

**TOFU FILLING:**

2 pounds (2 16-ounce packages) firm tofu

2 tablespoons minced garlic

1/4 cup chopped basil

1/4 cup chopped parsley (preferably Italian)

1 tablespoon chopped fresh oregano, or
   1 1/2 teaspoons dried oregano

1/2 teaspoon salt, or more, to taste

Fresh-ground black pepper to taste

2 pounds fresh spinach, large stems removed, or
   3 10-ounce packages frozen spinach, thawed
   and drained (optional)

**1.** Make the sauce: In a large, heavy saucepan over medium heat, heat the olive oil. Add the onions, and sauté them until they are soft, about 5 minutes. Add the garlic, and cook 5 minutes more. Then add the tomatoes, juice and all, along with the tomato paste, basil, and parsley. Stir well, turn the heat to low, and let the sauce simmer for 1 hour. Add the salt and pepper.

**2.** While the sauce is cooking, bring a large kettle of salted water to a boil. Boil the lasagna noodles for 9 minutes, then drain them and rinse them well.

**3.** Preheat the oven to 400°. Place the tofu blocks in a large bowl. Add the garlic, basil, parsley, and oregano. Add the salt and pepper, and mash all the ingredients together by squeezing pieces of tofu through your fingers. Continue until the ingredients are well mixed.

**4.** If you are using fresh spinach, bring ½ cup water to a boil in a large stockpot. Add the spinach, cover the pot, and boil the spinach for 3 minutes. Invert the pot over a colander, and let the spinach drain for 1 to 2 minutes.

**5.** Assemble the lasagna: Spread 1 cup of the tomato sauce in the bottom of a 9-by-13-inch casserole pan. Add a single layer of lasagna noodles, and sprinkle one-third of the tofu mixture over the noodles. If you are using fresh or frozen spinach, distribute it over the tofu. Next ladle on 1½ cups tomato sauce, and top it with another layer of the noodles. Then sprinkle another one-third of the tofu mixture over the noodles, top the tofu with 1½ cups tomato sauce, and place a final layer of noodles over the tomato sauce. Finally, top the noodles with the final one-third of the tofu, and spread the remaining tomato sauce over all.

**6.** Cover the pan with foil, and bake the lasagna for 30 minutes. Serve it hot.

Serves 8

# Poblanos Rellenos

This is a recipe from my friend Jon, a guy who loves to throw caution to the wind in his cooking. I can't claim that his version of chiles rellenos is authentic, but his recipe requires about half of the time and fat of the traditional one. The chiles need no roasting, no batter, and no deep-frying; they're simply stuffed and baked. There is no sauce to make; you'll find that the stuffed peppers are moist enough without it. Serve the peppers with plain boiled rice or Dirty Rice (page 203), and a simple tossed salad.

15 sundried or other dried tomato slices
1½ tablespoons canola or corn oil
20 pecans or walnuts, chopped
4 garlic cloves, minced
Kernels from 3 ears corn (about 1⅔ cups)
½ teaspoon salt
Fresh-ground black pepper to taste
6 ounces soft, mild chèvre (goat cheese)
1 cup cottage cheese
½ cup grated Monterey Jack or cheddar cheese
8 small poblano peppers (or 4 green bell
    peppers, or 8 Anaheim peppers)

**1.** Bring 2 cups water to a boil, and pour the water over the dried tomatoes in a small bowl. Let the tomatoes sit in the hot water for 10 minutes. Then drain the tomatoes, and chop them fine.

**2.** While the dried tomatoes are soaking, heat 1 tablespoon of the oil in a skillet, and add the pecans or walnuts. Cook them over low heat for 3 minutes, shaking the pan from time to time, until the nuts taste toasted; be careful not to burn them. Add the garlic, chopped dried tomatoes, and corn to the mixture. Cook an additional 2 to 3 minutes over medium heat, stirring. Remove the pan from the heat, and add the salt and pepper. Crumble the goat cheese into the mixture, and fold in the cottage cheese and Jack or cheddar cheese.

**3.** Preheat the oven to 350°. Stuff the peppers: Remove the stem, core, and seeds of each pepper without puncturing the sides. Stuff the peppers loosely with the filling, distributing it equally among the peppers.

**4.** Coat a casserole dish with the remaining ½ tablespoon of oil, and lay the stuffed peppers in the dish. Add a scant ¼ cup water, and cover the dish with a lid or foil. Bake the peppers for 30 to 45 minutes (bell peppers take longer than poblanos), until they are tender. Serve the peppers right away.

Serves 4

# Freezer Do's and Don'ts

✖ ✖ ✖

## Don't—

- Freeze much of anything over 6 months. The flavor deteriorates, and usually the texture does, too.
- Freeze potatoes, even in soup or stew. They become mushy.
- Freeze sauces, toppings, or fillings based on milk, cream, or sour cream. They will curdle or separate.
- Freeze fried foods.
- Freeze raw cabbage, celery, lettuce, or other greens.

## Do—

- Wrap food really well. Freezer-weight zippered bags (with the air squeezed out) are good, as is a double layer of plastic wrap. Or use rigid airtight containers. Allowing food to be exposed to air results in freezer burn, which will taint flavors.
- Blanch vegetables before freezing them.
- Leave adequate head space. Remember that food expands when it freezes.
- Label and date the food. I use a black marker and write on the plastic wrap.

## What You Can Freeze

Some foods keep longer and better in the freezer than in the pantry or refrigerator. If your freezer has extra room, it makes good sense to keep them there. These foods freeze well:

- *Nuts of all kinds*
- *Herbs such as rosemary, oregano, and marjoram (in zippered freezer bags)*
- *Pie dough and pie shells, and dry yeast*
- *Pesto*
- *Stewed tomatoes and tomato sauce*
- *Cooked beans*
- *Unsalted butter*
- *Fresh ginger (the skin scrapes off easily once ginger is frozen)*
- *Bagels, muffins, and other breads*
- *Bread scraps for crumbs*
- *Flours that are highly perishable or that you don't use often (such as chickpea, buckwheat, or rye)*
- *Stews, soups, stocks, and chili*
- *Uncooked veggie burgers*
- *Enchiladas (even with salsa on them)*
- *Unfilled crepes (separated by plastic wrap or waxed paper)*
- *Cooked rice and grains (for up to 2 months)*
- *Cakes that haven't been iced*
- *Fruit purées*
- *Leftover coconut milk (transferred from the can to a small airtight container)*
- *Leftover chipotles in adobo sauce*

# Potato, Jerusalem Artichoke, and Carrot Gratin

Thinly sliced potatoes, Jerusalem artichokes, carrots, and onions turn into a down-home casserole when baked with rosemary and vegetable stock. For slicing the vegetables, I prefer to use a mandoline, but a food processor with a slicing attachment or a sharp knife works fine, too.

Jerusalem artichokes are often labeled "sunchokes" in supermarkets. They resemble large gingerroots, and their unique, mild flavor is reminiscent of artichokes. But the Jerusalem artichoke is not even related to the conventional artichoke; it is a tuber in the sunflower family. Jerusalem artichokes are generally available from October through April.

2 1/2 pounds russet potatoes, peeled and sliced as thin as possible

2 cups thinly sliced onions

1 tablespoon minced garlic

3 tablespoons olive oil

2 teaspoons minced fresh rosemary, or 1 teaspoon dried rosemary

1 teaspoon salt

Fresh-ground black pepper to taste

1/2 pound Jerusalem artichokes, sliced as thin as possible

2 large carrots, peeled and sliced as thin as possible

1 1/4 cups Basic Vegetable Stock (page 79), or 1/2 cup white wine combined with 3/4 cup water

1/2 cup grated Parmesan cheese

**1.** Preheat the oven to 350°. In a large bowl, combine the potatoes with the onions, garlic, olive oil, rosemary, salt, and pepper. Toss well. Put half this mixture into a 9-by-13-inch casserole pan, then spread the Jerusalem artichokes and carrots over the potatoes. Spread the rest of the potato-onion mixture on top. Pour the stock or wine and water evenly over the vegetables, and bake them, uncovered, for 1 hour or until the vegetables are tender when poked with a knife.

**2.** Take the pan out of the oven, and sprinkle the vegetables with the Parmesan cheese. Increase the oven temperature to 400°, then return the pan to the oven. Bake 10 minutes more.

**3.** Remove the pan from the oven. Cut the gratin into squares, and serve. (The gratin is particularly good served on a bed of greens, such as arugula or watercress, dressed with olive oil and lemon juice.) This gratin is even better reheated the day after it's made.

Serves 6

# Spinach Pie

Although I love creamed spinach made with heavy cream, spinach is also delicious when creamed with protein-rich cottage cheese. Flaky buttered phyllo dough provides the crust for this pie, and cubed potatoes and carrots nestle in the creamed spinach. Complete this meal with a simple tossed salad.

1 medium russet or boiling potato (about
    ½ pound), peeled and cut into ½-inch cubes
1 large carrot, peeled and cut into ½-inch cubes
1 tablespoon olive oil
2 cups chopped onions
1 large garlic clove, minced
10 ounces fresh spinach (large stems removed)
1 cup low-fat or nonfat cottage cheese
2 or 3 pinches freshly grated nutmeg

1/2 teaspoon salt, or more, to taste
Fresh-ground black pepper to taste
4 phyllo sheets (available frozen in
    supermarkets)
3 tablespoons unsalted butter, melted

**1.** In a small pot of salted boiling water, cook the potato and carrot cubes until they are tender, about 10 minutes. Drain them, and run cold water over them for a few seconds.

**2.** In a heavy skillet, heat the olive oil over medium heat. Add the onions, and cook them, stirring frequently, for 5 minutes or until they have softened. Add the garlic, and sauté for 1 minute. Add the spinach in two or three batches, letting each batch wilt before you add more.

**3.** Take the spinach mixture off the heat, and spoon it into a food processor. Add the cottage cheese, the nutmeg, the ½ teaspoon salt, and pepper, and adjust the seasonings, if you like. Purée the mixture well. (If you don't have a food processor, chop the spinach mixture by hand. Stir it together with the cottage cheese, nutmeg, salt, and pepper.)

**4.** Preheat the oven to 400°. Lay a sheet of phyllo on your work surface, and brush it lightly with melted butter. Place another sheet of phyllo on top, and butter it. Do the same with the third and fourth sheets. Cut the layered phyllo in half crosswise, so that the pieces are 8½ by 11 inches.

**5.** Spoon the spinach filling into a shallow casserole approximately 8 by 10 inches in size. Add the potatoes and carrots, and stir them in. Place the phyllo layers over the filling. Turn under the edges as necessary to fit the pan. Bake the pie for 20 minutes or until the phyllo is golden brown. Cut the pie into portions, and serve.

**Variation:** Try adding ¼ cup raisins to the carrots and potatoes after they have simmered 5 minutes or so (in step 1). Proceed as directed.

Serves 2 to 3

# Deep-Dish Potato and Pumpkin Pie

Hearty and homey, this pie reminds me of the many meat pies and tarts of France. You can use butternut squash instead of the pumpkin, if you prefer, and you can make the pie dough either in a food processor or by hand. This tart needs only a green salad to make a complete meal.

- 1 3-pound pumpkin, or 1 2-pound butternut squash
- 2 large russet potatoes, cut in half lengthwise
- 1½ cups unbleached white flour
- ½ teaspoon salt
- ½ cup (1 stick) cold unsalted butter, cut into 8 pieces
- 4 to 5 tablespoons ice water
- 1 tablespoon olive oil
- 2 cups chopped onions
- 2 garlic cloves, minced
- Kernels from 2 ears corn (about 1⅓ cups)
- 6 ounces Monterey Jack cheese, grated (about 1¾ cups)
- 2 teaspoons fresh thyme, or 1 teaspoon dried thyme
- 2 pinches ground allspice
- ½ teaspoon salt
- Fresh-ground black pepper to taste

**1.** Preheat the oven to 400°. Split the pumpkin in half, spoon out the seeds, and place the pumpkin halves face down on a baking sheet. (If you're using butternut squash instead, cut it in half lengthwise, take out the seeds, and place the halves face down on a baking sheet.) Put the potatoes on the same baking sheet, or on a second sheet if all the vegetables can't fit on one. Bake the pumpkin (or squash) and potatoes for 1 hour. Remove them from the oven, and let them cool.

## Pumpkin for Dinner

*A*lthough sugar, or pie, pumpkins look like jack-o'-lantern pumpkins, sugar pumpkins are usually smaller and slightly sweeter. They are much better for cooking.

Here's one way to cook a sugar pumpkin as a savory dish: Cut off the skin with a large knife. Cut the pumpkin in half, remove the seeds and stringy masses, and cut the flesh into 1-inch cubes. Mix the cubes with olive oil, garlic, and herbs, and roast the cubes until they are tender. You can eat the roasted cubes as a side dish, or you can add them to chilis or stews.

**2.** To make the dough in a food processor fitted with a steel blade, put the flour and salt into the processor. Add the butter. Run the machine in spurts until the butter is in bits no bigger than pea-size. Add 4 tablespoons ice water, and run the machine in spurts again, just enough to bring the dough together. Turn the dough out onto a clean work surface, and knead the dough with your hands, adding a bit of water or flour if necessary, until the dough is soft, moist, and somewhat smooth. Do this fast, handling the dough as little as possible. Form the dough into a flattened ball.

To make the dough by hand, combine the flour, salt, and butter in a large bowl. With a pastry cutter or fork, cut the butter into the flour until the pieces of butter are no larger than peas. Add 4 tablespoons ice water, and stir briefly, just enough to incorporate the water. Add a touch more water or flour if necessary to make a soft and moist dough. Turn the dough onto a clean work surface, and, with the palm of your hand, smear the dough away from you about a handful at a time. Scrape up the dough, and form it into a flattened ball.

Chill the dough for at least 30 minutes. Preheat the oven to 375°.

**3.** Roll out the dough, and use it to line the bottom and sides of either a 9-inch square baking pan or a large (12-inch) deep-dish pie pan. Pierce the dough with a fork in three places. Line the sides of the pan with pieces of aluminum foil, wrap the foil over the edge of the pan, and crimp the foil gently to hold the dough in place. Bake the crust for 15 minutes. Remove the pan from the oven. Reduce the oven temperature to 350°.

**4.** While the crust bakes, make the filling: Heat the oil in a large skillet over medium heat. Add the onions, and cook them, stirring frequently, until they soften, about 5 minutes. Add the garlic, and cook for 3 to 4 minutes more, stirring frequently. Add the corn, and cook for 2 minutes more. Remove the skillet from the heat.

**5.** When the pumpkin (or squash) has cooled, spoon out the flesh, and put it into a large bowl. Cut the potato into ½-inch cubes, and add them to the bowl. Add the corn-onion mixture, the grated cheese, the thyme, the allspice, the salt, and the pepper. Spoon the mixture into the baked pie crust. (At this point you can refrigerate the pie for up to 24 hours before proceeding with the recipe.)

**6.** Bake the pie at 350° for 30 minutes, or until the vegetables and the cheese are piping hot. Serve immediately.

*Serves 4 to 6*

# All-American Pot Pie

When I eat this pie, chockablock full of America's most popular vegetables, I feel very American. I even considered adding something blue, so I could have all the colors of the flag in the pie, but blueberries were all I could think of, so I gave up the idea.

1 tablespoon butter
8 cups total any combination of the following
    vegetables: fresh corn kernels, 1/2-inch cubes
    of carrot, chopped red bell pepper, chopped
    zucchini, spinach leaves (firmly packed),
    sliced onions, and 1/2-inch cubes of potato
1 large garlic clove, minced
1 1/2 cups plus 3 tablespoons unbleached white
    flour
2 cups warmed milk, or a bit more
1 pinch fresh or dried thyme
1 teaspoon salt
Fresh-ground black pepper to taste
1/2 cup (1 stick) cold unsalted butter, cut into
    8 pieces
4 to 5 tablespoons ice water

**1.** Make the filling: In a 12- or 14-inch, preferably non-stick, skillet, heat the butter over medium heat. Add all of the vegetables, and sauté them for 5 minutes, stirring often. Add the garlic, and sauté for 5 minutes more, stirring. Sprinkle the 3 tablespoons flour over the vegetables, and stir the mixture over the heat for 2 minutes. Add the warmed milk slowly, stirring all the while to avoid lumps. Stir in the thyme. Bring the sauce to a simmer, and cook the mixture, stirring, until the sauce thickens. Continue to cook the vegetables until they become tender (especially the carrot and potato), adding a bit more milk if the sauce becomes too thick. Add ½ teaspoon of the salt and plenty of fresh pepper. Transfer the mixture to a 9- or 10-inch casserole or deep pie dish. (At this point you can cover the dish and chill it for up to 2 days, if you'd like to bake it later.)

**2.** To make the dough in a food processor fitted with a steel blade, put the 1½ cups flour and the remaining ½ teaspoon salt into the processor. Add the cold butter. Run the machine in spurts until the butter is in bits no bigger than pea-size. Add 4 tablespoons ice water, and run the machine in spurts again, just enough to bring the dough together. Turn the dough out onto a clean work surface, and knead the dough, adding a bit of water or flour if necessary, until the dough is soft, moist, and somewhat smooth. Do this fast, handling the dough as little as possible. Form the dough into a flattened ball.

To make the dough by hand, combine the 1½ cups flour, ½ teaspoon salt, and cold butter in a large bowl. With a pastry cutter or fork, cut the butter into the flour until the pieces of butter are no larger than peas. Add 4 tablespoons ice water, and stir briefly, just enough to incorporate the water. Add a touch more water or flour if necessary to make a soft and moist dough. Turn the dough onto a clean work surface, and, with the palm of your hand, smear the dough away from you about a handful at a time. Scrape up the dough, and form it into a flattened ball. Chill the dough for at least 30 minutes.

**3.** Preheat the oven to 400°. Roll the dough into a circle slightly larger in diameter than the casserole or pie dish. Place the circle of dough over the casserole, and pinch the dough along the rim so that it clings to the rim of the dish. Cut four 1-inch-long slits in the dough, and place the pie in the oven. Bake it for about 20 minutes, or until the filling is bubbling and the crust golden.

*Serves 4*

# Dixie Pot Pie

ere's a simple pot pie that doesn't need a cream sauce. The topping is a buttery biscuit and the filling is jam-packed with juicy vegetables that form their own sauce, with a little help from sherry and butter.

**FILLING:**
1 tablespoon butter
1/2 cup chopped onion
10 okra pods, cut into 1/2-inch rounds
2 medium tomatoes, chopped
1 medium sweet potato, peeled and cut into
   1/2-inch cubes
1/4 cup sherry
1/2 cup fresh or frozen lima beans
1 teaspoon salt
Fresh-ground black pepper to taste

**BISCUIT TOPPING:**
1 cup unbleached white flour
1/2 teaspoon baking powder
1/2 teaspoon salt
4 tablespoons cold unsalted butter, cut into
   8 pieces
1/4 cup milk, plus a bit more

**1.** Make the filling: In a large skillet over medium heat, melt

## Book Hunting

*I often shop for cookbooks in second-hand stores. Older cookbooks can be a great source of unusual recipes and inspiration. One of my favorites is* Thoughts for Food, *first published in 1938 by the Institute Publishing Company. The instructions in these pages are simple, and some of the ideas are surprisingly provocative. Recipes like Broth Braised Kohlrabi, Farmer's Chop Suey, Bouillon with Almond Balls, Persimmon Royale, Cucumber Relish, Sponge Dumplings, Celery Root Appetizer, and Corn Dodgers made me realize food wasn't always boring back in the thirties.*

the butter. Add the onion, and cook it, stirring often, until it softens, about 5 minutes. Add the okra, the tomatoes, the sweet potato, the sherry, and ½ cup water. Simmer the vegetables for 10 minutes, adding more water if they begin to stick to the pan. When the sweet potatoes are tender, add the lima beans. Season the vegetables with the salt and pepper.

**2.** Preheat the oven to 375°. Make the biscuit topping in a food processor or by hand:

To use a food processor, combine in it the flour, baking powder, salt, and butter. Run the machine until the mixture resembles sand. Add the milk, then run the machine in spurts until the dough comes together.

To mix the dough by hand, combine the flour, baking powder, and salt in a bowl. Cut in the butter with a pastry cutter or fork until the pieces are no larger than pea-size. Stir in the milk, and continue to stir until the dough comes together.

Roll out the dough on a floured surface to fit a 9-inch pie pan or a 9-inch square baking dish.

**3.** Transfer the vegetables to the 9-inch dish, and cover them with the biscuit top. (It shouldn't seal the pie, but just sit on top.) Using a pastry brush, brush the top of the pie with a bit of milk. Bake the pie for 15 minutes, until the top is golden. Serve the pie hot.

*Serves 4*

# Indian Saffron Pot Pie

This recipe is a kissing cousin of Indian Stew (page 472), which is also flavored with saffron and ginger. But here yogurt is used instead of coconut milk, and a buttery baked phyllo dough sits atop the stew. If you fall in love with the saffron-ginger combination after making this, and haven't yet made Indian Stew, you know which recipe to try next.

3 tablespoons butter
1 1/2 cups chopped onions
2 cups chopped green cabbage
1 garlic clove, minced
1 heaping teaspoon minced fresh ginger
1/2 teaspoon turmeric (optional)
2 carrots, peeled and cut into 1/4-inch-thick
　　rounds
1 medium potato, peeled and cut into 1/2-inch
　　cubes
1/3 cup red or brown lentils
1/4 teaspoon saffron
3 sheets phyllo dough
1/3 cup whole, low-fat, or nonfat yogurt
Salt and fresh-ground black pepper to taste

**1.** Heat 1 tablespoon of the butter in a large saucepan or large skillet over medium heat. Add the onions, and sauté them for 5 minutes, stirring frequently. Add the cabbage, and sauté 10 minutes more, stirring frequently. When the onions begin to brown, add the garlic, ginger, and, if you like, turmeric, and cook 2 minutes more.

**2.** Add the carrots, potato, lentils, saffron, and 2 cups water. Over high heat, bring the stew to a boil. Cover the pan, turn the heat to low, and cook for 20 minutes, or until the lentils and potato are tender. Take the pan off the heat.

**3.** Meanwhile, preheat the oven to 375°. Prepare the phyllo dough: Melt the remaining 2 tablespoons butter. Place one sheet of phyllo in front of you like a placemat. With a pastry brush, lightly butter the right half, and fold the left half over onto the buttered side. Lightly butter the top of the folded phyllo sheet, then place it to the side. Butter and fold the two other phyllo sheets in the same fashion, and stack the three folded sheets.

**4.** Add the yogurt to the still-warm stew, and season the stew with salt and pepper. Spoon it into a 8- or 9-inch square baking dish. Then lay the phyllo stack on top of the stew, and fold the

## Paprika, Mild and Hot

Paprika is made from ground sweet or mildly hot red peppers. Most paprikas are not very piquant, although all have at least a little kick. Generally, paprika is milder and sweeter than ground dried chiles from Mexico. Hotter paprikas can be found in Indian and Eastern European food stores and many supermarkets.

Although paprika is usually associated with Hungarian food, it's also used in Greece, Serbia, Croatia, Bulgaria, and Morocco. I often add a pinch or more of paprika to Italian tomato sauces or a spoonful to bean chilis.

edges under as necessary to fit.

**5.** Bake until the phyllo is golden, about 20 minutes. Cut the pie, and serve it hot.

**Variation:** Add 1½ cups fresh or frozen peas at the end of step 2, and stir well.

Serves 4

# Noodle Quiche

Letting noodles run around in quiche isn't something I would normally let happen, if the combination didn't taste so good. Here blue cheese, plum tomatoes, mushrooms, and an egg custard are poured over a bed of vermicelli noodles. The noodles take the place of a crust.

1 tablespoon butter
1 cup thinly sliced onion
½ pound mushrooms (any variety), sliced thin
3 plum tomatoes, sliced into ½-inch-thick rounds
½ teaspoon salt, plus more to taste
Fresh-ground black pepper to taste
2 cups whole or low-fat milk
2 eggs
1 teaspoon paprika (optional)
4 cups cooked vermicelli or spaghetti (about
    5 ounces dry noodles)
2 ounces Saga Blue, Cambozola, or Maytag
    Blue cheese (about 4 tablespoons)
2 tablespoons Parmesan cheese (optional)

**1.** Preheat the oven to 375°. Melt the butter in a large skillet over medium-high heat. Add the onion and sauté it, stirring occasionally, until it softens, about 5 minutes. Add the mushrooms, and sauté, stirring frequently, until the mushrooms are soft, about 10 minutes. Then add the tomatoes, and sauté 2 minutes more. Add ½ teaspoon salt and some pepper, and remove the skillet from the heat.

**2.** In a bowl, whisk together the milk, eggs, paprika if you're using it, and a bit of salt and pepper. Spread the pasta in a 9- or 10-inch pie plate. Distribute the blue cheese, in nine or ten small pieces, over the pasta. Then spoon the onion, mushrooms, and tomatoes over the cheese and pasta. Finally, add the custard mixture.

**3.** Bake the pie for 45 minutes, or until the filling is set. Sprinkle the pie with Parmesan cheese, if you like. Cut it into wedges, and serve it hot or warm.

Serves 6

# Nice Tomato and Crouton Omelet

I know that this recipe doesn't really belong in a chapter of baked things, but for lack of an omelet chapter, and because of its kinship to the frittata recipe that follows, it landed here.

The omelet is indeed nice, but its name comes from Nice, the city in Provence. In this part of France, omelets are made with olive oil, and they are often served cold at buffets and picnics, and warm for dinner.

I became fascinated with omelets at age ten. I'd make them every day after school in front of our bay window, pretending I was Julia Child and that the window was a live audience. Even then I most liked omelets with tomatoes in them. But only when I was sixteen, and came across a recipe for "Poor Man's Omelet," did I discover that an omelet could include croutons.

3 tablespoons olive oil
2 cups cubed French bread (I like 1-inch cubes)
1 garlic clove, minced
2 plum tomatoes, or 1 medium round tomato, chopped
3 eggs, lightly beaten
Salt and fresh-ground black pepper to taste
1 tablespoon chopped basil (optional)

**1.** In a well-seasoned or non-stick skillet or omelet pan, heat 2 tablespoons of the olive oil over medium heat. Add the cubes of bread, and cook them without stirring until they are golden on the bottom. Then toss them with a spatula, and let them brown on another side. Toss them again, and cook them until they have browned on at least three sides.

**2.** Add the garlic and the tomatoes, and cook for 2 minutes more, stirring. Then drizzle the remaining olive oil over everything, and pour the eggs into the pan, over the tomatoes and croutons. After 20 seconds or so the omelet will start to coagulate. Shake the pan gently so that the omelet comes loose from the pan. Then place a large plate over the pan, and hold the plate firmly in place while you invert the pan. Replace the empty pan over the heat, and slide the omelet from the plate back into the pan, cooked side up. Let the omelet cook about 1 minute more, until it is done to your liking. Then salt and pepper the omelet to your taste, slide it onto a plate (using a spatula, if necessary), and cut it in half. Serve the omelet hot, or chill it and serve it cold at a buffet or picnic. Garnish it with the basil, if you like, just before serving.

Serves 2

# Tomatillo Frittata

The successful marriage of tomatillos, tomatoes, and eggs happens without much effort in this straightforward frittata. Because the frittata is very flavorful, it's better for lunch or dinner than for breakfast, with slices of hearty bread that have been brushed with olive oil, then broiled until golden. Follow the cooking instructions carefully, because an overcooked frittata isn't worth feeding even to the birds.

1 tablespoon olive oil

1½ cups thinly sliced onions

8 small tomatillos, husked and sliced (about 1½ cups)

Salt and fresh-ground black pepper to taste

6 eggs, lightly beaten

2 small tomatoes, each cut into 8 wedges

2 ounces Ricotta Salata cheese, shaved or grated, or feta cheese, crumbled (about ½ cup)

**1.** Preheat the oven to 350°. Heat the oil in a 10-inch oven-proof non-stick skillet over medium heat. Add the onions, and cook them for 10 minutes, stirring occasionally, until they are lightly browned. Add the sliced tomatillos, and cook for 5 minutes more, stirring often. Season with salt and pepper.

**2.** Pour the eggs over the onions and tomatillos. Stir with a plastic spatula for 60 seconds. Let the eggs rest for a few seconds, then push the frittata toward one side of the pan so the uncooked egg runs underneath. When the frittata is still moist but no longer runny, place the tomato wedges on top, and sprinkle the cheese over all. Place the pan in the oven for 3 minutes or until the frittata is just set. Sprinkle it with salt and pepper, and serve it right away.

Serves 4

## Tomatillo-ville

*L*ooking like baby green tomatoes swaddled in their own green blankets, tomatillos are an unusual and tasty fruit. A member of the nightshade family but only distantly related to the tomato, tomatillos are curiously tart and can impart delicious flavor to many dishes. Just remove the husks, and purée the tomatillos in a blender with a splash of water. Add this purée to fresh and cooked salsas, pasta dishes and gazpachos, or even cook the purée down as you would a tomato sauce and use it on pizzas. Fresh tomatillos are available in many supermarket produce sections, and they also come parboiled in cans.

# CHAPTER 16

# Pizza Zone

# Pizza Dough

Don't be intimidated by the thought of making pizza dough. Making your own pizza crust is a lot easier than making most loaf breads, since pizza dough uses few ingredients and needs only one rising. Besides, pizza possibilities are too exciting to limit yourself to your local pizzeria's repertoire. Wonderful ingredients—such as wild mushrooms, goat cheese, fresh herbs, potatoes, and roasted garlic—are just waiting to sit atop your homemade pizza crust.

If you want to make just two individual pizzas, freeze the remainder of the dough for later use.

²/₃ cup lukewarm water
1 pinch sugar
1¹/₂ teaspoons dry yeast
1 tablespoon olive oil
2 cups unbleached white flour, plus a bit more,
    as needed
1 teaspoon salt

**1.** To make the dough by hand, stir together ⅓ cup water and the sugar in a large bowl. Sprinkle the yeast over this mixture, and let it stand until it is foamy, about 10 minutes. Stir in the remaining ⅓ cup water, the olive oil, the 2 cups flour, and the salt. Blend with a large spoon until the contents form a dough. Knead the dough on a floured surface, incorporating more flour, if necessary, to keep the dough from sticking. Knead the dough until it is smooth and elastic, about 5 to 10 minutes.

To make the dough in a food processor with a plastic dough blade or in a heavy-duty mixer, proof the yeast as described, but use a small bowl. Then combine the yeast mixture with the olive oil, 2 cups flour, and salt in the food processor or mixer. If you are using a food processor, run it until the mixture forms a ball, adding more water or flour by the tablespoon if the dough is too dry or wet. Process for 15 seconds more. If you are using a mixer, use the hook attachment, and mix the dough on the lowest speed until a ball is formed, adding a bit of water or flour as necessary. Knead the dough in the mixer for 5 minutes.

**2.** Put the dough into a deep, oiled bowl, and turn it to coat it with the oil. Let the dough rise, covered with plastic wrap, in a warm place for 1 hour or until it is doubled in bulk. Punch down the dough, and form it into four balls. Each will make a serving-size pizza.

Variations:

- Rosemary Crust—Mix ½ teaspoon chopped fresh rosemary into the flour before adding the flour to the yeast mixture.
- Semolina Crust—Substitute 1 cup semolina for 1 cup of the unbleached white flour, and mix the semolina and flour before adding them to the yeast mixture. This makes a crisp crust, which some people prefer to an all-flour crust.
- Cracked-Pepper Crust—Crack about 1½ teaspoons peppercorns with a rolling pin or in a mortar. Mix the cracked peppercorns into the flour before proceeding with the recipe.
- Whole-Wheat Crust—Substitute ⅔ cup whole-wheat flour for ⅔ cup of the unbleached white flour. Mix the two flours together before adding them to the yeast mixture.
- Cornmeal Crust (Mexican-inspired pizzas)—Substitute 1 cup cornmeal for 1 cup of the flour, and mix the flour and cornmeal together before adding them to the yeast mixture.

*Makes dough for 4 single-serving pizzas*

# Shiitake and Potato Pizzas

People who have just come back from Italy tell me about the wonderful pizzas they've had—pizza with fried eggs, pizza with whole olives, dessert pizzas, fish pizzas! Potato pizza is something I've heard a lot about. These individual potato pizzas with shiitakes are one of those dishes whose sum is greater than the parts.

2 Yellow Finn or red new potatoes, cut in half
2 tablespoons olive oil
2 cups sliced onions
2 garlic cloves, minced
2 cups sliced shiitake mushroom caps (discard the stems)
Salt and fresh-ground black pepper to taste
1/2 batch (2 balls) Pizza Dough (page 443)
1 tablespoon cornmeal
1/4 cup grated Parmesan cheese
1 tablespoon chopped oregano

**1.** Bring a pot of salted water to a boil. Add the potatoes, and cook them until they are just tender (check them often; they must not overcook, or they will break into pieces). Drain them and let them cool.

**2.** Meanwhile, heat the oil in a large skillet over medium heat, and add the onions. Cook them, stirring occasionally, for 5 minutes. Add the garlic and the mushrooms, and cook, stirring frequently, for 10 minutes. Season with salt and pepper. Then slice the cooked potatoes into thin oval rounds.

**3.** Preheat the oven to 450°. On a floured surface, roll out one ball of dough to a round about 8 inches in diameter. Sprinkle a baking sheet with the cornmeal, and place the round on the baking sheet. Roll out the second ball, and place the round on the baking sheet (or on another one, if necessary). Place the potato slices on top of the two rounds. Top the potatoes with the shiitake-onion mixture.

**4.** Bake the pizzas for 10 minutes, or until the crust is firm. Sprinkle them with the Parmesan cheese and oregano, cut them into quarters, and serve.

Variation: Instead of the oregano, a tablespoon of truffle oil drizzled over the finished pizza is sublime.

Makes 2 pizzas
(serves 2)

## Make Your Own Shiitake Oil

*My friend Tom Tenuta came up with this way to flavor oil with shiitake mushrooms: Soak 2 ounces dried shiitake caps (about 2 cups) in hot water for 1 hour. Strain the shiitakes, pat them dry, slice them, and transfer them to a pan. Add 3 cups vegetable oil, and heat the mixture until it is warm to the touch. Pour the oil and mushrooms into a glass or plastic container. Let the oil stand uncovered for 2 hours, then cover it and chill it for at least 24 hours. It keeps for up to one month, refrigerated.*

*Try the oil drizzled on pasta or pizza, or add it to cooked grains or seared greens. The aroma is intoxicating.*

# Goat Cheese Pizzas with Tomato Confit

The tomatoes on this pizza are confit—"preserved"—with vinegar and sugar, and the result is intense tomato flavor. The fried shallots, a popular Vietnamese garnish on salads and soups, suit the sweet tomato confit and add texture to every bite. Don't worry that the 3 tablespoons oil will make for a greasy pizza; the oil is used to crisp the shallots, and most of it remains in the pan.

3 tablespoons peanut, canola, or corn oil
1 cup sliced shallots
Salt and fresh-ground black pepper to taste
1 tablespoon butter
2½ cups chopped plum tomatoes
1 tablespoon sugar
3 tablespoons red wine vinegar
½ teaspoon dried thyme
2 garlic cloves, minced
½ batch (2 balls) Pizza Dough (page 443)
1 tablespoon cornmeal
¼ cup soft, mild chèvre (goat cheese) or
    crumbled feta cheese

**1.** In a small skillet, heat the oil over medium-high heat. When it is quite hot, add the shallots. Let them fry until they are crispy and brown, but not burnt. (Remove a few slices to paper towels to test whether they are crispy.) Remove the shallots with a slotted spoon onto paper towels. Season them with salt and pepper.

**2.** In a large, heavy pot over medium heat, melt the butter. As it begins to brown, add the tomatoes and the sugar. Cook the tomatoes for 10 to 15 minutes, stirring frequently, until most of the liquid is gone. Add the red wine vinegar, thyme, and gar-

## Dried Fig Pizza

*At a Boston restaurant called Figs, my favorite pizza is the fig pizza. It's topped with a bit of Gorgonzola cheese and fig jam made from dried figs and balsamic vinegar, then sprinkled with shredded scallion and olive oil. The pizza is absolutely delicious.*

*Available all year, dried figs are intensely flavorful. The main commercial varieties are Black Mission, which are purple-black on the outside and reddish on the inside, and Calimyrna, tan on the outside with a succulent brown interior. Dried figs contain high levels of calcium and fiber. Some are treated with sulfites, so be sure to check the label if you or a family member is allergic to these chemicals.*

lic. Simmer the confit, uncovered, for 15 minutes or until it has thickened considerably, gently stirring it occasionally during the cooking. Season with salt and pepper, and take it off the heat.

**3.** Preheat the oven to 450°. Roll out each ball of dough on a floured surface to a round about 8 inches in diameter. Transfer both rounds to a baking sheet sprinkled with the cornmeal (you may need two baking sheets, depending on their size). Bake the pizzas without topping for 4 minutes; do not let them brown.

**4.** Remove the baking sheet(s) from the oven. If the pizza rounds have inflated, poke them with a knife. Spread the tomato confit onto the two rounds. Dot the pizzas with the goat cheese or feta cheese. Return the rounds to the oven for 5 minutes more. Remove the pizzas from the oven, and top them with the shallots. Cut the pizzas into quarters, and serve.

Makes 2 pizzas
(serves 2)

# White Pizzas

I'll never forget my first white pizza. I had it on the Upper West Side of Manhattan at a cheap pizza shop. My friend David took me there, and when he ordered a slice of white pizza I did the same. The pizza was absolutely fabulous: soft, white ricotta cheese, laced with garlic and herbs and dotted with droplets of olive oil, on a tender crust. I came home to Boston hoping to discover pizza shops that made white pizza, but to no avail. I was ready to disrupt my life and move to New York City for white pizza until I thought about how much I would miss the Cuban milkshakes at my neighborhood sub shop. I decided to stay put.

2 tablespoons olive oil
2 cups sliced onions
3 large garlic cloves, minced
1 teaspoon chopped fresh rosemary, or
    1/2 teaspoon dried rosemary
Salt and fresh-ground black pepper to taste
2 cups ricotta cheese, whole-milk or part-skim
1/3 cup grated Parmesan cheese
1 batch (4 balls) Pizza Dough (page 443)
2 tablespoons cornmeal

**1.** Heat the oil in a large skillet over medium heat. Add the onions, garlic, and rosemary, and cook them, stirring frequently, for 5 to 7 minutes, until the onions soften. (Do not brown the onions, unless you want to call the pizza a brown pizza.) Add salt and pepper. Set the skillet aside.

**2.** Mix together the ricotta and Parmesan cheeses in a small bowl. Set the bowl aside.

**3.** Preheat the oven to 450°. On a floured surface, roll one ball of pizza dough to a round about 8 inches in diameter. Place the round on a baking sheet that has been sprinkled with the cornmeal. Roll out the other three balls of dough. Lay one on the baking sheet with the first round, and two on a second cornmeal-sprinkled baking sheet.

**4.** Evenly distribute the onion mixture over all four pizzas. Then drop the ricotta mixture by the teaspoonful evenly onto the pizzas. Bake the pizzas for about 10 minutes, rotating the baking sheets between the lower and higher racks about 5 minutes into the cooking. The pizzas are done when they are firm on the bottom.

Variations: Add steamed spinach, seared zucchini, pan-fried mushrooms, roasted eggplant, artichoke hearts, or other vegetables. Spread the vegetables on the pizza 5 minutes before the baking is done, when you rotate the pans.

Makes 4 pizzas (serves 4)

# Fennel Pizzas
# with White-Bean Purée

This recipe is dedicated to my parents. Since my father underwent open-heart surgery last year, my parents have altered their diets. They no longer eat red meat or poultry six days a week, and they have reduced their fat consumption considerably. This pizza has only a scant amount of saturated fat but contains a good amount of protein. Aside from the health benefits, fennel is my mother's favorite vegetable.

1 large fennel bulb
4 tablespoons olive oil (1 tablespoon should be
    extra-virgin, for drizzling on top of the
    pizza)
2 to 3 garlic cloves, minced
Salt and fresh-ground black pepper to taste
1½ cups (1 15-ounce can) cooked and drained
    white beans
1 tablespoon cornmeal
½ batch (2 balls) Pizza Dough (page 443)
¼ cup grated Asiago cheese (optional)

**1.** Preheat the oven to 400°. Trim the fennel stalks, leaving only an inch or two. Split the fennel bulb in half, and cut out the small, hard core. Slice the fennel thin, and put it into a bowl. Add 2 tablespoons of the olive oil, the garlic, and the salt and pepper. Toss well, and put the fennel slices into a roasting pan. Roast the fennel for about 10 minutes, until it is tender. Keep the oven on.

**2.** Meanwhile, put the white beans into a food processor with salt, pepper, 1 tablespoon of the olive oil, and 2 tablespoons water. Blend the mixture, but not to a purée; it should have some texture.

**3.** On a floured surface, roll each ball of dough to a circle about 8 inches in diameter. Place both circles on a baking sheet sprinkled with the cornmeal (you may need two baking sheets, depending on their size).

**4.** Turn the oven to 450°. With a plastic spatula, spread the bean purée on the two pieces of pizza dough. Distribute the fennel on top of the purée. Bake the pizzas in the lower third of the oven for 10 minutes or until the crust is firm. Cut the pizzas into quarters, drizzle them with the remaining 1 tablespoon olive oil (I like to use extra-virgin), and sprinkle them with the grated Asiago, if you like. Serve the pizzas hot.

Makes 2 pizzas (serves 2)

# Curried Onion and Spinach Pizzas

C urry on pizza? Believe me, curry and pizza together taste as if they were made for each other. This shouldn't be surprising, since a pizza crust is not unlike an Indian flatbread.

For the topping on this pizza, onions are caramelized with spices in olive oil; the spinach is added at the last minute. The pizza is sprinkled with mozzarella cheese, cashews, and cilantro. I usually save some of this tasty pizza for the next day's lunch—it's great eaten cold right from the fridge.

1 tablespoon olive oil

2 cups sliced onions

1½ teaspoons curry powder, store-bought or homemade (page 36)

½ teaspoon fennel seeds

1 garlic clove, minced

5 cups packed spinach leaves, large stems removed

Salt and fresh-ground black pepper

## Pizza Pit Stop

❀

*Do you want to make pizza top-pings but not the dough? Your wish can be granted if you buy ready-made dough from a pizzeria. Many pizzerias (and even supermarkets) will sell pizza dough in 1- to 2-pound bags, at a very good price. Buy a good quantity of dough, and divide it, using a sharp chef's knife, into 5- to 6-ounce pieces (each large enough for a personal pizza). Then put each piece of dough into a small plastic bag, and freeze it. When you want to make pizza, thaw the bag or bags of dough for 1 to 2 hours at room temperature, until the dough is soft. Pizza making will now be a snap—all you need to worry about is what goes on top.*

½ batch (2 balls) Pizza Dough (page 443)
1 tablespoon cornmeal
½ to 1 cup grated mozzarella cheese
2 tablespoons chopped cashews
1 tablespoon chopped cilantro

**1.** Heat the oil in a large, heavy skillet over medium heat, and add the onions. Cook the onions for 10 minutes, stirring occasionally, until they are light brown. Add the curry powder, fennel, and garlic, and cook, stirring, for 1 minute.

**2.** Add the spinach and 1 tablespoon water, and stir until the spinach wilts. Season well with salt and pepper.

**3.** Preheat the oven to 450°. On a floured surface, roll each ball of dough to a round about 8 inches in diameter, and place both rounds on a baking sheet sprinkled with the cornmeal (you may need two baking sheets, depending on their size). Spoon the onion-spinach mixture onto the two pizzas.

**4.** Bake the pizzas in the bottom third of the oven for 5 minutes. Remove them, then sprinkle on the mozzarella and the cashews. Cook the pizza for 3 minutes more. Top each pizza with cilantro, cut it into quarters, and serve.

Makes 2 pizzas
(serves 2)

# Summer Squash and Herbed Ricotta Pizzas

Roasted summer squash is exquisite on a pizza. The crisp, chewy pizza crust really shows off the subtle flavor and texture of the soft, sweet squash. Here a rich layer of herbed ricotta cheese lies between the two, and a nest of thinly sliced, browned onions sits on the very top.

1 medium to large summer squash
2 tablespoons olive oil
Salt and fresh-ground black pepper
2 cups sliced onions
1 garlic clove, minced
½ cup ricotta cheese, whole-milk or part-skim
3 tablespoons chopped basil or cilantro
½ batch (2 balls) Pizza Dough (page 443)
1 tablespoon cornmeal

**1.** Preheat the oven to 400°. Slice the squash into ¼-inch-thick rounds. Place them on a baking sheet, drizzle 1 tablespoon of the olive oil over them, and sprinkle them with salt and pepper. Bake them for 15 minutes or until they are tender and just beginning to brown at the edges. Leave the oven on.

**2.** Heat the remaining 1 tablespoon olive oil in a large skillet over medium heat. Add the onions, and cook them, stirring occasionally, for 10 minutes or until they begin to brown. Then add the garlic, and stir for 1 minute. Take the skillet off the heat, and season the onions with salt and pepper.

**3.** In a bowl, combine the ricotta cheese and the basil or cilantro. Season with salt and pepper, and stir well.

**4.** Raise the oven temperature to 450°. On a floured surface, roll out each ball of dough to a round 8 inches in diameter. Transfer both rounds to a baking sheet sprinkled with the cornmeal (you may need two baking sheets, depending on their size). With a spoon, spread the ricotta cheese onto the dough, leaving a bit of a bare border. Lay the summer squash over the ricotta cheese, and form a small nest of onions in the middle of the pizza. Bake the pizza for 10 minutes or until the crust begins to turn golden around the edge. Cut the pizzas into quarters, and serve.

Variation: If you are watching your fat intake, you can omit the ricotta cheese. Toss the herbs onto the pizza once it has been cooked, and sprinkle on a tablespoon or two of grated Parmesan or Asiago cheese as well.

Makes 2 pizzas (serves 2)

## Gold Star for Butternut Squash

*Butternut squash has three out-standing virtues. It is rich in vitamins and minerals, especially vitamin A, riboflavin, and potassium. It has a long shelf life; un-cut, it can keep for up to five months after harvest in a cool place. Best of all, but-ternut squash has a sweet, buttery flavor, richer and sweeter than that of most win-ter squashes.*

*Try butternut squash roasted: Peel it, seed it, and cut it into smaller pieces. Toss it with some minced garlic, salt and pepper, and a few tablespoons olive oil. Roast the squash in a 400° oven until the pieces are tender (about 20 minutes).*

# Butternut Squash Pizzas with Rosemary

I had the best lunch of my life at the Chez Panisse Cafe in Berkeley a few years ago. As soon as I tasted the butternut squash, sage, and Asiago pizza, I went into a euphoric state that lasted for hours. The flavors were so true, so vivid that it seemed the ingredients had been created just to be on a pizza together. Here is my version of that great pizza.

1 cup sliced onion
½ butternut squash, peeled, seeded, and sliced
    very thin
1 teaspoon chopped fresh rosemary (or sage),
    or ½ teaspoon dried rosemary (or sage)
Salt and fresh-ground black pepper to taste
3 tablespoons olive oil
½ batch (2 balls) Pizza Dough (page 443)
1 tablespoon cornmeal
2 tablespoons grated Asiago or Parmesan cheese

**1.** Preheat the oven to 400°. Place the onion and the squash in a roasting pan. Add the rosemary (or sage), the salt and pepper, and 2 tablespoons of the olive oil. Toss well. Bake the vegetables for 20 minutes or until the onions are browning and the squash is tender.

**2.** Increase the oven temperature to 450°. On a floured surface, roll each ball of dough into an 8-inch round. Place the rounds on a baking sheet sprinkled with the cornmeal (you may need two baking sheets, depending on their size). Distribute the squash mixture over the two rounds. Bake the pizzas for 10 minutes or until the crust is firm.

**3.** Sprinkle the pizzas with the cheese, and drizzle them with the remaining olive oil. Cut each pizza into quarters, and serve.

Makes 2 pizzas (serves 2)

# Poblano and Jack Cheese Pizzas

The poblano chiles in these pizzas pack a punch. If you haven't much heat tolerance, substitute Anaheim chiles for the poblanos or use only one poblano instead of two. The roasted corn contributes an enticing crunch to this pizza, and chopped cilantro provides a classic Mexican flavor.

2 poblano peppers
1 ear corn, shucked
½ batch (2 balls) Pizza Dough or the Cornmeal
    Crust variation (page 443)
1 tablespoon cornmeal
1 tomato, sliced thin
Salt and fresh-ground black pepper to taste
3 ounces grated Monterey Jack cheese (about
    3/4 cup)
1 tablespoon extra-virgin olive oil
2 tablespoons chopped cilantro

**1.** Preheat the oven to 400°. Roast the peppers in a roasting pan for 25 minutes. Add the ear of corn to the roasting pan, and roast the vegetables for 10 minutes more. Leave the oven on.

**2.** Let the peppers and corn cool for 10 minutes. When the peppers are cool enough to handle, remove their skins and seeds. Then slice the peppers into thin strips. Cut the corn kernel from the ear.

**3.** Increase the oven temperature to 450°. On a floured surface, roll each ball of dough into a round about 8 inches in diameter. Place both rounds on a baking sheet sprinkled with the cornmeal (you may need two baking sheets, depending on their size). Sprinkle the corn over the rounds, then lay the tomato slices over the corn. Distribute the poblano strips over all. Salt and pepper the pizzas.

**4.** Bake the pizzas for 8 minutes, then remove them from the oven. Sprinkle the Monterey Jack cheese over the pizzas, and bake an additional 2 minutes or until the cheese is melted. Drizzle the olive oil over the two pizzas, and garnish with cilantro. Cut the pizzas into quarters, and serve.

Makes 2 pizzas
(serves 2)

# Calzones with Mushroom Pesto

For this dish, mushrooms are chopped fine, then sautéed with garlic, olive oil, walnuts, and herbs. This "pesto" is tucked into calzones with a bit of goat cheese or ricotta.

The mushroom pesto is also excellent with pasta, such as radiatore or fusilli. Just add 3 tablespoons water and 2 tablespoons more olive oil to the pesto (omit the goat cheese). Toss the pesto with hot cooked pasta (you'll need 1 pound dry pasta), and sprinkle with grated Parmesan cheese.

2 medium portobello mushrooms (about
⅓ pound)
10 ounces white button mushrooms
3 to 4 large garlic cloves
2 tablespoons olive oil
2 tablespoons chopped parsley, or 1 tablespoon
chopped oregano, thyme, or sage
¼ cup chopped walnuts, lightly toasted
½ teaspoon salt
Fresh-ground black pepper to taste
1 batch (4 balls) Pizza Dough (page 443)
2 tablespoons cornmeal
½ cup soft, mild chèvre (goat cheese) or
ricotta cheese

**1.** Cut off and discard the dirt-laden base of each portobello stem. Chop the mushrooms and garlic fine in a food processor, in two batches, if necessary; do not blend them to a purée. Or use a knife to mince them very fine. In a large, heavy skillet, heat the oil over medium heat. Add the mushrooms and garlic. With a wooden spoon, stir in the chopped parsley, oregano, thyme, or sage, and cook for 10 minutes, stirring frequently. Add the walnuts, salt, and pepper.

**2.** Preheat the oven to 450°. On a floured surface, roll each ball of dough into a round about 8 inches in diameter. Sprinkle two baking sheets with the cornmeal. Place the four rounds of dough on the two baking sheets, and put ¼ of the mushroom mixture in the center of each round. Sprinkle the goat cheese or ricotta cheese over the mushrooms. Moisten the edge of each round with water, and fold the calzone over. Squeeze the edges tightly together with your fingers.

**3.** Bake the calzones for about 15 minutes, or until they are golden brown on the outside. Serve them hot.

Makes 4 calzones (serves 4)

# Tomato and Grated Zucchini Calzones

Grated zucchini is flash-sautéed over high heat, tomatoes are squeezed of their excess juice, and then the vegetables are combined with Parmesan cheese and basil to form a refreshing and fast filling for these calzones. Use a smallish zucchini in this recipe; large ones are too seedy and watery.

I suggest serving these calzones with a green salad dressed with Caramelized Balsamic Vinaigrette (page 158). A little caramelized dressing drizzled over the calzone is both pretty and delicious, too.

2 tablespoons olive oil
1 1/2 cups sliced onions
1 small zucchini, grated (about 2 cups)
1 garlic clove, minced
1/4 cup grated Parmesan cheese
Salt and fresh-ground black pepper to taste
2 medium tomatoes
1/2 batch (2 balls) Pizza Dough (page 443)
1/4 cup chopped basil leaves
1 tablespoon cornmeal

**1.** In a large skillet (preferably non-stick), heat 1 tablespoon olive oil over medium-high heat. Add the onions, and cook them for 5 minutes or until they soften, stirring occasionally. Transfer the onions to a plate.

**2.** Place the skillet over high heat, and add the remaining 1 tablespoon olive oil. When the oil is very hot (but before it begins to smoke), add the grated zucchini and the garlic. Stir frequently, making sure the zucchini does not burn. After 2 minutes, take the skillet off the heat, and add the Parmesan cheese, salt, and pepper.

**3.** Cut the tomatoes in half crosswise, and squeeze out the excess juice and most of the seeds. Chop the tomatoes, put them into a bowl, and season them well with salt and pepper.

**4.** Preheat the oven to 450°. On a floured work surface, roll out each ball of dough to an 8-inch round. Put half of the tomatoes, then the zucchini, into the middle of one round. Sprinkle with half of the chopped basil. Fill the second round of dough the same way. Moisten the edge of each round with water, and fold the calzone over, pressing with your fingers to seal the calzone tight. Place the calzones on a baking sheet sprinkled with the cornmeal.

**5.** Bake the calzones for 15 minutes, or until they are golden brown. Serve them hot.

Makes 2 calzones (serves 2)

# Tomato, Swiss Chard, and Ricotta Calzones

Swiss chard is a good source of vitamins A and C and iron. For this calzone you can use either green chard or the slightly stronger-flavored red.

2 tablespoons olive oil
2 cups sliced red onions
2 large garlic cloves, minced
3 plum tomatoes, chopped
1 bunch Swiss chard, leaves chopped, stems diced
3/4 cup ricotta cheese
1/2 teaspoon salt
Fresh-ground black pepper to taste
1 batch (4 balls) Pizza Dough (page 443)
2 tablespoons cornmeal

**1.** Heat the olive oil in a large skillet over medium heat. Add the red onions, and cook them, stirring occasionally, for 5 minutes. Add the garlic and the tomatoes. Cook for 5 minutes more, stirring frequently. Add the Swiss chard, and cook, stirring frequently, for 6 to 8 minutes or until the chard is tender. Drain off any remaining liquid. Add the ricotta cheese, and season the mixture well with salt and pepper.

**2.** Preheat the oven to 450°. On a floured surface, roll each ball of dough into an 8-inch round. Sprinkle two baking sheets with the cornmeal. Place two rounds of dough on each baking sheet. Put a portion of the vegetable compote in the center of each round. Moisten the edge of each round with a bit of water, and fold the round in half. Squeeze the edges tightly together with your fingers.

**3.** Bake the calzones for about 15 minutes, or until they are golden brown on the outside. Serve them hot.

Makes 4 calzones (serves 4)

## Swiss Chard

Both white and red chard are growing in popularity, thanks to their likable flavor and their nutritional value. Available from spring through fall, chard is a good source of vitamins A and C and iron.

Some chefs remove the large central stems of chard leaves and braise the stems as a side dish, using the leaves separately. If you want to cook the stems with the leaves, choose young, thin-stemmed chard. Or dice the stems and ribs fine, and braise or pan-fry them along with the leaves.

Chard makes a good substitute for spinach in many dishes. Try chard in minestrone-style soups. I love it as a side dish, simply seared with some sesame oil, sesame seeds, and a touch of soy sauce.

# CHAPTER 17

# Big Chilis & Hot Stews

# Chili Verde

This terrific recipe is from my friend Jeff. A chef by trade, Jeff is very opinionated about chile peppers. I have heard him say that if he were president he would try to make it illegal for any bowl of chili to contain less than 25 percent fresh chiles. A lot of people would be locked up (or paying for their crimes by working on chile farms), because many chili recipes call for chile powder but no fresh chiles at all.

1 pound dried navy beans
6 Anaheim peppers
4 poblano peppers
3 to 4 jalapeño peppers
2 tablespoons olive oil
2 medium white onions, chopped fine
4 garlic cloves, minced
1 tablespoon ground cumin seeds
1 tablespoon ground coriander seeds
2 pounds tomatillos, husked and chopped
Kernels from 3 ears corn (about 2 cups)
1 red bell pepper, seeded and chopped fine
1/4 cup hulled, unsalted pumpkin seeds, chopped
2 tablespoons tequila (optional)
Juice of 1 lime
1 1/2 teaspoons salt
Fresh-ground black pepper to taste
1/2 cup chopped cilantro
2 tablespoons sour cream

**1.** Soak the beans overnight, or use the quick-soak method: Boil the beans in plenty of water for 5 minutes. Remove the pan from the heat, and let the beans soak for 1 hour.

**2.** Drain the soaked beans, and rinse them well with cold water.

**3.** Char the chile peppers (all three varieties) over a low flame, using tongs to rotate them so they char evenly. (If you do not have a gas stove, roast the peppers in a 450° oven for 15 minutes or until the skins are blistering.) Let the peppers cool, then remove their skins, and chop the flesh into small pieces. Reserve the seeds from the poblanos and jalapeños if you like a spicy chili.

**4.** In a large pot, heat the oil over medium heat, and add the onions and garlic. Cook them for 5 minutes, stirring occasionally. Add the cumin and coriander, and cook for 2 minutes more. Add the rinsed beans and 2 quarts water. Bring the chili to a boil, turn down the heat, and simmer the chili for 1½ hours, stirring every now and then and adding a little water periodically to keep the beans covered.

**5.** When the beans are almost soft, stir in the chopped roasted peppers (including the jalapeño seeds, if you like), the tomatillos, the corn, and the red bell pepper. Simmer for 30 minutes more. Then add the pumpkin seeds, tequila (if you're using it), lime juice, salt, pepper, and cilantro. Serve the chili in bowls, each garnished with a dollop of sour cream.

The leftover chili will keep well for 4 to 5 days in a tightly sealed container in the refrigerator; it also freezes well.

**Variation:** A tasty addition to this chili is 2 cups cooked hominy. Add it with the tequila, lime juice, and cilantro, and cook just until the hominy is heated through.

*Serves 4*

# Three-Chile Chili

This chili will bring out the chile lover in you. To take it full throttle, use the maximum amounts of chiles called for in the recipe, or play it safe by staying near the minimums. Either way, the chiles will impart their complex flavor and fragrance to this melange of tomato, zucchini, and rice.

3 tablespoons canola or corn oil

3 cups chopped onions

2 poblano peppers, chopped

2 red bell peppers, seeded and chopped

4 garlic cloves, minced

1/2 to 2 teaspoons ground chiltepin peppers or chile flakes

2 teaspoons ground cumin or whole cumin seeds

1/2 to 1 habanero or Scotch bonnet pepper, minced (reserve the seeds)

1 1/2 cups uncooked white or brown long-grain rice

3 cups chopped fresh or canned plum tomatoes

1 medium zucchini, cut into small pieces

Kernels from 3 ears corn (about 2 cups)

1 3/4 cups (1 15-ounce can) cooked kidney beans, rinsed and drained

1 teaspoon salt, or more, to taste

Fresh-ground black pepper to taste

2 tablespoons sour cream

**1.** In a large pot, heat the oil over medium heat. Add the onions and the chopped peppers. Cook for 10 minutes, stirring occasionally. Add the garlic, ground chile peppers or chile flakes, cumin, and the habanero or Scotch bonnet pepper. Cook, stirring frequently, for 5 minutes. Add the rice, and stir to coat the rice with the oil and spices.

**2.** Add the tomatoes and 5 cups water. Bring the mixture to a boil, then cover the pot, and turn the heat to low. If you are using white rice, simmer the chili for 20 minutes; if you are using brown rice, simmer for 35 minutes.

**3.** Uncover the chili, and add the zucchini, corn, and beans. Stir well, and cook the chili 10 minutes more or until the zucchini and rice are tender.

**4.** Season the chili with salt and pepper. If you'd like more heat, add some of the reserved habanero seeds. Serve the chili in large bowls with dollops of sour cream.

Serves 6

# Tomato and Lentil Chili

Inspired by 1950s-style beef chili in which the gravy is thickened with flour, this is one of the few chilis I know that you can start making at six in the evening to eat at seven. For a real treat, make this chili with the small, jewel-like French lentils (also called *lentilles du Puy*); they are sold in specialty food stores and some whole-foods markets.

1/2 cup butter or canola or corn oil
4 cups chopped onions
6 garlic cloves, minced
1 tablespoon ground cumin seeds
1/4 cup chili powder
1/2 teaspoon ground cinnamon
1/2 teaspoon chile flakes
1/2 cup unbleached white flour
4 1/2 to 5 cups water or Roasted Vegetable Stock
     (page 80)
2 carrots, chopped into 1/2-inch cubes
2 green bell peppers or poblano peppers, seeded
     and cut into 1/2-inch squares
3 1/2 cups (1 28-ounce can) peeled plum
     tomatoes
3 ripe medium tomatoes, chopped
3 cups dried brown or French lentils
1 to 2 chipotle peppers, dried and soaked in hot
     water 30 minutes, or canned in adobo sauce
     (optional)
1 cup light-colored beer
1 to 1 1/2 teaspoons salt
1/2 teaspoon fresh-ground black pepper
1/4 cup chopped cilantro
1/2 cup sour cream (optional)

**1.** In a large, heavy saucepan, melt the butter or the oil over medium heat. Add the onions, and cook them for 5 minutes. Add the garlic, cumin, chili powder, cinnamon, and chile flakes. Cook 2 minutes more.

**2.** Add the flour, and cook the mixture for 5 minutes, stirring frequently. Slowly whisk in 2 cups of the water or stock. Whisk until you have a smooth, thick gravy, then add 2½ cups more liquid, and whisk again. Add the carrots and the peppers. Then add the canned tomatoes, squeezing them one by one before dropping them into the chili, so that they are somewhat crushed. Add the fresh tomatoes, the lentils, the chipotles (if you're using them), and the beer. Add the salt and pepper. Turn the heat to high, and when the chili starts to boil, turn down the heat. Simmer the chile for 40 minutes, stirring occasionally, until the lentils are tender.

# Vegetarian Chili—an Oxymoron?

Some Texans would say that a true bowl of red consists of beef, chiles, spices, and not much else. No bell peppers, no tomatoes, and definitely no beans. But other Texans have broken these rules, and have won many competitions with their unconventional chilis. Still, the idea of a vegetarian chili has been rather daunting to me. Leaving meat out of chili seems a little like using tofu instead of turkey for Thanksgiving. But I do believe chili can transcend its meat-laden history. "The meat is the medium, but the chile is the message," write Cheryl and Bill Jamison in *Texas Home Cooking.* So I've just changed the medium; the message is at least as strong as ever.

Chile aficionados know that chile peppers offer more than just heat. Each chile variety has its own unique flavor, and this flavor varies depending on whether the chile is green or ripe, fresh or dried. In the recipe for Three-Chile Chili (page 462), fresh peppers provide a lovely fragrance and flavor; using only chili powder would bring the dish down a few notches. Combining different chile varieties also adds to the excitement of this dish. Another way to ensure a richly flavored chili is to grind dried ancho or New Mexican chile pods instead of using packaged chili powder. So base your chili on plenty of good fresh or dried chile peppers, and no one will ask, "Where's the meat?"

**3.** Take the pan of chili off the heat. Fish out the chipotle peppers (if you've used them), chop them, and return them to the pan. Add the cilantro. If the chili seems too thick, thin it with a little water. Spoon the chili into bowls, dollop sour cream on top, and serve.

Serves 8

# White-Bean Chili with Scarlet Salsa

On its own, White-Bean Chili is a very simple and unassuming dish. But add the Scarlet Salsa, and you have a spicy, fiery meal. I serve this chili with hot Ten-Minute Cornbread (page 18).

**WHITE-BEAN CHILI:**
2 cups dried Great Northern or navy beans
1½ tablespoons olive oil
2 cups chopped onions
6 garlic cloves, minced
6 cups chopped green cabbage
2 teaspoons chopped fresh oregano, or 1 teaspoon
    dried oregano
1 russet potato, peeled and cut into ½-inch cubes
½ medium rutabaga, peeled and cut into ½-inch
    cubes (about 4 cups)
1 teaspoon salt, or more, to taste
Fresh-ground black pepper to taste

**SCARLET SALSA:**
1 ancho pepper
1 chipotle pepper in adobo sauce, minced
½ red bell pepper, seeded and chopped fine
½ red onion, chopped fine

1 tablespoon olive oil
¼ cup lime juice (from about 2 limes)
⅓ cup chopped cilantro
Salt to taste

·■·■·■·■·■·

**1.** Soak the beans overnight in cold water, or use the quick-soak method: Bring the beans to a boil in a large saucepan. Remove the pan from the heat, and let the beans soak for 1 hour. Drain the soaked beans, and rinse them well with cold water.

**2.** In a large pot, cover the drained beans with plenty of water, and bring the water to a boil. Cook the beans at a gentle boil: for Great Northern beans, for 2 to 2½ hours, or until they are tender; for navy beans, for 1 to 1½ hours, or until they are tender. Drain the beans, reserving 3 cups of the cooking liquid (if less than 3 cups liquid remain, add water to the reserved liquid to bring the total to 3 cups).

**3.** In a large, heavy pot, heat the olive oil over medium heat. Add the onions, and sauté them for 5 minutes, stirring occasionally, until they soften. Add the garlic and cabbage. Turn the heat to low, and cook for 5 more minutes, stirring occasionally.

**4.** Add to the pot the 3 cups reserved bean liquid (or water), the oregano, the potato, the rutabaga, and the salt. Cook for 25 minutes over medium heat, or until all the vegetables are tender. Add the beans, and mix well. Add the black pepper and, if you like, more salt.

**5.** Make the salsa while the chili cooks: Using tongs, place the ancho pepper over a medium flame or in a dry skillet. Turn the chile often to char it evenly. Let the chile cool, then chop it well, discarding most of the seeds. Place the chopped chile in a bowl and mix it with the remaining ingredients, including salt to taste.

**6.** Serve the chili in large bowls, with a spoonful of the salsa on top of each serving.

Serves 4 to 6

# Sweet-Potato
# and
# Barley Chili

If you don't much like beans or lentils, this is the chili for you. Boniatos are white-fleshed sweet potatoes; they are less sweet and somewhat drier than orange sweet potatoes. Now grown in Florida as well as Central America, boniatos are sold in Latin American markets and some supermarkets, as are chipotle peppers. If you can't find boniatos, orange sweet potatoes will do fine.

1/2 cup dried pearled or hulled barley
2 tablespoons olive oil
2 cups chopped onions
5 garlic cloves, minced
1 1/2 teaspoons cumin seeds
1 tablespoon chili powder
2 cups (about 12) chopped husked tomatillos
2 green bell peppers, seeded and cut into
    1/2-inch squares
1 large boniato or 2 small sweet potatoes
    (about 1 1/4 pounds), peeled and cut into
    1/2-inch cubes
3 cups water or Basic Vegetable Stock
    (page 79)
1 teaspoon salt
1 to 2 chipotle peppers, dried or canned in
    adobo sauce
Fresh-ground black pepper to taste
4 tablespoons sour cream (optional)

**1.** Bring the barley and 1½ cups lightly salted water to a boil. Reduce the heat, and simmer the barley, covered, for 1 hour. Drain the barley, if any water remains.

**2.** In a large saucepan, heat the olive oil over medium-high heat. Cook the onions, stirring occasionally, for 10 minutes or until they brown at the edges. Add the garlic, cumin, and chili powder. Cook for 3 minutes more, stirring frequently.

**3.** Add the tomatillos, bell peppers, boniato or sweet potatoes, water or stock, and salt. Chop the chipotle pepper(s) if they are canned; keep them whole if they are dried. Add them to the chili. Let the chili simmer for 25 minutes, or until the vegetables are tender.

**4.** Remove the chipotle(s) if they were dried. Seed them, chop them fine, and return them to the chili (add the seeds if you want more heat). Add the black pepper and the barley. Stir well, taste, and adjust the seasonings. Serve the chili in bowls, with dollops of sour cream on top, if you like.

Serves 4

# Indonesian Bean-Curd Stew

Coconut milk, ginger, and coriander provide the prominent flavors in this fragrant stew, chockablock full of tofu, green beans, zucchini, and carrots. (Other vegetables will work as well; try substituting mushrooms, eggplant, okra, peppers, or even spinach for any of the vegetables.) Serve the stew over basmati rice or quinoa, or alone in big bowls as you would chili.

2 tablespoons lime juice (from about 1 lime)
2 teaspoons minced fresh ginger
1 teaspoon salt, or more, to taste
8 ounces tofu, cut into ½-inch cubes
1 tablespoon canola or corn oil
2 cups chopped onions

1 large garlic clove, minced
1 teaspoon ground coriander seeds
$\frac{1}{2}$ teaspoon ground cumin seeds
$\frac{1}{4}$ teaspoon ground cloves
1 cup coconut milk (you can freeze any left in
    the can for later use)
2 cups water or Basic Vegetable Stock (page 79)
3 small carrots, peeled and cut into $\frac{1}{4}$-inch
    rounds
$\frac{1}{4}$ teaspoon chile flakes
$1\frac{1}{2}$ cups 1-inch-long pieces green beans
1 small zucchini, cut into $\frac{1}{2}$-inch cubes
2 tablespoons chopped cilantro (optional)
Fresh-ground black pepper to taste

**1.** Marinate the tofu: In a bowl, combine the lime juice, fresh ginger, and $\frac{1}{2}$ teaspoon salt. Stir, and add the chopped tofu. Leave the tofu in the marinade for 30 minutes, tossing it once or twice.

**2.** Heat the oil in a large skillet over medium heat. Add the onions, and sauté them until they have softened, stirring frequently. Add the garlic, coriander, cumin, and cloves, and cook, stirring constantly, for 2 minutes. Add the coconut milk, water or stock, and $\frac{1}{2}$ teaspoon salt, and bring the stew to a simmer. Simmer it for 10 minutes, uncovered.

**3.** Add the carrots and chile flakes, and simmer the stew for 5 minutes. Then add the tofu and its marinade, the green beans, and the zucchini, and simmer the stew 8 minutes more.

**4.** Stir in the cilantro, if you're using it. Add salt and pepper to taste, and serve the stew.

Variation: Fresh curry leaves, available in Indian markets, add a delicious flavor to this dish. Add two curry leaves with the coconut milk in step 2, and discard them before serving the stew.

Serves 4

# Curried Lentil Stew

This full-flavored lentil, carrot, and potato stew is especially good served over rice or steamed millet.

1 tablespoon butter
1 cup chopped onion
2 garlic cloves, minced
1 teaspoon curry powder, store-bought or
    homemade (page 36)
1/4 teaspoon ground cardamom
1/2 teaspoon ground cloves
2 pinches ground cinnamon
1 teaspoon fresh thyme leaves, or 1/2 teaspoon
    dried thyme
1 large carrot, peeled and cut into 1/4-inch rounds
1 medium potato, peeled and cut into 1/2-inch
    cubes
1 1/4 cups water
1/2 cup dried brown lentils
2 medium tomatoes, chopped
1/2 cup sherry
1/2 teaspoon salt, or more, to taste
Fresh-ground black pepper to taste
3 tablespoons chopped cilantro (optional)

**1.** Melt the butter over medium heat in a large saucepan. Add the onion, and cook it, stirring occasionally, until it begins to brown at the edges, about 10 minutes. Add the garlic, curry powder, cardamom, cloves, cinnamon, and thyme. Cook, stirring constantly, for 2 minutes. Add the carrot and potato, then the water and lentils. Cover the pan, and let the mixture simmer for 15 minutes. Add the tomatoes, sherry, salt, and pepper, and simmer for 5 to 10 minutes more, until the potatoes and lentils are tender.

**2.** Serve the stew on its own or over mounds of rice or millet, garnished, if you like, with the chopped cilantro.

*Serves 4*

# Indian Stew

A secret of this vegetable, chickpea, and lentil stew, as for many Indian dishes, is to cook the onions until they turn golden brown. This gives the sauce a sweet, rich flavor. You can vary the vegetables according to your tastes and your refrigerator's current stocks. If you have an Indian grocery store nearby, try grilled pappadums as an accompaniment.

1 tablespoon canola or corn oil
2½ cups chopped onions
2 garlic cloves, minced
1 heaping tablespoon minced fresh ginger
2 teaspoons ground coriander seeds
1½ teaspoons ground cardamom
1½ teaspoons cumin seeds
1 teaspoon turmeric
1 teaspoon salt, plus more to taste
1 quart water or Basic Vegetable Stock (page 79)
¼ teaspoon saffron
1 cup red lentils (available at Indian groceries)
   or brown lentils
2 russet potatoes, peeled and cut into ½-inch
   cubes
4 carrots, cut into ½-inch cubes
½ bunch broccoli, broken and cut into small
   pieces
½ cup cooked chickpeas (garbanzo beans)
12 okra, sliced into ½-inch-thick rounds
   (optional)
1 teaspoon fresh-ground black pepper

## Pappadums

People should not have to go through life deprived of pappadums. Pappadums are wafer-thin discs made from wet-ground moong or urad dal, *that is, mung beans or urad beans. Crisp and delicious when cooked, even slightly addictive, pappadums make an excellent accompaniment to any Indian meal. Pan-fry them in a little vegetable oil, or heat them in a dry skillet. In either case, cook each pappadum on one side until little bubbles appear all over. Turn the pappadum, cook it for another minute on the other side, and serve it. Pappadums can also be cooked over an open flame until they swell. They are available in packages in Indian groceries.*

**1.** Heat the oil in a large pot. Add the onions, and cook them over medium heat, stirring occasionally, for 10 minutes or until the onions brown. Add the garlic, ginger, coriander, cardamom, cumin, turmeric, and salt. Sauté for 3 minutes more, stirring frequently.

**2.** Add the stock or water, saffron, and lentils, and bring the mixture to a boil. Simmer for 10 minutes. Add the potatoes and carrots, and simmer for 10 minutes more or until the potatoes and lentils are just tender. Add the broccoli, chickpeas, and, if you like, okra, and cook for 5 minutes more. Add the pepper and more salt to taste, and spoon the stew into bowls.

Variation: Try using one green plantain, peeled and cut into ½-inch cubes, instead of the potatoes.

Serves 4

# Hominy and Corn Stew

When hominy is cooked for a long time, it becomes soft as dumplings. Combining soft hominy with fresh corn and red beans, this stew is hearty but not heavy. Like many stews, it is even better the day after it is made.

1 pound small dried red beans or black beans
3 tablespoons canola or corn oil
4 cups chopped onions
4 to 6 large garlic cloves, minced
¼ cup chili powder
2 teaspoons cumin seeds
1 to 3 jalapeños, chopped fine (include the seeds
    if you like more heat)
⅓ cup masa harina or cornmeal
4 carrots, chopped
5½ cups water

8 cups canned hominy, drained of about half its
    liquid
12 ounces light-colored beer
Kernels from 4 ears corn (about 2²/₃ cups)
1 teaspoon salt, or more, to taste
Fresh-ground black pepper to taste
¼ cup chopped cilantro

**1.** Soak the beans overnight, or use the quick-soak method: Boil the beans in plenty of water for 5 minutes. Remove the pan from the heat, then let the beans soak for 1 hour.

**2.** Drain the soaked beans, and rinse them well with cold water.

**3.** In a large saucepan, heat the oil over medium heat. Add the onions, and cook them, stirring occasionally, for 10 minutes. Add the garlic, chili powder, cumin, and jalapeños, and cook, stirring often, for 5 minutes.

**4.** Add the beans, masa harina or cornmeal, carrots, water, hominy, and beer. Bring the mixture to a boil, then turn the heat to low. Simmer the stew, stirring occasionally, for 1½ hours or until the beans are tender.

**5.** Add the fresh corn, and cook 10 minutes more. Add the salt and pepper to taste. Serve the stew sprinkled with chopped cilantro.

Serves 6

# Sancocho

Meat is usually a central ingredient in this popular dish from the Dominican Republic, but the parsley-cilantro seasoning mix known as *recaito* is what really distinguishes sancocho from other stews. Besides leaving out the meat, I've changed little from the traditional recipe. Green plantains are cooked until tender with sweet potatoes and yuca. With bits of cilantro and habanero or Scotch bonnet peppers flavoring the stew, meatless sancocho is delicious. Serve sancocho over rice, as the Dominicans always do, or on its own.

2 green plantains
1 ½-pound yuca (also known as cassava and manioc)
1 tablespoon butter
1 cup minced onion
2 tablespoons minced parsley
2 tablespoons minced cilantro
1 teaspoon minced habanero or Scotch bonnet pepper
1 to 2 garlic cloves, minced
1 medium sweet potato or small boniato, peeled and cut into ½-inch cubes (about 2 cups)
10 to 20 okra (optional)
1 to 2 teaspoons salt, to taste

**1.** Cut the ends off the plantains. Make three lengthwise cuts, from end to end, through the skins of each plantain. Then peel away the skins with a paring knife. Cut the plantains into ½-inch cubes.

**2.** Cut the ends off the yuca. Stand it on end, and, with lengthwise cuts of a large chef's knife, peel the yuca. Quarter the yuca lengthwise. Stand each quarter on end, and cut away the core. Discard the core pieces. Cut the rest of the yuca into ½-inch cubes.

**3.** Heat the butter in a large saucepan over medium heat. Add the onion, parsley, cilantro, chile pepper, and garlic. Cook for 5 minutes, stirring occasionally. Add the plantains, yuca, sweet potato, and, if you like, okra. Stir well. Add 3½ cups water and the salt to taste. Bring the stew to a boil, then lower the heat and simmer it for 1 hour or until all the vegetables are soft. Season the sancocho with more salt, if you like, and serve it hot, with or without rice.

*Serves 4*

# Tagine of Eggplant and Olives

Moroccan tagines come in hundreds of varieties, from lamb tagines to vegetable tagines to eel tagines. This one features tomatoes, eggplant, and chickpeas, enlivened by spices, raisins, and olives. Tagines are usually eaten with couscous, but I prefer quinoa; the two are similar in texture and weight, but quinoa has more protein and fiber.

3 tablespoons olive oil
2 cups chopped onions
3 garlic cloves, minced
1½ teaspoons paprika
½ teaspoon ground ginger
½ teaspoon ground cumin seeds
6 plum tomatoes, chopped
½ cup water
1 small pinch saffron
1 eggplant, cut into ½-inch cubes
¼ cup raisins
1 cup Greek Victoria, Royal, or other green
    olives, pitted
Salt and fresh-ground black pepper to taste
1 cup cooked chickpeas (garbanzo beans)
½ lemon, sliced into 4 wedges

**1.** In a heavy saucepan, heat the olive oil and the onions over medium heat. Sauté the onions for 5 minutes, stirring frequently. Add the garlic, paprika, ginger, and cumin, and sauté for 2 minutes more. Add the tomatoes, water, saffron, eggplant, raisins, olives, and salt and pepper. Turn the heat to low, and simmer the tagine for 30 minutes.

**2.** Add the chickpeas to the vegetables. Taste, and adjust the seasonings. Serve the tagine in soup crocks over mounds of quinoa or couscous, with a lemon slice atop each serving.

*Serves 4*

## Must You Salt Eggplant?

*Eggplant is sliced, salted, and left to stand to draw out its bitterness. Eggplant that is truly fresh, however, doesn't need to be salted. When buying eggplant, choose ones that are taut, shiny, and light for their size. Much of the bitterness of an eggplant lies in or near the skin, so if you're not sure your eggplant is fresh, you probably should peel it. When I'm using an eggplant that feels a tad too soft or heavy, I cut it into rounds or cubes, salt it liberally, and let it sit for 20 minutes before rinsing it and cooking it.*

# Thai Sweet-Potato and Coconut Stew

This stew, made with zucchini, red pepper, carrot, onion, tofu, and noodles, takes less than 15 minutes to prepare once the noodles have soaked. You can save even more time by buying the fried garlic; it is sold in plastic jars in Asian markets. Green curry paste is sold in Asian markets, too, in small, tuna-size cans. Save the leftover curry paste in an airtight container in the refrigerator; it will keep for up to 2 months.

3 ounces dried rice vermicelli noodles

4 tablespoons canola or corn oil

4 garlic cloves, minced

1 cup thinly sliced onion

1 red bell pepper, seeded and chopped

1 medium sweet potato, peeled and cut into
 1/2-inch cubes

1 small zucchini, halved lengthwise, then cut
 into 1/4-inch-thick half moons

1 carrot, peeled and cut into thin diagonal slices

8 ounces firm or very firm tofu, cut into
 1/2-inch cubes

3/4 cup coconut milk (you can freeze the
 remainder of the can for later use)

2 kaffir lime leaves, or 1 lemongrass stalk, cut
 crosswise into thirds

1 1/2 tablespoons Thai or Vietnamese fish sauce,
 or 1 1/2 tablespoons soy sauce

1 to 3 teaspoons canned green curry paste,
 to taste

1/2 teaspoon salt

Fresh-ground black pepper to taste

2 tablespoons chopped cilantro leaves

**1.** Put the rice noodles into a bowl, cover them with warm water, and let them soak for 30 minutes.

**2.** In a large skillet, heat 2 tablespoons of the oil with the garlic. Fry the garlic until it is light brown (no darker, or it will taste bitter). Transfer the garlic to a paper towel–lined plate.

**3.** Discard the oil remaining in the skillet, wipe the skillet clean, and pour into it the remaining 2 tablespoons oil. Over medium heat, sauté the onion, bell pepper, sweet potato, zucchini, and carrot for 3 to 4 minutes. Add the tofu, the coconut milk, ¾ cup water, the kaffir lime leaves or lemongrass, the fish or soy sauce, and the curry paste. Simmer for 15 minutes or until the sweet potato is tender.

**4.** Drain the rice noodles, and add them to the stew. Simmer for 2 minutes, adding a bit more water if the stew has become too dry. Add the salt and pepper. Serve the stew in bowls, sprinkled with the fried garlic and the cilantro.

Serves 4

# African Potato Stew

This stew has its origins in Kenya and other parts of South and East Africa. It is a comforting and unusual mixture of potato, sweet potato, cauliflower, collard greens, and raisins. It is good served with hot couscous, basmati rice, or quinoa, and a dollop of Harissa (page 31) or hot sauce.

2 tablespoons canola or corn oil
2 cups chopped onions
1 garlic clove, minced
1 tablespoon minced fresh ginger
2 teaspoons poppy seeds
1 teaspoon mustard seeds
1 tablespoon ground coriander seeds
¼ teaspoon ground cloves

# Calcium Concerns

*Rather than con-suming a lot of dairy products, we can get calcium from the same place that cows get it—grains and dark, leafy greens. In China, where osteoporosis is unknown in rural areas, people get their calcium mainly from greens. Although they consume only half the calcium that Americans do, this is apparently plenty for them. Leafy greens such as kale, collard greens, bok choy, broccoli, and Swiss chard are all good sources of calcium. Other foods, including tortillas, packaged tofu, beans, chickpeas, lentils, okra, almonds, sesame seeds, sea vegetables, figs, quinoa, and winter squashes, are also good sources of calcium.*

2 russet potatoes, peeled and cut into ¹/₂-inch cubes
1 teaspoon salt
¹/₂ cauliflower head, cut into bite-size florets
1 sweet potato, peeled and cut into ¹/₂-inch cubes
4 cups thinly sliced collard greens
¹/₄ cup raisins
1 tablespoon apple cider vinegar
Salt and fresh-ground black pepper to taste

**1.** Heat the oil in a large pot over medium heat. Add the onions and garlic, and cook them for 5 minutes, stirring occasionally, until the onions soften. Add the ginger, the poppy and mustard seeds, the ground coriander, and the cloves. Cook, stirring frequently, for 2 minutes.

**2.** Add the potatoes to the pot, and stir well. Stir in 4 cups water. Turn the heat to high. When the mixture comes to a boil, add the 1 teaspoon salt, stir, and turn the heat to low. Simmer the stew, uncovered, for 5 minutes, stirring occasionally.

**3.** Stir in the cauliflower, sweet potato, collard greens, and raisins. Continue to cook for 10 minutes, or until the potatoes and sweet potatoes are tender.

**4.** Season the stew with the vinegar, salt, and pepper, and add more water if the stew is too dry. Serve it hot.

**Variation:** If you like, you can add 1 cup cooked chickpeas with the cauliflower in step 3.

Serves 4

# Jambalaya

This dish from New Orleans traditionally combines various meats with rice, herbs, and spices. Creating a vegetarian jambalaya was a challenge, but the taste and aroma of the bay, oregano, and thyme come through much more clearly in this version.

1½ tablespoons butter

3 cups chopped onions

2 red or green bell peppers, seeded and chopped

2 cups finely chopped scallions

2 garlic cloves, minced

1 cup chopped parsley

1 tablespoon chopped fresh oregano, or
   1 teaspoon dried oregano

1 teaspoon fresh thyme leaves, or 1 teaspoon
   dried thyme

3 bay leaves

2 pinches cayenne

1¼ cups uncooked white rice

4 plum tomatoes, chopped fine

1 tablespoon tomato paste

3¾ cups water

⅓ cup dried lentils

1 teaspoon salt, or more, to taste

2 ears corn, each cut into 4 pieces

20 olives, preferably imported, pitted

Fresh-ground black pepper to taste

**1.** In a heavy-bottomed stockpot, melt the butter over medium heat. Add the onions, bell peppers, and scallions. Sauté for 10 minutes, stirring often.

**2.** Add the garlic, parsley, oregano, thyme, bay leaves, and cayenne. Sauté, stirring often, for 2 minutes. Add the rice, and mix well. Add the tomatoes, tomato paste, water, lentils, and salt. Turn the heat to high, and bring the stew to a boil. Stir until the tomato paste is fully incorporated, then cover the pot, and reduce the heat to low. Simmer the stew for 25 minutes.

**3.** Add the corn pieces and the olives, and cook the stew for about 5 minutes more, until the lentils and rice are tender. Season with black pepper and, if you like, more salt. Serve the stew right away.

Serves 4

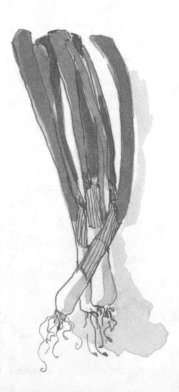

# Sweet Thing

# Say It Ain't So

*S ad to say, one cup of coconut milk has about the same amount of saturated fat as a 16-ounce chuck steak. But who can deprive themselves of those luscious Thai soups and curries made with coconut milk? My solution is to cut down on coconut milk rather than to cut it out. To cut the fat further, you can buy reduced-fat co-conut milk, although I find that the flavor is not as intense, so I just want to use more.*

*Coconut milk will sour within a week in the fridge, so if you don't want to use the whole can at once, freeze the remainder in an airtight container.*

# Mango with Coconut-Buttermilk Granita

G ranita is an Italian ice, similar to sorbet but more granular in texture. The flavors in this particular granita are drawn from the Caribbean. You can use three or four nectarines or peaches if no ripe mangoes are available. Keep in mind that the granita needs to freeze for 3 hours before you serve it.

1 14-ounce can coconut milk
8 1/4-inch slices fresh ginger
2/3 cup sugar
1 quart buttermilk
2 ripe mangoes
8 lime wedges
Mint sprigs (optional)

**1.** In a large saucepan, heat the coconut milk with the ginger until the mixture is very hot but not boiling. Take the pan off the heat, cover it, and let the mixture stand for 15 minutes. Add the sugar, and bring the mixture to a boil. Stir until the sugar is dissolved.

**2.** Take the mixture off the heat again, and add the buttermilk. Pour the mixture through a strainer into a wide bowl or casse-role pan (but not too wide to fit into your freezer). Freeze the granita about 2 hours, until it is nearly frozen, then fluff it with a fork. Return the granita to the freezer for another hour.

**3.** Peel the mangoes with a sharp vegetable peeler or a paring knife. Cut the flesh away from the pit in large pieces. Slice the mango into thin strips.

**4.** Lay the mango strips in shallow glass bowls or in wine glasses. Spoon the granita on top of the mango, then garnish with the lime wedges and the mint, if you'd like. Serve the granita at once.

*Serves 8*

# Pomegranate Ice
# with Mascarpone Cream

Brilliantly colored by pomegranate juice, this dessert demands attention. The tart yet sweet flavor of the pomegranate ice makes for an appealing contrast with the mascarpone-thickened cream (you can substitute sour cream for the mascarpone if the latter is unavailable). Served in martini or champagne glasses, topped with a few pomegranate seeds or perhaps a mint sprig, there isn't a dessert I can think of that is more sophisticated.

¼ cup water
½ cup plus 1 teaspoon sugar
2 pomegranates
½ cup heavy cream
1 teaspoon sugar
3 tablespoons mascarpone cheese (an Italian
    cream cheese available at cheese shops and
    Italian markets)
1 tablespoon dark rum

**1.** In a small saucepan, combine the water and ½ cup sugar. Bring the syrup to a boil, and take it off the heat.

**2.** Cut the pomegranates in half. Remove about 1 tablespoon seeds, put them into a cup, and reserve them in the refrigerator for the garnish. Squeeze the juice out of the pomegranates either with your hands or with a juicer that presses the juice out. Strain the juice if necessary. You should have ¾ cup juice.

**3.** Combine the pomegranate juice with the sugar syrup in a small bowl. Freeze the mixture in the bowl for 45 minutes, then break it up with a fork. Freeze it 30 minutes more, and break it up again. Freeze it for at least 2 hours more.

**4.** When you're ready to serve, whip the cream and 1 teaspoon sugar with an electric mixer or whisk until the cream has thickened but is not stiff. Whisk in the mascarpone and the rum, and beat until the cream is almost stiff.

**5.** Spoon the ice into small glasses, such as martini or champagne glasses. Then spoon the cream on top. Garnish each glass with a few pomegranate seeds, and serve.

**Variation:** For a fun and zesty twist, add about ¼ teaspoon fresh-ground black pepper to the sugar syrup and pomegranate juice.

*Serves 4*

# Butter Bananas with Toasted Cashews

This dessert is terrific both on its own and with vanilla ice cream. I'm not quite sure why bananas taste so good when they are cooked with butter; this is just one of the small wonders of life.

2 tablespoons butter
2 bananas, peeled and halved lengthwise
1 pinch nutmeg
1 tablespoon brown sugar or maple syrup
2 tablespoons dark rum or orange juice
2 tablespoons chopped cashews, lightly toasted

**1.** In a large skillet, melt the butter over medium heat. Add the bananas, and sprinkle the nutmeg over them. Sprinkle the brown sugar, or drizzle the maple syrup, over them as well. Cook the bananas for 5 minutes, turning them once or twice.

**2.** Add the rum or orange juice, and let it bubble and thicken for 1 minute. Take the pan off the heat, and serve the bananas with the sauce spooned over them and with the cashews atop the sauce.

*Serves 2*

# Lemon Curd Dip
# with Cherries and Berries

The first lemon curd I tasted was made by a talented pastry chef in New York City named Paul Geltner. He was teaching a French pastry class in a tiny restaurant in Greenwich village, and I got to attend at half-price because I washed all the dishes afterward. The best part was that after each class we could bring home our creations. Since I was in college at the time, this meant bringing a very expensive and sophisticated *gâteau* or tart back to the unruly gang at my dorm. I'd get about ten yards down the hall before my dorm-mates would attack the pastry. Within minutes, it would be demolished.

Although the lemon curd was used as a filling for a fruit tart in Paul's class, I use it here more casually, as a dip for fresh berries and cherries.

4 large eggs
1 cup sugar
²/₃ cup lemon juice
¼ cup (½ stick) unsalted butter, cut into small pieces
½ pound fresh cherries
1 pint attractive strawberries

**1.** In a bowl, whisk together the eggs. Whisk in the sugar, then the lemon juice. Pour this mixture into a heavy-bottomed saucepan. Place the saucepan over medium-low heat, and whisk the mixture constantly until it is very hot, about 5 minutes. Continue to whisk the mixture until it thickens (don't worry if the sauce bubbles or boils a little), about 5 minutes more.

**2.** Take the saucepan off the heat. Add the butter in three or four parts, whisking all the while. Pour the sauce into an attractive bowl, and chill it for at least 1½ hours.

## Lemon Trivia

In culinary terms, fruit is distinguished by a single trait, its sweetness. Most fruits have a sugar content of 10 to 15 percent; in some tropical fruits, the sugar content can reach 60 percent. Lemons contain 1 percent sugar. So you can see why the word lemon got its secondary meaning, as in "This new car of mine's a lemon; it breaks down every five minutes." Lemons are a big disappointment in the sugar department; they don't have nearly enough sugar to match their high acidity level.

**3.** Place the strawberries and the cherries in another bowl or on a plate. Serve the curd as a dip with the fruit.

*Serves 6 to 8*

# Lavender Rice Pudding with Raspberries

Lavender is used as a culinary herb throughout France. The herb mixture *herbes de Provence*, used in soups and stews, usually contains lavender, and many Parisian chefs infuse *crème Anglaise* with lavender. American chefs like to add lavender to honey ice cream. In this rice pudding, the aromatic presence of lavender seems to float over the creamy rice kernels. Dried lavender can be found in many whole-foods stores.

7¹/₂ cups milk, or a bit more
1¹/₂ teaspoons dried lavender
2 3-inch strips of lemon rind
²/₃ cup uncooked white rice (I use jasmine rice)
²/₃ cup sugar
¹/₂ pint raspberries

**1.** In a medium heavy-bottomed saucepan, heat the milk with the lavender and lemon rind. When the milk starts to simmer, add the rice. Turn the heat to low, and stir a bit. Cook the mixture, uncovered, for 2 hours over very low heat, stirring at least three times an hour. Add the sugar 10 minutes before the cooking is done.

**2.** Stir well, and remove the pieces of lemon rind. Transfer the pudding to a bowl, and chill it for at least 2 hours, uncovered. Fold in the berries just before serving the pudding, adding a bit of milk if the pudding is too thick.

*Serves 6*

# Creamy Coconut Pudding

This coconut milk and ginger pudding makes a great foil for fresh summer fruit. Serve the pudding in a wine goblet layered with berries, mango, papaya, pineapple, or melon, with a wedge of lime on the goblet's lip. Coconut pudding is especially suitable after a spicy, full-flavored meal.

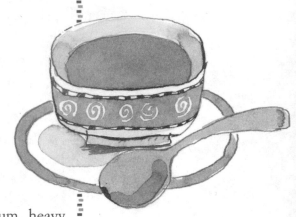

2 cups milk
2 tablespoons minced fresh ginger
4 egg yolks
3/4 cup sugar
1/4 cup cornstarch
1 14-ounce can coconut milk
1 tablespoon unsalted butter

**1.** Bring the milk and ginger to a boil in a medium, heavy saucepan, and immediately take the pan off the heat so that it doesn't boil over. Let the ginger steep in the milk for 15 minutes, then pour the milk through a fine-mesh strainer into a bowl.

**2.** In another small bowl, whisk together the egg yolks and about ½ cup of the strained milk. Add the sugar and cornstarch, and whisk until the mixture is smooth. While whisking, slowly add the coconut milk and the rest of the milk.

**3.** Return the mixture to the saucepan, and place the pan over medium heat. Whisk constantly until the pudding begins to boil. Continue whisking for 2 minutes. Add the butter, and whisk until it is melted.

**4.** Pour the pudding into a bowl, and cover it tightly with plastic wrap so a skin doesn't form. Chill the pudding for at least 2 hours before serving.

Makes 6 to 8
servings

# Pumpkin Bread Pudding

Here's a way to enjoy an underused vegetable, the pumpkin. Split and seed a small sugar (pie) pumpkin, and bake it at 350° for about an hour, till it's tender (see the Note following the recipe for ideas on using the leftover pumpkin flesh). Or just open a can of puréed pumpkin.

This homey and light bread pudding has the burnt-sugar topping that one usually encounters with a *crème brûlée*. The pudding is best eaten warm with vanilla ice cream.

About ½ baguette, cut into 2-inch-thick slices
3 extra-large eggs
3½ cups whole or low-fat milk
½ teaspoon freshly grated nutmeg
1 tablespoon minced fresh ginger, or 2 teaspoons
    ground ginger
1 teaspoon vanilla extract
½ cup white sugar
1 cup baked pumpkin flesh (you don't need to
    purée it) or canned pumpkin purée
¾ cup brown sugar

**1.** Preheat the oven to 350°. Cover the bottom of a 10-by-13-inch baking dish with a single layer of the sliced bread. In a large bowl, whisk together the eggs, milk, nutmeg, ginger, vanilla, white sugar, and pumpkin. (If you are using fresh pumpkin, the pumpkin will be somewhat lumpy.) Pour this mixture over the bread slices. Push down on the bread slices so they soak up the liquid. Let them soak for 10 minutes.

**2.** Bake the pudding in the lower third of the oven for 45 to 50 minutes, until a knife inserted into the pudding comes out clean. Let the pudding cool for 10 minutes.

**3.** Sprinkle the brown sugar evenly over the pudding. Place the pudding under the broiler, keeping the oven door slightly open. Keeping close watch, broil the sugar until it begins to bubble. Remove the pudding and let it cool.

I like to serve the bread pudding warm with ice cream, or at room temperature; some like it cold. The topping will lose its candy-like crunch after 5 to 6 hours in the refrigerator.

Note: If you've baked a pumpkin, are you wondering what to do with the rest of it? Jamaican Rice Mix-Up (page 208) uses two pounds of pumpkin. You can also substitute pumpkin for the butternut squash in Roasted Squash Soup (page 118). Or chop the pumpkin, and add it to African Tomato and Peanut Soup (page 96) near the end of the cooking.

Serves 6 to 8

# Chocolate Blackout Pudding

A delirious dessert with intense chocolate flavor, this pudding is cooked over the stove, then chilled. The consistency is creamy and smooth, like that of the Jell-O chocolate pudding I loved as a child, but the flavor is far superior.

3 cups whole or low-fat milk
4 tablespoons cornstarch (or 5 tablespoons
    arrowroot)
1 egg yolk
1 egg
1/2 cup plus 2 tablespoons sugar
2 tablespoons good quality cocoa, preferably
    Dutch-processed
3 ounces unsweetened chocolate, cut into small
    pieces
4 ounces semisweet or bittersweet chocolate, cut
    into small pieces, or 4 ounces chocolate chips
2 teaspoons vanilla extract
1 tablespoon brandy or Grand Marnier (optional)
Whipped cream (optional)

## Chocolate Bites

*Although chocolate originated in the New World, the people of Switzerland are the planet's champion chocolate consumers. The Swiss manage to eat about 22 pounds a year per person (that's about 1 ounce per day, or 6 percent of their daily calorie intake). Americans consume only about half this amount (14 pounds a year); the English, Germans, and Belgians fall somewhere in between.*

*My favorite chocolates for baking are Valrona and Côte d'Or bittersweet for special occasions (both are French), and VanLeer bittersweet, a less expensive chocolate from Pennsylvania. For eating, I like Ghirardelli bittersweet.*

**1.** In a small bowl, combine ½ cup of the milk with the cornstarch, and whisk well. Add the yolk, whole egg, sugar, and cocoa, and whisk well.

**2.** In a large, heavy saucepan, heat the remaining 2½ cups milk over medium-high heat until it begins to boil. Then pour about half of the milk into the cornstarch mixture, stirring all the time. Pour this mixture back into the saucepan. Place the pan over low heat, and whisk constantly for about 5 minutes, until the pudding thickens. The pudding should get very thick, like cold yogurt.

**3.** Remove the pan from the heat, and add the unsweetened and sweetened chocolate, the vanilla, and, if you'd like, the brandy or Grand Marnier. Stir until the chocolate is melted.

**4.** Ladle the pudding into mugs or cups, and chill it for at least 1½ hours. Serve it cold, topped with whipped cream, if you like.

**Variation:** Have you ever had *frozen* pudding? If not, here's your chance to experience one of life's great pleasures. Instead of ladling the pudding into mugs or cups in step 4, transfer it to a plastic storage container, and freeze the pudding, covered, for at least 3 to 4 hours. The outer part of the pudding will be frozen, the inner part creamy and very cold. Spoon the frozen pudding into mugs or cups, and serve it plain or with whipped cream.

*Makes 6 servings*

# Spiced Crème Caramel

The flavors of Sichuan peppercorns, cloves, and cardamom subtly infuse this crème caramel. I was inspired to invent this dessert while I was eating *pudeen,* a saffron-flavored crème caramel, at the Helmand, an Afghan restaurant in Cambridge, Massachusetts. I thought it would be fun to experiment with different spices. Although each spice is intensely flavored, together they make a mellow blend.

Allow several hours for the crème caramel to chill before serving.

* * * * * * *

2¼ cups sugar
3¼ cups milk
½ teaspoon whole Sichuan peppercorns
½ teaspoon whole black peppercorns
½ teaspoon whole cloves
½ teaspoon crushed whole cardamom, or
    ¼ teaspoon ground cardamom
4 eggs
3 egg yolks

* * * * * * *

**1.** Preheat the oven to 325°. Have at hand 6 oven-proof 1-cup ramekins or a 9-inch round cake pan. (Ramekins are preferable; if you use a cake pan, you'll need to check the custard often to avoid overcooking the outer part.)

In a heavy saucepan, combine 1½ cups sugar and ¼ cup water, and stir well. Place the pan over high heat, and let the sugar syrup boil until it becomes a deep golden color, about 10 minutes. Immediately take the pan off the heat. Very carefully, pour or spoon the caramel into the cake pan, or divide it equally among the ramekins.

**2.** In another saucepan, combine the milk with the four spices. Bring the milk to a boil, and quickly take it off the heat. Cover the saucepan, and let the spices steep in the milk for 10 minutes.

**3.** In a large bowl, whisk together the whole eggs and the yolks. Add the remaining ¾ cup sugar, and whisk well. Place a fine sieve over the bowl, and pour half of the hot milk through the sieve into the bowl. Quickly set the sieve aside, and stir with a spoon (do not whisk). Place the sieve over the bowl again, and pour in the rest of the milk. Stir well.

**4.** Ladle the custard into the ramekins or the cake pan. Prepare a water bath: Bring 2 quarts water to a boil. Place the ramekins or cake pan in a large roasting pan. Carefully pour in boiling water around the ramekins or cake pan until the water rises at least halfway up the sides of the custard. Cover the roasting pan with foil, and carefully place it in the oven.

**5.** Bake the custard for about 45 to 50 minutes if you're using ramekins, or 50 to 60 minutes if you're using a cake pan. The custard is done when it is barely firm to the touch. Remove the roasting pan from the oven, and let the crème caramel cool in the water bath. Then remove the cake pan or ramekins, cover them with plastic wrap, and chill the crème caramel for at least 3 hours.

**6.** To serve the crème caramel, run a knife along the inside edge of the ramekins or cake pan. Invert the crème caramel onto a large platter, if you've used a cake pan, or, for ramekins, onto small serving plates. Lift off the pan or ramekins. If you've used a cake pan, cut the crème caramel into wedges, and top them with the cold caramel sauce left in the cake pan.

Serves 6 to 8

# Banana Cream Pie with Chocolate Lining

After making many, many banana cream pies, using all sorts of cream fillings, I have returned to the old-fashioned pastry cream that was popular in the pies of the 1950s, with my own additions of lemon juice and whiskey. I think this filling outshines the fancy, more complicated fillings popular today. The thin layer of chocolate that rests on the graham-cracker crust adds a delicious contrast to the cream filling, and complements the subtle flavor of the bananas. I do not have the willpower to turn down a piece of this pie no matter how full I am.

1½ cups graham-cracker crumbs

¼ cup (½ stick) butter, melted

2 tablespoons brown sugar

2 ounces dark chocolate

2 tablespoons heavy cream

3 cups whole or low-fat milk

¾ cup white sugar

2 eggs

½ cup unbleached white flour

2 tablespoons Irish whiskey, or 2 tablespoons
    vanilla extract

4 ripe bananas

2 tablespoons lemon juice (from about ½ lemon)

1 cup heavy cream, whipped with 1 to 2
    tablespoons Irish whiskey

**1.** Preheat the oven to 375°. Combine the graham-cracker crumbs with the butter and brown sugar in a medium bowl, and stir well. Transfer the mixture to a 10-inch pie plate, and pat it evenly along the bottom and sides. Bake the crust for 7 to 9 minutes, or until the edges darken slightly. Let the crust cool.

**2.** Melt the chocolate with the 2 tablespoons cream over simmering water in the top of a double boiler or in a heat-proof bowl set on top of a saucepan. Whisk the chocolate and cream until they form a smooth liquid. Take the pan off the heat, and spoon the chocolate mixture onto the graham-cracker crust. Let the chocolate cool for at least 15 minutes.

**3.** Meanwhile, make the filling: Heat the milk in a heavy-bottomed saucepan. When the milk is just about to boil, take the pan off of the heat. In a medium bowl, whisk together the sugar, eggs, and flour. Slowly add the hot milk to the bowl, whisking constantly. Then transfer the mixture to the saucepan. Whisking almost constantly, bring the mixture to a boil over medium heat, and continue whisking while it boils for 3 minutes. Take the pan off the heat, and add the whiskey or the vanilla. Let the filling cool for 20 minutes.

**4.** Slice the bananas, and toss them with the lemon juice. Lay the banana slices on the chocolate-lined crust. Pour the filling over, and chill the pie for at least 2 hours. Serve it with the whiskey-spiked whipped cream.

Serves 8

# Jon's Rhubarb-Raisin Pie

My friend Jon, who grows rhubarb in his backyard, worked with me to perfect this traditional New England pie. Raisins add texture to the filling, and their sweetness balances the tartness of the rhubarb.

**CRUST:**
3 cups unbleached white flour
1 teaspoon salt
1/2 cup (1 stick) cold unsalted butter, cut into
      8 pieces
1/2 cup vegetable shortening (or more cold
      unsalted butter, cut into 8 pieces)
6 tablespoons or more ice water

**FILLING:**
1/4 cup triple sec liqueur
3/4 cup raisins
1 1/2 pounds rhubarb stems, cut into 1/2-inch
      pieces
1/4 cup unbleached white flour
1 cup sugar
Juice and grated rind of 1/2 orange
3 eggs, beaten

**EGG WASH:**
1 egg, beaten

**1.** To make the pie dough in a food processor fitted with a steel blade, combine the 3 cups flour, the salt, the butter, and the vegetable shortening (or more unsalted butter). Run the machine for 10 seconds, or until the mixture has the consistency of sand. Add the ice water about 2 tablespoons at a time, running the machine in short spurts after each addition, until the dough starts to come together.

To make the dough by hand, combine the 3 cups flour, salt, butter, and shortening (or more butter) in a large bowl. With a pastry cutter or fork, cut the butter and shortening into the flour until the mixture has the consistency of sand. Add the ice water about 2 tablespoons at a time, and mix well after each addition.

Transfer the dough to a floured work surface, and form it into two balls. Chill the dough for 30 minutes.

**2.** Make the filling: Combine the triple sec and raisins in a saucepan. Bring the mixture to a boil, then take the pan off the heat. Let the raisins steep for 10 minutes. In a large bowl, meanwhile, combine the rhubarb with the ¼ cup flour, the sugar, and the orange rind. Add the 3 beaten eggs, the raisins and triple sec, and the orange juice, and mix well.

**3.** Preheat the oven to 425°. On a floured surface, roll each ball into a 10-inch circle. Line a 9-inch pie pan with one circle of dough. Spoon the rhubarb mixture into the pie shell. Place the second circle of dough on top of the filling. Crimp the bottom and top pieces of dough together around the rim, and make three slits in the top crust. Brush the egg wash evenly over the top of the pie, and place the pie in the lower third of the oven.

**4.** Bake the pie at 425° for 10 minutes, then reduce the heat to 350°. Bake the pie for 35 to 40 minutes longer, until the crust is a deep golden brown.

Makes 1
9-inch pie

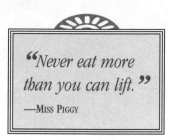
# Grandmarie's Sweet-Potato Pie

I had the good fortune to work as a private chef for the Bridges, a small but very big-hearted family in Newton, Massachusetts. Maria Bridge's mother, Gladys ("Grandmarie") Alexander, who grew up in North Carolina, had cultivated a large following for her sweet-potato pie. She never measured anything in it—she liked to make it a bit different every time—until family and friends pressed her finally to write down the recipe. Lucky for me that she did so, because I hated sweet-potato pie before this one came along. It's best hot from the oven, with a scoop of vanilla ice cream.

1 medium sweet potato (about 2/3 pound),
    cut in half
1 9-inch store-bought or homemade unbaked
    pie shell
3/4 cup brown sugar
1/3 cup white sugar
2 eggs
12 ounces evaporated milk
1/4 cup (1/2 stick) unsalted butter, melted
1 teaspoon freshly grated nutmeg
1/2 teaspoon ground cinnamon
1 pinch salt

**1.** Put the sweet-potato halves into a saucepan, and cover them with water. Bring the water to a boil, then turn down the heat, and simmer the sweet potatoes for 30 minutes or until they are tender. Drain and skin the halves.

**2.** While the sweet potatoes cook, preheat the oven to 400°. If you're using a store-bought shell, leave it in its foil base; if you've made the shell yourself, put it in a 9-inch pie pan.

Crimp pieces of foil tightly around the side of the pie crust to hold it in place as it bakes. Pierce the base of the crust three times with a fork. Bake the shell for 15 minutes. Let it cool, then remove the foil. Lower the oven temperature to 350°.

**3.** With a potato masher, food processor, or electric mixer, mash or purée the sweet potatoes. In another bowl, whisk together the sugars and the eggs. Whisk in the evaporated milk, melted butter, nutmeg, cinnamon, and salt. Add the sweet potatoes, and stir until the mixture is smooth. Pour the filling into the pie shell.

**4.** Bake the pie for 45 minutes or until it has set. Let it cool for 10 minutes, then serve it; or let it cool completely, and wrap and chill it for later reheating.

**Variation:** This pie is also delicious with a graham-cracker crust. In a bowl, mix together 2 cups graham-cracker crumbs (ground from one package of crackers), ⅓ cup brown sugar, and ½ cup melted butter. Press the mixture into the bottom and halfway up the side of a 9-inch pie pan. Pour the filling into the shell, and bake the pie as directed.

Makes 1
9-inch pie

# Cornmeal
# Strawberry
# Cake

Strawberries are seldom baked, perhaps because they are so delicious fresh. In this delectable cornmeal cake, however, sliced strawberries are incorporated into the batter, moistening the cake and infusing it with their sprightly flavor.

1¹/₃ cups cornmeal
²/₃ cup unbleached white flour
¹/₂ teaspoon salt
1 teaspoon baking powder
³/₄ cup (1¹/₂ sticks) unsalted butter, softened
1¹/₄ cups sugar
4 large eggs, beaten
1 teaspoon vanilla extract
¹/₂ cup plain whole, low-fat, or nonfat yogurt or
    buttermilk
1 cup sliced strawberries
Ice cream or whipped cream

**1.** Preheat the oven to 350°. Butter a 9-inch cake pan or a Bundt pan. In a large bowl, mix together the cornmeal, flour, salt, and baking powder.

**2.** In another bowl, mix together the butter and sugar with a sturdy wooden spoon, but be careful not to cream them. Stir about half of the beaten eggs into the sugar and butter. Then add the rest of the eggs, and stir well.

**3.** Add the vanilla to the yogurt or buttermilk. Add half of the flour mixture to the egg mixture, and stir well, but do not beat. Add the yogurt or buttermilk, and stir again. Then add the remaining flour mixture. Fold in the strawberries, and pour the batter into the prepared pan.

**4.** Bake the cake for 45 to 50 minutes or until a knife inserted into the cake comes out clean.

**5.** Let the cake cool in its pan on a rack for 30 minutes, then run a knife around the side, and invert the pan onto a plate. Serve the cake warm or at room temperature, with whipped cream or ice cream.

**Variation:** Use 1 cup blueberries instead of the strawberries.

Makes 1 9-inch cake

# Lemongrass-Ginger Cheesecake

Lemongrass and ginger are unusual flavors for a cheese-cake, but they work together well here. With a base of ricotta cheese and sour cream, this cheesecake is not as heavy as a cream-cheese cheesecake. Be sure to make the cheesecake well in advance; it needs to chill for at least 3 hours after you bake it.

Lemongrass can be found in Asian markets, whole-foods stores, and some supermarkets.

.......

1 3/4 cups graham-cracker crumbs
2/3 cup brown sugar
1/4 cup (1/2 stick) unsalted butter
1 lemongrass stalk
2 1/2 cups ricotta cheese, whole-milk or part-skim
1/2 cup white sugar
3 large eggs
1/2 cup whole, low-fat, or nonfat sour cream
1/4 cup chopped crystallized ginger

.......

**1.** Preheat the oven to 350°. In a bowl, stir together the crumbs and the brown sugar. Melt the butter, and pour it over the crumb mixture. Stir with a spoon until the butter is fully incor-porated. Pour the mixture into a 9-inch springform cake pan (the sides of the pan should be at least 3 inches tall). Press the mixture evenly onto the bottom of the pan.

**2.** With a sharp chef's knife, cut off the bulbous bottom third of the lemongrass stalk. Remove the tough outer leaves from this piece, cut it into thin slices, then mince it. Measure 2 table-spoons of the minced lemongrass for the cheesecake, and save the rest for another use.

**3.** In a large bowl, whisk together the ricotta, sugar, and eggs. Stir in the sour cream and lemongrass. Add the crystallized

---

## Lemongrass

*Although I often suggest lemon rind as a substitute for lemongrass, some differences between the two are worth mentioning. Both con-tain the aromatic compound citral, but lemongrass has a light aroma and a strong, somewhat sour flavor, whereas lemon rind is intensely fragrant but milder in flavor.*

*To use lemongrass, you can cut the entire length of the scallion-shaped herb into long pieces, smash it with the broad side of the cleaver, and add it to Asian-style soups or stews, removing it just before serving. Or you can mince the bulb end of lemongrass and add it to a stir-fried dish or curry paste. Look for lemongrass in Asian markets and in the produce sec-tions of large super-markets.*

ginger, and stir well. Pour the filling onto the crumb crust.

**4.** Bake the cheesecake on a baking sheet for 45 to 55 minutes in the lower third of the oven. The cheesecake is done when a knife inserted into the filling comes out clean. Let the cheesecake cool for ½ hour, then chill it in its pan for at least 2½ hours.

**5.** Loosen the cheesecake with a butter knife, then remove the side of the springform pan. Slice the cheesecake, dipping the knife in hot water between slices, and serve.

*Makes 1 9-inch cheesecake*

# Lemon-Walnut Pound Cake

The flavor of butter is so pleasing in a pound cake, the dense texture of the cake so gratifying, that one small slice is all I need to keep me happy. This is a very lemony pound cake. One might think it's soaked in lemon syrup, but in fact the flavor comes from the lemon rind and juice in the batter. For the best taste, be sure to toast the walnuts lightly before adding them to the batter.

Juice and grated rind of 2 lemons
¼ cup dark rum
1 cup currants
2¼ cups unbleached white flour
1 teaspoon baking powder
½ teaspoon salt
1 cup plus 6 tablespoons (2¾ sticks) unsalted
    butter, softened
1⅓ cups sugar
6 eggs, beaten
1¼ cups chopped walnuts, lightly toasted

**1.** In a saucepan, combine the lemon juice, rum, and currants. Simmer them for 1 minute, then take the pan off the heat.

**2.** Butter and flour a 12-inch cake pan or two 9-by-5-by-3-inch loaf pans. Preheat the oven to 350°.

**3.** In a large bowl, sift 2 cups of the flour with the baking powder and salt.

**4.** With an electric mixer or by hand, combine the butter, sugar, and grated lemon rind. Beat the mixture for 8 minutes (at medium-high speed, if you're using an electric mixer). Add the dry ingredients, and beat slowly, just long enough to incorporate them. Add the eggs slowly, in 3 batches, one by one, mixing after each addition.

**5.** Drain the currants, and add the soaking liquid to the cake batter. Mix well. Then toss the currants with the remaining ¼ cup flour. Add this mixture and the walnuts to the cake batter. Spoon the batter into the prepared pan(s). Bake the cake for approximately 1 hour, until a knife inserted in the center comes out clean.

**Note:** This pound cake keeps well in the refrigerator, tightly wrapped, for 2 weeks.

Makes 1 12-inch cake
or 2 loaves

# Dairy-Free
# Almond-Orange Cake

When I was pastry chef at a restaurant in New York City, I created this cake for a vegan wedding. I was happy to find out that everyone there, non-vegans included, really enjoyed the cake. If *you* are getting married, you can easily multiply the recipe.

## ORANGE-ALMOND CAKE:

1 cup whole almonds, lightly toasted
2 cups unbleached white flour
1½ teaspoons baking powder
½ teaspoon baking soda
½ teaspoon salt
⅔ cup canola oil
1 cup soy milk
⅔ cup honey
1 tablespoon vanilla extract
½ teaspoon almond extract or 1 teaspoon
    maple extract
2 teaspoons finely grated orange rind

## CHOCOLATE ICING:

5 ounces semisweet or bittersweet chocolate (my
    favorite brand is Sweet River), broken into
    small pieces, or 5 ounces chocolate chips
4 tablespoons soy margarine
2 tablespoons honey
3 drops vanilla extract, or 1 tablespoon Amaretto

**1.** Preheat the oven to 350°. Grease a 9- or 10-inch cake pan by rubbing or spraying it with a bit of oil. Grind the almonds in a food processor or blender (you'll need to grind them in two batches if you use a blender). Transfer the almonds to a large bowl. Add the flour, baking powder, baking soda, and salt. Mix well.

**2.** In a smaller bowl, combine the canola oil, soy milk, honey, vanilla, almond or maple extract, and the orange rind. Pour about half of this mixture into the flour mixture, and stir briefly. Add the remaining liquid, and stir until the batter is smooth. Pour it into the prepared pan.

**3.** Bake the cake for 40 to 45 minutes, or until a knife inserted into the cake comes out clean. Let the cake cool in its pan on a rack for 15 minutes, then loosen the cake with a sharp knife. Place a plate on top of the pan, and invert the cake onto the plate. Let the cake cool completely.

**4.** Make the icing: Melt the chocolate in the top of a double boiler or in a bowl set over a saucepan of simmering water. Once the chocolate is melted, add the margarine 1 tablespoon at a time, whisking after each addition. Whisk in the honey and vanilla or liqueur.

**5.** Ice the cake, using a cake spatula or butter knife. If the cake won't be eaten within 5 hours, store it in the refrigerator.

Serves 8

# Mexican Brownies

Is there really such a thing as a Mexican brownie? I doubt it. I was trying one day to create a cookie with the Mexican flavors of chocolate, cinnamon, and almonds. I ended up with a brownie—of a delightfully different sort. These are a little more gooey than your average brownie, but if you let them cool for an hour they'll firm up. Their flavor and texture practically demand whipped cream or vanilla ice cream on top or on the side.

7 ounces semisweet or bittersweet chocolate, cut
      into small pieces, or chocolate chips
1/2 cup (1 stick) unsalted butter, cut into 8 pieces
1/2 teaspoon ground cinnamon
1 cup sugar
1/2 cup unbleached white flour
2 eggs
1 teaspoon vanilla extract
1/2 cup chopped almonds, lightly toasted (optional)

**1.** In the top of a double boiler or in a heatproof bowl set on top of a saucepan, melt the chocolate and butter over simmering water. Take the mixture off the heat, and let it cool for 5 minutes.

**2.** Meanwhile, preheat the oven to 350°. Butter an 8-by-8-inch baking pan. In a small bowl, combine the cinnamon, sugar, and flour. Mix well.

**3.** With a whisk, beat 1 egg into the cooled chocolate. Add the second egg and the vanilla, then beat again. Using a wooden spoon, stir in the flour mixture and, if you like, the almonds. Stir until the dry ingredients are fully incorporated. Pour the batter into the prepared pan, and bake the brownies for 25 to 30 minutes, until they are firm but still moist inside.

**4.** Let the brownies cool for at least 1 hour before removing them from the pan. Transfer them to a plate, and serve them. They keep well, individually wrapped, in the refrigerator for a week.

*Makes 12 brownies*

# Cinnamon Snaps

When I asked all my friends if there was a recipe they would like to see in my cookbook, two suggested this one. I probably wouldn't have thought to include Cinnamon Snaps otherwise, but they are my friends, after all, and I'd have hated to leave them snap-less.

2 cups unbleached white flour
1½ teaspoons baking soda
½ teaspoon salt
3 to 4 teaspoons ground cinnamon, to taste
1 teaspoon ground allspice
3/4 cup (1½ sticks) unsalted butter, softened
½ cup plus ⅓ cup white sugar
½ cup plus 3 tablespoons dark brown sugar
1 egg

1. In a small bowl, combine the flour, baking soda, salt, cinnamon, and allspice, and mix well.

2. With an electric mixer or by hand, beat the butter. When it is creamy, add the ½ cup white sugar and all of the brown sugar. Beat the mixture until it is soft and fluffy. Add the egg, and beat well again.

3. With a wooden spoon, stir the flour mixture into the butter and sugar, bit by bit, until the flour is fully incorporated. Chill the dough for at least 30 minutes.

4. Preheat the oven to 350°. Put the remaining ⅓ cup white sugar onto a plate. Form the dough into 1-inch balls, and roll each ball in the sugar. Place the cookies at least 3 inches apart on an ungreased baking sheet, and lightly press down on each cookie. Bake the cookies for 6 to 8 minutes, then let them cool on racks.

Makes 24 cookies

# Peanut Espresso Cookies

These are currently at the top of my list of favorite cookies. If you have no espresso maker at home, you'll have to go to your nearest espresso shop to order a "solo," or single espresso, or save some from your morning "doppio," or double espresso. These cookies will be a bit chewy in the center if you cook them as instructed here.

1 cup (2 sticks) unsalted butter, softened
3/4 cup brown sugar
3/4 cup white sugar
1/2 teaspoon salt
2 eggs, beaten
1/4 cup brewed espresso

## An Elegant and Simple Dessert

*In the dead of winter, it's sometimes nice to serve a really delicious cup of homemade hot chocolate instead of dessert. You can prepare the chocolate ahead of time, too.*

*For eight cups chocolate, heat ½ gallon whole or low-fat milk in a pot. When the milk is hot, add two 2-inch strips of orange peel, 3 tablespoons brown sugar, six whole allspice berries, and two cinnamon sticks. Keep the milk over very low heat for 10 minutes, then take the pan off the heat, and let the spices steep 10 minutes more. Coarsely chop 8 ounces of semisweet chocolate. Strain the milk into a new pot, and whisk in the chocolate.*

1/2 cup peanut butter, at room temperature
1 3/4 cups unbleached white flour
2 teaspoons baking soda
1 cup dry-roasted, unsalted peanuts

**1.** Preheat the oven to 350°. With an electric mixer or by hand, cream the butter with the two sugars. Add the salt, eggs, and espresso, and mix well. Add the peanut butter, and mix just until the batter is smooth.

**2.** In a separate bowl, stir together the flour and the baking soda. Add this mixture to the batter in four parts, mixing between additions. Add the peanuts, and stir just long enough to distribute them throughout the batter. The batter will be quite wet.

**3.** Drop the batter by the tablespoonful on ungreased baking sheets, spacing the cookies about 3 inches apart. Bake them for 5 to 7 minutes (they will still be very soft on top, but brown around the edges).

**4.** Let the cookies cool on the baking sheets for 3 minutes, then remove them with a spatula. Store them in an airtight container.

Makes 40 large cookies

# Five-Spice Biscotti

Biscotti accommodate all sorts of spice combinations. Sometimes I use just one or two spices, but in this recipe I use a whopping six (the five in five-spice powder plus nutmeg). You can buy five-spice powder in a Chinese market or well-stocked supermarket, or you can mix your own according to the recipe on page 38. These cookies are wonderful with coffee in the afternoon or for dessert with vanilla or ginger ice cream.

3 large eggs
1 cup sugar
2 teaspoons five-spice powder
1/4 teaspoon ground nutmeg
1/2 cup unsalted butter (1 stick), melted
3 1/3 cups unbleached white flour, or a bit more
1 teaspoon baking powder
1/2 teaspoon baking soda
1/2 teaspoon salt
1 1/4 cups whole almonds

**1.** Preheat the oven to 350°. Grease two baking sheets. In a large bowl, whisk together the eggs, sugar, and spices. Add the melted butter, and stir well.

**2.** In another bowl, mix together the 3 1/3 cups flour, the baking powder, the baking soda, the salt, and the almonds. Add half of this mixture to the egg mixture. Stir well with a wooden spoon. Add the second half of the flour mixture and stir until a smooth dough forms, adding a tablespoon or two of flour if the dough seems too tacky. (With floured hands, you should be able to form a small piece of dough into a ball.)

**3.** Place half the dough on one of the greased baking sheets. Form it into a large log, then flatten the log until it is 5 to 6 inches wide and 10 inches long. Do the same with the second half of the dough, using the second baking sheet.

**4.** Bake the logs for 35 minutes, until the logs are firm but give slightly when pressed with a finger. Remove the baking sheets from the oven, and reduce the oven temperature to 325°.

**5.** While the logs are still warm, carefully transfer them with a large spatula to a cutting board. Cut them crosswise into 1/2-inch-thick diagonal slices. Lay the cookies on their sides on the baking sheets, and bake the cookies 15 minutes more.

**6.** Let the cookies cool. Stored in an airtight container, they will keep well for 2 weeks.

Makes about 20 biscotti

# Almond Macaroons

A couple of years ago I went through a macaroon phase; I tried over and over to bake the perfect macaroon. Almond macaroons are one of my favorite cookies, because they have a lot of almond flavor and are chewy and crispy at the same time. Also, they aren't loaded with fat, as most cookies are. These macaroons are composed of only three ingredients—almonds, egg whites, and sugar.

2²/₃ cups almonds
2¹/₄ cups sugar
5 large egg whites

**1.** Grind the almonds very fine in two batches in a food processor or blender. If you use a blender, start with ¼ cup almonds, and add more through the lid opening.

**2.** Transfer the ground almonds to a large bowl, add the sugar, and stir well. Then add the egg whites, one at a time, stirring after each addition. Chill the mixture for 15 minutes. Preheat the oven to 350°.

**3.** Dust one or two baking sheets with flour. Put pieces of dough the size of a ping-pong ball 3 inches apart on the baking sheet(s).

**4.** Bake the cookies for 20 to 25 minutes, until they're lightly browned. Let them cool for 5 minutes, then carefully remove them with a spatula. Store them in an airtight container.

Makes 20
large macaroons

## Fruit for Dessert

When I don't have the time to make a complicated dessert, I make a fruit melange. I usually use only two or three fruits; my favorites are strawberries, lychees (canned), mangoes, plums (with their skins on), pineapple, pears, figs, clementines (a seedless variety of mandarin oranges), blueberries, watermelon, and other melons. Dried dates and apricots make good additions. I also include a spoonful of honey and some lemon or lime juice to heighten the fruit flavors. Fresh chopped mint or candied or fresh ginger is also nice. Or perhaps a splash of liqueur…

# Chocolate Ice-Cream Sandwich Wafers

These cookies are wonderful sandwiching ice cream of any flavor, but I especially like to use coffee ice cream, particularly when it's made with espresso.

10 tablespoons unsalted butter, softened
1¼ cups sugar
1 large egg, beaten
2½ ounces unsweetened chocolate, melted and
    cooled
2 tablespoons cocoa, preferably Dutch-processed
1⅔ cups unbleached white flour
½ teaspoon salt

**1.** With an electric mixer, beat the butter with the sugar until the mixture is fluffy and pale. Add half of the beaten egg, and beat for 2 minutes more (save the rest of the egg for another use). With a wooden spoon, stir in the melted chocolate.

**2.** With the back of a wooden spoon, push the cocoa through a sieve into the cookie batter. Stir well. Add half of the flour and all of the salt to the bowl, and stir well again. Add the rest of the flour, and stir until the flour is fully incorporated. Chill the dough for 1 hour. Preheat the oven to 350°.

**3.** Divide the dough into two equal pieces. With well-floured hands, make four large balls from each piece; you will have eight dough balls in all. Place the dough balls 5 inches apart on baking sheets. Flatten each dough ball until it is ¼ inch thick and 4 inches in diameter. Bake the cookies for 4 to 5 minutes only; they should be soft to the touch when you remove them from the oven. Let them cool on the baking sheets for 5 minutes, then remove them with a spatula. Serve them in pairs, sandwiching ice cream.

Makes 8 large cookies for 4 sandwiches

# CHAPTER 19

# Cool Drinks

# Minty Lemonade

Lemonade bought in a bottle or mixed from a dry powder is a far cry from the real stuff. This carbonated, minted version is very tasty.

1/4 cup sugar
10 fresh mint leaves
6 tablespoons lemon juice (from about
    1 1/2 lemons)
5 to 6 medium or 3 large ice cubes
Ice for the glasses
1 1/3 cups soda or seltzer water
2 lemon wedges

**1.** In a blender, blend the sugar and mint on high speed for 5 seconds or until the leaves are ground. Add the lemon juice, and blend on high for 5 more seconds. Then add the ice cubes, and blend the mixture until most of the ice is crushed.

**2.** Pour the mixture into two large glasses filled with ice, then divide the soda or seltzer water between the two glasses, and stir well. Top each drink with a lemon wedge, and serve.

*Makes 2 large drinks*

# Ginger Iced Tea

This honey-sweetened ginger tea is caffeine-free. With its simple and refreshing flavor, it's a great lunch beverage and a reliable thirst quencher on a hot day.

2 tablespoons honey
1 tablespoon finely grated fresh ginger
2 tablespoons lemon juice (from about ½ lemon)
2 cups hot water
Ice for the glasses
2 lemon wedges

**1.** In a bowl, combine the honey, ginger, lemon juice, and hot water. Stir well, and let the mixture sit for 30 minutes. (You can refrigerate the mixture for up to 1 week.)

**2.** Pour the tea through a strainer into two large glasses filled with ice. Top each drink with a lemon wedge, and serve.

Makes 2 large drinks

# Sparkling Grape Soda

Much better than any grape soda in a can, this is a real pick-me-up.

1¼ cups seedless green grapes
¼ cup lightly packed mint leaves
¼ cup sugar
¼ cup lime juice (from about 2 limes)
1 teaspoon finely grated fresh ginger
Ice for the glasses
1½ cups soda or seltzer water

**1.** Combine the grapes, mint leaves, and sugar in a blender. Blend on high speed for 10 seconds. Add the lime juice and grated ginger, and blend again for a few seconds.

**2.** Pour the mixture through a sieve or fine-meshed strainer

---

## Popcorn Possibilities

Popcorn is great for munching and a good source of fiber. I like to bring popcorn on road trips and to the movies. The reason I bring my own popcorn to the movies is that theater popcorn is loaded with saturated fat. Homemade popcorn can be low in calories and devoid of any saturated fat. I use only one to two tablespoons of olive or peanut oil when I cook a large pot of popcorn. I add the kernels only when the oil is very hot, then I keep the heat high and shake the pot constantly until most of the kernels are popped. Once the popcorn is ready, I like to add salt, a teaspoon of sugar, and a few pinches of powdered ginger, curry powder, or even ground Sichuan pepper. Yum.

into a bowl, pressing with a rubber spatula to extract as much liquid as possible. Pour the grape liquid into two large glasses filled with ice. Top each glass with half of the soda or seltzer water, and stir. Serve right away.

Variation: Freeze some green grapes beforehand to use instead of ice cubes.

Makes 2 large drinks

# Mango Lassi

Here is my version of the famous Indian drink. You can buy pomegranate molasses at Middle Eastern and some Indian grocery stores. I prefer the Lebanese brand Cortas. If you cannot find any, lime juice is a fine substitute.

1 ripe mango
2 tablespoons sugar
1 cup plain whole, low-fat, or nonfat yogurt
8 medium or 4 large ice cubes
1 teaspoon pomegranate molasses, or 1
    tablespoon lime juice (from about 1/2 lime)
1/2 cup water

**1.** Peel the skin off of the mango either with a sharp vegetable peeler or a paring knife. Then cut the flesh away from the pit, cutting as close to the pit as possible.

**2.** Put the mango and the other ingredients into a blender, and purée the mixture until it is smooth. Pour it into two large glasses, and serve.

Makes 2 large shakes

# Banana-Cardamom Lassi

No flavor combination beats banana and cardamom. These two also appear together in Cardamom Banana Bread (page 8), but here you can enjoy them in liquid form.

½ cup plain whole, low-fat, or nonfat yogurt
1 ripe banana
1 teaspoon finely grated fresh ginger
2 tablespoons lime juice (from about 1 lime)
1½ tablespoons honey
¼ teaspoon ground cardamom
4 medium or 2 large ice cubes
½ cup water

**1.** In a blender, combine the yogurt, banana, ginger, lime juice, honey, and cardamom, and blend on high speed until the contents are puréed.

**2.** Add the ice and water, and blend again until the ice is pulverized. Pour the lassi into two glasses, and serve.

Makes 2 drinks

# Strawberry-Melon Lassi

My friend Alan Santos-Buch, when making his first strawberry daiquiri, picked all the seeds off two strawberries before I and some friends asked him what he was doing. He was noticeably relieved when we told him that strawberry seeds are okay in daiquiris. In a lassi, too, the seeds are almost indiscernible.

½ cup plain whole, low-fat, or nonfat yogurt

10 medium strawberries
2 cups cubed cantaloupe
1½ tablespoons honey
4 medium or 2 large ice cubes
1 pinch ground cinnamon (optional)
1 tablespoon lemon juice

**1.** In a blender, blend on high speed the yogurt, strawberries, cantaloupe, honey, and ice for 10 seconds or until the ice is pulverized.

**2.** Add the cinnamon, if you like, and the lemon juice. Blend again for a few seconds. Pour the lassi into two large glasses, and serve.

Makes 2 drinks

## Lassi Come Home

The lassi, India's yogurt-based shake, is not only nutritious and delicious; it also dampens the fire of spicy foods (yogurt is the key ingredient here). This drink has a multitude of variations: Fennel seeds, cumin seeds, mint, lemon zest, cardamom, ginger, rose petals, honey, coconut milk, and cloves are just some of the aromatic flavorings used. Fruits such as green mangoes, bananas, apples, peaches, and grapes are blended with yogurt as well. Have fun inventing your own versions.

# Watermelon Lassi Cooler

Watermelon is a fruit that is undeniably refreshing. Try one of these drinks on a hot day, and you will come back to life.

2½ cups seedless watermelon chunks
1 tablespoon lime juice (from about 1 lime)
2 tablespoons sugar
⅔ cup plain whole, low-fat, or nonfat yogurt
5 medium or 2 or 3 large ice cubes

**1.** In a blender, purée the watermelon, lime juice, sugar, and yogurt.

**2.** Add the ice cubes, and blend on high speed until the ice is pulverized. Pour the lassi into two large glasses, and serve.

**Variation:** Mint is an excellent addition to this drink. Add 2 tablespoons chopped mint to the blender along with the ice.

Makes 2 drinks

# Honey-Ginger Lassi

The nutmeg and honey balance the sharp taste of ginger in this lassi, making for a smooth and mellow drink. Try this drink warm, too; see the Variation following the recipe.

2$\frac{1}{2}$ cups whole or low-fat milk
$\frac{1}{4}$ cup honey
1 heaping tablespoon finely grated fresh ginger
2 pinches freshly grated nutmeg
8 medium or 4 large ice cubes
Ice for the glasses

**1.** Combine all of the ingredients except the ice in a blender. Blend for 30 seconds to froth the milk.

**2.** Add the ice cubes, and blend until the ice is pulverized. Pour the lassi into large glasses filled with ice, and serve.

Variation: The same ingredients can make a soothing warm drink. Increase the milk to 3 cups, and heat it almost to a boil. Add the honey, ginger, and nutmeg, and stir well. Omit the ice. You'll have enough for two people. Serve the drink in mugs.

Makes 2 drinks

# Nectarine-Coconut Frappe

This drink, although tropical in spirit, is designed for us poor folks who can't grab a coconut from a backyard tree and buy papayas from a neighborhood fruit truck. The coconut milk here is canned, and nectarines take the place of papayas. In case you've never been to Boston, a frappe is simply what Bostonians call a shake.

## Ginger Basics

Ginger is not really a root; it is an underground stem, a rhizome. Fresh ginger rhizomes are heavy for their size; when ginger feels light and its skin is wrinkled, you know it has been sitting around for a while. Ginger that has been in the ground for a long time is fibrous and sharp in flavor; slice it into rounds to impart flavor to stir-fry dishes, Asian soups, and dipping sauces. Less mature ginger is less fibrous, less intense in flavor, and perfect for mincing. You can judge the maturity of ginger by looking where the knobs have broken; the more fibers visible, the older the ginger is.

Most people prefer to peel ginger before mincing it, although this isn't really necessary.

3 cups (about 4) peeled and chopped nectarines
1 cup canned coconut milk (you can freeze the
    remainder in the can for later use)
2 tablespoons sugar
2 tablespoons lime juice
6 medium or 3 large ice cubes
Ice for the glasses

**1.** In a blender, purée the nectarines with the coconut milk, sugar, and lime juice.

**2.** Add the ice cubes, and blend on high speed until the ice is pulverized. Pour the mixture into a glass filled with ice, and serve.

Makes 2 drinks

# Guanabana Batido

A batido is a Cuban shake that combines fruit, milk, and ice. My favorite batido is guanabana. Although I have yet to see guanabanas, or soursops, sold fresh in this country, the juice is available canned (under the Goya label) in Latin American markets and many supermarkets.

3/4 cup guanabana juice
2 tablespoons lemon juice (from about 1/2 lemon)
1/2 cup whole or low-fat milk
2 tablespoons sweetened condensed milk
5 medium or 2 or 3 large ice cubes

**1.** In a blender, combine all of the ingredients. Blend on high speed until the ice is pulverized.

**2.** Pour the mixture into two large glasses, and serve.

Makes 2 drinks

## Guanabana Relief

*N*othing can lift me from the swelter of a hot day the way a guanabana batido can. Guanabana, or soursop, is a tropical fruit that looks like a large green prickly pear. Inside, the flesh of the guanabana is soft, white, and fibrous, with big brown seeds. When the juice is extracted and sweetened with sugar, the flavor is sublime, like a mix between peach and vanilla. In Jamaica, guanabanas are made into a drink for those with amorous intentions. Called a "Front End Lifter," the drink is 1 part Dragon Stout (a dark beer), 1 part guanabana juice, and 1 part milk.

# Mango Batido

Mango is easily overpowered by other flavors. In this simple batido, though, the full flavor of mango rings clear.

1 very ripe mango
1½ tablespoons sweetened condensed milk
1 cup whole milk
1 tablespoon lime juice (from about ½ lime)
4 medium or 2 large ice cubes
Ice for the glasses

**1.** Peel the mango with a sharp vegetable peeler or paring knife. Discard the skin. Cut away as much flesh as possible from the pit. Put the mango flesh into a blender, and blend well.

**2.** Add the condensed milk, fresh milk, lime juice, and ice cubes. Blend on high speed for 10 seconds or until the ice is pulverized. Pour the mixture into two large glasses filled with ice, and serve.

Makes 2 drinks

# CHAPTER 20

# Breakfast Any Time

## Thrifty Living

*E*ating less meat or no meat will help keep your food budget under control, but there are ways to keep even more change in your pocket. Avoid shopping in the "gourmet" section of supermarkets or in "gourmet" stores. Instead, shop in whole-foods stores, where flours, grains, beans, legumes, nuts, and spices are sold in bulk. If you have the time, visit ethnic markets. Olives, pita bread, grains, and legumes are fresh and inexpensive in Syrian, Greek, and Lebanese markets. Soy sauce, tofu, wheat noodles, rice, and some produce are at rock-bottom prices in Asian markets. Try Indian food stores, Latin American markets, and other ethnic markets as well.

# Muesli

This is what I eat for breakfast when I'm concerned about my nutrition or just sick of bagels (I ate this every day, in fact, until I moved next to a bagel shop). Muesli may seem like a strange breakfast cereal at first, since it's quite different from crispy, light packaged cereals, and it takes some chewing prowess. But you may come to love as much as I do the different textures of the dried fruit, wheat germ, oatmeal, walnuts, and other ingredients. Besides, muesli is much less expensive than those overpriced boxed cereals.

It's best to let the milk soak in for about 5 minutes before you dive into the muesli. Fresh berries or bananas, of course, are always a welcome addition.

4½ cups rolled oats
½ cup toasted wheat germ
½ cup wheat bran
½ cup oat bran
1 cup raisins, currants, or chopped dried fruit such as apricots or apples
½ cup chopped walnuts or almonds
¼ cup brown sugar
¼ cup shelled, unsalted sunflower seeds (optional)

**1.** Mix all of the ingredients in a large bowl.

**2.** Serve muesli in bowls with milk and, if you like, fresh berries or sliced fresh fruit.

Stored in an airtight container, muesli keeps for 2 months at room temperature.

Makes 8 cups

# Breakfast Grits

I'm not from the South, and neither is my brother-in-law Stuart, but we both love grits. During Stuart's college years in upstate New York, he'd cook up three or four eggs every morning, and eat them with sliced tomato on buttered toast and on a big pile of grits. Soon, everyone on campus started calling him "Egg," and the nickname stuck. Hopefully, the enthusiasm he has spread for eating eggs with grits will outlast his nickname.

3 cups water
1/2 teaspoon salt
1 cup fine- or medium-ground hominy grits
    (don't buy instant grits)
Fresh-ground black pepper to taste
1 tablespoon butter
1/2 cup grated sharp cheddar cheese (optional)

**1.** Bring the water and salt to a boil in a saucepan. Whisk in the grits, and continue to whisk for 1 minute, turning the heat to low once the mixture is bubbling.

**2.** Cook the grits, stirring frequently with a spoon or whisk, for 10 to 15 minutes. Take the grits off the heat, and add the pepper, the butter, and, if you're using it, the cheese. Stir until the butter (and the cheese) is melted.

Serves 4

# Grilled Poblano Frittata

Ordering a frittata in a restaurant can be perilous—the open-faced omelet is likely to be covered with too many vegetables and overcooked. Cooking your own frittata at home is a better bet. I like to make a large one, as in this recipe, and cut it into pieces at the table. You can make the salsa and grill the poblanos a day in advance, if you like. By the way, this doesn't have to be a breakfast dish—try it for brunch or lunch.

3 poblano peppers
3 medium tomatoes
1 small onion, minced
2 tablespoons lime juice (from about 1 lime)
3 tablespoons minced cilantro
1/2 jalapeño pepper (optional), minced (include the seeds if you like more heat)
Salt and pepper to taste
3 corn tortillas
1 tablespoon olive oil
6 to 7 eggs, lightly beaten
1 cup grated Monterey Jack cheese

**1.** Make the *pico de gallo* salsa: Place the poblano peppers and the tomatoes over a medium gas flame, either on a grill or right on the burners. Rotate the vegetables every few minutes so that the skins don't completely blacken. Remove the vegetables once their skins are blistering and just partially charred. (The tomatoes will char faster, so remove them first.) Let the vegetables cool a bit.

**2.** Remove the skins of the vegetables with a paring knife. Cut the poblanos into ½-inch-wide strips, and set them aside. Cut the tomatoes into ½-inch cubes, and put them into a bowl.

**3.** Add to the bowl the onions, lime juice, cilantro, jalapeño (if you're using it), and salt and pepper. Chill the salsa if you won't be making the frittata within the next few hours.

**4.** Make the tortilla chips: Preheat the oven to 350°. Stack the tortillas, and cut the stack into six wedges. Spread the pieces on a baking sheet, lightly salt them, and bake them for 10 minutes or until they are crisp. Remove the chips from the oven, but keep the oven on.

**5.** Make the frittata: Heat the olive oil in a 10- or 12-inch non-stick oven-proof skillet over medium heat. Add the eggs, and stir them for the first minute of cooking with a plastic spatula. Let the eggs rest for a few seconds, then push the frittata to one side of the pan so the uncooked egg runs underneath. When the frittata is still moist but no longer runny, sprinkle it with salt, pepper, and the grated Jack cheese. Place the poblano strips in a star shape on top of the cheese. Bake the frittata in the oven for 3 to 4 minutes or until it is just set. Remove the skillet from the oven, and stick the tortilla chips around the edge of the frittata. Take the skillet to the table, and cut the frittata into wedges. Serve with the *pico de gallo.*

Serves 4

# Curried Poached Eggs

The quantities of spices in this recipe may seem hefty, but most of the spice mixture remains in the water in which the eggs are cooked.

- 1 tablespoon butter
- 1 garlic clove, minced
- 1 tablespoon ground coriander seeds
- 1 teaspoon ground cumin seeds
- 1 tablespoon curry powder, store-bought or homemade (page 36)
- 2 teaspoons turmeric
- 1 teaspoon salt
- 1/2 teaspoon fresh-ground black pepper
- 2 cups water
- 8 eggs

## Turmeric

One of the earliest spices ever used (it was used before 2500 B.C.), turmeric dyes bright yellow anything it touches, such as your nice white Formica counter or your new food processor bowl. Turmeric is what gives curry powder its color. Turmeric is also what gives hotdog mustards their bright yellow color (the intense yellow-gold color called mustard in the world of fashion should really be called turmeric). Although the flavor of turmeric, with slight hints of lemon and clove, is mild when the spice is used in moderation, abundant amounts make foods unpleasantly bitter.

**1.** In a large skillet, melt the butter over medium heat. Add the garlic, spices, and salt and pepper. Cook for 2 to 3 minutes, stirring often. Add the water, and bring the mixture to a boil. Reduce the heat.

**2.** Break four eggs, one at a time, as close to the simmering water as possible, and drop them into the water. Simmer them for 3 minutes, until the eggs become opaque and lose their sheen. Lift the eggs out with a slotted spoon. Cook the remaining four eggs the same way.

Serve the eggs on toasted whole-grain bread. They are wonderful with a spoonful of Tomato-Raisin Chutney (page 45).

*Serves 4*

# Wrapped Mexican Eggs

This tasty dish will feed a crowd without demanding much attention from the cook. Scrambled eggs with tomatoes, cheese, and bell peppers are stuffed inside flour tortillas, then topped with a salsa verde. The entire casserole can be assembled the night before and baked right before serving. Because of the slow baking and the addition of cheese and sour cream, the eggs don't overcook or dry out.

**SALSA VERDE:**
1½ pounds tomatillos, husked and cut in half
2 garlic cloves, cut in half
1½ cups coarsely chopped onions
⅓ cup coarsely chopped cilantro
1 cup water
1 jalapeño pepper, chopped (optional)
½ teaspoon salt

**FILLING:**
4 medium tomatoes, chopped fine
1 tablespoon olive oil
2 green bell peppers, seeded and sliced very thin
16 eggs, beaten
1 teaspoon salt
Fresh-ground black pepper to taste
1 cup grated Monterey Jack cheese

8 12-inch flour tortillas
½ cup whole, low-fat, or nonfat sour cream
½ cup grated Monterey Jack cheese

1. Make the salsa: In a blender or food processor, purée the salsa ingredients (you may need to do this in batches). In a saucepan, bring the salsa verde to a simmer, and simmer it for 5 minutes. Transfer it to a bowl, and set the bowl aside.

2. Make the filling: Put the chopped tomatoes into a sieve, and let them drain for 10 minutes or more.

3. In a large skillet, heat the oil over medium heat. Add the peppers, and sauté them until they are soft, about 5 to 10 minutes. Add the eggs, then turn the heat to low. Stirring occasionally with a wooden spoon, let the eggs cook until they begin to set. Take the skillet off the heat, and add the salt, the pepper, 1 cup Jack cheese, and the drained tomatoes.

4. Lay a flour tortilla on a work surface. Spread about ⅔ cup of the egg filling down the middle of the tortilla. Drop 1 tablespoon of the sour cream on top of the eggs. Fold in the sides of the tortilla to partly cover the egg mixture, then roll the tortilla, folding in the outer edges as you roll, to enclose the egg mixture completely. Continue this process with the remaining filling and tortillas. Place the filled tortillas close together in a 10-by-16-inch casserole dish. (At this point you can cover the dish, and chill it for up to 24 hours.)

5. Preheat the oven to 375°. Pour the salsa over the filled tortillas, and sprinkle them with the ½ cup grated cheese. Cover the dish with foil, and bake the casserole for 15 minutes (25

minutes if it has been chilled). Remove the dish from the oven, and serve one stuffed tortilla per person.

Serves 8

# Herbed Cream-Cheese Omelet

Somehow, when cream cheese is mixed with herbs and melted in an omelet, it acquires a wonderful taste that you wouldn't even associate with cream cheese.

When making omelets, don't be proper. Keeping food warm in the oven so everyone can eat together is a nice gesture for your guests, but it's terrible for the omelets. Omelets should be eaten as they're made; otherwise they lose their delicate quality. Serve this omelet with buttered toast topped with sliced tomato.

4 ounces cream cheese, softened
½ cup chopped herbs (I like to combine dill,
    basil, and a touch of oregano or thyme;
    cilantro on its own is nice)
Salt and fresh-ground black pepper to taste
3 tablespoons butter
8 eggs, beaten two at a time

**1.** Mix the cream cheese with the herbs in a bowl, adding salt and pepper to taste. Set the bowl aside.

**2.** Heat one-quarter of the butter in a well-seasoned omelet pan or 8-inch non-stick skillet over medium-high heat. When the butter is hot and bubbling, swirl it around in the pan. Just before the butter begins to brown, add 2 beaten eggs. Lower the heat. After 10 seconds or so, the omelet will coagulate. Push the omelet to one side of the pan with a spoon or spatula, and let the raw egg run over the cleared skillet. Repeat this

**"** *It is said that eggs and wine do not marry. I personally take great pleasure in drinking a young, light-bodied, relatively dry white wine with scrambled eggs.* **"**

—RICHARD OLNEY, *SIMPLE FRENCH FOOD*

one more time, then take the skillet off the heat. Dab one-quarter of the herbed cream cheese along the middle of the omelet from one side to the other. Season the omelet with additional salt and pepper, if you like. If it has not completely set, place the pan over medium heat for a half minute longer. When the omelet is set, slide it from the pan onto a plate so that the omelet rolls up and the herbed cream cheese runs along the length of the roll. Serve it right away.

**3.** Make three more omelets the same way, making sure the pan and butter get good and hot before adding the beaten eggs. Serve each one as soon as it is cooked.

Serves 4

# Johnnycakes

Johnnycakes are one of my favorite kinds of pancakes. Throughout my years as a cook, and especially when I was a chef at a bed-and-breakfast inn, I've had many different versions of this traditional corn pancake from Rhode Island. There are two basic styles of johnnycake—the thick cake and the thin cake. The thick cakes are so thick that they are split and buttered like English muffins. Both kinds contain the same basic ingredients—corn, salt, and water. In my version (a thick johnnycake), I add some buttermilk, butter, and a bit of baking powder. The leavening keeps the cake moist but not gummy, and the buttermilk and butter provide richness and flavor. These cakes are traditionally served only with butter, but I like them with a touch of maple syrup as well.

2½ cups cornmeal, preferably labeled organic or
    stone-ground
1½ teaspoons salt
6 to 7 tablespoons unsalted butter
3 tablespoons buttermilk or plain whole, low-fat,
    or nonfat yogurt

1 teaspoon baking powder
1 teaspoon baking soda

**1.** Put the cornmeal and salt into a large bowl. Bring 2 cups water to a boil with 1 tablespoon of the butter, and pour this over the cornmeal. Stir well with a wooden spoon, and then let the batter sit for 10 minutes. It will thicken a bit.

**2.** Stir the buttermilk or yogurt into the batter. Sprinkle the baking powder and soda over the batter, and stir well.

**3.** On a griddle or in a large skillet, melt ½ tablespoon butter over medium-low heat. With lightly floured hands, take hold of about 2 tablespoons of the batter and form a cake 2½ inches in diameter and ¾ inch thick. Form 3 more cakes in this manner. Place the johnnycakes on the griddle or in the pan, and cook them for 4 to 5 minutes or until they are golden brown on one side. Turn them, and cook them for 4 minutes more. Take the cakes off the heat, and keep them warm in a slow oven.

**4.** Melt another ½ tablespoon of butter, and repeat the process of forming and cooking four cakes. Continue this process until all the batter is used; you should have about 16 cakes in all.

**5.** Split the johnnycakes in half horizontally. Cut 3 tablespoons butter into 16 thin pieces, and place one thin piece of butter in the middle of each cake. (Use additional butter if you have more than 16 cakes.) Serve four cakes per person, with maple syrup.

Makes 16 to 20 cakes (serves 4 to 5)

# Best Buckwheat Pancakes

Sometimes buckwheat flour can be overwhelming, but in this recipe the flavor is just right. Have these pancakes with some butter and maple syrup, but don't drown them in syrup, or you'll lose the lovely buckwheat flavor.

1 cup buttermilk (or ²/₃ cup plain whole, low-fat,
   or nonfat yogurt mixed with ¹/₃ cup water)
1 large egg
3 tablespoons butter, melted
6 tablespoons unbleached white flour
6 tablespoons buckwheat flour
1 teaspoon sugar
¹/₂ teaspoon salt
1 teaspoon baking soda

1. In a medium bowl, whisk together the buttermilk (or thinned yogurt), egg, and melted butter. In another bowl, mix together the dry ingredients. Add the dry ingredients to the wet, and stir only until they are incorporated, no longer.

2. Heat a griddle or large skillet to medium hot, and grease it with a bit of butter or oil. Spoon the batter onto the griddle or into the skillet to form 4-inch pancakes, and cook them 3 minutes per side. Keep the first batch warm in a slow oven while you make more pancakes, until all the batter is used. Serve the pancakes right away, with maple syrup.

Makes 8 4-inch pancakes
(serves 2 to 3)

# Oat-Corn
# Pancakes

Marion Cunningham's wonderful volume, *The Breakfast Book,* inspired me to experiment with eggless batters for pancakes. These oat-corn pancakes are beautiful in their simplicity. They contain no eggs, no spices, no sugar—just the essentials to produce delicate, crispy pancakes. Serve them with butter and maple syrup, and, if you like, fresh fruit.

## When Pancakes Become Too Popular

*Some years ago I worked at a tiny cafe in Boston that was well known for its brunches. We served potatoes Santa Cruz (pan-fried new potatoes with carrots, tofu, and garlic) and eggs on cornbread with black beans and salsa. But what really got people going were the pancakes: pumpkin, banana, zucchini, strawberry—you name it. Our griddle was average in size, and we often ran into a pancake traffic jam. When orders would back up, I would tell those ordering about the "pancake waiting list." This made the pancakes seem much more special, which of course only added customers to the waiting list.*

2 tablespoons unsalted butter
1 cup rolled oats
1 cup yellow cornmeal
1 teaspoon salt
¼ teaspoon baking soda
2 cups buttermilk

**1.** In a skillet, melt the butter over medium heat. Let the butter become nut-brown, then remove the skillet from the heat.

**2.** In a food processor, grind the oats. Transfer them to a bowl. Mix in the cornmeal, salt, and baking soda. Add the buttermilk, and stir well. Stir in the butter.

**3.** Heat a griddle or large skillet to medium hot, and grease it lightly with butter or oil. With a small ladle, pour the batter onto the griddle or into the skillet to form 4-inch pancakes. Cook until bubbles appear on top of the pancakes, then flip them, and cook them 2 minutes more. Keep them warm in a slow oven while you make the remaining pancakes. Serve the pancakes hot.

Makes about 15 pancakes
(serves 4 to 5)

# Whole-Wheat Pancakes

When pancakes are good, there is no food in the world that can rival them. The two secrets to these pancakes are, first, that butter is cut into the flour, and, second, that buttermilk is used instead of milk. The result is very light, tender pancakes.

1 cup whole-wheat flour
²/₃ cup unbleached white flour
¹/₃ cup wheat germ or rolled oats
1¹/₂ teaspoons baking powder
¹/₂ teaspoon baking soda
2 tablespoons brown sugar
1 teaspoon salt
5¹/₃ tablespoons (²/₃ stick) cold unsalted butter
2¹/₂ cups buttermilk
2 large eggs, beaten

**1.** In a food processor or in a large bowl, combine the whole-wheat flour, white flour, wheat germ or oats, baking powder, baking soda, brown sugar, and salt. Cut the butter into small pieces with a knife, and add the butter to the other ingredients. Either run the processor in short spurts or cut with a pastry cutter or fork until the mixture has a sand-like consistency. If you've used a food processor, transfer the mixture to a large bowl.

**2.** Make a well in the center of the flour-butter mixture, and add the buttermilk and eggs. Stir until the liquids are fully incorporated.

**3.** Heat a griddle or large skillet over medium heat, and grease the surface with a bit of butter or oil. Ladle the batter onto the surface to form 4-inch pancakes. Once bubbles form on the top of the pancakes, flip them over, and cook them on the other side for about 2 minutes. Keep them warm in a slow oven while you make the rest of the pancakes. (If you don't want to use all the batter at once, you can keep it for up to 3 days in an airtight container in the refrigerator.) Serve the pancakes warm with maple syrup.

Makes about 16 pancakes
(serves 4 to 5)

# Portuguese Bread French Toast

Besides eating it fresh from the bakery, one of the best uses for Portuguese sweet bread is in baked French toast. Because the bread is so light, it soaks up a lot of batter and becomes too fragile to pan-fry. Pouring the custard over the slices of bread and baking it in the oven solves the problem, takes less effort, and produces delicious results. Serve the French toast with maple syrup.

5 eggs
4 cups milk
¹/₄ cup sugar
¹/₂ teaspoon ground cinnamon
¹/₂ teaspoon freshly grated nutmeg
1 teaspoon grated orange rind
1 small (8-inch round) loaf Portuguese sweet bread (or challah)
2 tablespoons unsalted butter, cut into small pieces

**1.** Preheat the oven to 350°. In a bowl, whisk together the eggs, milk, sugar, cinnamon, nutmeg, and orange rind.

**2.** Cut the bread into seven or eight slices, and lay them, overlapping, in a large baking dish (I use a 13-by-18-inch dish). Pour the custard over the bread, covering every slice. The bread should not be entirely submerged, though; the higher parts should become toasted and crispy. Dot the bread with the butter.

**3.** Bake the French toast in the oven for 35 to 45 minutes or until the custard is set (when a knife inserted in it comes out clean). Serve it immediately.

Serves 6

# Poppy Seed
# French Toast

The pleasant crunch and mild flavor of poppy seeds make this French toast a nice way to start the day. I like to use the semisoft, inexpensive French bread or Italian bread found at supermarkets, but other breads work well, too.

3 tablespoons poppy seeds
3 eggs
2 cups whole or low-fat milk
1 teaspoon vanilla extract
1 pinch freshly grated nutmeg
2 tablespoons sugar
12 slices sandwich bread (preferably thick-sliced), or 24 1-inch slices soft French bread
2 to 4 tablespoons butter

**1.** In a bowl, whisk together the poppy seeds, eggs, milk, vanilla, nutmeg, and sugar.

**2.** Heat a griddle or large skillet over medium heat.

**3.** Dip one slice of the bread into the egg batter, then quickly take it out (I gently squeeze some of the batter back into the bowl so the bread isn't dripping wet). Melt 1 tablespoon of the butter over the griddle or in the skillet, and add the dipped bread. Continue dipping bread slices, stirring the batter frequently so all the poppy seeds don't sink to the bottom, and laying the bread on the griddle or in the skillet until no more bread will fit. Cook the slices for about 2 minutes per side, or until they are golden. Keep the French toast warm in a slow oven while you melt more butter and use the rest of the bread and batter. Serve the French toast with maple syrup.

Serves 4

## Maple Syrup

It takes one mature maple tree to produce the 10 gallons of sap needed to make just 4 cups of maple syrup. This is why maple syrup is so expensive. Maple syrup is made throughout the northeastern United States and southeastern Canada. For pancakes, I prefer grade A medium or dark amber syrup; it is slightly heavier than the fancy or extra-light syrup. For baking I use the very dense grade B maple syrup, which is sold in some whole-foods and specialty food stores.

# Sweet-Potato Muffins

It occurs to me that I have been carrying on, in front of all my readers, a love affair with sweet potatoes. They've made their way into every chapter of this book, making me wonder if perhaps I am overly attached to this vegetable. But I can't leave sweet-potato muffins out of the book, since they surely deserve as much acclaim as zucchini and carrot muffins already get.

1 cup plus 2 tablespoons brown sugar
$^{1}/_{2}$ cup canola or corn oil
1 teaspoon vanilla extract
2 eggs
2 cups unbleached white flour
2 teaspoons baking powder
1 teaspoon ground cinnamon
1 teaspoon freshly grated nutmeg
$^{1}/_{2}$ teaspoon ground allspice
$^{1}/_{2}$ teaspoon salt
2 large sweet potatoes (about 1$^{1}/_{3}$ pounds),
    peeled and finely grated, to make 4 cups
$^{1}/_{2}$ cup raisins
1 cup chopped walnuts

**1.** Preheat the oven to 350°. Butter or oil a tin or tins to hold twelve muffins.

**2.** In a small bowl, whisk together the brown sugar, oil, vanilla, and eggs.

**3.** In a large bowl, mix together the flour, baking powder, spices, salt, and grated sweet potatoes. Make a well in the center, and pour in the egg mixture. Stir the egg mixture, gradually incorporating it with the flour mixture. Stir in the raisins and walnuts. Spoon the batter into the tins. I like to fill each tin to the rim to make a large cap (no, the batter doesn't overflow). Bake the muffins for 25 to 30 minutes or until a knife inserted into a muffin comes out clean.

**4.** Take the muffin tin(s) out of the oven. Run a paring knife carefully around each muffin, then invert the pan, and knock one edge against your work surface to release the muffins. Serve the muffins right away.

Makes 12 muffins

# Two-Blue Muffins

In these doubly true-blue muffins, the intensely dark blue of the berries bleeds into the blue cornmeal interior. The combination is so gorgeous that I'm waiting for the New York clothing designers to showcase their newest fashions in blueberry–blue cornmeal colors. (Although you will lose some color, you can substitute easier-to-find yellow cornmeal for blue, if you can't locate the blue kind.)

In case you don't care one way or another about the color of your muffins, you'll be glad to know that these taste every bit as good as they look.

1/4 cup unsalted butter
1/4 cup honey
1 1/2 cups blue cornmeal (available in whole-foods
    stores and some supermarkets)
2/3 cup unbleached white flour
1 1/2 teaspoons baking powder
1/2 teaspoon baking soda
1 teaspoon salt
2 tablespoons water
1 cup plain whole, low-fat, or nonfat yogurt
1 egg
1 cup blueberries

## Porridge Fit for a King

My brother-in-law, Stu, loves good food, which is why his name appears more than once in this book. Here I must mention his affection for hot oatmeal. Stu doesn't eat rolled oats; he prefers steel-cut oats from Ireland, which he says are more flavorful. To make oatmeal for two from steel-cut oats, bring 3 cups water to a boil with ½ teaspoon salt. Add ¾ cup oats, and turn the heat down. Cook the oatmeal over low heat, stirring from time to time, for 20 minutes. Serve the oatmeal in bowls, with any combination of the following: milk, butter, maple syrup, brown sugar, and cinnamon.

**1.** Preheat the oven to 400°. Butter or oil a muffin pan that can hold at least eight muffins. In a small saucepan, melt the butter with the honey, then remove the pan from the heat.

**2.** In a large bowl, mix together the cornmeal, flour, baking powder, baking soda, and salt. Make a well in the center, and pour in the honey-butter mixture. Add the water, yogurt, and egg. Stir to mix the ingredients thoroughly (but do not overmix). Stir in the blueberries. Spoon the batter into the muffin pan. Bake the muffins in the center of the oven for 15 to 20 minutes, or until a knife inserted into a muffin comes out clean.

**3.** Take the pan out of the oven, and run a paring knife around each muffin. Invert the pan, and knock one side of it against your work surface to release the muffins. Serve the muffins immediately, with honey or butter.

*Makes 8 muffins*

# Oatmeal-Currant Scones

These scones are a bit lighter than most because they contain milk and not cream. They also contain nutritious, fiber-rich oatmeal.

Like all scones, these are best eaten hot from the oven. Freeze any that are left over, even if you'll be eating them the next morning. Let them thaw in the refrigerator overnight, then heat them at 275° until they're warm.

¼ cup orange juice or Grand Marnier
¼ cup water
1 cup currants
2 cups rolled oats
3 cups unbleached white flour

1 teaspoon salt
2 teaspoons baking powder
1 teaspoon baking soda
3 tablespoons sugar
1 cup (2 sticks) cold unsalted butter, each stick
    cut into 8 pieces
1¹/₃ cups cold milk

**1.** Preheat the oven to 375°. Heat the orange juice or Grand Marnier and the water in a small pan, and add the currants. Simmer the mixture for 1 minute, then let it sit until it is cool a bit.

**2.** In a food processor, grind the oats with the flour, salt, baking powder, baking soda, and sugar. Add the butter, and run the machine in short spurts until it has the consistency of sand. Transfer the mixture to a large bowl.

**3.** Add to the bowl the milk and the currants with their liquid. Stir until the mixture comes together. Form the dough into a ball with your hands, adding a bit of milk if necessary. Press or roll out the ball of dough until it is 1 inch thick. Cut the dough into 16 squares or triangles.

**4.** Bake the scones on an ungreased baking sheet for 15 minutes or until they are lightly browned on the edges. Serve them warm with butter and jam.

*Makes 16 scones*

# Harry's Famous Home Fries

When I was growing up, my father used to guard three or four baked potatoes at dinner so he could make his "famous" home fries the following morning. He would cook

## Green Eggs, No Ham

❀

Once I was a brunch chef at a tiny cafe in Boston. By 5:30 on Sunday mornings, I would be down in the cellar cracking over one hundred eggs into a 5-gallon bucket for the day's omelets. I'd beat the vat of eggs with a mammoth whisk, then I would move on to making the cranberry cooler, a cranberry-juice beverage. One day, after I made the cranberry beverage, I poured it directly into the eggs. There was no logic to this; my brain just malfunctioned. Within seconds, the eggs turned an interesting green. Fortunately, my "Green Eggs, No Ham, and Green Home-Fries" special (the potatoes were smothered in herbs) sold out quickly.

the onions until they were nearly black, and then let the potatoes develop a dark brown crust. As I helped him, he would tell me that if we canned his home fries we could make a million dollars.

▪▪▪▪▪▪▪▪▪▪

1/4 cup butter
2 medium onions, sliced thin
3 large baked russet potatoes, chilled
1 garlic clove, minced
3/4 teaspoon salt, or more, to taste
1/4 teaspoon fresh-ground black pepper

▪▪▪▪▪▪▪▪▪▪

**1.** In a heavy skillet, melt the butter over medium heat. Cook the onions for 10 to 15 minutes, stirring occasionally, until they turn dark brown.

**2.** Meanwhile, cut the potatoes (without peeling them) into 1/2-inch cubes. Add them and the garlic to the onions.

**3.** Turn the heat to medium-low, and cook the potatoes, without stirring, for 15 minutes or until they develop a golden crust on the bottom. Then toss them, and let them cook, untouched, for 15 minutes more. Toss them again, sprinkle them with the salt and pepper, and serve.

Serves 4

# Potato, Red Lentil, and Brown Onion Hash

Fried in butter, the potatoes and red lentils make this hash doubly crunchy. Enjoy this dish with fried or poached eggs. This hash is another good use for leftover baked potatoes.

▪▪▪▪▪▪▪▪▪▪

1 cup red lentils (available from Indian grocers
   or whole-foods stores)
2 tablespoons butter, or a bit more
2 cups chopped onions
3 baked and cooled medium russet potatoes, cut
   into ½-inch cubes
1 teaspoon salt
¼ teaspoon fresh-ground black pepper, or more,
   to taste

**1.** Cook the lentils: Bring 2½ cups water to a boil in a saucepan. Add the lentils, and simmer them, uncovered, for 10 to 15 minutes or until they are just tender. Drain the lentils, and set them aside.

**2.** In a large skillet over medium heat, melt 2 tablespoons butter, then add the onions. Cook them, stirring, until they begin to brown, about 10 minutes. Add the potatoes, salt, and pepper. Let the mixture sit over medium heat without stirring for 10 minutes.

**3.** Stir in the lentils, and cook the hash for 5 minutes more, adding more butter if the pan seems dry. The hash should form a crust on the bottom. Toss the hash, and let the bottom crust up for 5 minutes.

   Serve the hash immediately, or keep it over low heat until you are ready to serve it.

Serves 4

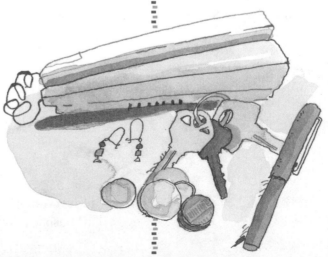

# CHAPTER 21

# What's for Dinner?

These days, the less time it takes to cook something, the more likely we are to make it. I therefore wrote this book so that each entrée is a meal in itself. On a weeknight, it may be hard to find the time to cook anything more.

If you want to try the easiest, speediest recipes this book has to offer, here are a few suggestions. The grain and pasta chapters (9 and 10) contain many of the simpler recipes in this book. Or try the soup and salad chapters (4 and 5). Most of the soup recipes are easy, and you can probably make enough soup to last two nights. For variety, you can make a different salad each night. Or how about a burger (chapter 13)? Make enough burger mixture for two meals, and have burgers three or four days apart. Or you could make quesadillas or burritos (both in chapter 14). These are very quick and simple dishes, and a good salsa is all you need to complete the meal.

I hope there will be days when you'll want to try a new dish regardless of the speed and ease of the recipe. Cooking holds so much opportunity for satisfaction, learning, and innovation. We often forget the simple pleasure of making something new, or of improvising on dishes we know. But time invested in leisurely cooking pays off. Some of the best times I've had have been in my kitchen, whether at home or at work, with good food to cook and the radio on. My mind begins racing with culinary possibilities as I start collecting foods and seasonings on my worktable. Then all of a sudden I'm doing five things at once, and my stomach churns with excitement as my mind's eye pictures the finished dishes I'm in the midst of creating. This is when I feel that everything is right with the world.

Some people plan their dinners a week or a day in advance, some plan them the day they make them, and others don't plan at all—they cook free-style with whatever's in their refrigerator, cupboard, or garden. For a beginner, the free-style option is practically out of the question, first because there's probably no food in the house, and second because we are not born with culinary knowledge and skill. Yet planning dinner can take a lot of time; you need to read cookbooks, find recipes, write shopping lists, and so on. So what do you do if you want to start cooking better meals?

Start slowly. My mother is living testimony that this approach works. When she married my father in the 1950s she knew how to cook spaghetti and chicken divan. She started cooking from books and magazines once or twice a week, and by trial and error she developed a repertoire of favorites. Now, forty years later, my mom has dozens of favorites to choose from, many of them exotic and challenging. So aim to try a new recipe just once a week, and maintain your current dinner habits for the rest of the week. This way, improving your skills in the kitchen won't be an overwhelming job.

In the meantime, there are many ways to get quick relief from a limited culinary repertoire without studying recipes at all. Order a cheese pizza from your local pizzeria, bring it home, and add your own toppings—perhaps sautéed shiitakes, or maybe spinach or fennel seared with olive oil and garlic. If you're getting sick of take-out pizza, how about visiting a taqueria? A burrito provides a lot of protein and carbohydrates as well as good flavor. If a Chinese, Japanese, Korean, Thai, or Vietnamese restaurant is nearby, pick up a take-out menu. There you should find many healthful options, like soups, stir-fried dishes, and stews. Or develop some favorite sandwiches that are hearty, easy, and satisfying enough for dinner (one of my favorites is the Spinach and Mozzarella Grilled Cheese Sandwich with Chile Dipping Sauce on page 389). Or buy all sorts of salad fixings, and make dressings for them. Mesclun, green beans, tomatoes, cucumbers, zucchini, and peppers are just some of the vegetables that can be eaten raw. Or use your homemade dressings on cooked vegetables, such as new potatoes, artichokes, cut corn, or roasted veggies.

When planning a dinner with more than one course, the concept of pairing complementary dishes comes into play. The most important thing to know is that menu planning is a highly personal endeavor; there are no absolute rights or wrongs. You are entitled to your whims and fancies. With that said, here are some loose guidelines.

Each course should appeal in a way that the previous one has not. Avoid overuse of any particular kind of food. Not many people want to eat cream sauces with three consecutive

## Vegetarian Dinner for $3.50

*Around the country, taquerías are opening up. In these small, mostly independent restaurants, you can get a freshly made taco or burrito very fast. My favorite taquería in Boston is Ana's. A grilled-vegetable super burrito from Ana's keeps me fueled for over half a day. For the super burrito, a huge steamed tortilla is wrapped tightly around spiced rice, soft kidney beans, freshly grilled vegetables (like butternut squash, zucchini, and eggplant), guacamole, and salsa. I get my complementary proteins, a host of vitamins and minerals, and barely any fat, all for $3.50.*

## Worthy Reading

If you're looking for more information on the nutritional qualities of foods as well as general cooking advice, I recommend the book Good Food, *by Margaret Wittenberg (Crossing Press, 1995). In this knowledgeable, well-organized guide, Wittenberg reports on hundreds of foods and provides loads of useful information for the avid cook. In the chapter on dried fruit, for example, she describes fifteen dried fruits, their history, their varieties, and ways to cook them.*

courses, for example. Nor does anyone want three courses of puréed foods. The same is true of sweet, sour, and hot foods. If the first course is Yuca "Potato" Salad (page 132), a main course of Your Pad Thai or Mine (page 277) would be too sour, because both dishes use lime juice as a predominant ingredient. Both dishes are also very starchy. A better choice to follow Pad Thai would be Chilled Mango Soup (page 90). Be careful also not to use the same strong flavors (such as saffron, artichokes, ginger, kasha, or habanero peppers) in two or three dishes. Unless you are expressing your undying love for the food and are celebrating its very existence, once is enough for a pungent ingredient to appear during a meal.

As you will see if you look at the menus that follow, I think it's fun to combine in one meal dishes that are inspired by cuisines from different parts of the world. East Asian food can be a challenge in this regard: generally, combining various East Asian dishes in a meal is easier than pairing East Asian dishes with foods from outside the region. Asian main dishes do work well with many first-course Western salads, such as Bistro Avocado Salad (page 138) or Bibb Salad with Anise Croutons (page 136). Asian entrées also go well with many broth-based soups, such as Garlic Soup with Bread (page 97). And Asian main dishes work well with American desserts, especially simple ones such as Chocolate Blackout Pudding (page 490) with Cinnamon Snaps (page 505). But because East Asian food is usually light, heavy dishes from other continents can ruin the harmony of a mostly Asian meal.

In general, when you plan a meal you want to strive for variety and balance, and trust your instincts. Following are some examples to get you started.

# Menus for Occasions Big and Small

Because so much of the discussion about wines is about how to pair them with meat, chicken, or fish, I thought it might be useful to provide wine recommendations for vegetarian meals. Don't take the presence of wine recommendations in these menus to mean that the meal wouldn't be good without your own choice of wine (or beer), or with no wine at all. I'm grateful to Walter Clay for his advice on these wine selections.

### FORMAL SUNDAY DINNER FOR FRIENDS
*Asparagus Wasabi Tempura*
*Lima Minestrone*
*Pappardelle with Asparagus and Herbed Cream*
*Pomegranate Ice with Mascarpone Cream*
*Cinnamon Snaps*
*Wine: an Italian white such as Pinot Grigio or Gavi*

### DINNER FOR ADVENTUROUS EATERS
*Saffron-Scented Plantain Soup*
*Long and Winding Bean Slaw, or French Lentil Salad with*
*Caramelized Balsamic Vinaigrette*
*Persian Basmati Rice with Cinnamon and Pistachios*
*Chickpea-flour Dumplings in Spinach-Tomato Sauce*
*Lavender Rice Pudding with Raspberries*
*Wine: a California Chardonnay or a Provençal rosé*
*Dessert wine: a Muscat from Roussillon*
*or a Muscat Beaumes-de-Venise*

### PIZZA WITH FRIENDS
*Root Soup with Three Herbs*
*Fennel Pizzas with White-Bean Purée*
*Summer Squash and Herbed Ricotta Pizzas*
*Poblano and Jack Cheese Pizzas*
*Mixed greens (such as watercress, red-leaf lettuce, endive, and Boston lettuce) tossed with Caesar Revamped dressing*
*Wine: a Chianti, Sangiovese, Valpolicella, or Dolcetto,*
*or a Portuguese red*

### DIXIE DINNER
*Corn and Sweet-Potato Chowder*
*Ten-Minute Cornbread*
*Dixie Pot Pie*
*Fava Bean Succotash*
*Grandmarie's Sweet-Potato Pie*
*Wine: a Chardonnay on the sweet side*
*or a Tokay Pinot Gris from Alsace*

### SOUTH-OF-THE-BORDER DINNER
*Chile and Zucchini Quesadillas with
Roasted Corn and Garlic Salsa
Real Tamale Pie
Gunsmoke Slaw
Mango with Coconut-Buttermilk Granita
Beer: a Mexican dark beer*

### ITALIAN CUCINA DINNER
*Lima Minestrone
Italian Bread-and-Tomato Salad
Zucchini Risotto Cakes with Provençal Sauce
Five-Spice Biscotti with espresso ice cream
Wine: a Chianti, Sangiovese, or Valpolicella*

### GREEK SUPPER
*Planet Moussaka
Brown lentils with olives, parsley, chopped onion,
and Three-Citrus Vinaigrette
Paximade (sweet Greek bread), grapes, and melon wedges
Wine: a big Chardonnay, white Rioja, or Greek white wine*

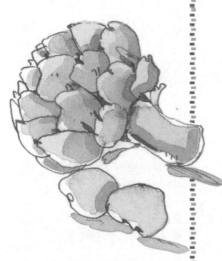

### MEDITERRANEAN DINNER PARTY
*Green Grape and Tomatillo Gazpacho
Tagine of Eggplant and Olives over quinoa
Bibb lettuce, cherry tomato, and goat cheese salad with
Caramelized Balsamic Vinaigrette
Lemon Curd Dip with Cherries and Berries
Wine: a Valpolicella or Dolcetta*

### ASIAN DINNER
*Shiitake Consommé with Transparent Noodles
Thai Tofu with Red Curry Sauce over Coconut-Scallion Rice
Almond Macaroons
Fruit cup of lychees, oranges, melon, mango, and mint
Wine: a Gewürztraminer from Alsace
or a California Sauvignon Blanc*

## NO-FUSS DINNER AFTER A DAY AT WORK
*Eggplant, Tomato, and Mozzarella Sandwiches*
*Butter Bananas with Toasted Cashews, and vanilla ice cream*
*Wine: a Sauvignon Blanc or a light red such as*
*Merlot or Côtes du Rhône*

## NO-FUSS DINNER NUMBER TWO
*Tagine of Eggplant and Olives over quinoa*
*Arugula salad with balsamic vinegar and olive oil*
*Wine: a Chianti, Sangiovese, Valpolicella, or Zinfandel*

## NO-FUSS DINNER NUMBER THREE
*Tomato, Corn, and Black-Bean Gazpacho*
*Potato and Cheddar Quesadillas and your favorite hot sauce*
*Sweet Fried Plantains*
*Wine: a Sauvignon Blanc or a California Chardonnay*

## I-JUST-LOST-MY-JOB SUPPER
## (DINNER ON A TIGHT BUDGET)
*Tomato-Lentil Soup*
*Crusty bread*
*Green Slaw*
*Banana Cream Pie (without the chocolate)*
*Wine: some leftover Chianti or any*
*two-for-$5 Cabernet in the bin*

## RENT-A-GOOD-MOVIE DINNER
*Lambless Shepherd's Pie*
*Spanish Swiss Chard with Raisins and Hazelnuts*
*Chocolate Blackout Pudding*
*Wine: a Vouvray or a California Chardonnay*
*on the sweet side*

## DECAF CAPPUCCINO CHAT
## (OR TEA TIME, OR BOOK CLUB CHAT)
*High-Tea Cucumber Sandwiches*
*Dried Cranberry–Pecan Coffeecake*
*Irish Soda Bread*
*Cornmeal Strawberry Cake*
*Cappuccino made with decaffeinated espresso; or tea*

" *If you accept the premise that nothing is sacred and all things are possible, it won't bother you a bit to use sour cream instead of heavy cream. You don't have to tell your friends that what they're eating isn't 'by the book.'* "

—ALICE MAY BROOK, *ALICE'S RESTAURANT COOKBOOK*

> " *The qualities of an exceptional cook are akin to those of a successful tightrope walker: an abiding passion for the task, courage to go out on a limb, and an impeccable sense of balance.* "
>
> —BRYAN MILLER

## BIRTHDAY BRUNCH
*Mango Batido*
*Potato, Red Lentil, and Brown Onion Hash*
*Brown Soda Bread*
*Curried Poached Eggs*
*Dairy-Free Almond-Orange Cake*
*Coffee*

## SPRING CELEBRATION
*Fava Minestrone (a variation on Lima Minestrone)*
*Pappardelle with Asparagus and Herbed Cream*
*Young spring lettuce with Coriander-Honey Dressing*
*Jon's Rhubarb-Raisin Pie*
*Wine: a Chianti or Moscato d'Asti or an Italian Chardonnay*

## COOL SUMMER NIGHT'S MEAL
*Corn and Tomato Chowder*
*Pasta with Baby Red Lentils and Ginger*
*Creamy Coconut Pudding*
*Wine: a Côtes du Rhône or a Châteauneuf-du-Pape*

## SUMMER PICNIC
*Orzo with Olives, Broccoli, and Basil*
*Roasted New Potato Salad*
*Irish Soda Bread with butter*
*Pan Bagna*
*Lemon-Walnut Pound Cake*
*Wine: a Pinot Grigio or a Côtes du Rhône*

## SUMMERTIME GRILLING PARTY
*Charred-Tomato Salsa with Grilled Bread*
*Peanut Millet with Grilled Curried Vegetables*
*Sorbet or sherbet with fresh fruit*
*Wine: a chilled crisp Alsace Pinot Blanc or Riesling,*
*or a California Sauvignon Blanc*

## WEATHERING THE SUMMER HEAT
*Spinach Patties with Cumin-Orange Raita*
*Quinoa-Sorrel Salad*
*Mango slices with lemon sorbet*
*Wine: a Pinot Grigio or a chilled Beaujolais*

### TOMATO AND ZUCCHINI BUMPER-CROP DINNER
*Risotto with Tomato, Corn, and Basil*
*Crumbed Zucchini*
*Simple tomato salad with olive oil, salt,*
*pepper, and a squeeze of lime*
*Wine: a Côtes du Roussillon, Côtes du Rhône,*
*or Pinot Grigio*

### EATIN' AFTER APPLE PICKIN'
*Roasted Fennel with Green Apples*
*Deep-Dish Potato and Pumpkin Pie*
*Celery Root and Apple Slaw*
*Sautéed apples with maple syrup and ice cream*
*Wine: a Riesling Kabinett or a crisp Sauvignon Blanc*

### WINTER SNOWSTORM PARTY
*Root Soup with Three Herbs*
*Dark Boston Brown Bread*
*Farro Risotto with Shiitakes in Roasted Acorn Squash*
*Pumpkin Bread Pudding*
*Wine: a Pinot Noir, a simple red Burgundy,*
*or a Chardonnay*

### DINNER AFTER SKATING
*African Tomato and Peanut Soup*
*No-Fry Spicy Potato Skins*
*Jamaican Burgers on bulky rolls with Mango Ketchup*
*Peanut Espresso Cookies*
*Hot cocoa*
*Wine: a Zinfandel with gumption (or beer)*

### WINTER DINNER BY THE FIRE (OR SPACE HEATER)
*Carrot-Fennel Soup*
*Baked Rigatoni with Broccoli and Gorgonzola*
*Watercress and curly endive salad with*
*Roasted Shallot Dressing*
*Wine: a Chianti, Barbaresco or Barolo, or Chinon*
*(Cabernet Franc) from the Loire*

# Index